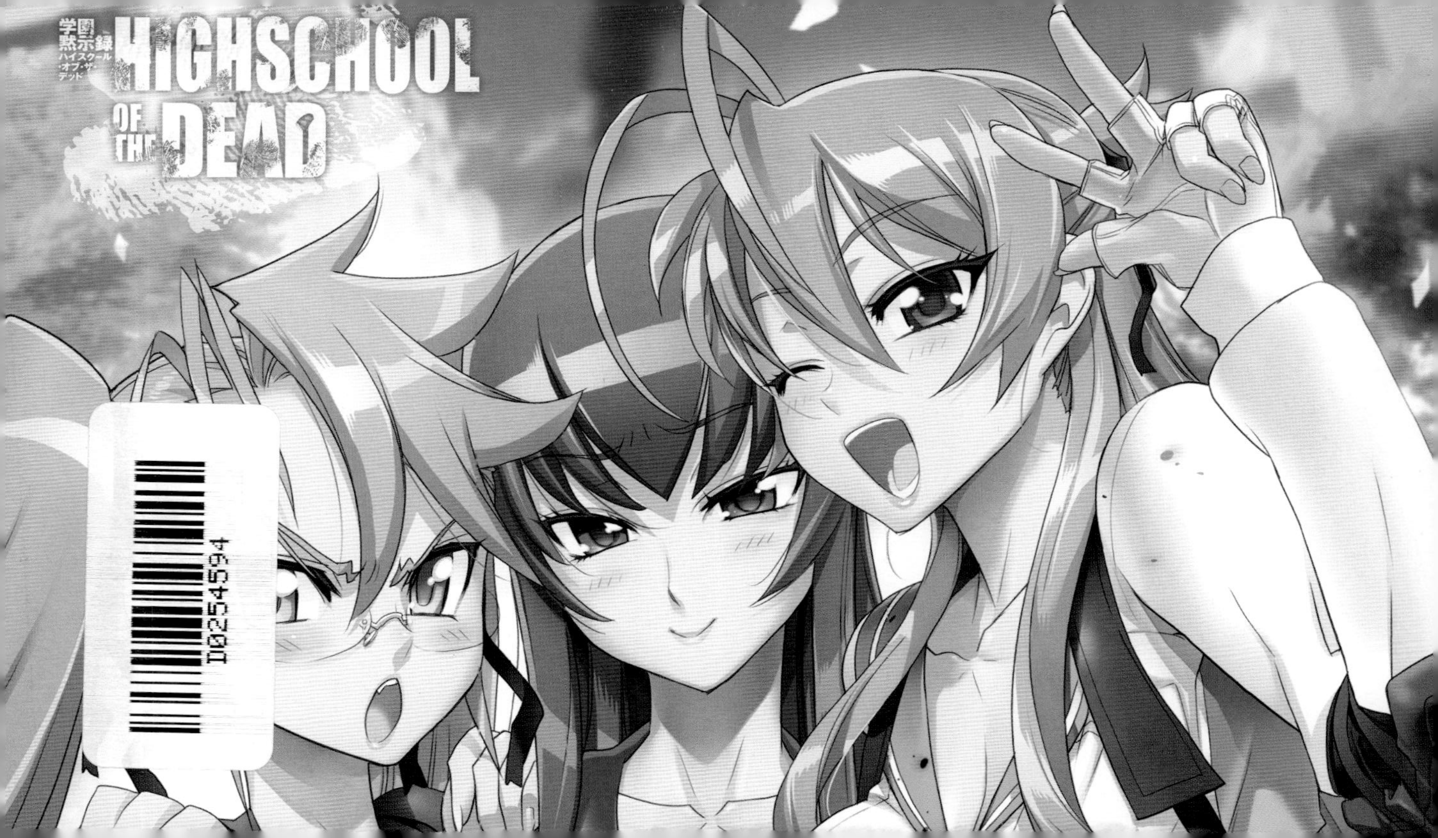
学園黙示録
ハイスクール・オブ・ザ・デッド
HIGHSCHOOL OF THE DEAD

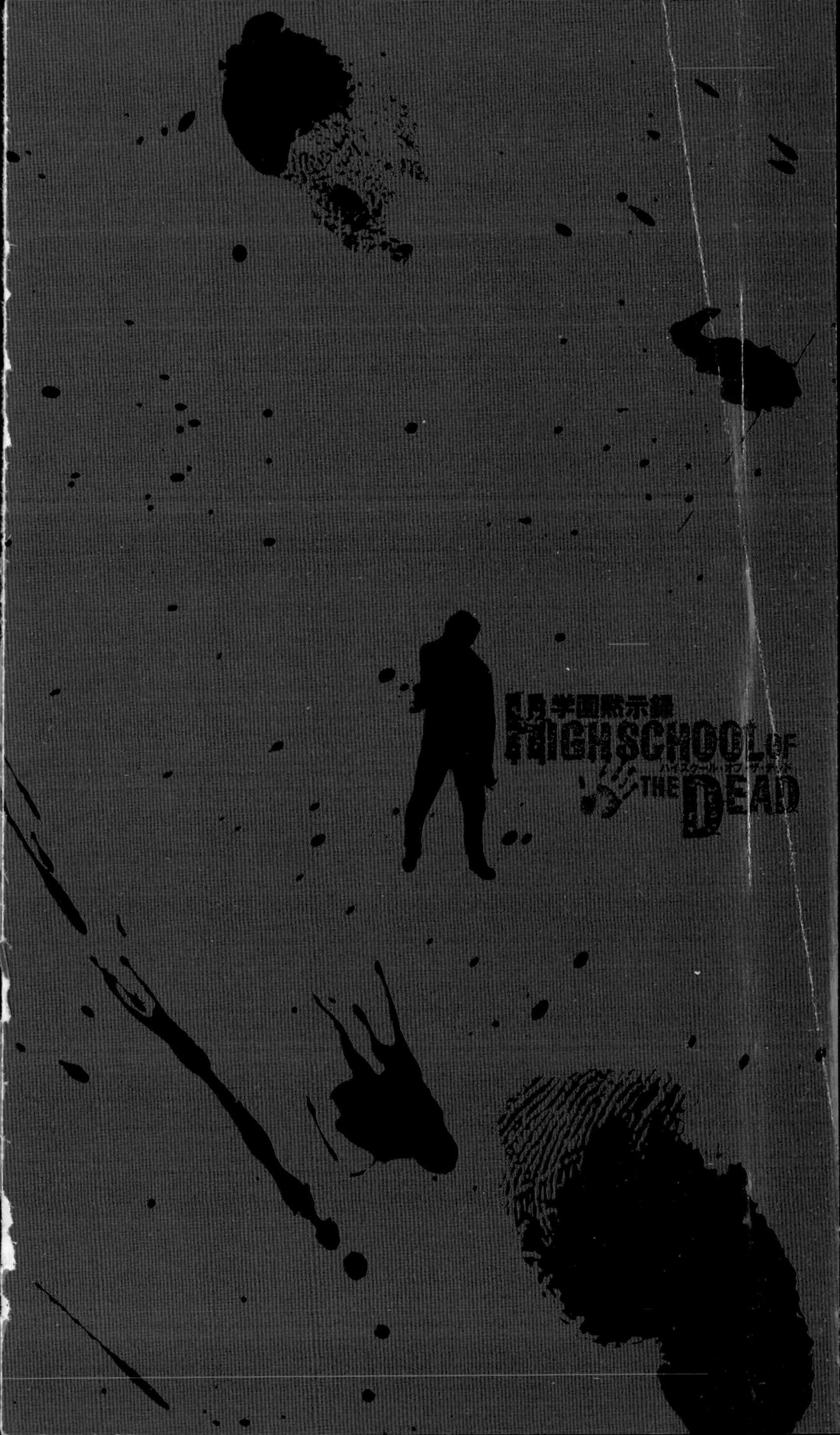
学園黙示録
HIGHSCHOOL OF THE DEAD
ハイスクール・オブ・ザ・デッド

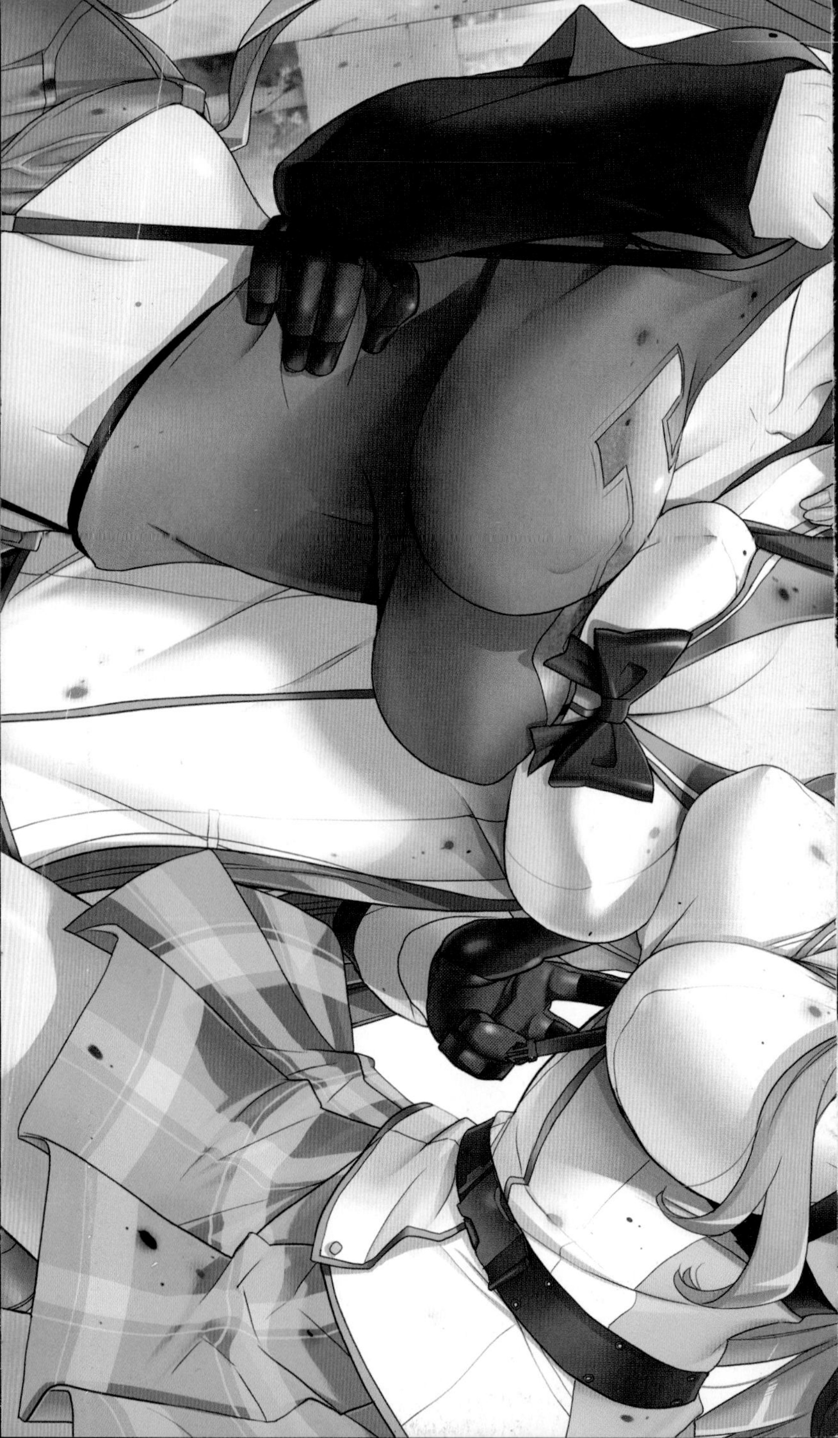

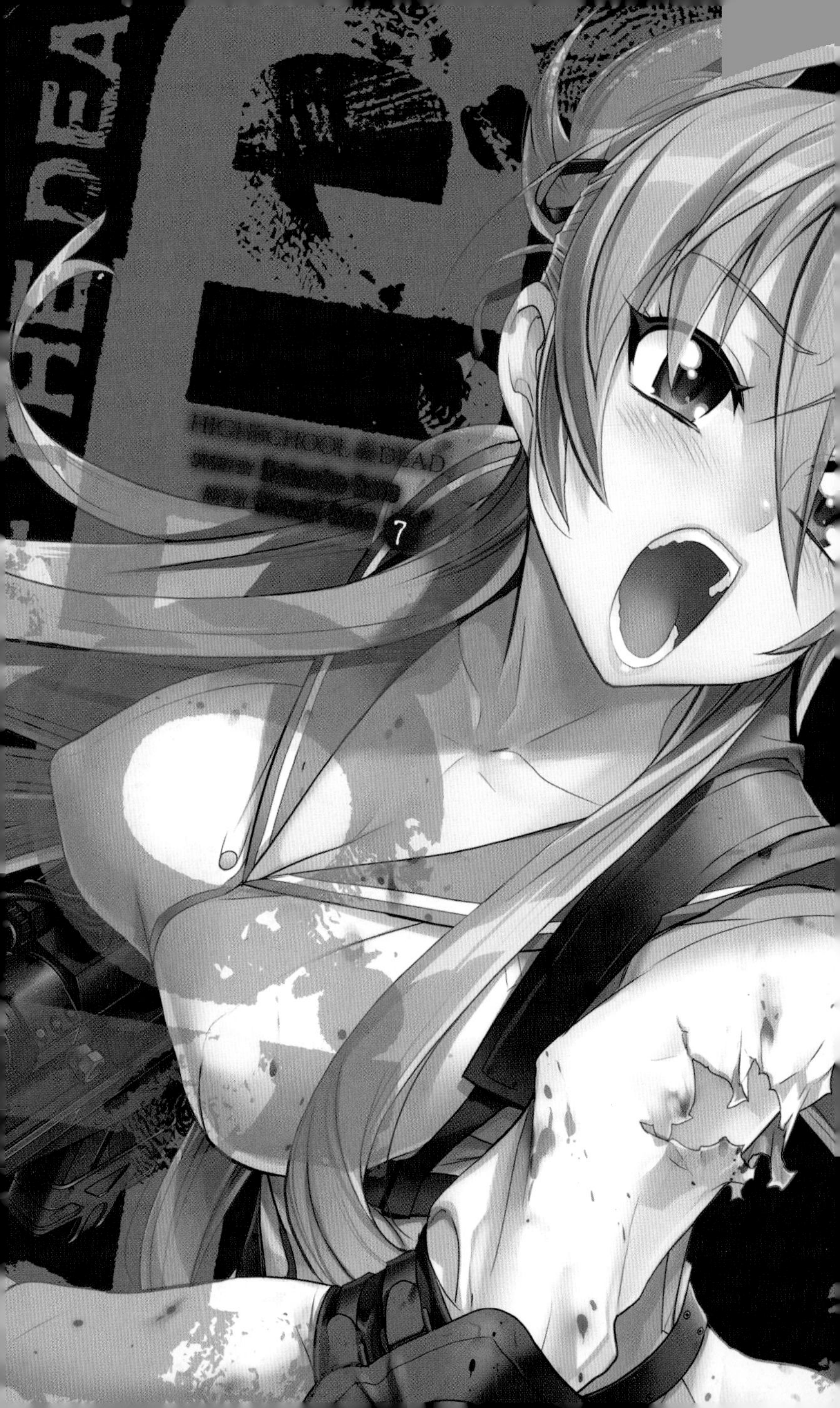
7

CONTENTS

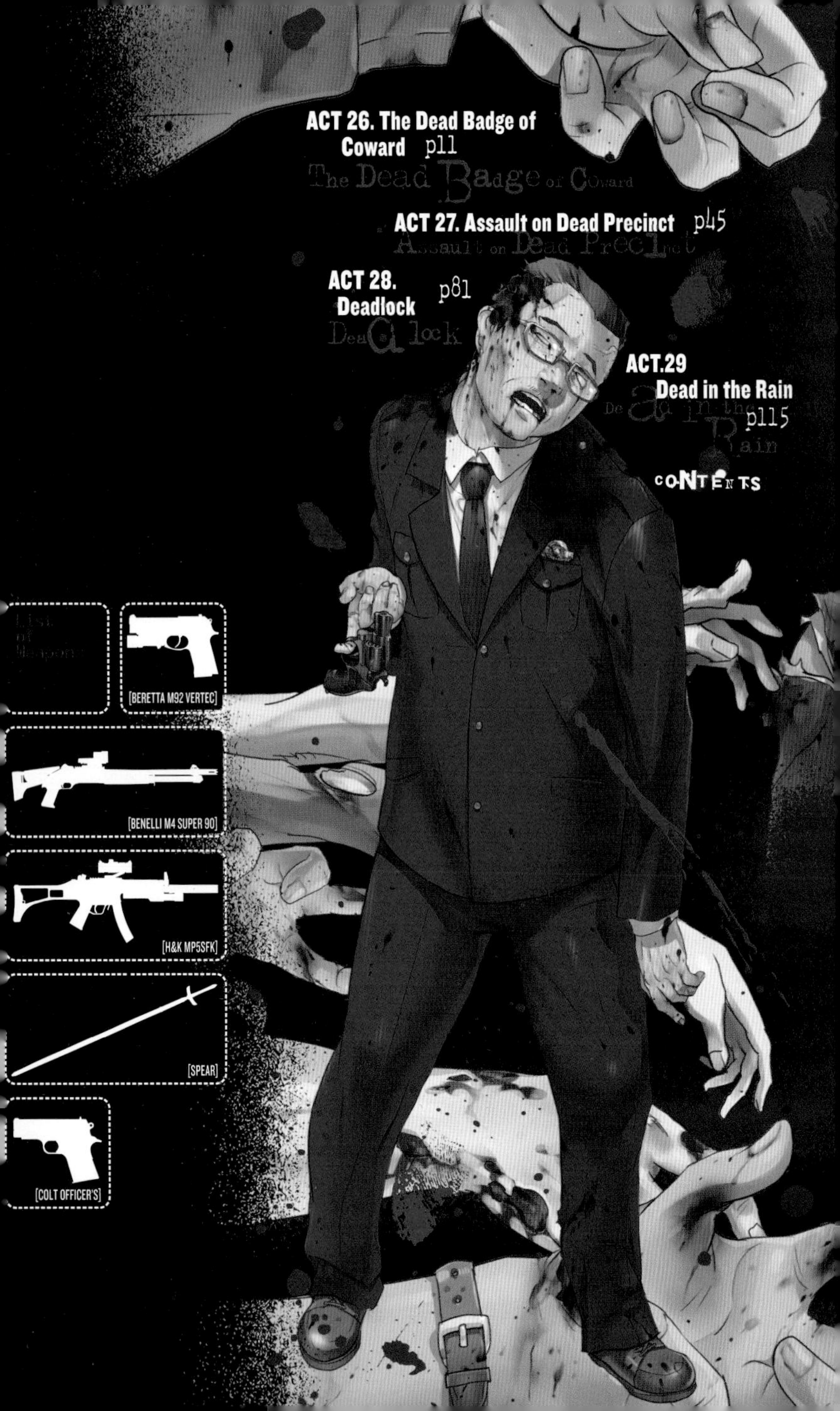
[BERETTA M92 VERTEC]
[BENELLI M4 SUPER 90]
[H&K MP5SFK]
[SPEAR]
[COLT OFFICER'S]

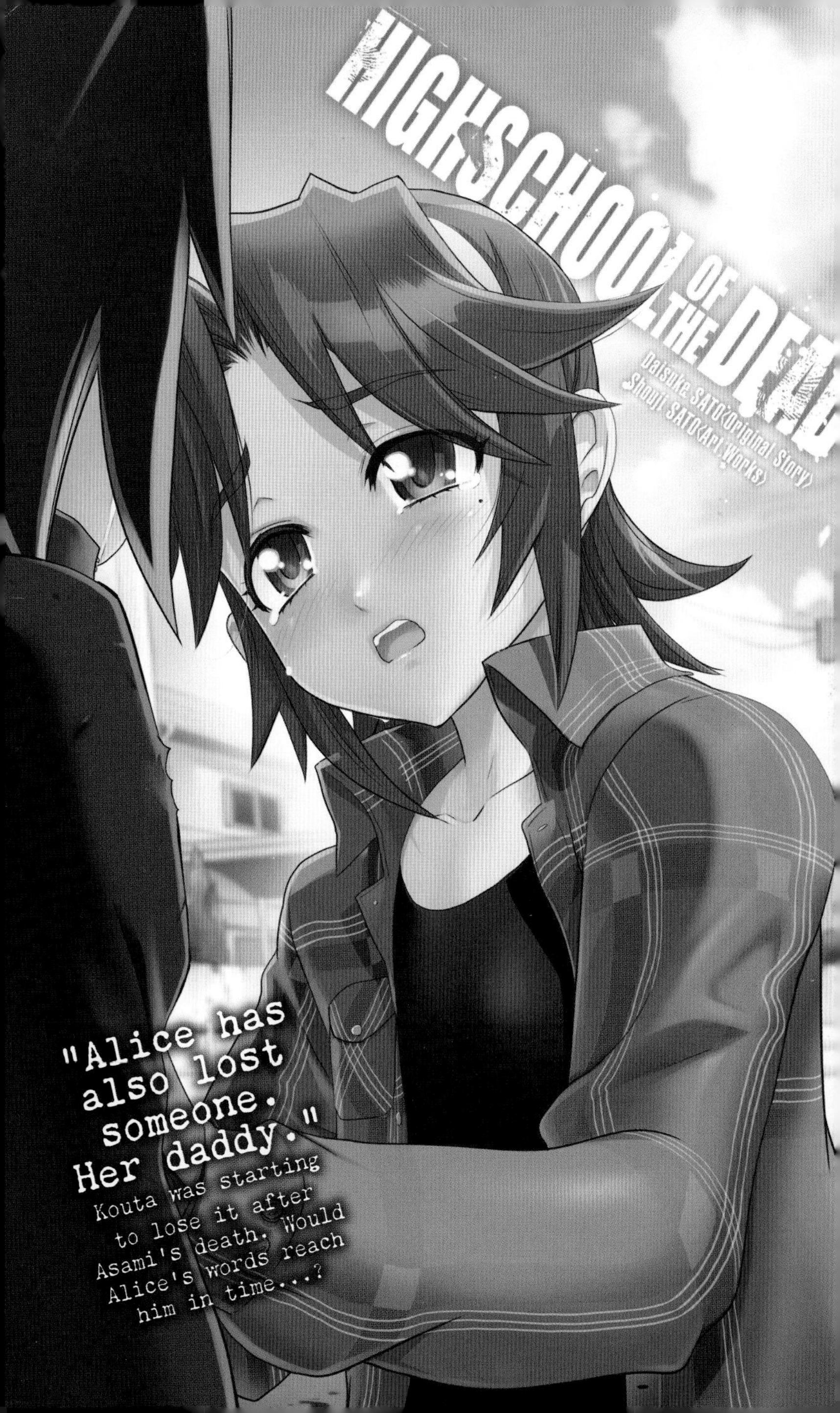
HIGHSCHOOL OF THE DEAD
Daisuke SATO〈Original Story〉
Shouji SATO〈Art Works〉
"Alice has also lost someone. Her daddy."
Kouta was starting to lose it after Asami's death. Would Alice's words reach him in time...?

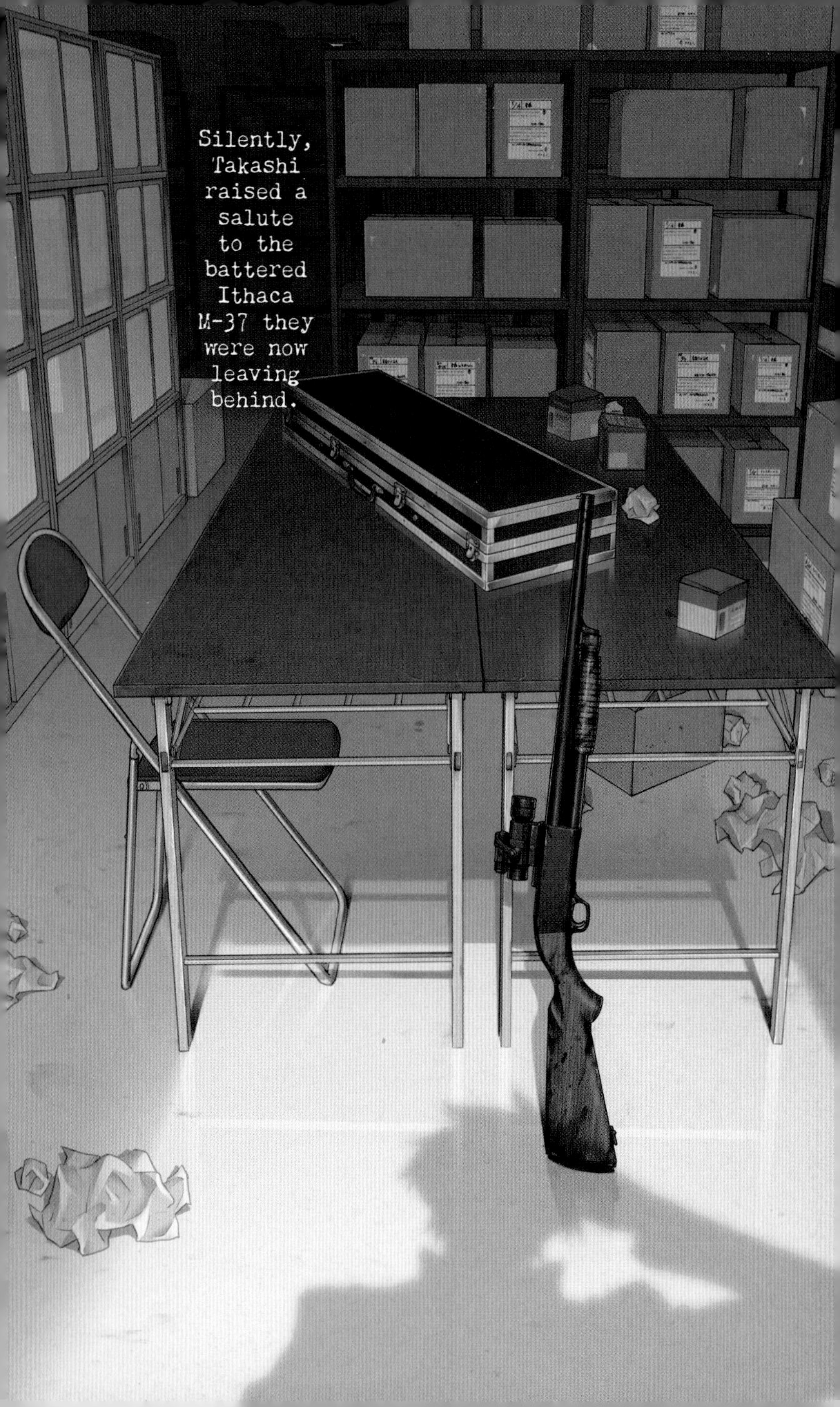
Silently, Takashi raised a salute to the battered Ithaca M-37 they were now leaving behind.

HIGHSCHOOL OF THE DEAD

7

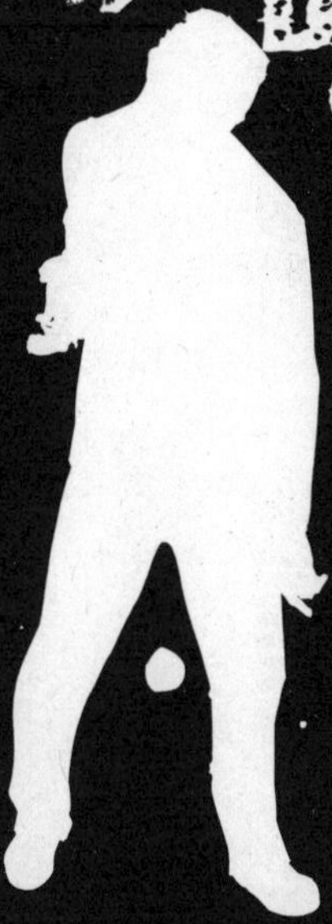

STORY BY

Daisuke Sato

ART BY

Shouji Sato

That was the day our once peaceful world fell apart. A, second-year at the private school Fujimi High, Takashi Komuro escapes from the living dead, known as "them," when they suddenly storm his campus. He and his childhood friend, Rei Miyamoto, join Saya Takagi, Kouta Hirano, Saeko Busujima, and the school nurse, Shizuka Marikawa, and flee the school, seeking refuge in the home of a friend of Marikawa-sensei's. Late that night, they rescue a little girl named Alice Maresato and welcome her into their group.

The next morning, the team heads to the Takagi estate and is saved along the way by Saya's mother and offered temporary sanctuary in the Takagi mansion. At the same time, an EMP attack is launched, and in the ensuing chaos, "they" breach the Takagi estate.

After fleeing the estate, the group reaches the safety of the shopping mall, where they join up with Officer Asami Nakaoka and another group of refugees. Some friction erupts between the two parties, but thanks to Kouta's quick thinking, they manage to avert a disaster between the two. The incident leads Asami to begin to develop feelings for Kouta. In order to save a senior among the refugees, a small party travels to a nearby hospital, resulting in another victim. To make matters worse, the officer who had gone out for help, Asami's senpai, has been turned into one of "them," filling the air within the mall with a sudden sense of doom.

When the security of the mall is breached, "they" infiltrate, and the team takes Asami with them as they head to Takashi and Rei's homes on foot. However, on the way there, Asami goes to rescue a high schooler surrounded by "them," sacrificing herself to save him. Responding to Asami's pleas to let her die a human death, Kouta points his gun at her and pulls the trigger.

ACT.26 The Dead Badge of Coward

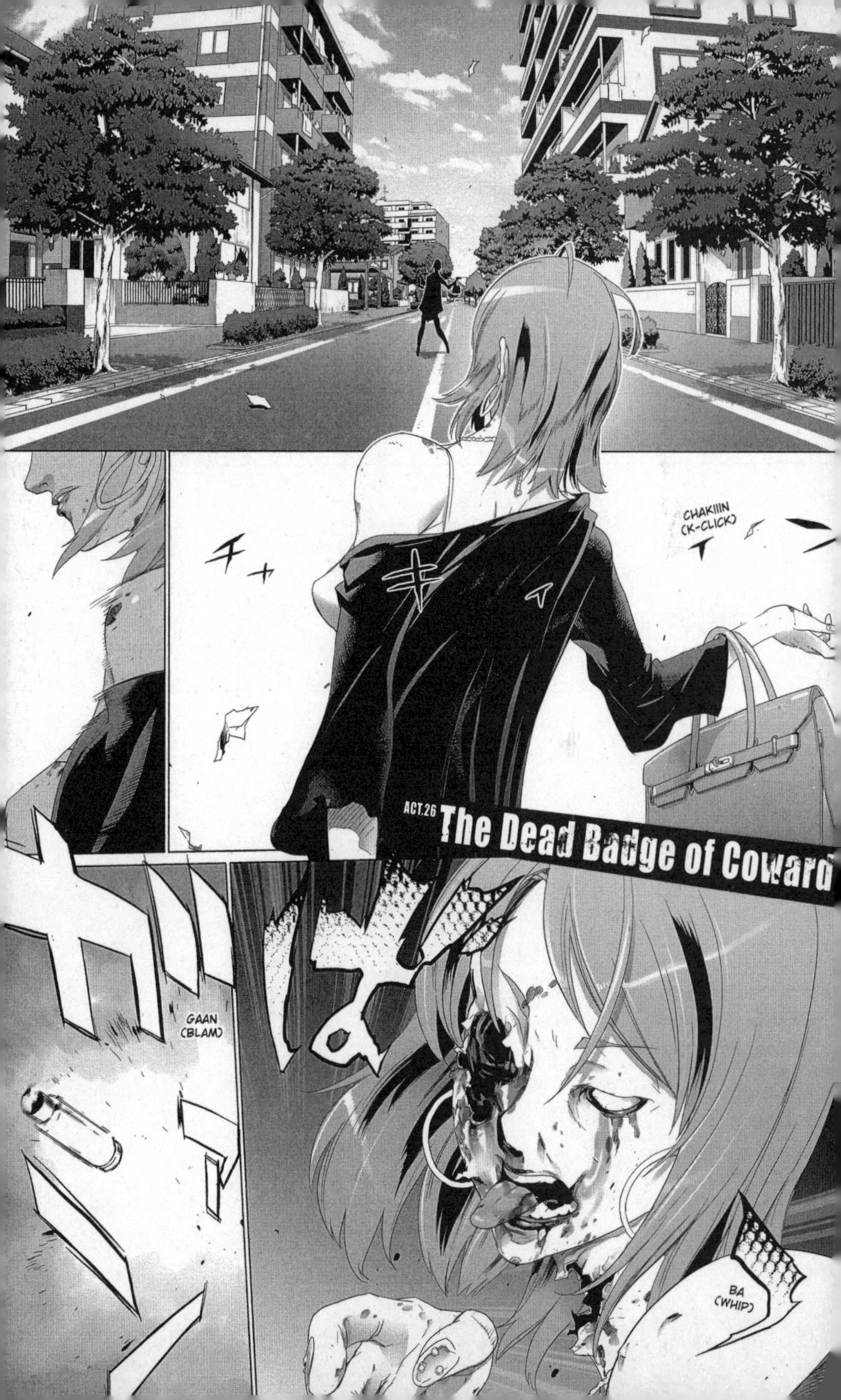

チャキイ
CHAKIIIN (K-CLICK)
BA (WHIP)
GAAN (BLAM)

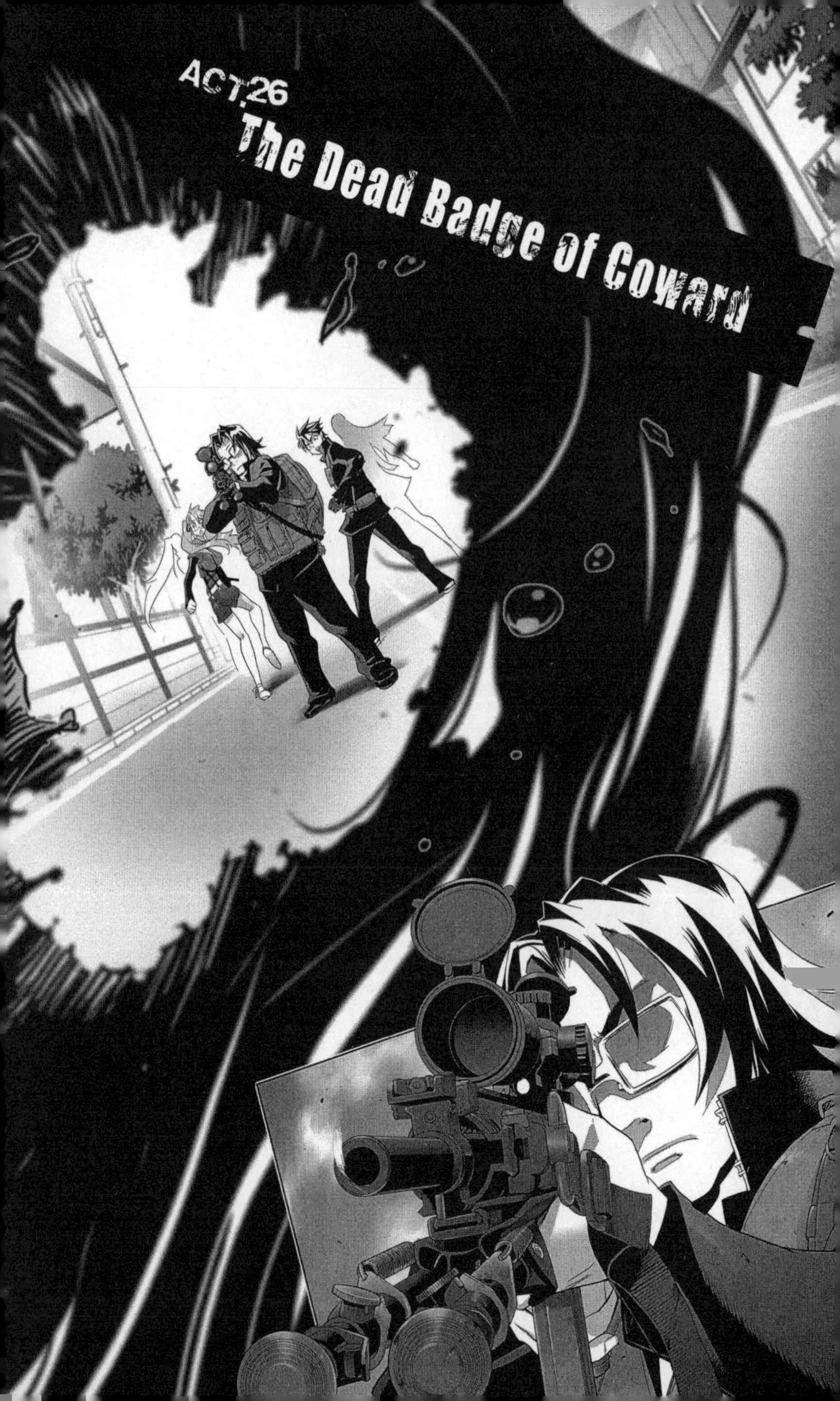

ACT.26
The Dead Badge of Coward

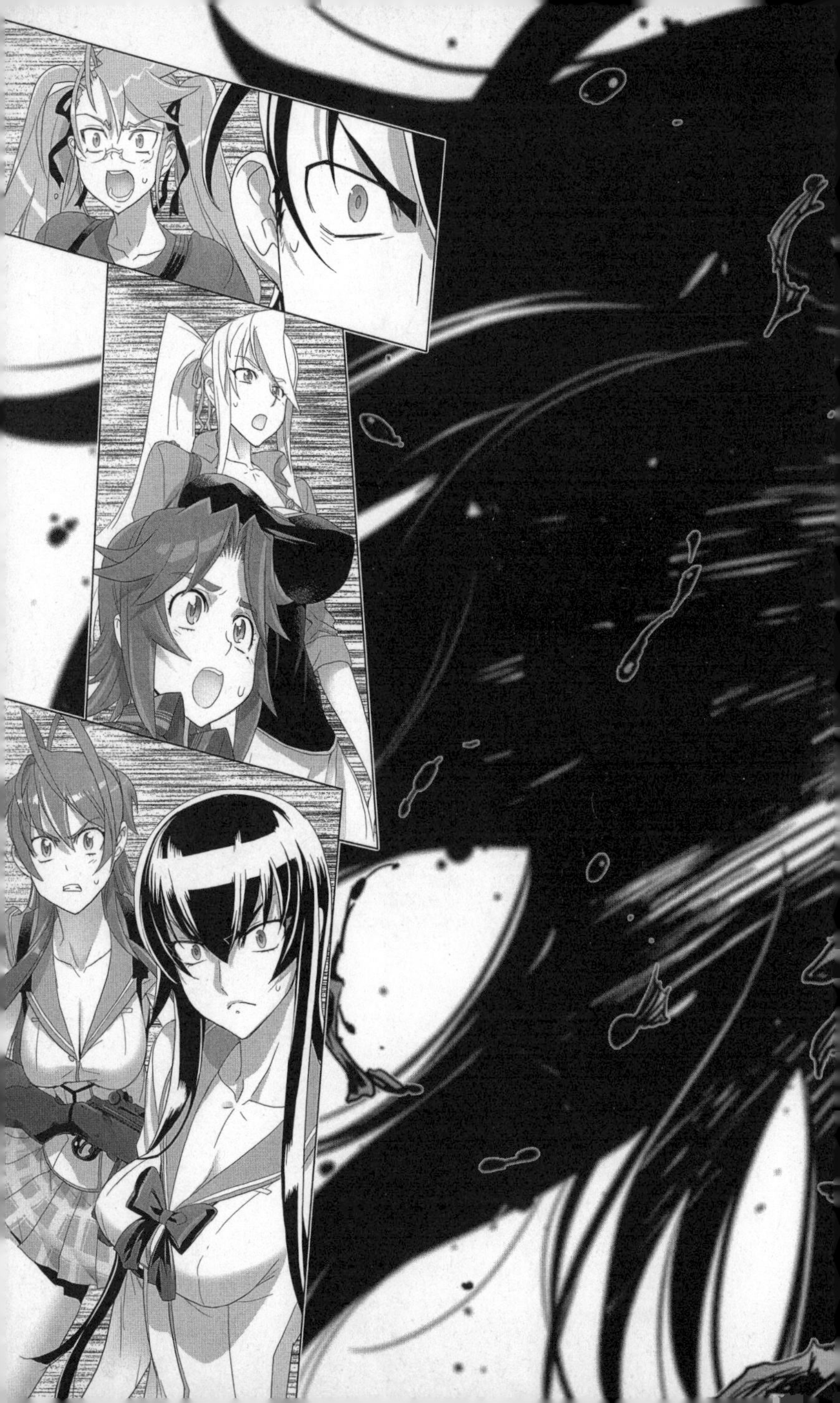

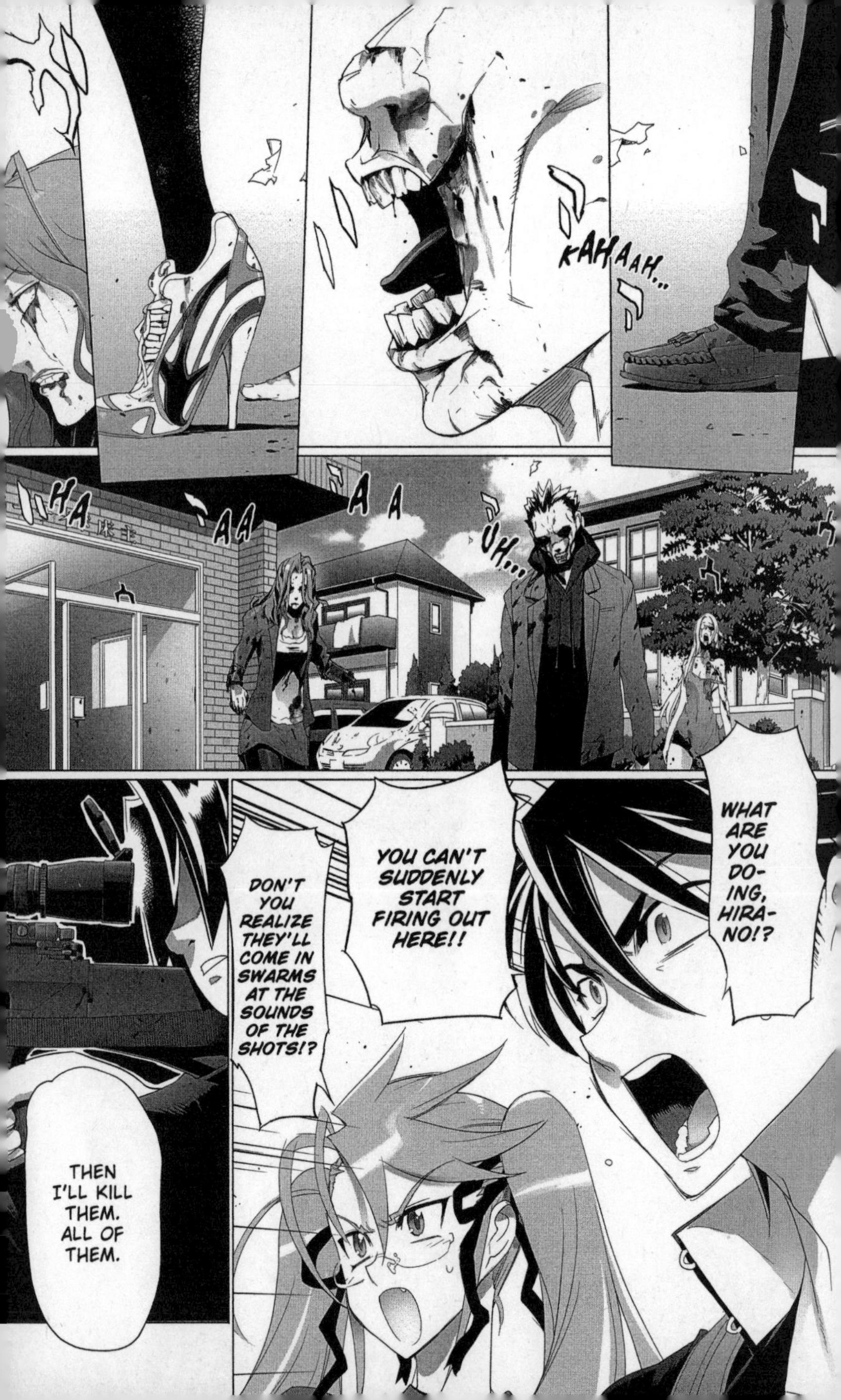
KAHAAAH...
HA AA
A A
UH...
WHAT ARE YOU DOING, HIRANO!?
YOU CAN'T SUDDENLY START FIRING OUT HERE!!
DON'T YOU REALIZE THEY'LL COME IN SWARMS AT THE SOUNDS OF THE SHOTS!?
THEN I'LL KILL THEM. ALL OF THEM.

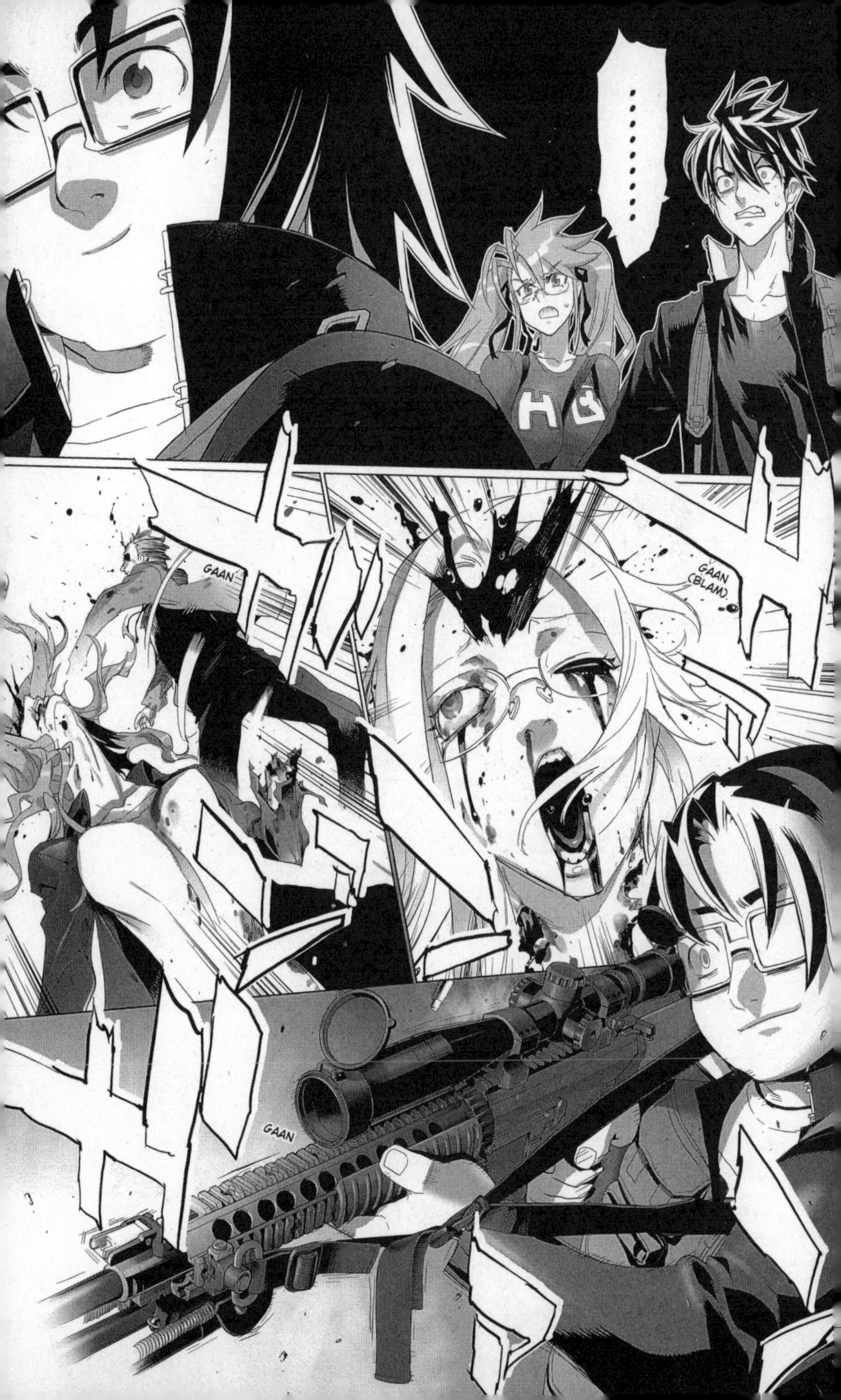
......
GAAN
(BLAM)
GAAN
GAAN

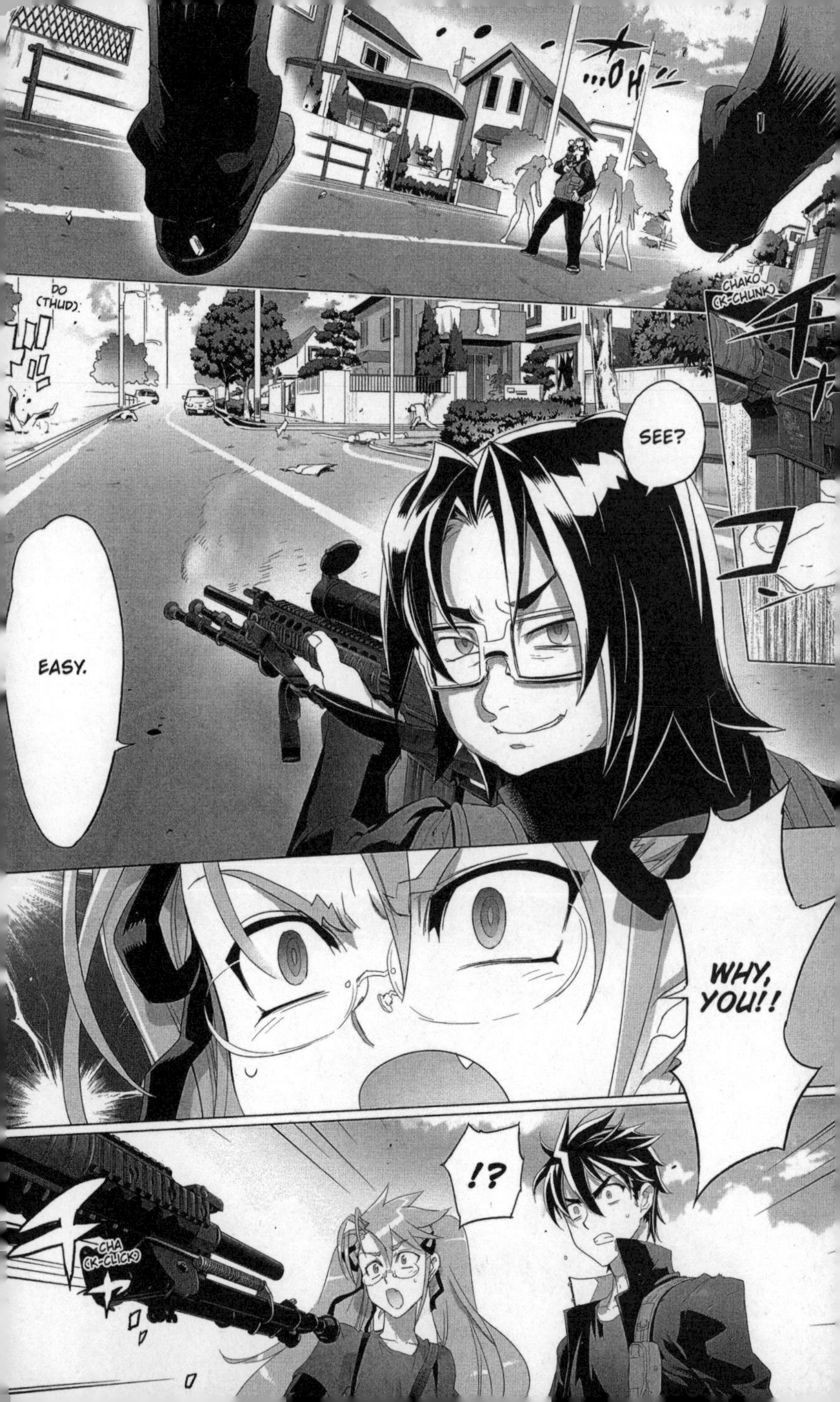

...OH!!
CHAKO (K-CHUNK)
SEE?
DO (THUD)
EASY.
WHY, YOU!!
!?
CHA (K-CLICK)

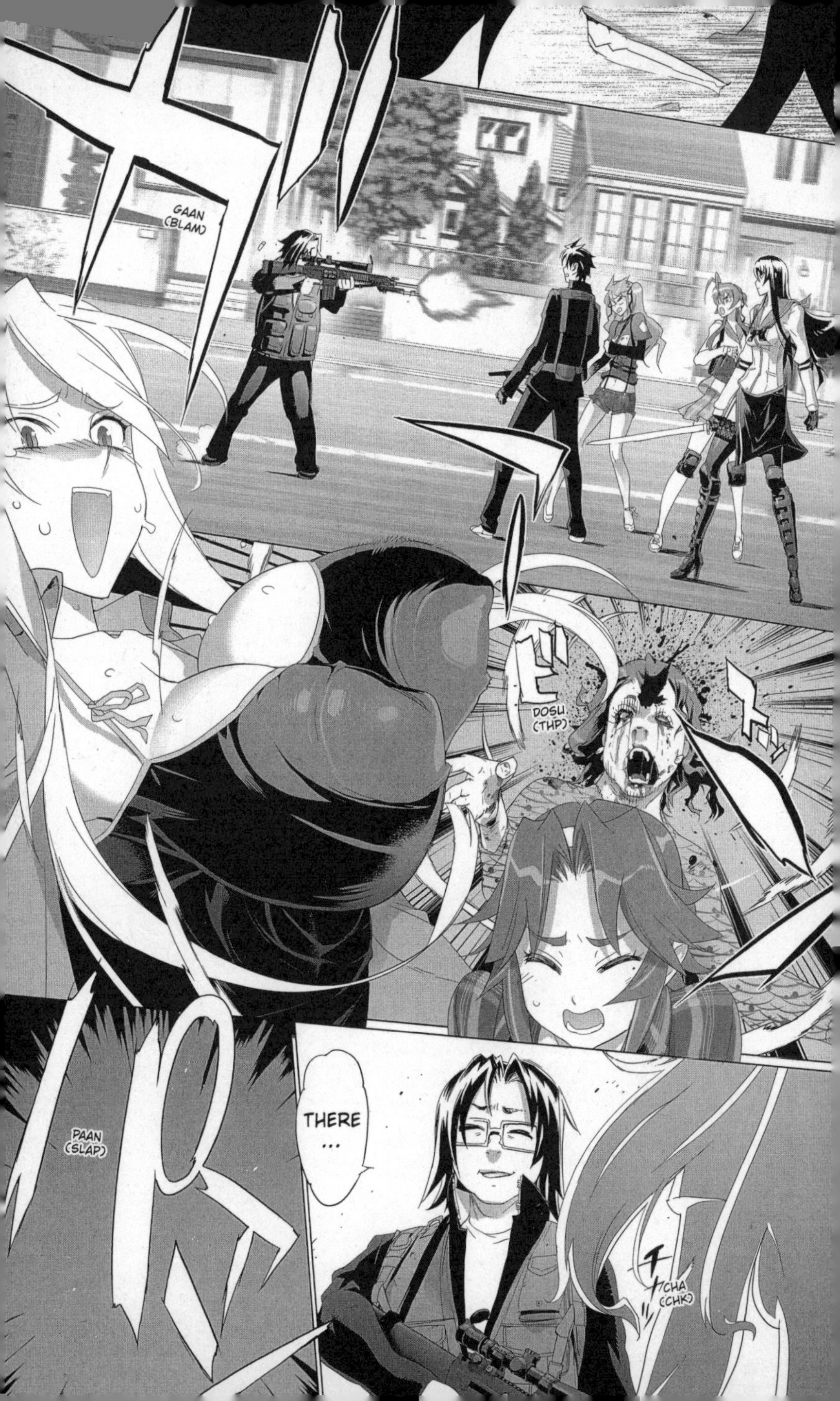
GAAN (BLAM)
DOSU (THP)
THERE ...
PAAN (SLAP)
CHA (CHK)

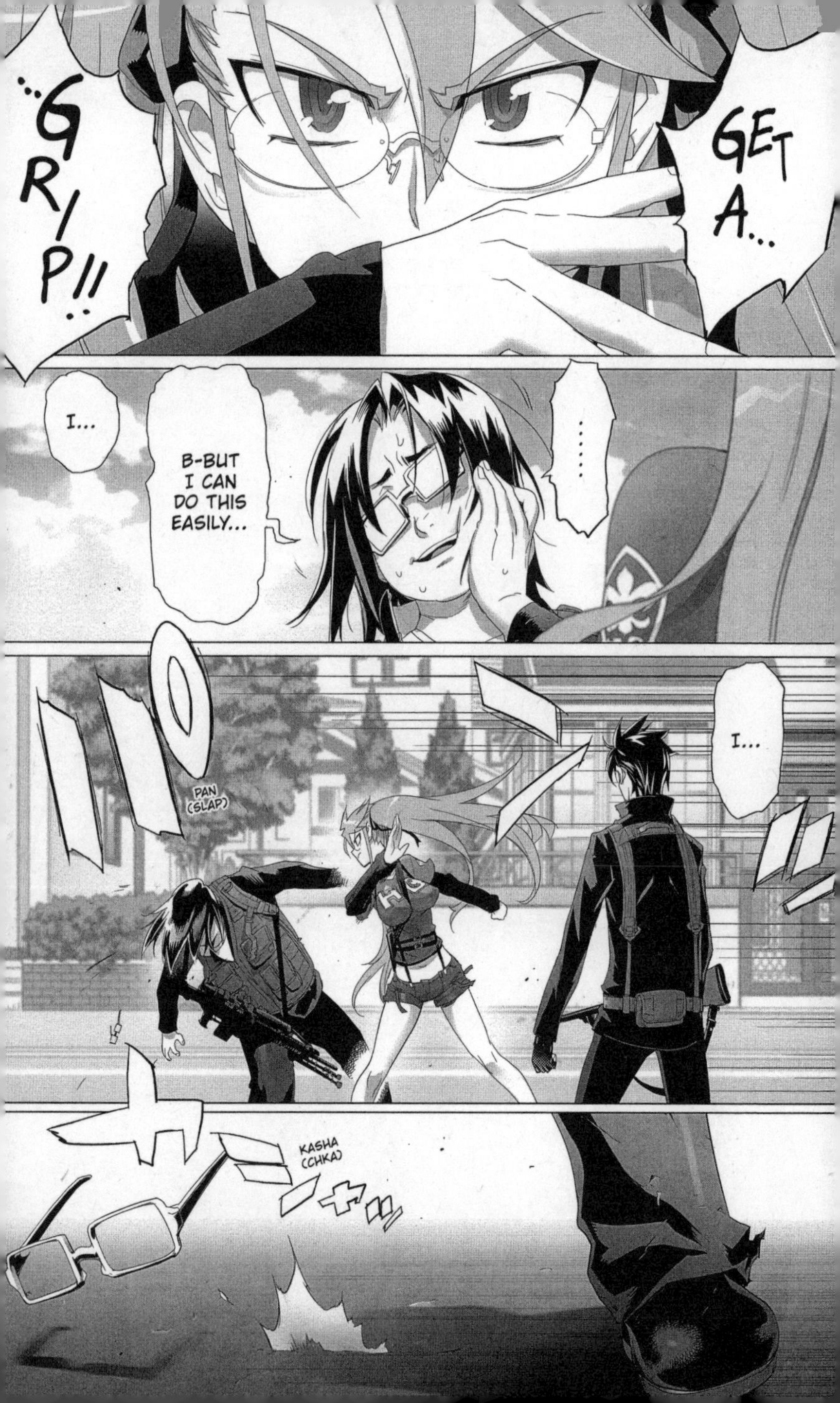
GET A...
...GRIP!!
......
B-BUT I CAN DO THIS EASILY...
I...
I...
PAN (SLAP)
KASHA (CHKA)

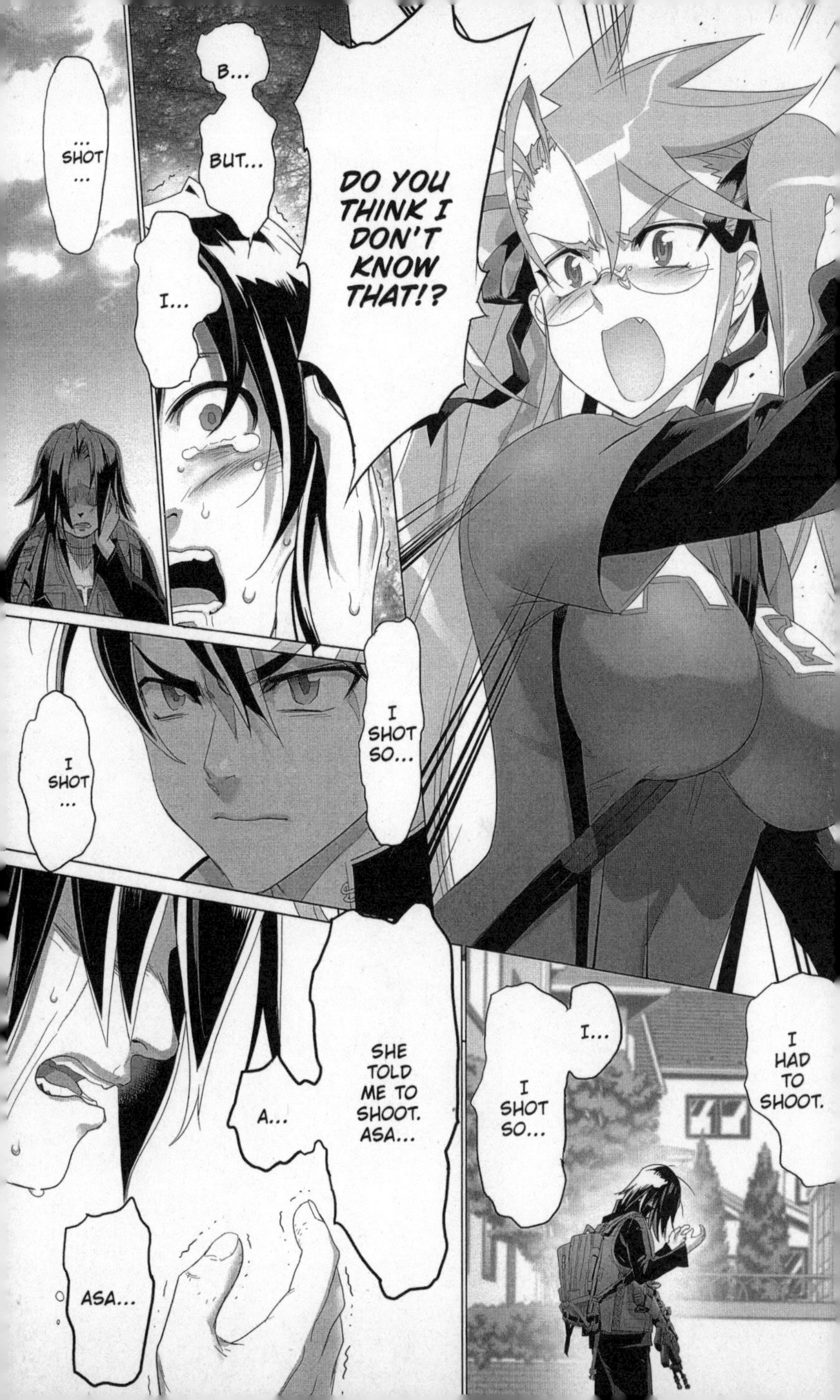
DO YOU THINK I DON'T KNOW THAT!?
B...
BUT...
I...
...SHOT...
I SHOT SO...
I SHOT...
I HAD TO SHOOT.
I...
I SHOT SO...
SHE TOLD ME TO SHOOT. ASA...
A...
ASA...

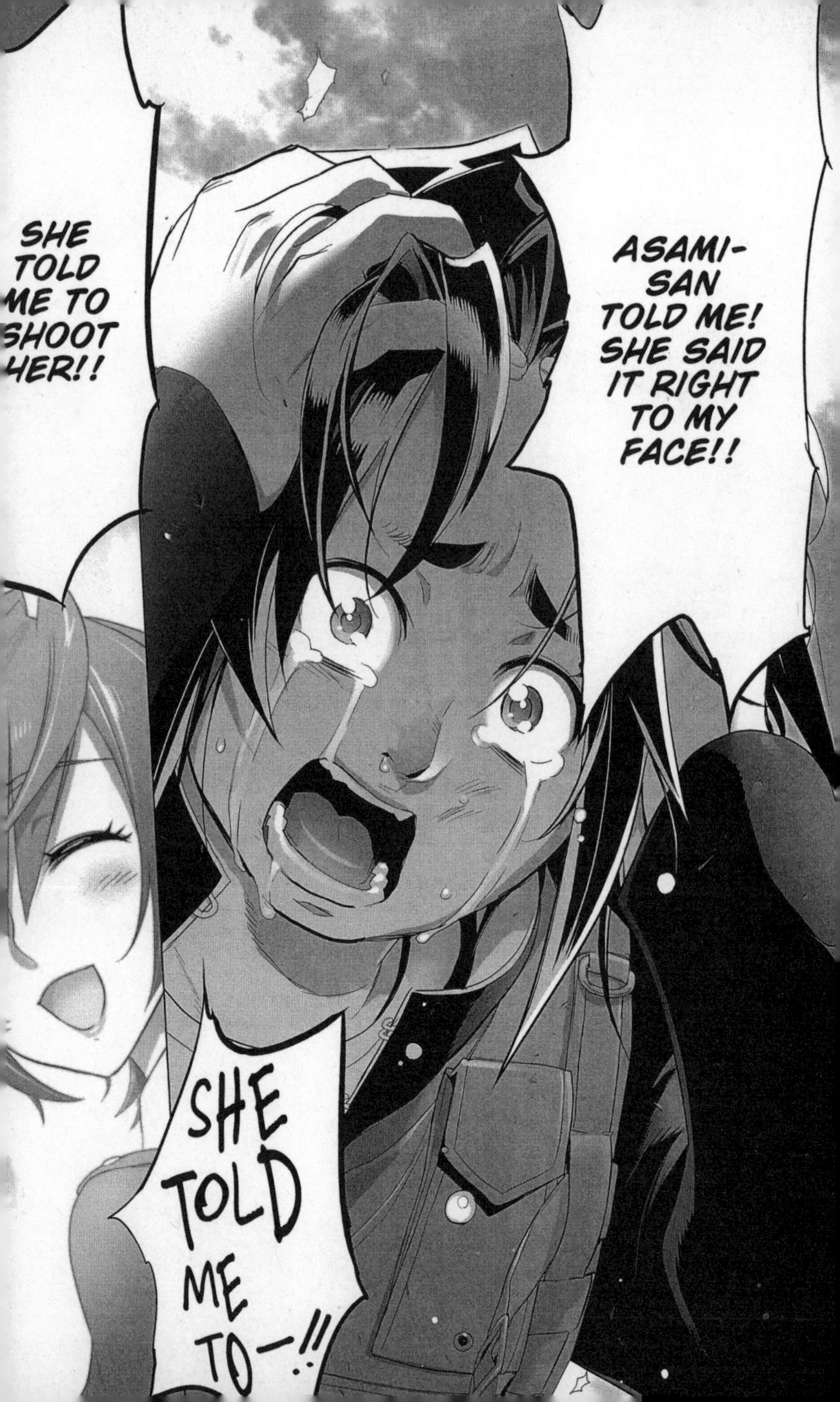
ASAMI-SAN TOLD ME! SHE SAID IT RIGHT TO MY FACE!!
SHE TOLD ME TO SHOOT HER!!
SHE TOLD ME TO—!!

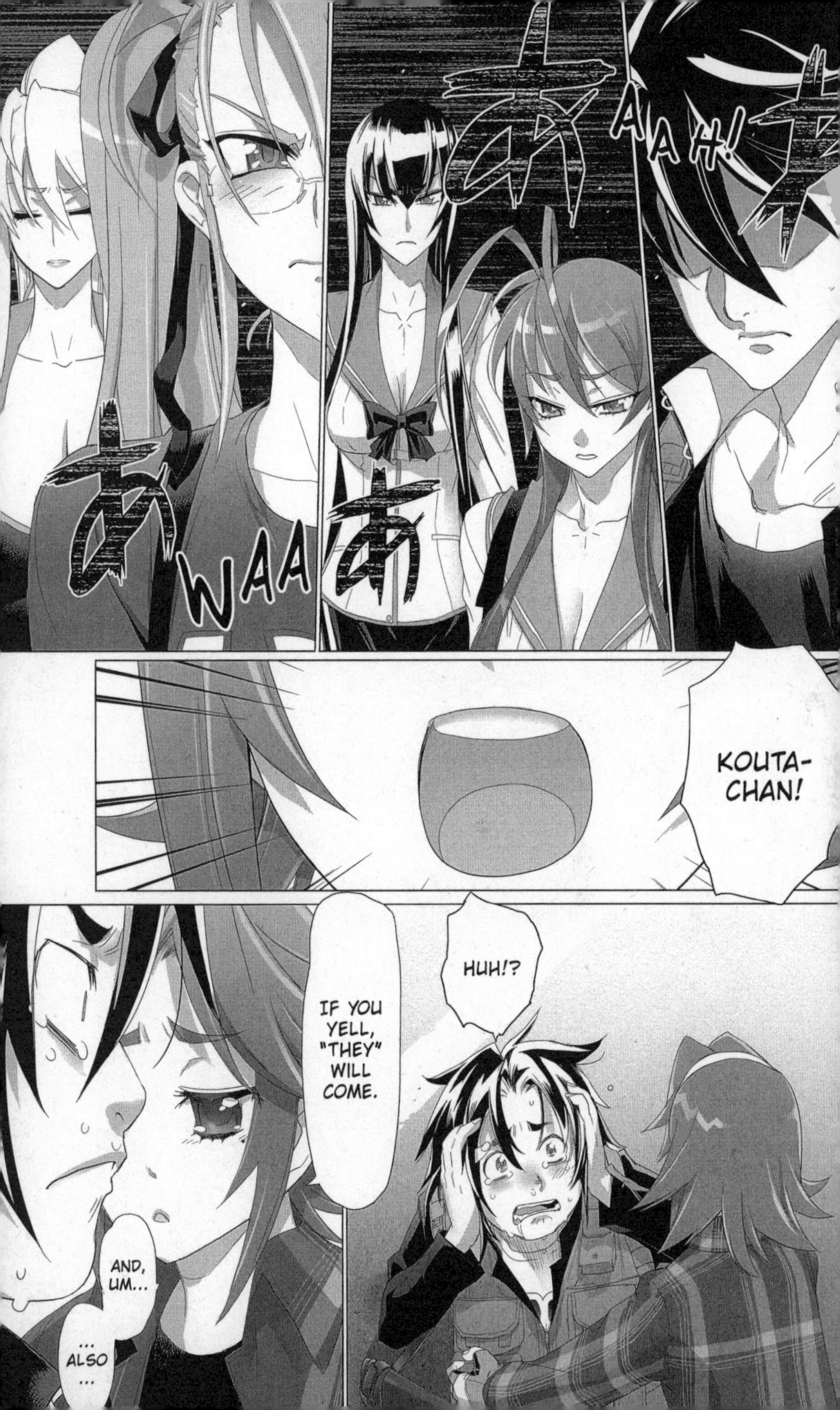

あ AAH! あ
あ WAA あ
KOUTA-CHAN!
HUH!?
IF YOU YELL, "THEY" WILL COME.
AND, UM...
...ALSO...

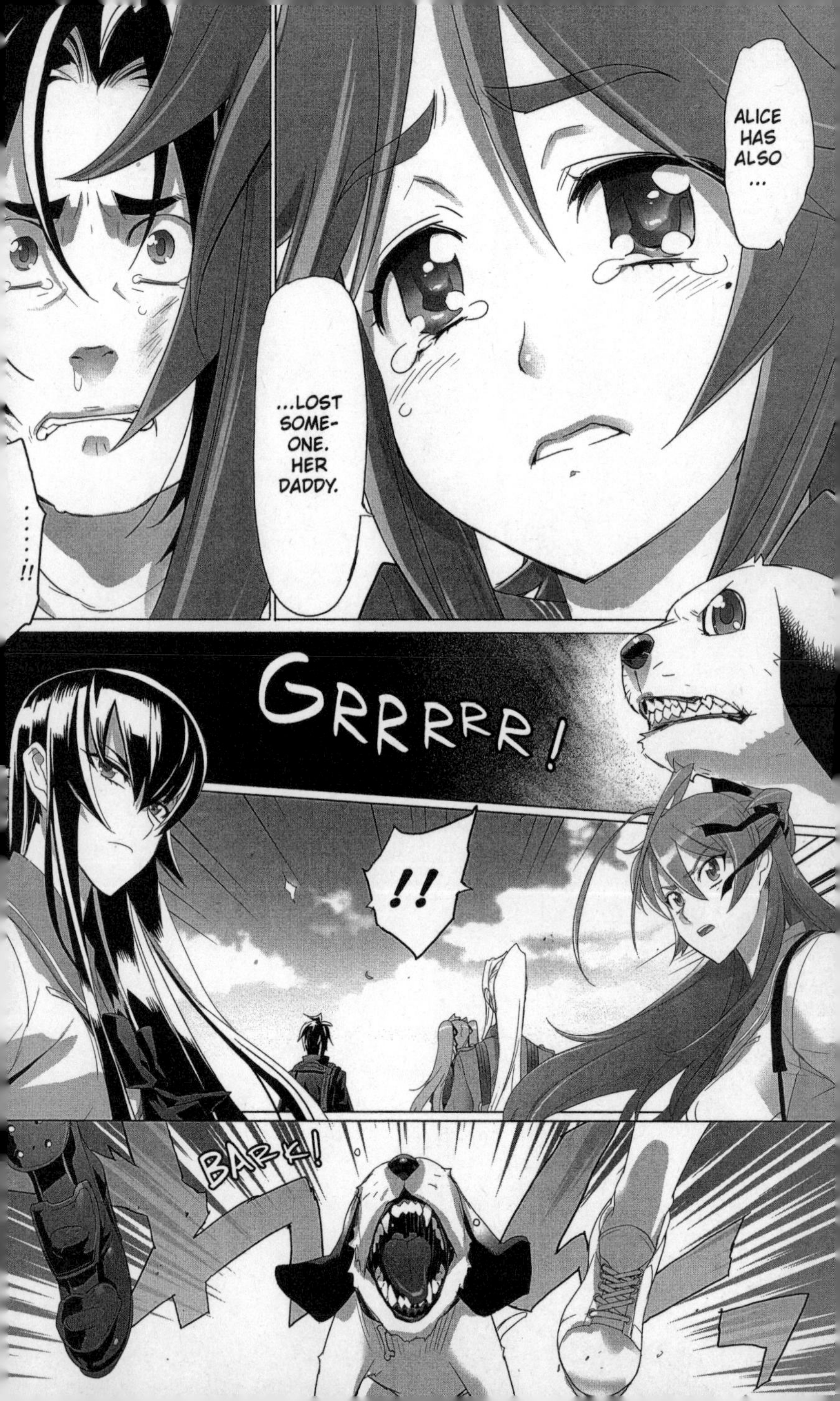
ALICE HAS ALSO ...
...LOST SOME-ONE. HER DADDY.
......!!
GRRRRRR!
!!
BARK!

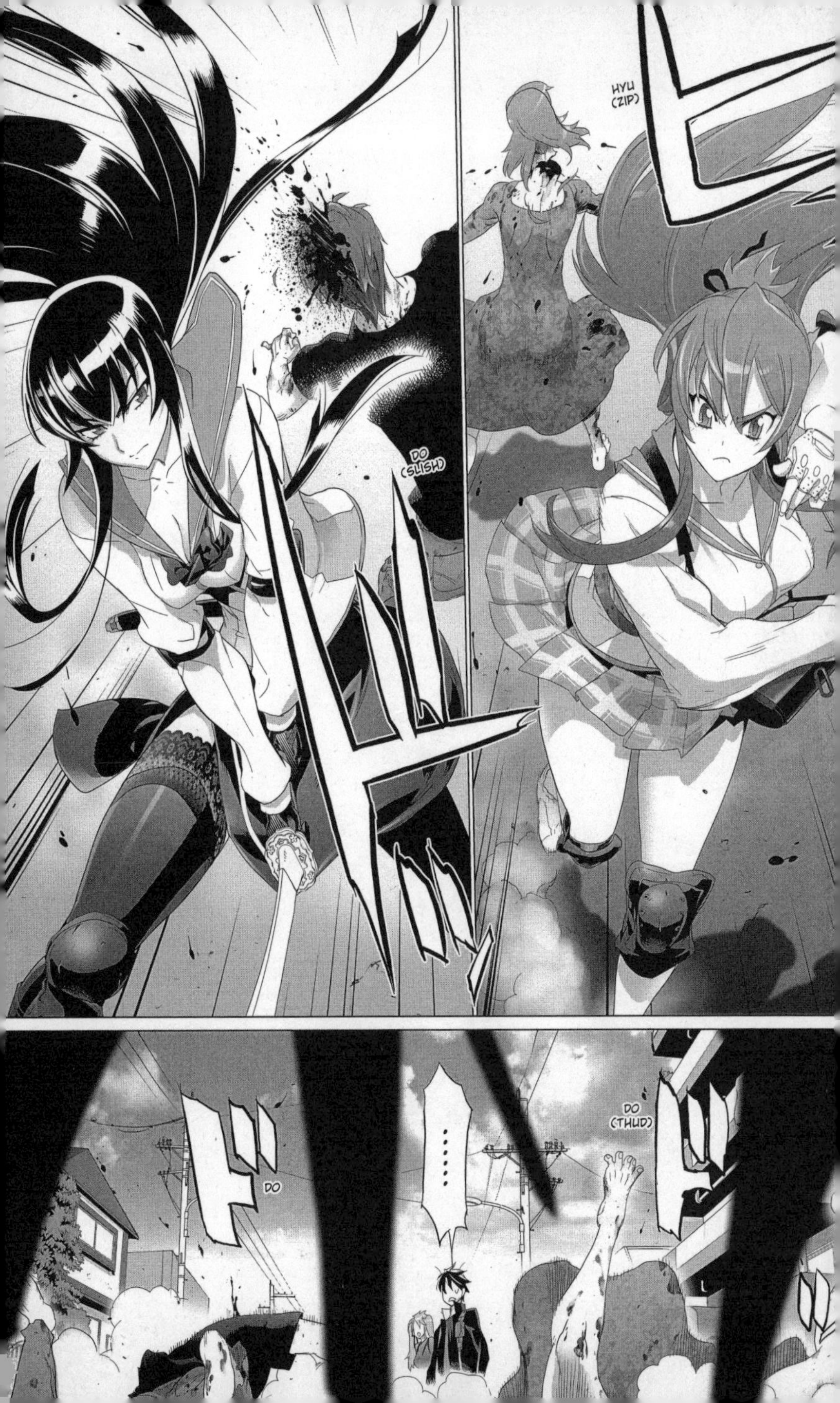
HYU
(ZIP)
DO
(SLISH)
DO
(THUD)
......
DO

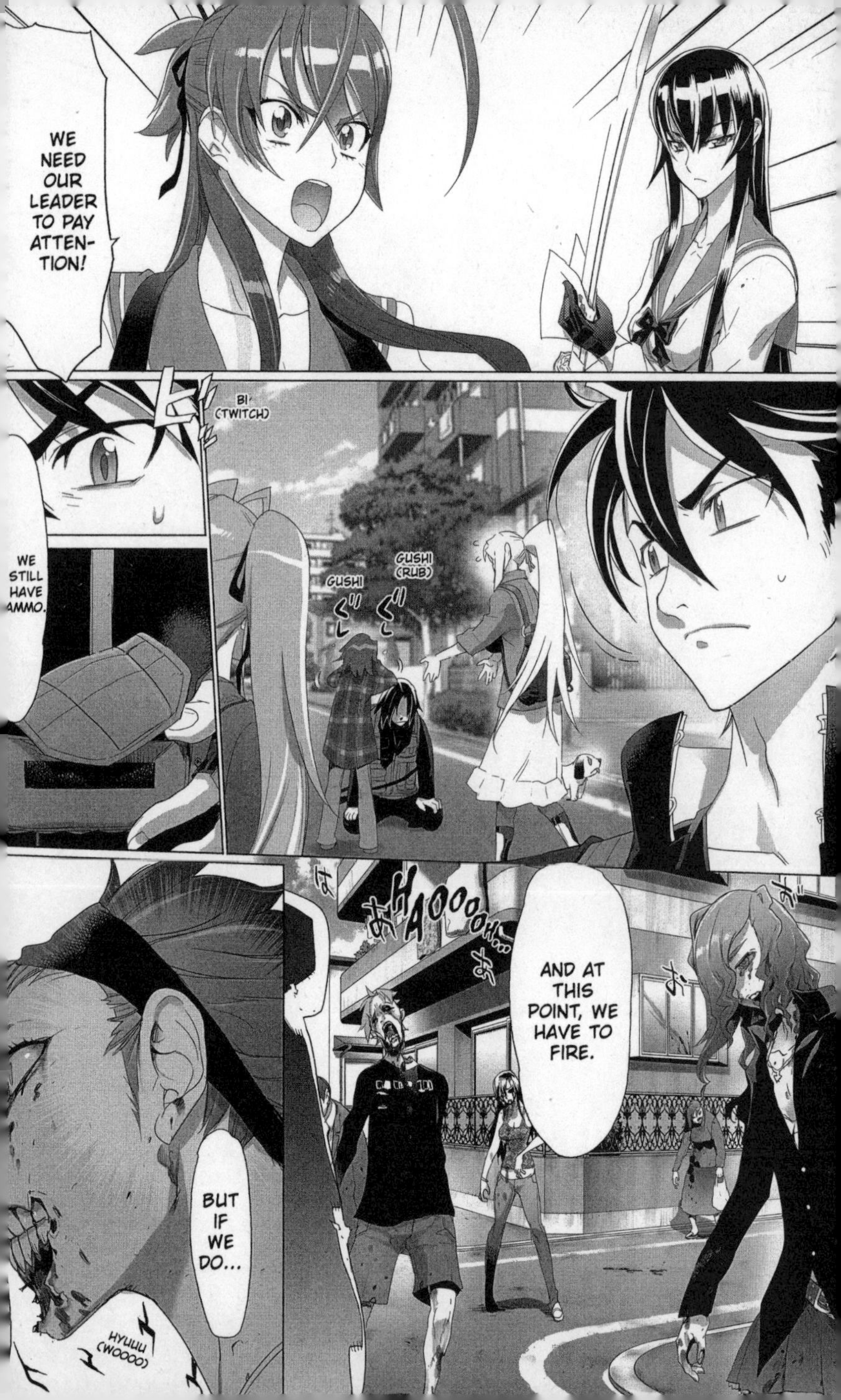
WE NEED OUR LEADER TO PAY ATTEN-TION!
GUSHI (RUB)
GUSHI
BI (TWITCH)
WE STILL HAVE AMMO.
AND AT THIS POINT, WE HAVE TO FIRE.
HAOOOOH...
BUT IF WE DO...
HYUUU (WOOOO)

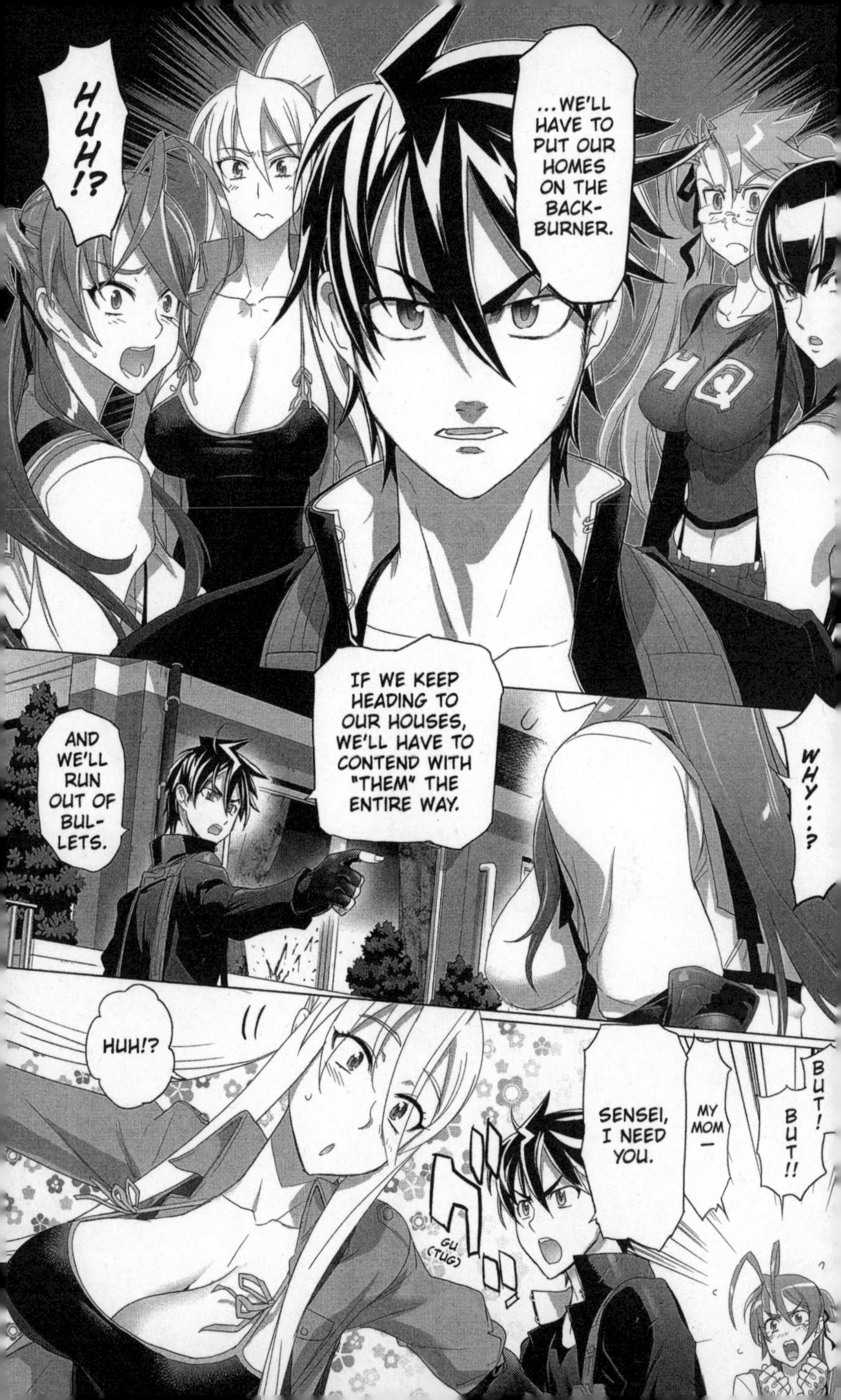
...WE'LL HAVE TO PUT OUR HOMES ON THE BACK-BURNER.
HUH!?
WHY...?
IF WE KEEP HEADING TO OUR HOUSES, WE'LL HAVE TO CONTEND WITH "THEM" THE ENTIRE WAY.
AND WE'LL RUN OUT OF BUL-LETS.
BUT! BUT!!
MY MOM —
SENSEI, I NEED YOU.
HUH!?
GU (TUG)

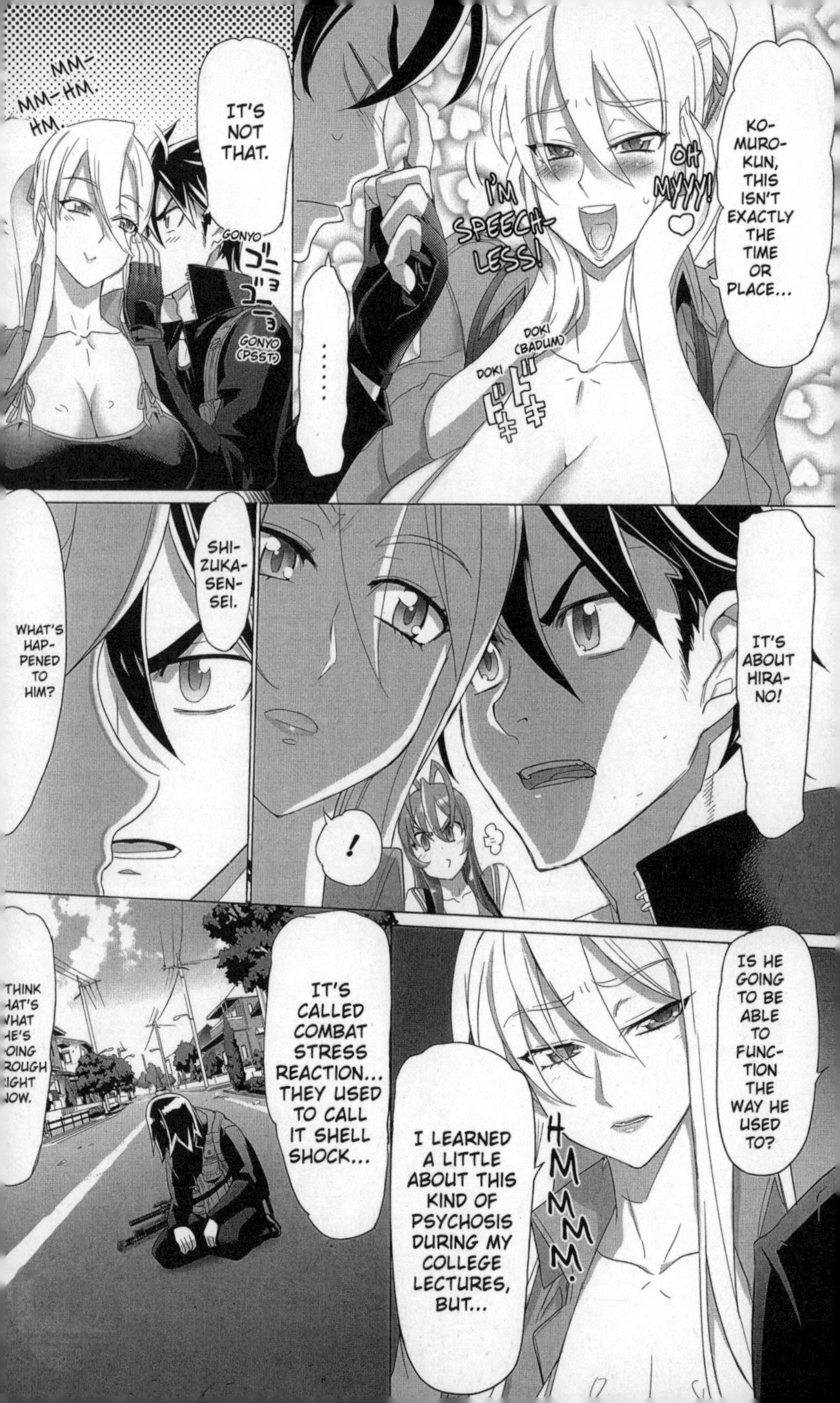
KO-MURO-KUN, THIS ISN'T EXACTLY THE TIME OR PLACE...
OH MYYY!
I'M SPEECH-LESS!
DOKI (BADUM) DOKI
......
IT'S NOT THAT.
MM-MM-HM. HM.
GONYO
GONYO (PSST)
IT'S ABOUT HIRA-NO!
!
SHI-ZUKA-SEN-SEI.
WHAT'S HAP-PENED TO HIM?
IS HE GOING TO BE ABLE TO FUNC-TION THE WAY HE USED TO?
HMMMM.
I LEARNED A LITTLE ABOUT THIS KIND OF PSYCHOSIS DURING MY COLLEGE LECTURES, BUT...
IT'S CALLED COMBAT STRESS REACTION... THEY USED TO CALL IT SHELL SHOCK...
THINK HAT'S WHAT HE'S OING ROUGH IGHT NOW.

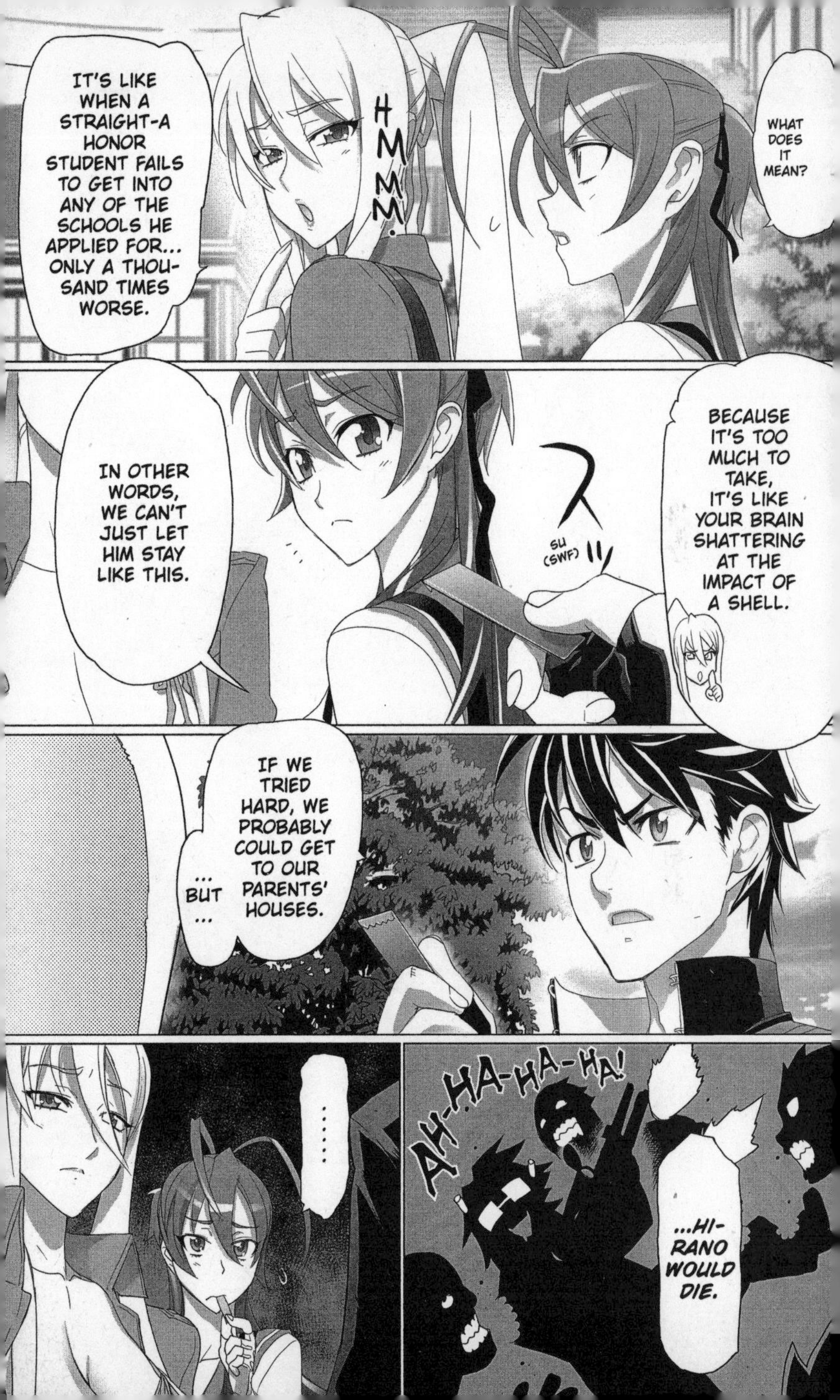
WHAT DOES IT MEAN?
HMMM.
IT'S LIKE WHEN A STRAIGHT-A HONOR STUDENT FAILS TO GET INTO ANY OF THE SCHOOLS HE APPLIED FOR... ONLY A THOUSAND TIMES WORSE.
BECAUSE IT'S TOO MUCH TO TAKE, IT'S LIKE YOUR BRAIN SHATTERING AT THE IMPACT OF A SHELL.
SU (SWF)
IN OTHER WORDS, WE CAN'T JUST LET HIM STAY LIKE THIS.
IF WE TRIED HARD, WE PROBABLY COULD GET TO OUR PARENTS' HOUSES.
...BUT...
AH-HA-HA-HA-HA!
...HI-RANO WOULD DIE.
......

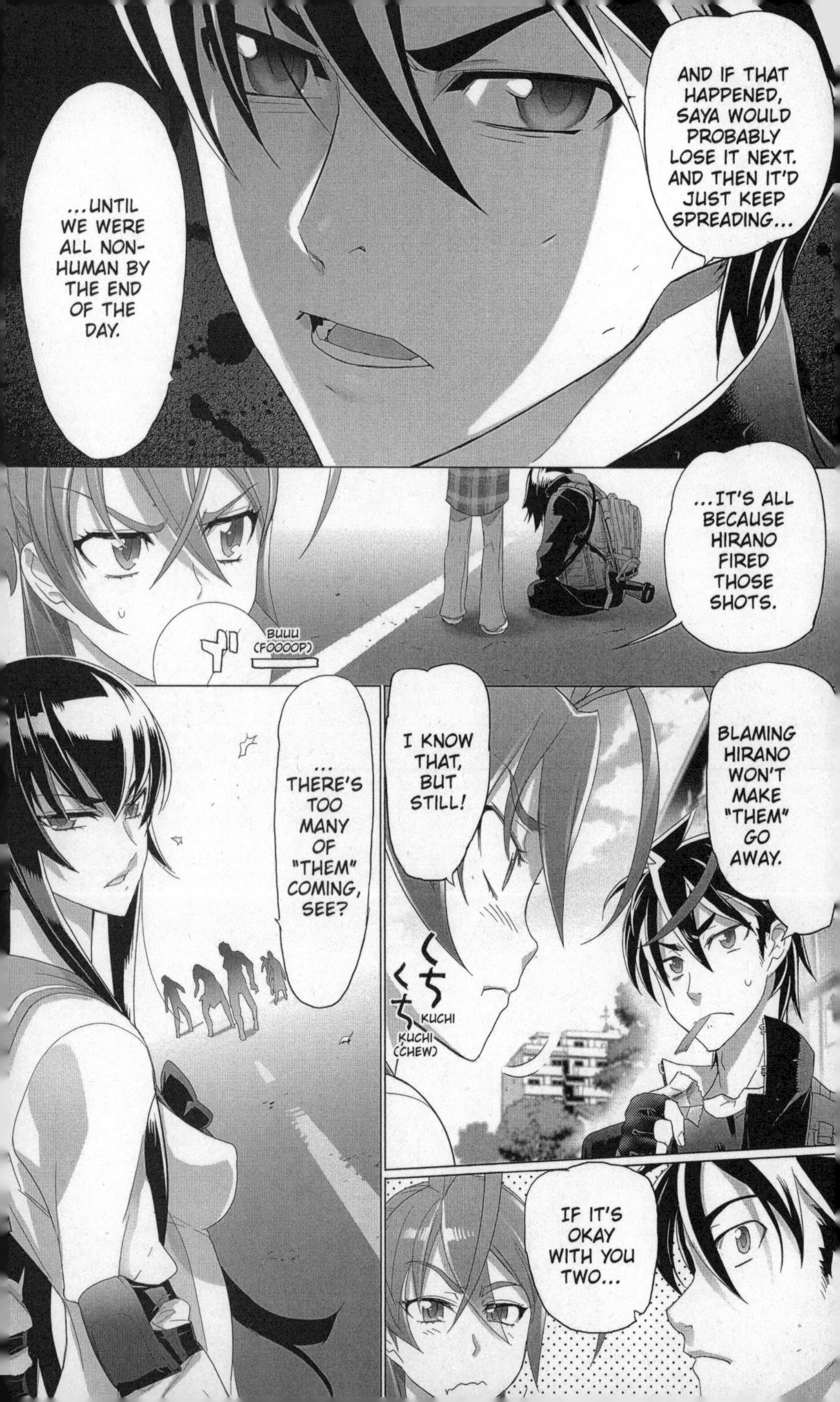
AND IF THAT HAPPENED, SAYA WOULD PROBABLY LOSE IT NEXT. AND THEN IT'D JUST KEEP SPREADING...
...UNTIL WE WERE ALL NON-HUMAN BY THE END OF THE DAY.
...IT'S ALL BECAUSE HIRANO FIRED THOSE SHOTS.
BUUU (FOOOOP)
BLAMING HIRANO WON'T MAKE "THEM" GO AWAY.
I KNOW THAT, BUT STILL!
KUCHI KUCHI (CHEW)
IF IT'S OKAY WITH YOU TWO...
... THERE'S TOO MANY OF "THEM" COMING, SEE?

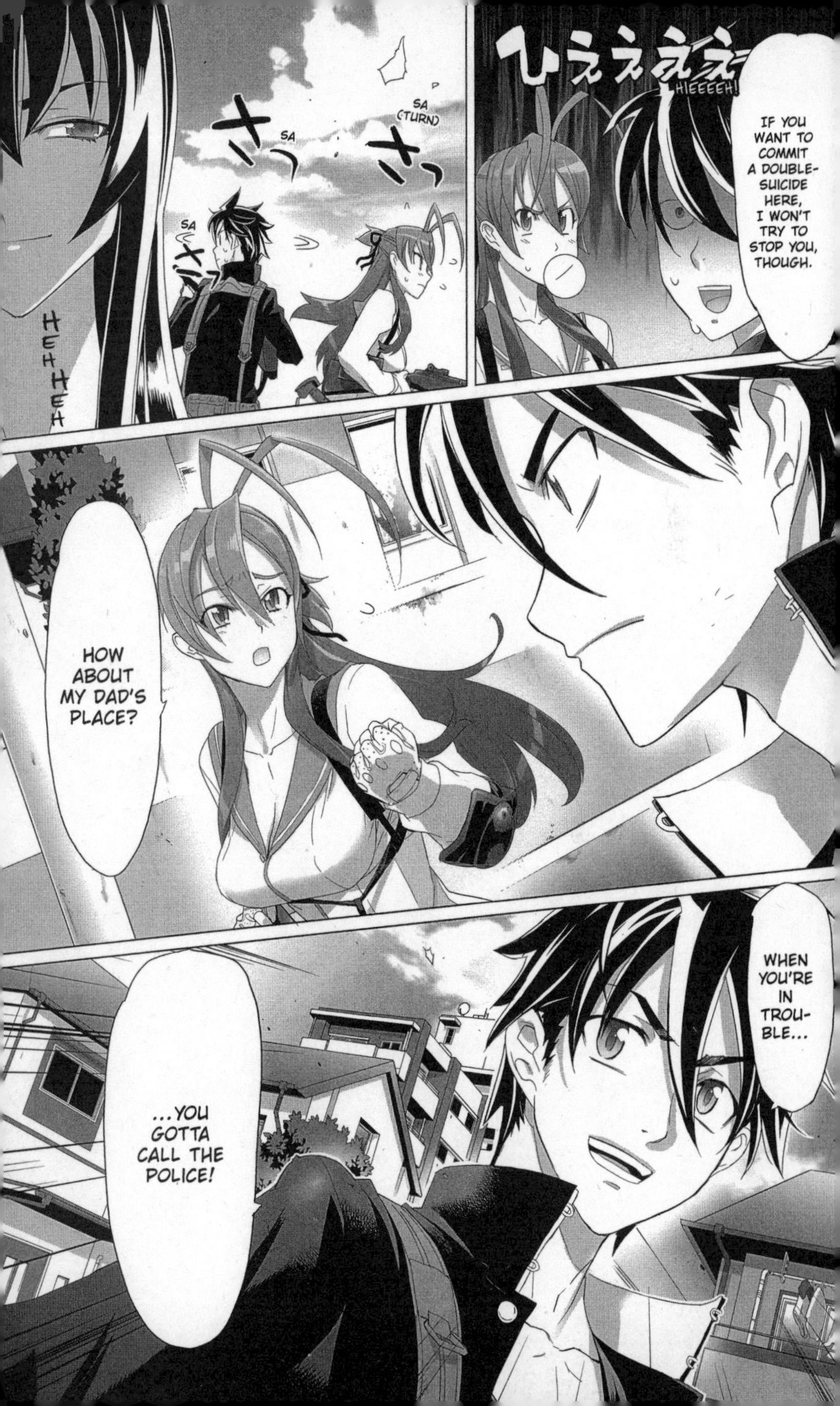
ひえええええ
HIEEEEH!
IF YOU WANT TO COMMIT A DOUBLE-SUICIDE HERE, I WON'T TRY TO STOP YOU, THOUGH.
さっ
SA (TURN)
さっ
SA
SA
HEH HEH
HOW ABOUT MY DAD'S PLACE?
WHEN YOU'RE IN TROU-BLE...
...YOU GOTTA CALL THE POLICE!

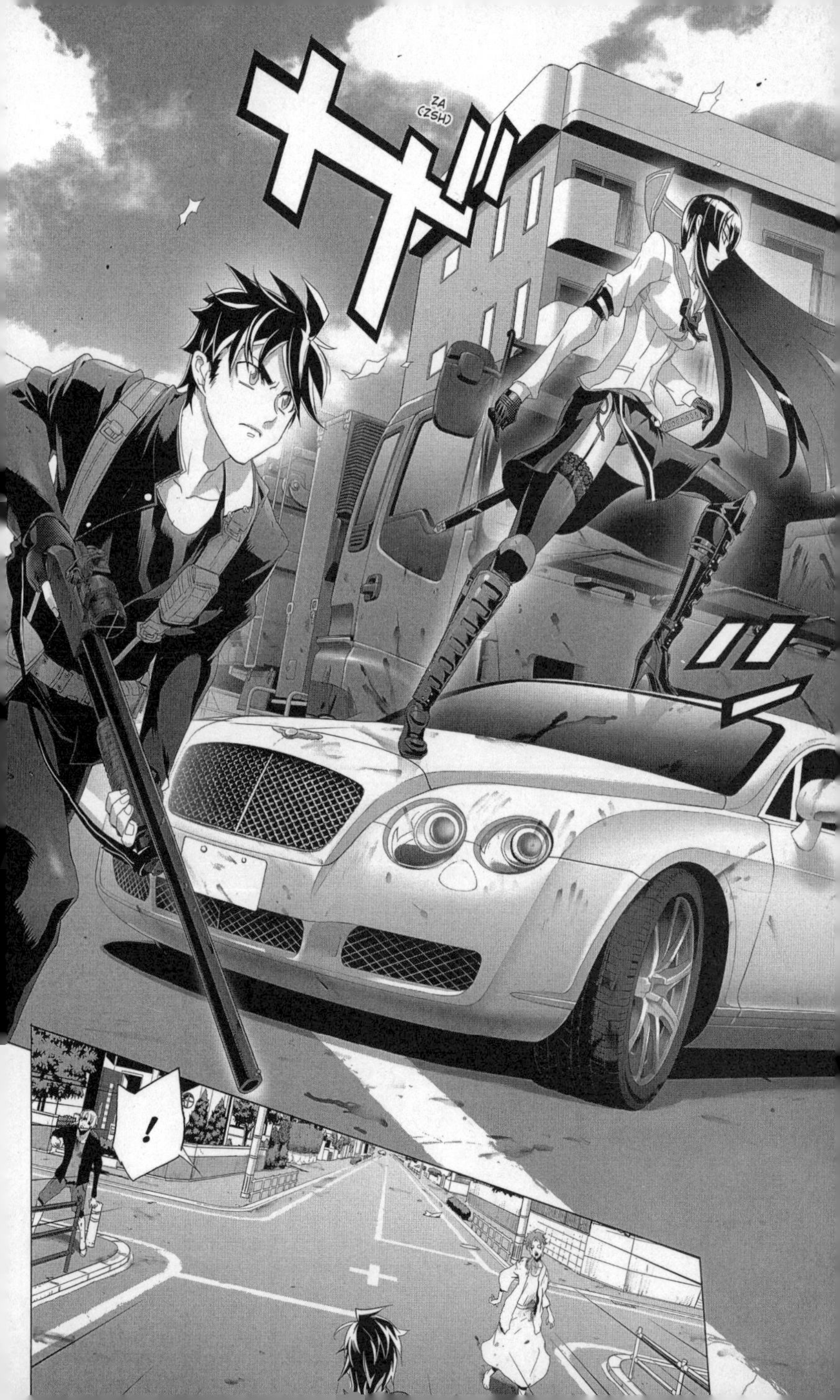
ZA
(ZSH)
!

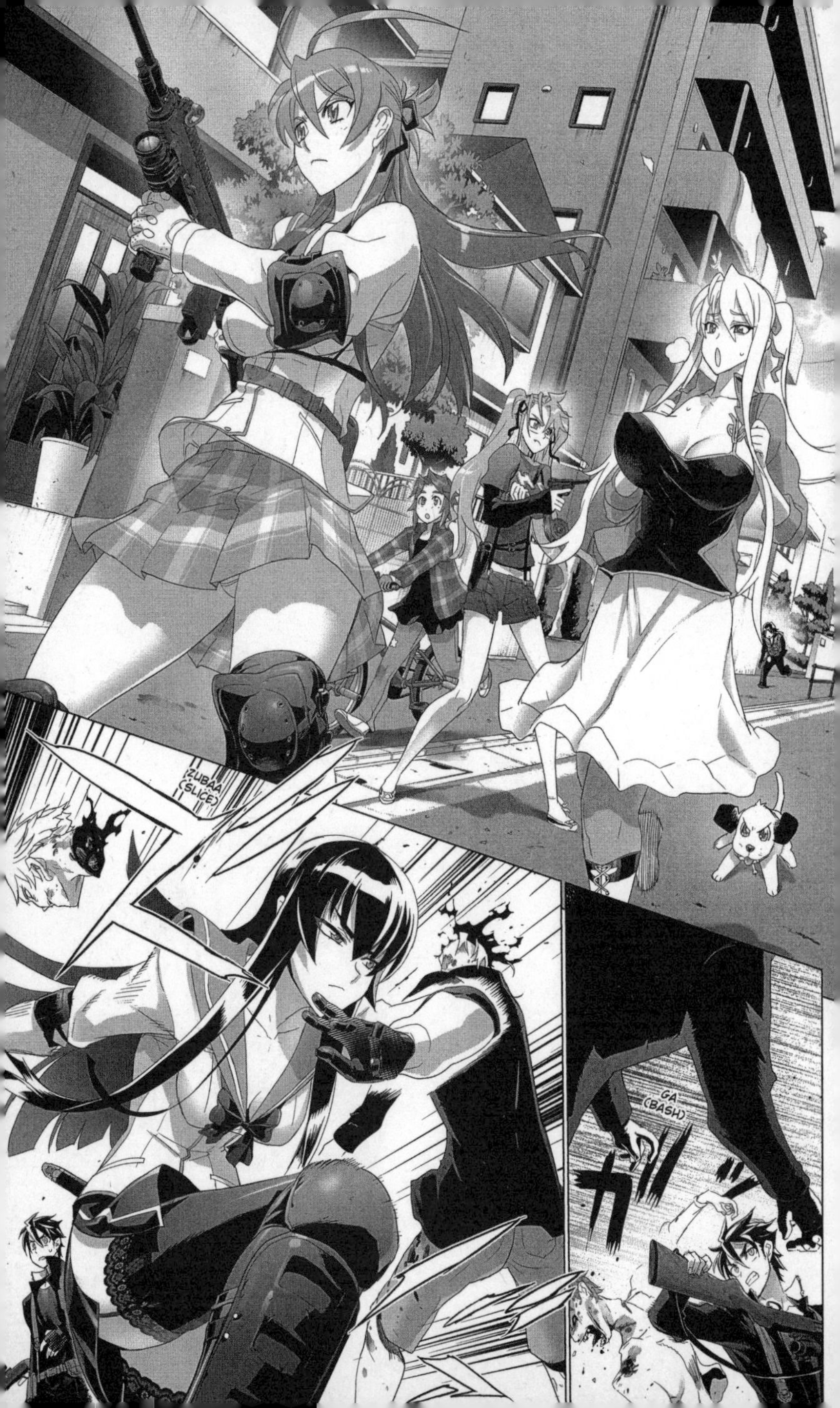
GA
(BASH)
ZUBAA
(SLICE)

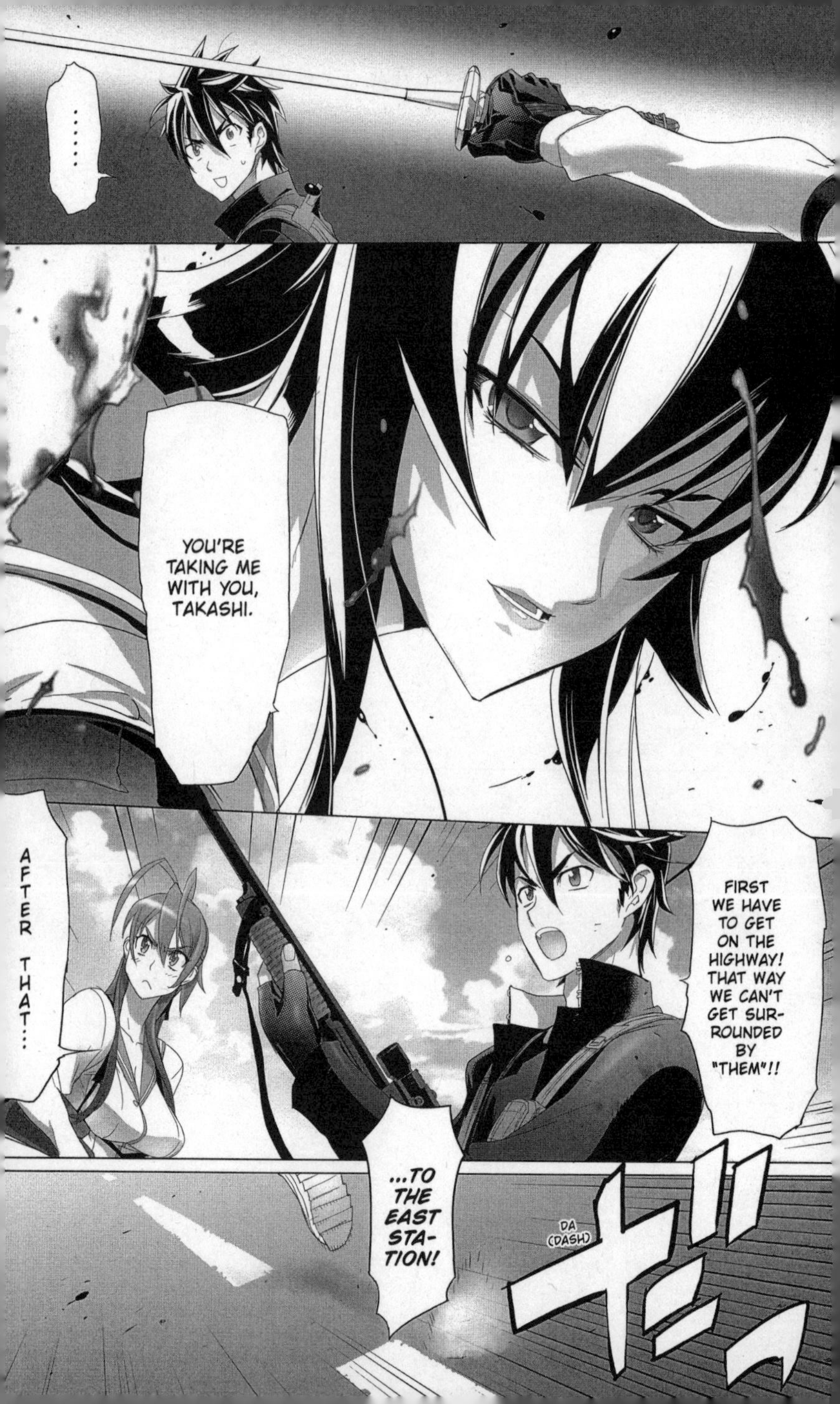
……
YOU'RE TAKING ME WITH YOU, TAKASHI.
FIRST WE HAVE TO GET ON THE HIGHWAY! THAT WAY WE CAN'T GET SUR-ROUNDED BY "THEM"!!
AFTER THAT…
…TO THE EAST STA-TION!
DA (DASH)

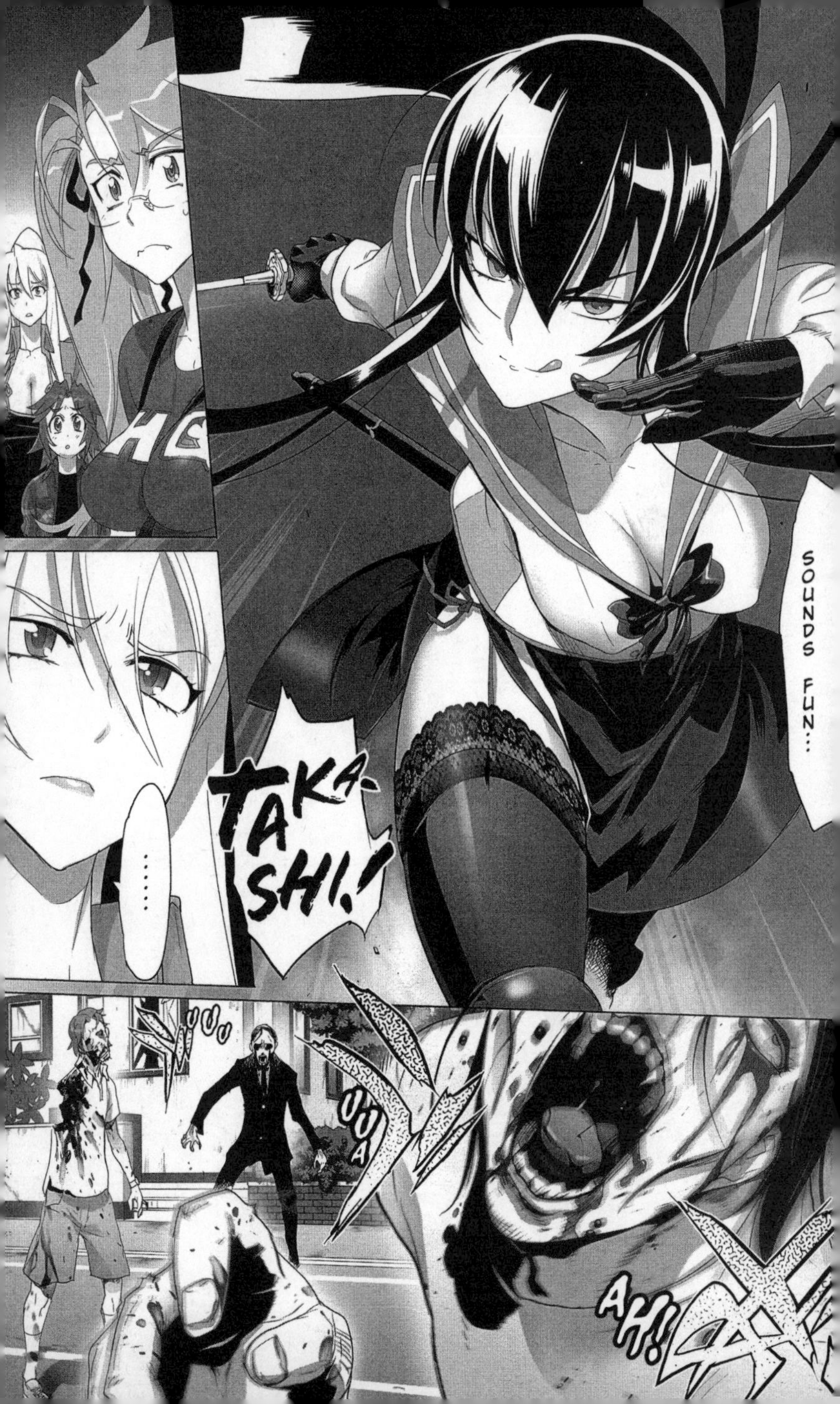
SOUNDS FUN...
TAKASHI!
......
AH!
UUUA
UUU

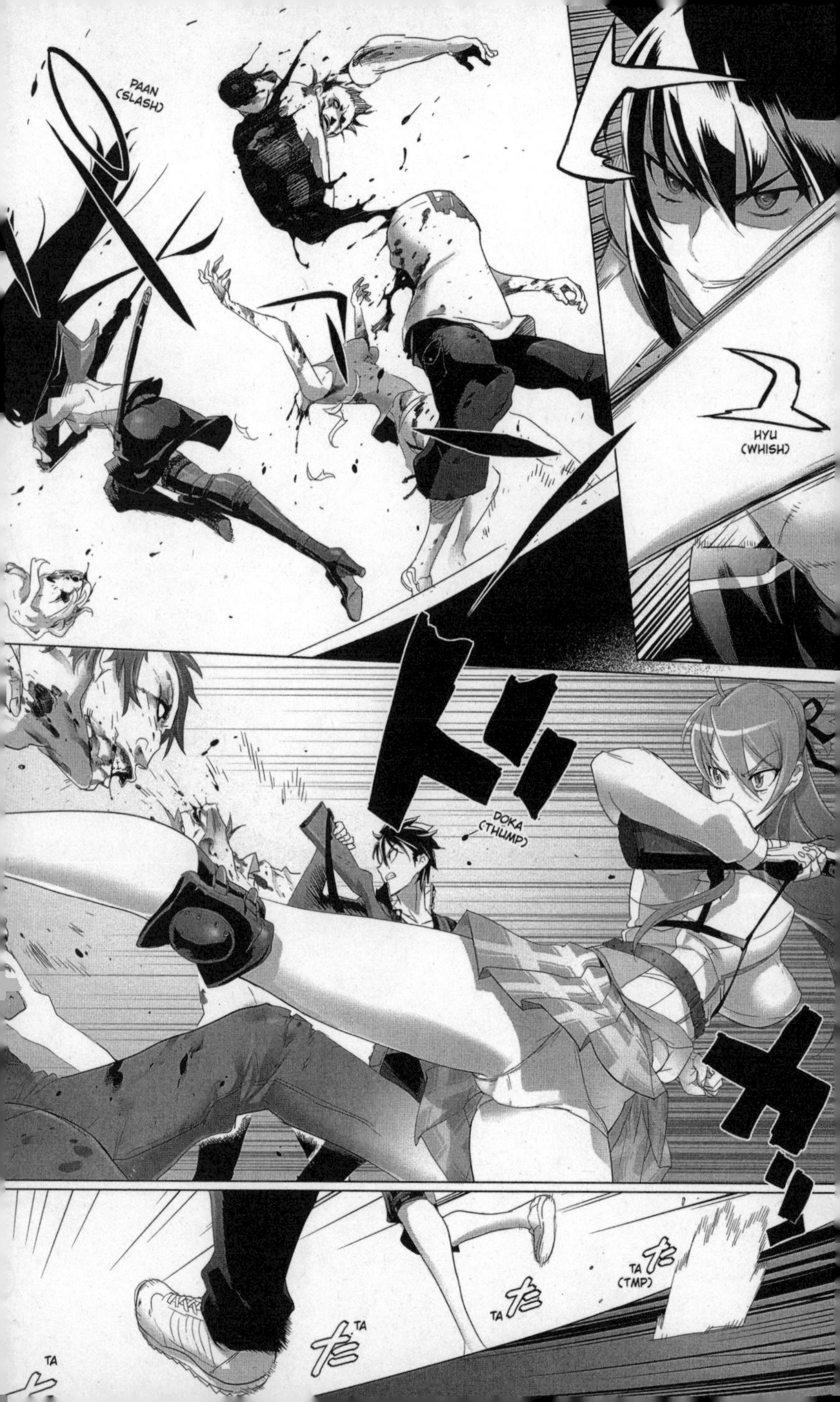

HYU
(WHISH)
PAAN
(SLASH)
ドッ
DOKA
(THUMP)
TA
(TMP)
た
TA
た
TA
た
TA

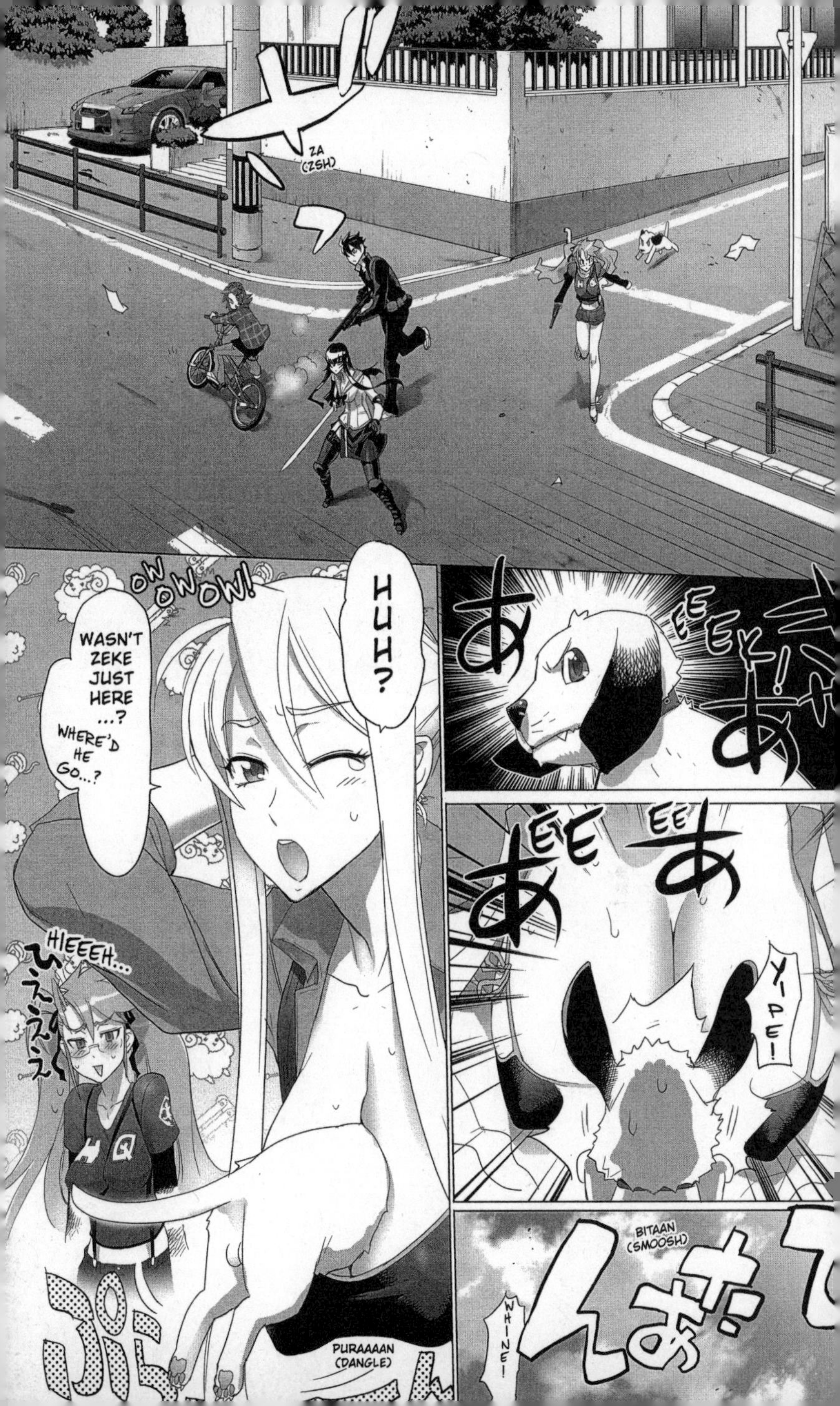

ZA (ZSH)
EEEK!
EE
EE
YIPE!
BITAAN (SMOOSH)
WHINE!
HUH?
OW OWOW!
WASN'T ZEKE JUST HERE ...?
WHERE'D HE GO...?
HIEEEH...
PURAAAAN (DANGLE)

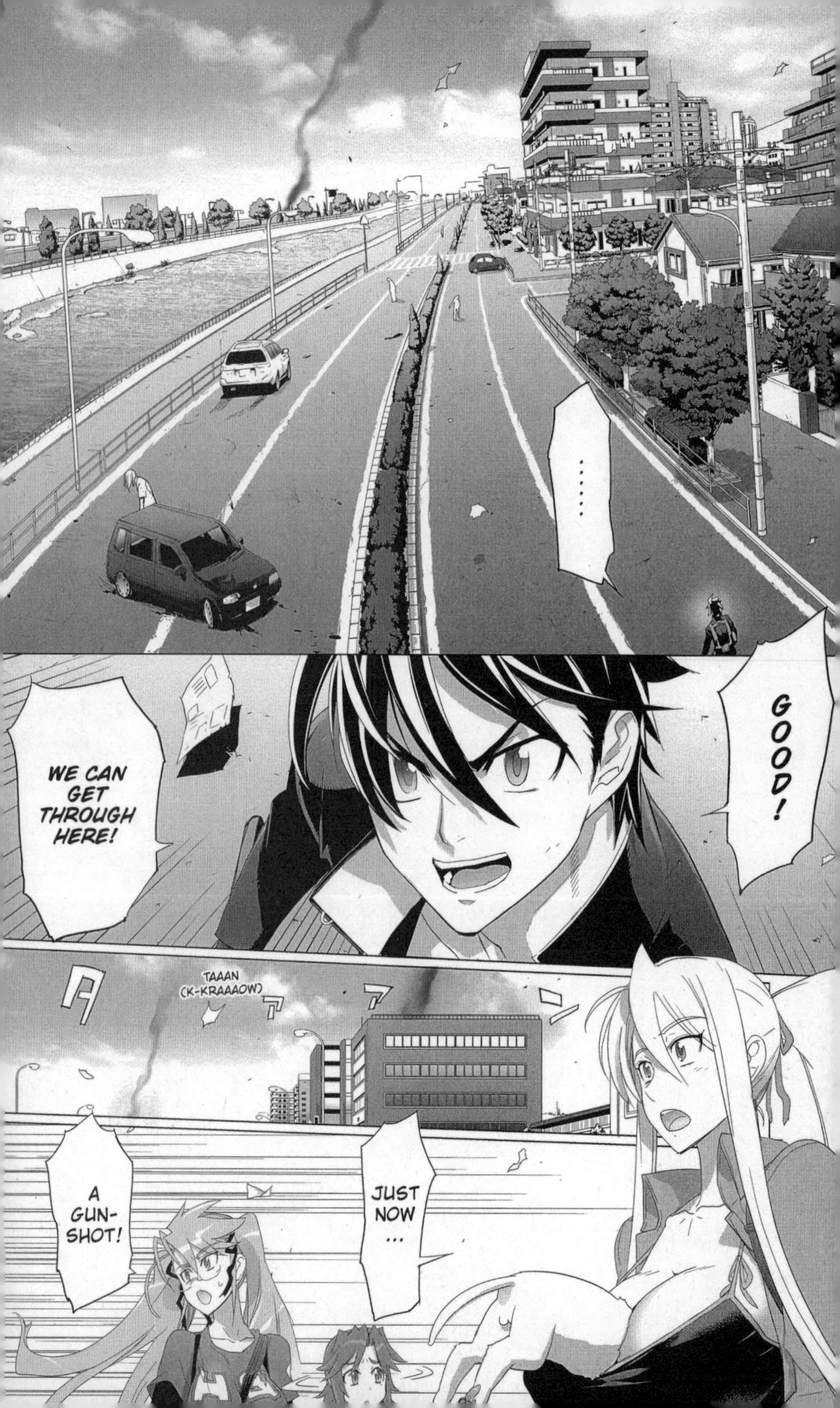
......
GOOD!
WE CAN GET THROUGH HERE!
TAAAN (K-KRAAAOW)
JUST NOW ...
A GUN-SHOT!

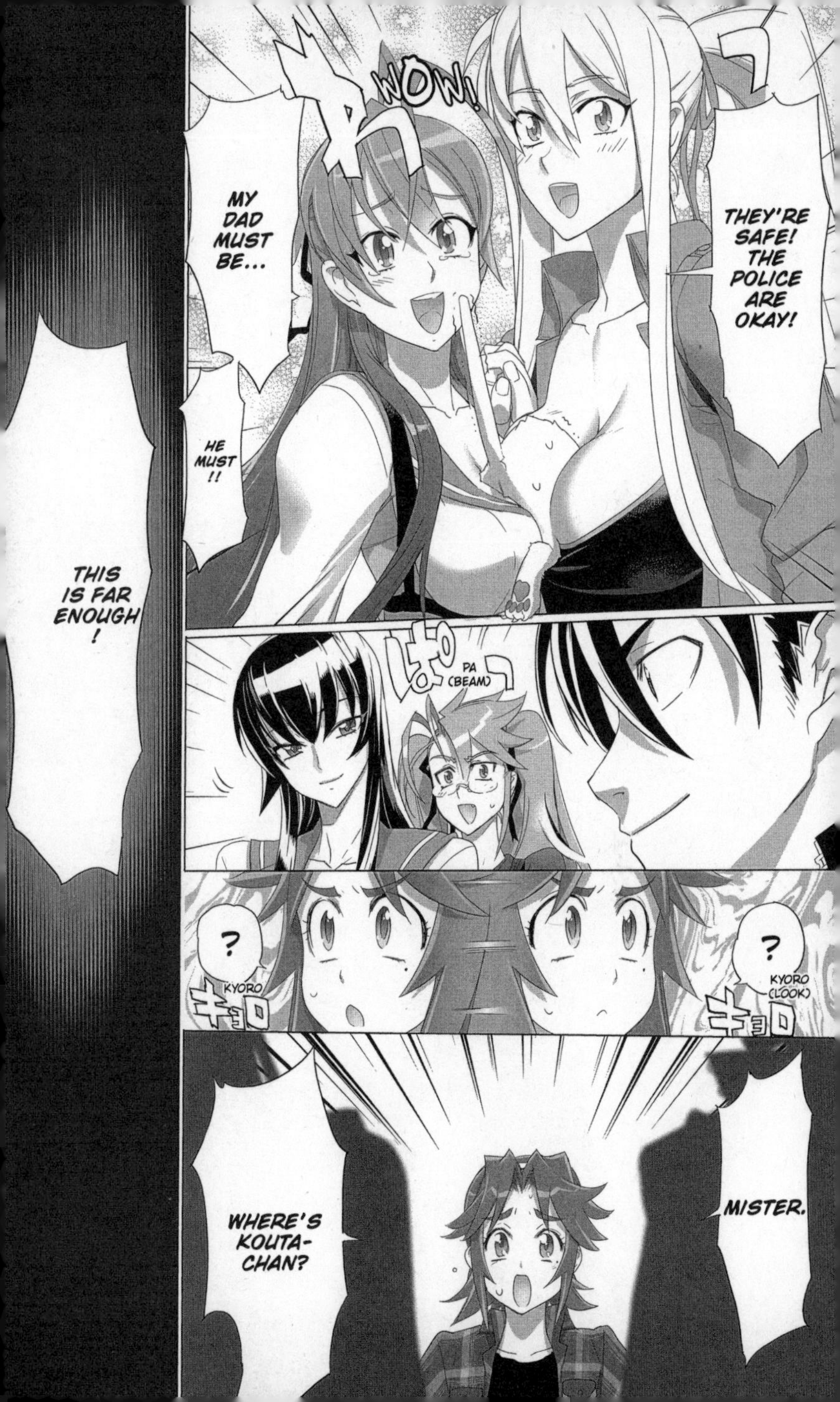
WOW!
THEY'RE SAFE! THE POLICE ARE OKAY!
MY DAD MUST BE...
HE MUST!!
ぱっ
PA (BEAM)
?
キョロ
KYORO (LOOK)
?
キョロ
KYORO
MISTER.
WHERE'S KOUTA-CHAN?
THIS IS FAR ENOUGH!

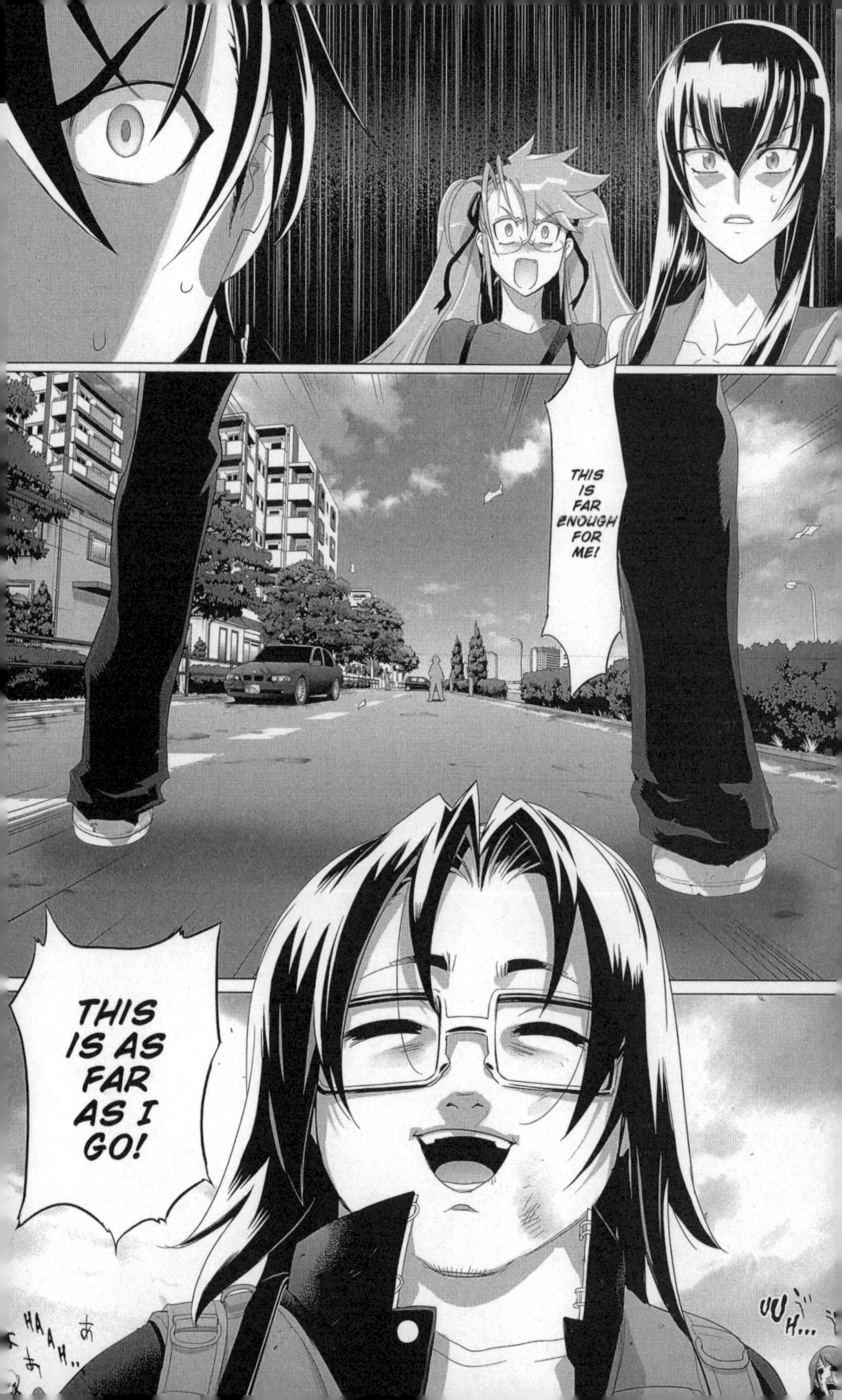
THIS IS FAR ENOUGH FOR ME!
UUH...
THIS IS AS FAR AS I GO!
HAAAH..

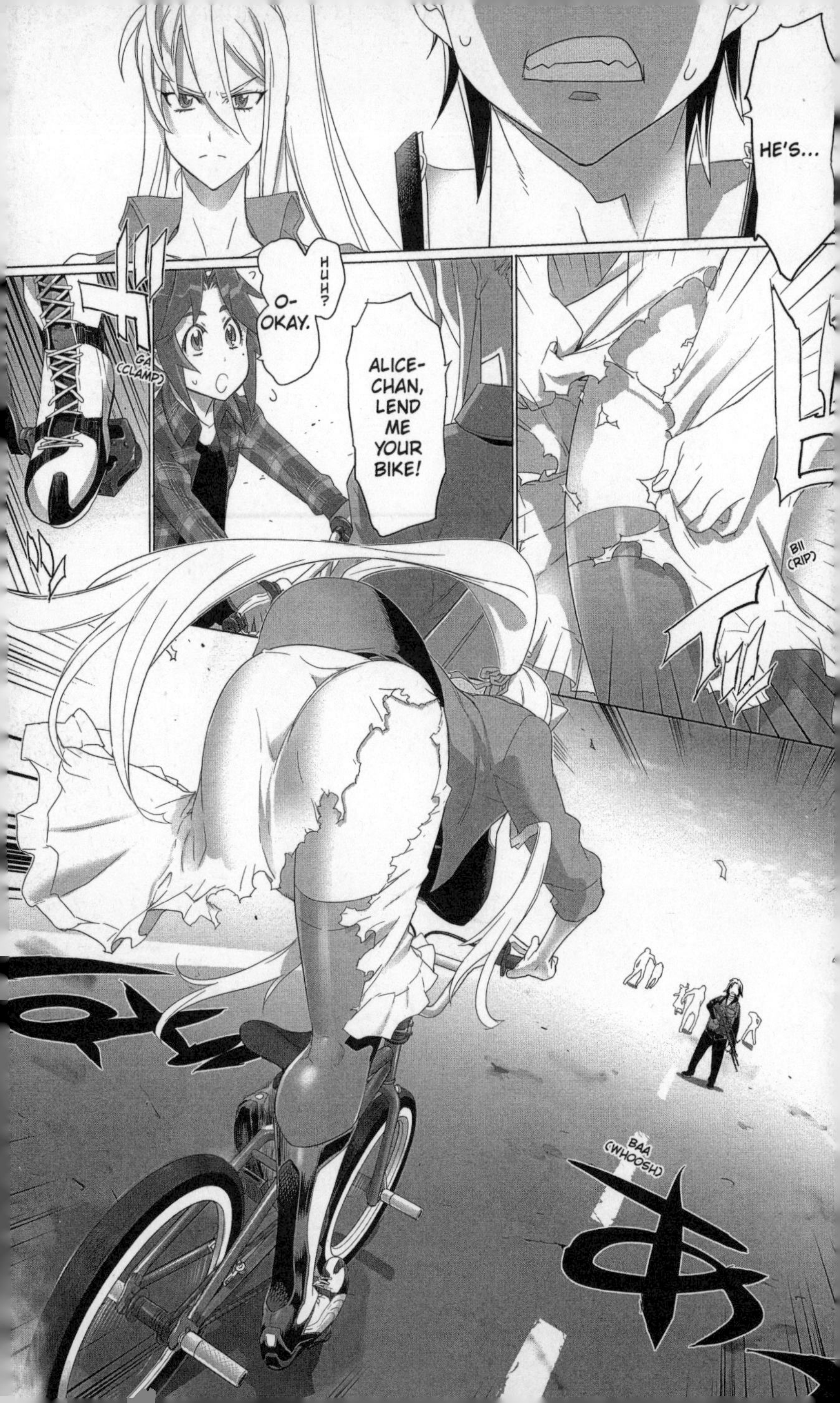
HE'S...
BII (RIP)
ALICE-CHAN, LEND ME YOUR BIKE!
HUH?
O-OKAY.
GA (CLAMP)
BAA (WHOOSH)

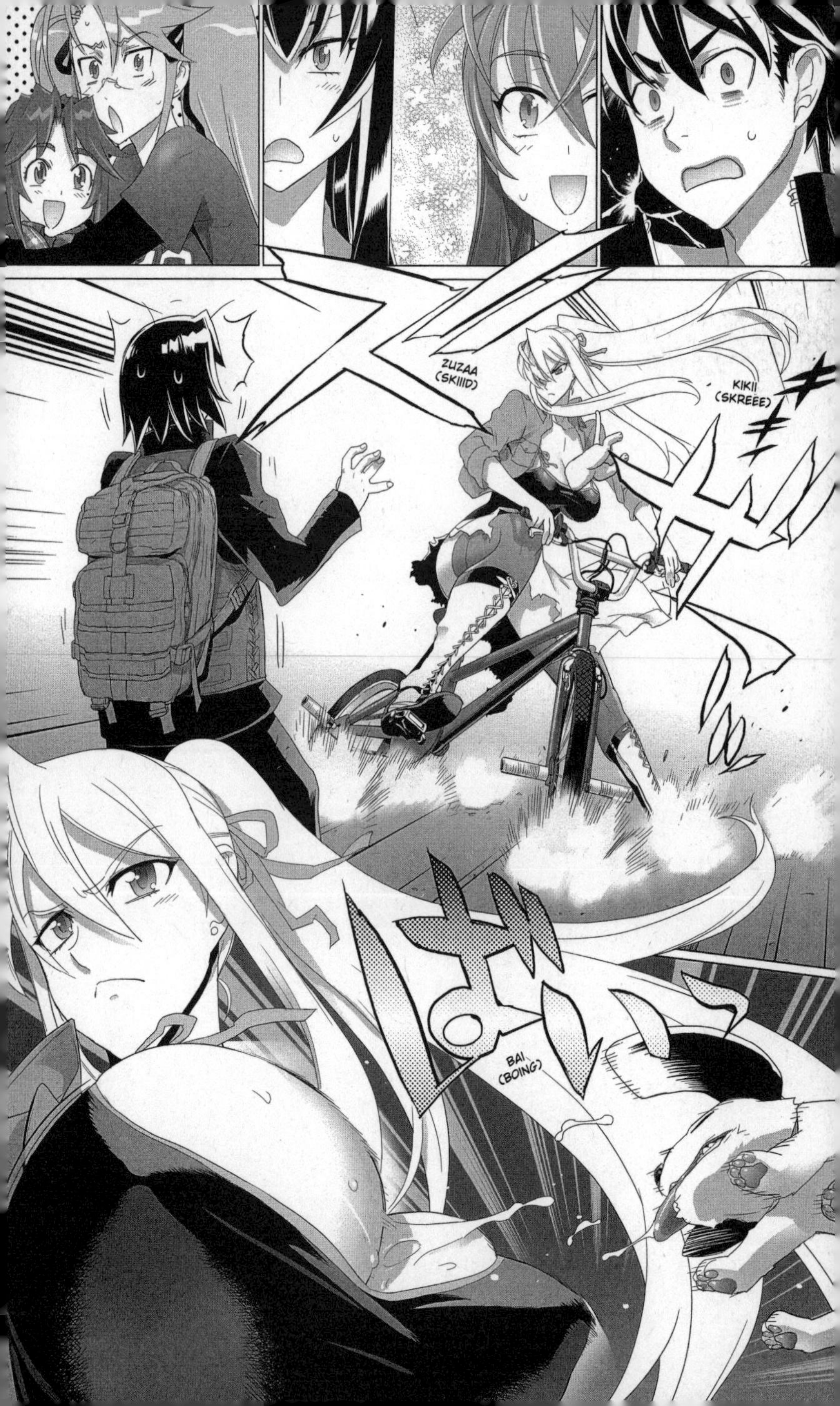
KIKII (SKREEE)
ZUZAA (SKIIID)
BAI (BOING)

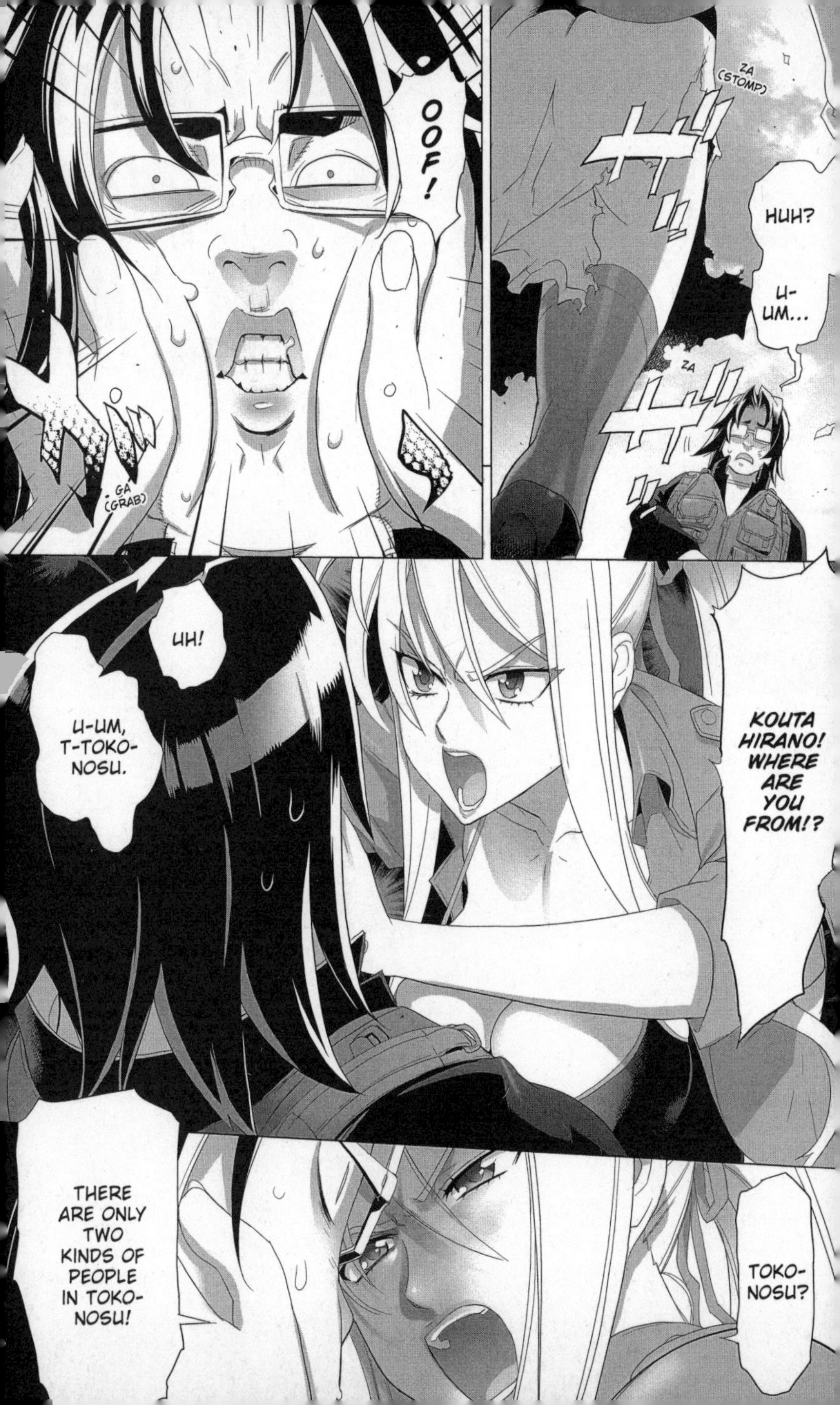
ZA (STOMP)
HUH?
U-UM...
ZA
OOF!
GA (GRAB)
KOUTA HIRANO! WHERE ARE YOU FROM!?
UH!
U-UM, T-TOKO-NOSU.
TOKO-NOSU?
THERE ARE ONLY TWO KINDS OF PEOPLE IN TOKO-NOSU!

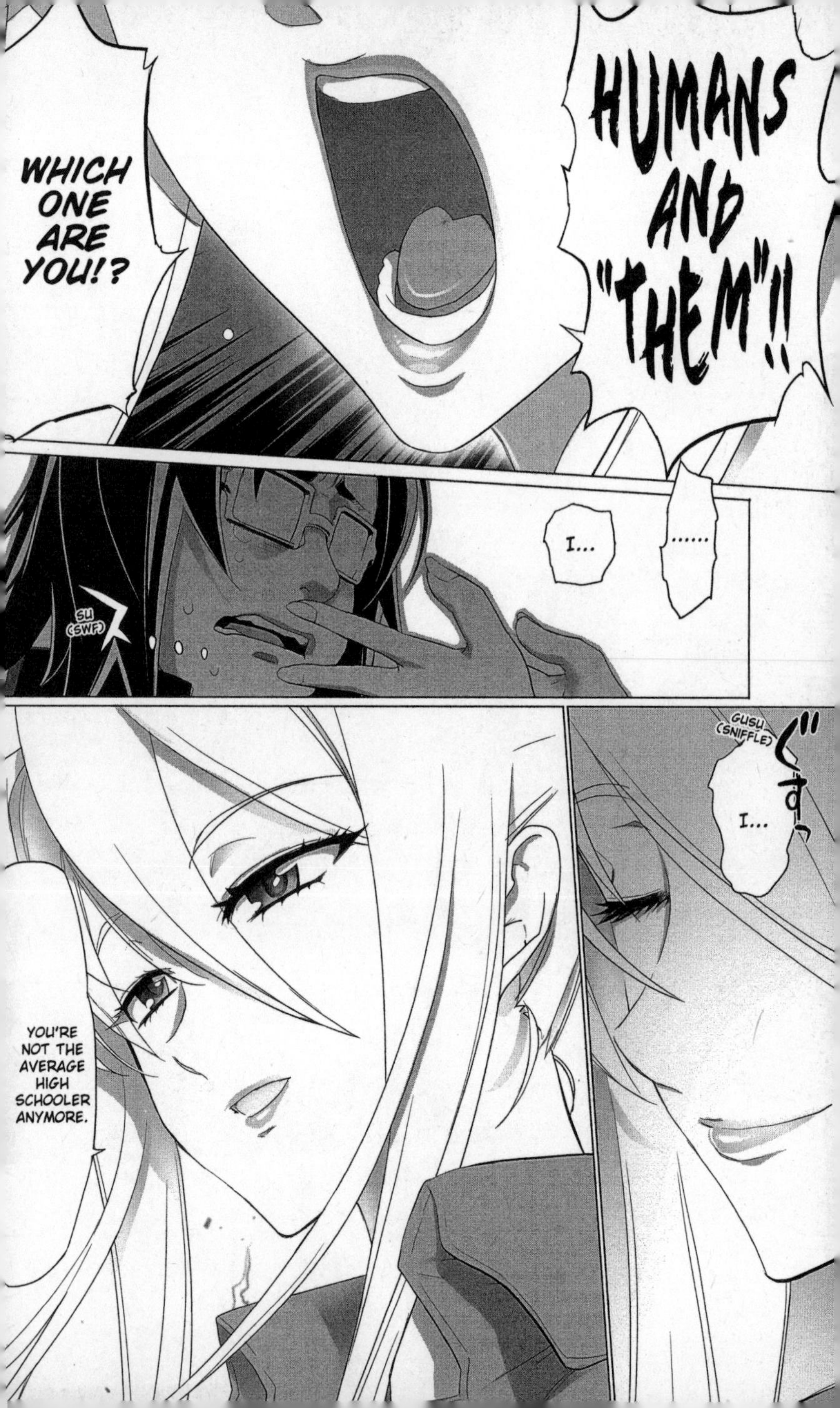
HUMANS AND "THEM"!!
WHICH ONE ARE YOU!?
......
I...
SU (SWF)
GUSU (SNIFFLE)
ぐす
I...
YOU'RE NOT THE AVERAGE HIGH SCHOOLER ANYMORE.

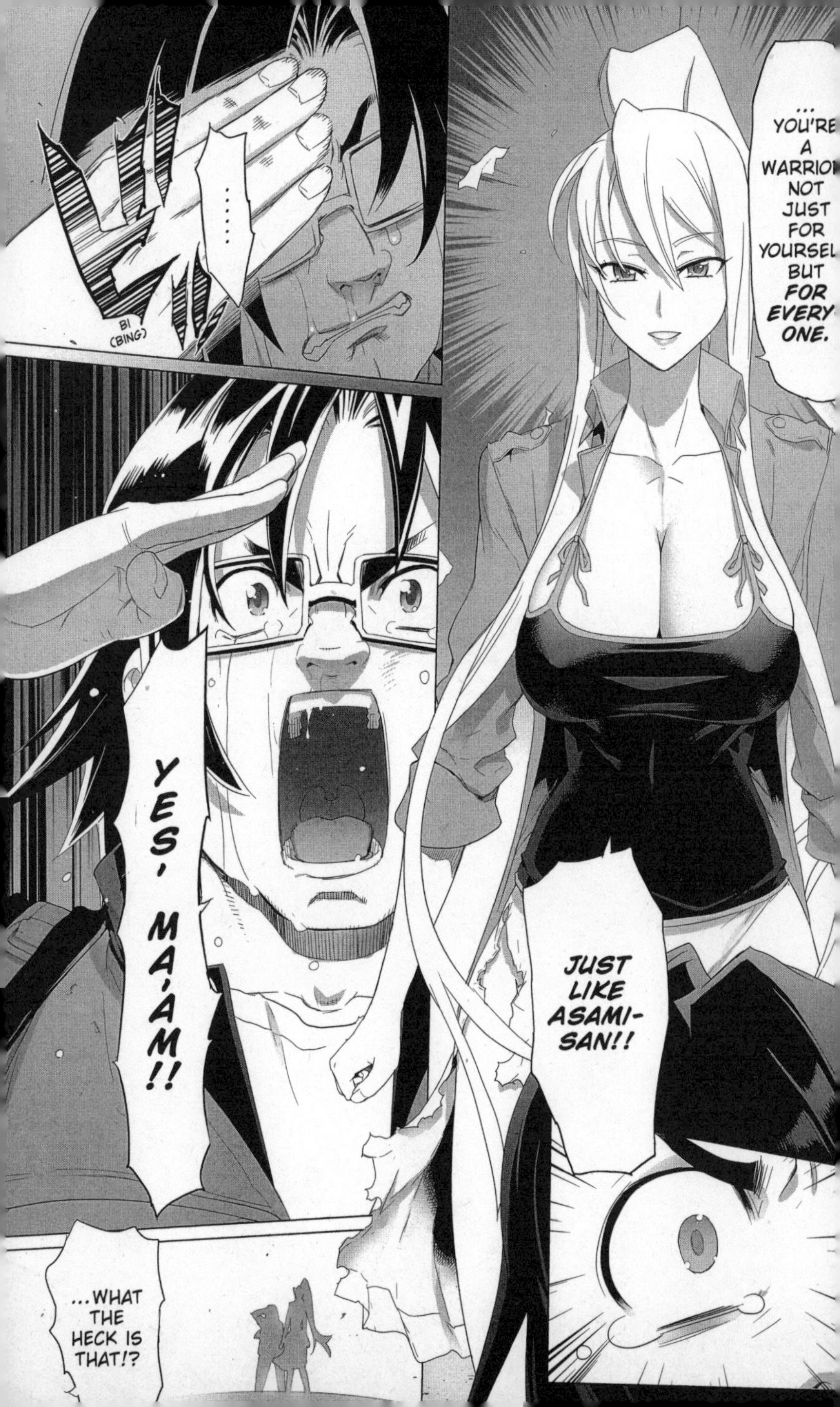

... YOU'RE A WARRIO NOT JUST FOR YOURSEL BUT FOR EVERY ONE.
JUST LIKE ASAMI-SAN!!
......
BI (BING)
YES, MA'AM!!
...WHAT THE HECK IS THAT!?

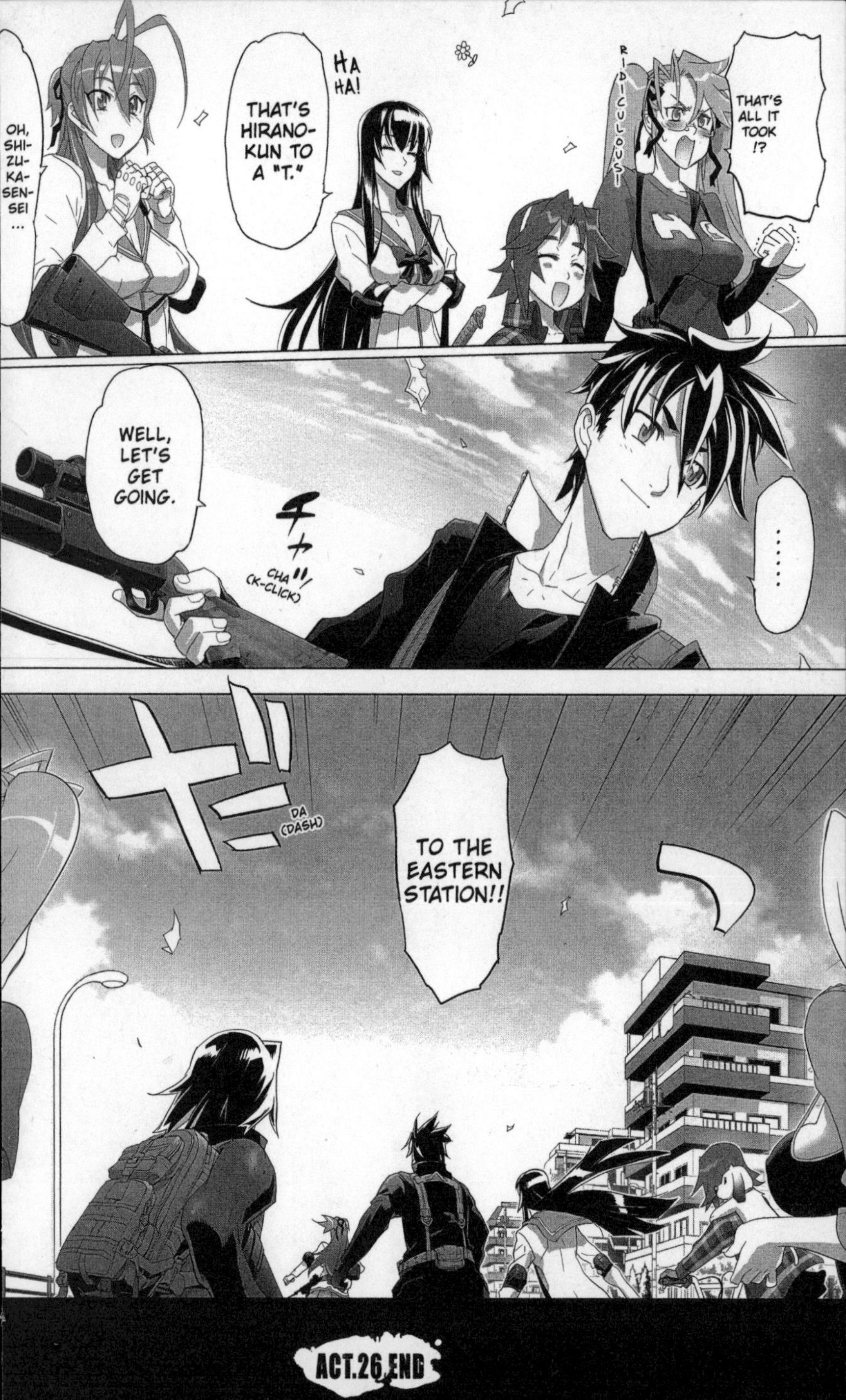
RIDICULOUS!
THAT'S ALL IT TOOK!?
HA HA!
THAT'S HIRANO-KUN TO A "T."
OH, SHIZUKA-SENSEI...
......
CHA (K-CLICK)
WELL, LET'S GET GOING.
TO THE EASTERN STATION!!
DA (DASH)
ACT.26 END

あ
KNOCK IT...
あ
AAAUH!
あ
...OFF!
ARGH!
GASU (THWACK)
I HATE GUYS WHO WON'T LAY OFF!
AGREED!!
GA (STAB)
DOKA (WHACK)
ACT.27 Assault on Dead Precinct
IS THAT TRUE, SENSEI?
HMMM. WELL, IT HAS ITS TIME AND PLACE.
GRRR.
... THAT'S AN ADULT WOMAN, FOR YOU.
WHAT DID YOU JUST SAY!?

ACT.27 Assault on Dead Precinct

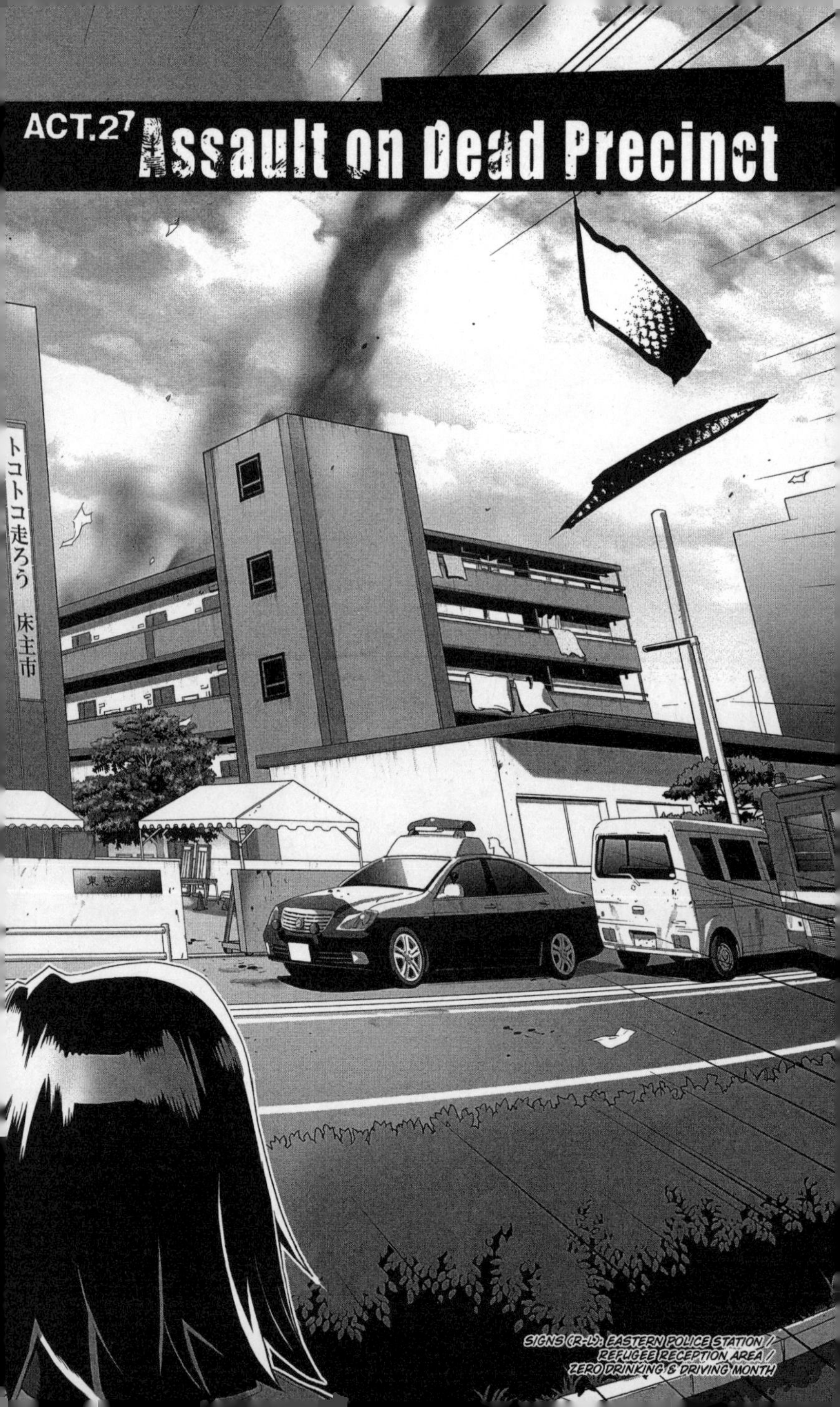
トコトコ走ろう 床主市
SIGNS (R-L): EASTERN POLICE STATION /
REFUGEE RECEPTION AREA /
ZERO DRINKING & DRIVING MONTH

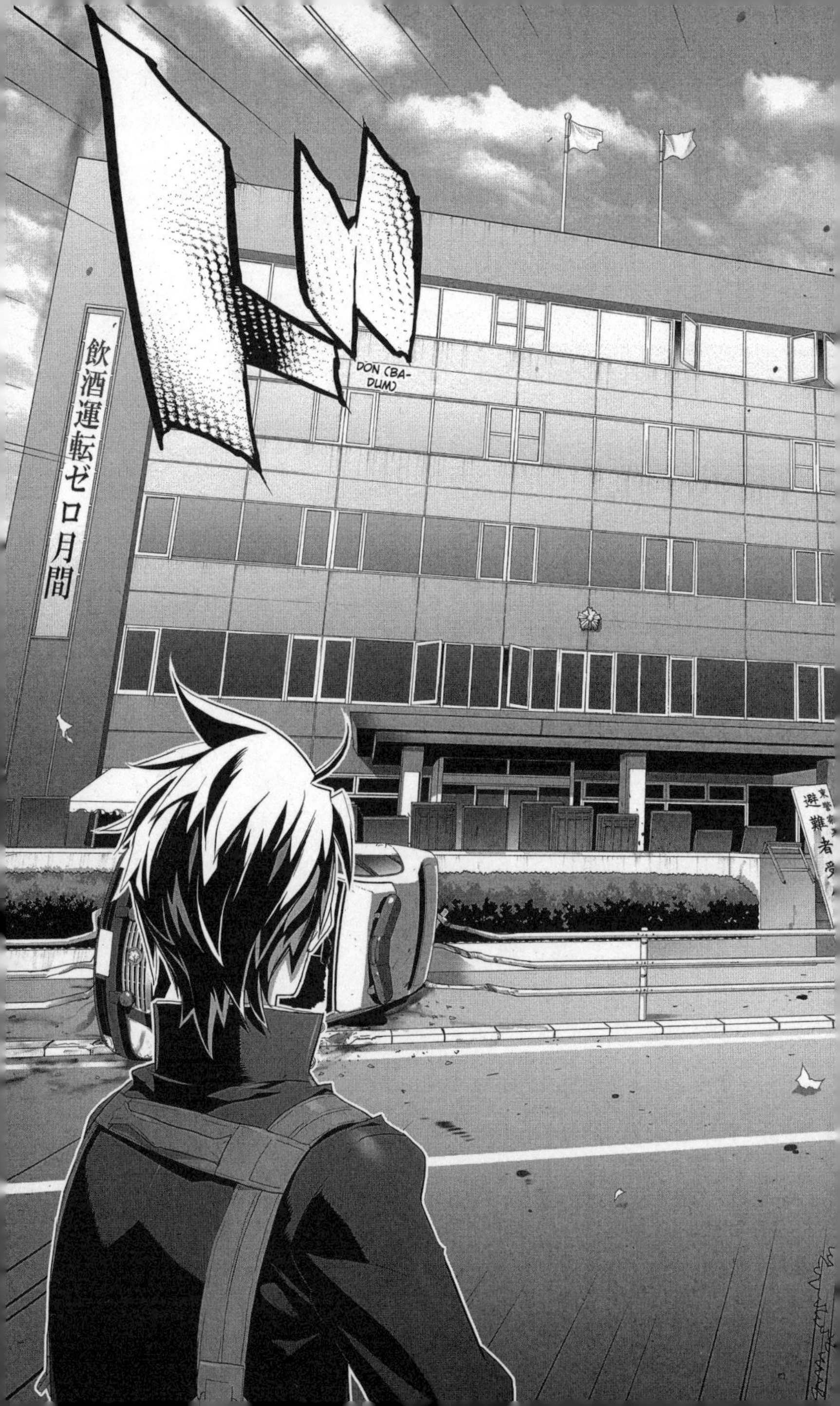
DON (BA-DUM)
飲酒運転ゼロ月間
避難者

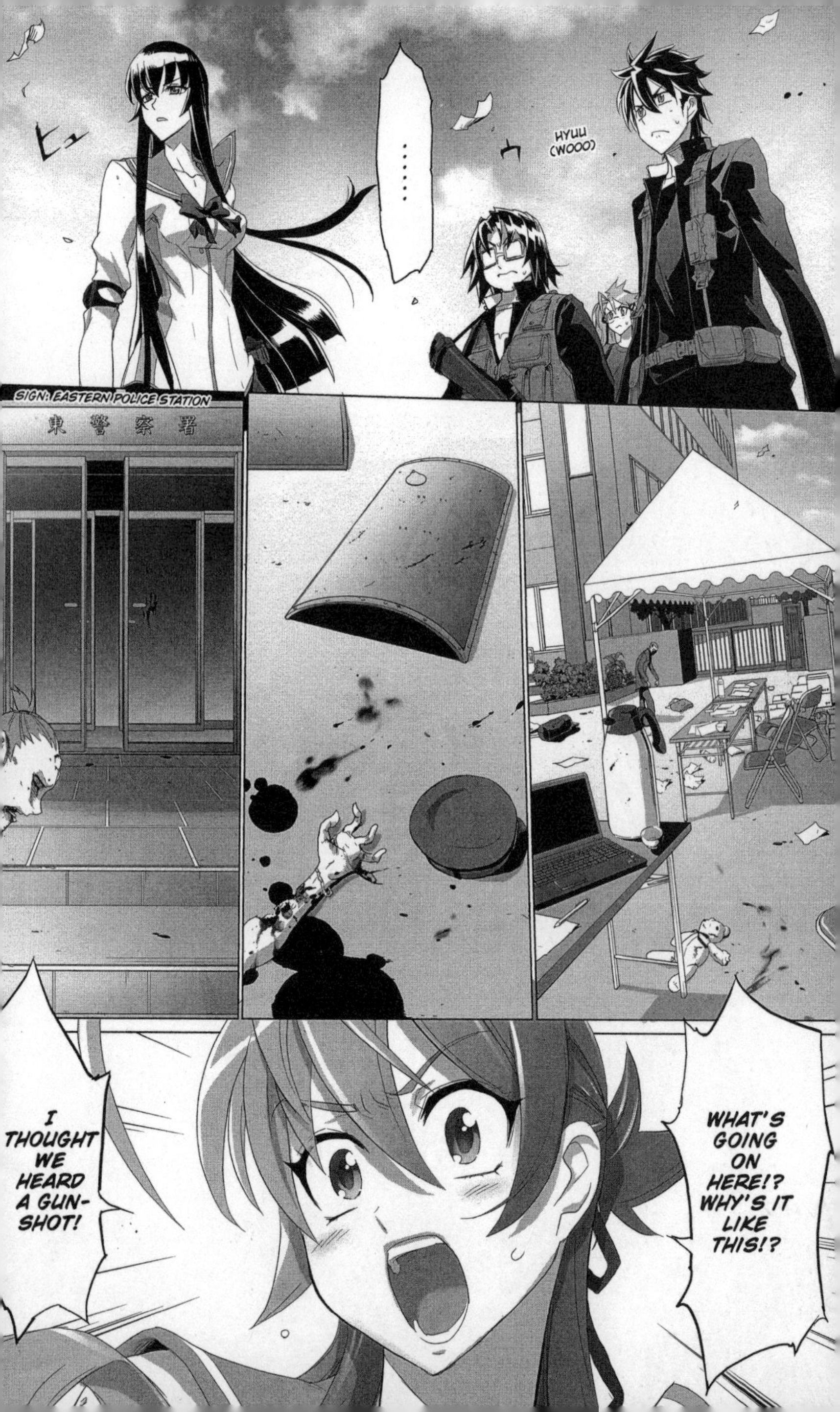
HYUU (WOOO)
......
SIGN: EASTERN POLICE STATION
東警察署
WHAT'S GOING ON HERE!? WHY'S IT LIKE THIS!?
I THOUGHT WE HEARD A GUN-SHOT!

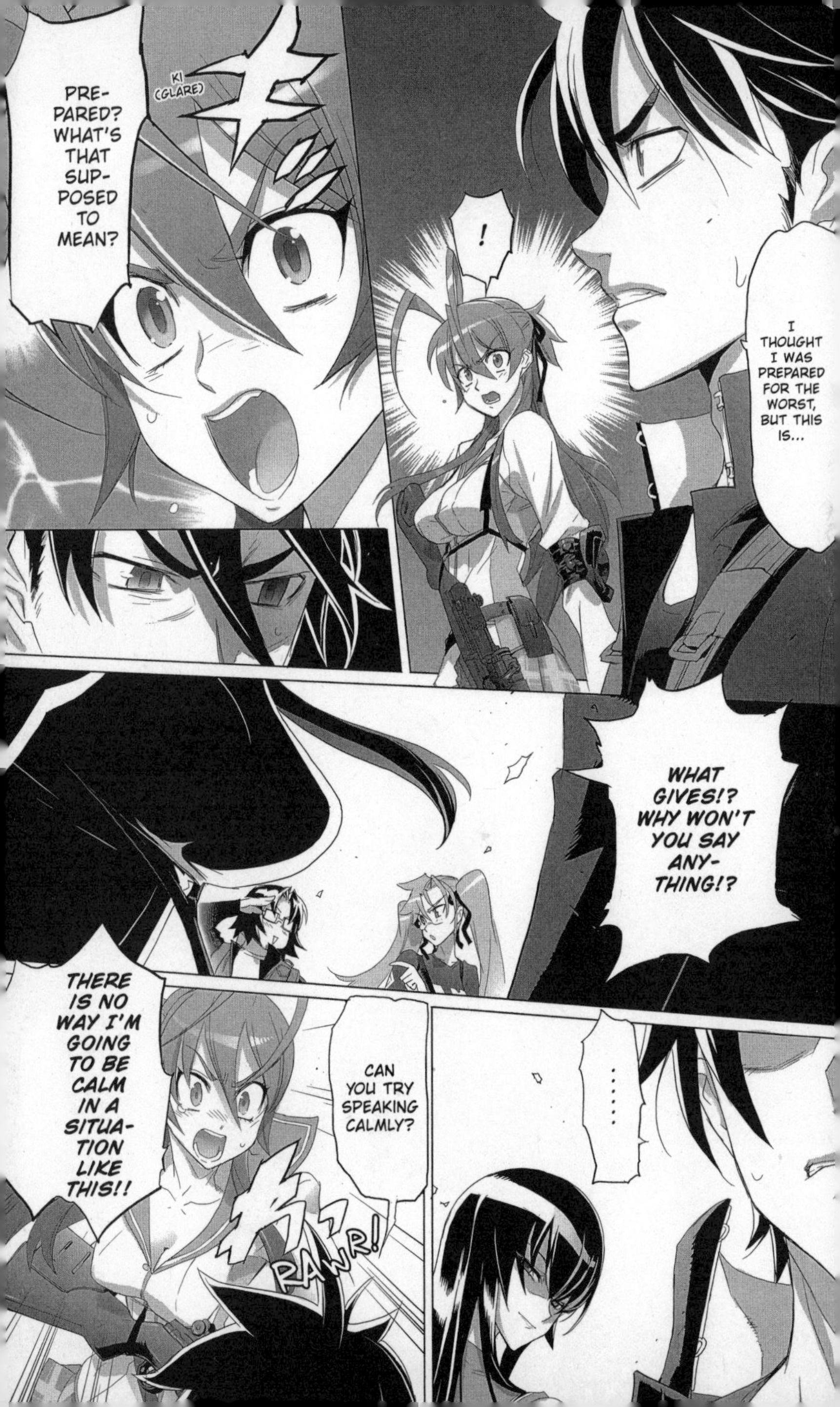
I THOUGHT I WAS PREPARED FOR THE WORST, BUT THIS IS...
!
PRE-PARED? WHAT'S THAT SUP-POSED TO MEAN?
KI (GLARE)
WHAT GIVES!? WHY WON'T YOU SAY ANY-THING!?
......
CAN YOU TRY SPEAKING CALMLY?
THERE IS NO WAY I'M GOING TO BE CALM IN A SITUA-TION LIKE THIS!!
RAWR!

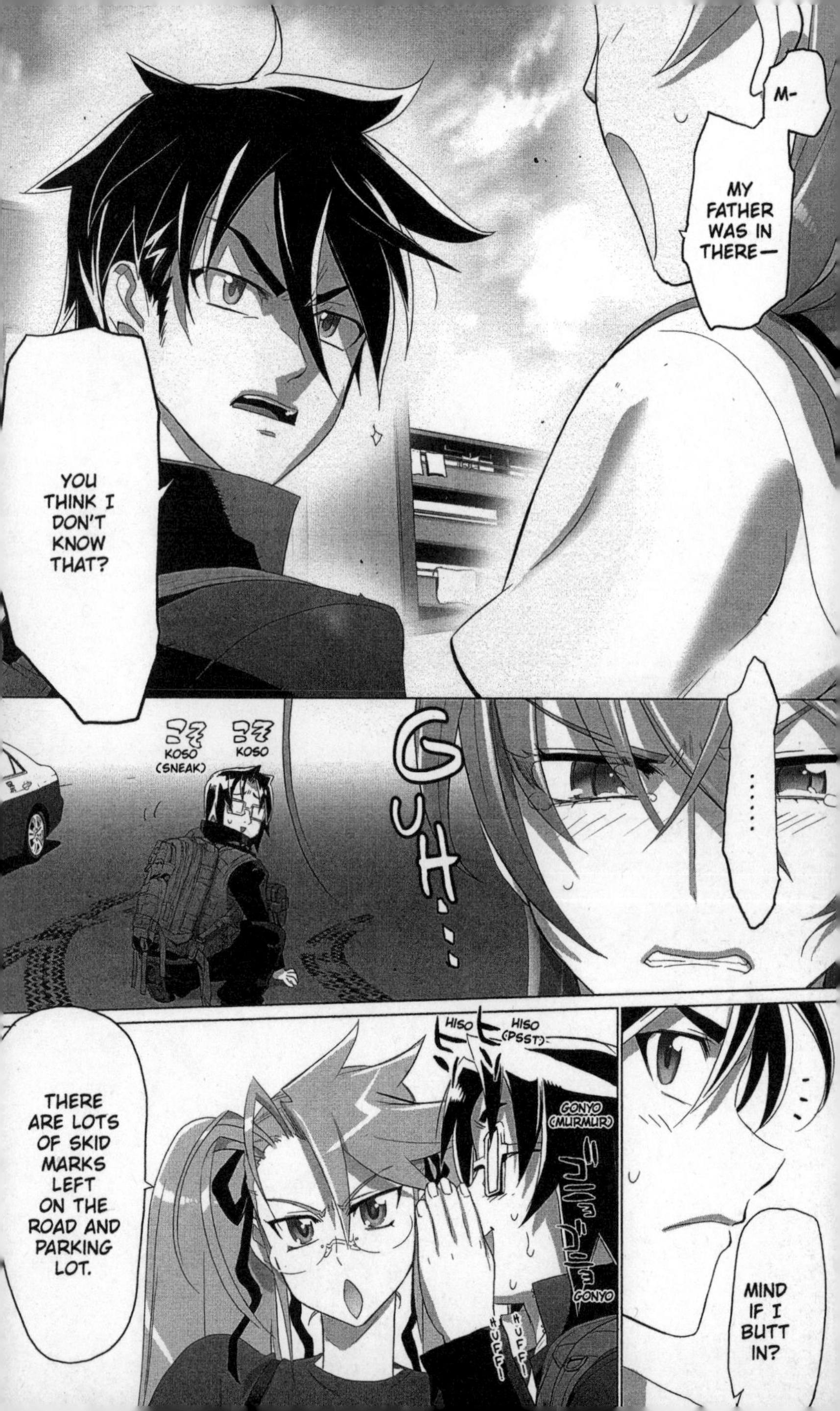

M-
MY FATHER WAS IN THERE—
YOU THINK I DON'T KNOW THAT?
......
GUH...
KOSO KOSO (SNEAK)
...
MIND IF I BUTT IN?
HISO HISO (PSST)
GONYO (MURMUR) GONYO
THERE ARE LOTS OF SKID MARKS LEFT ON THE ROAD AND PARKING LOT.
HUFF HUFF

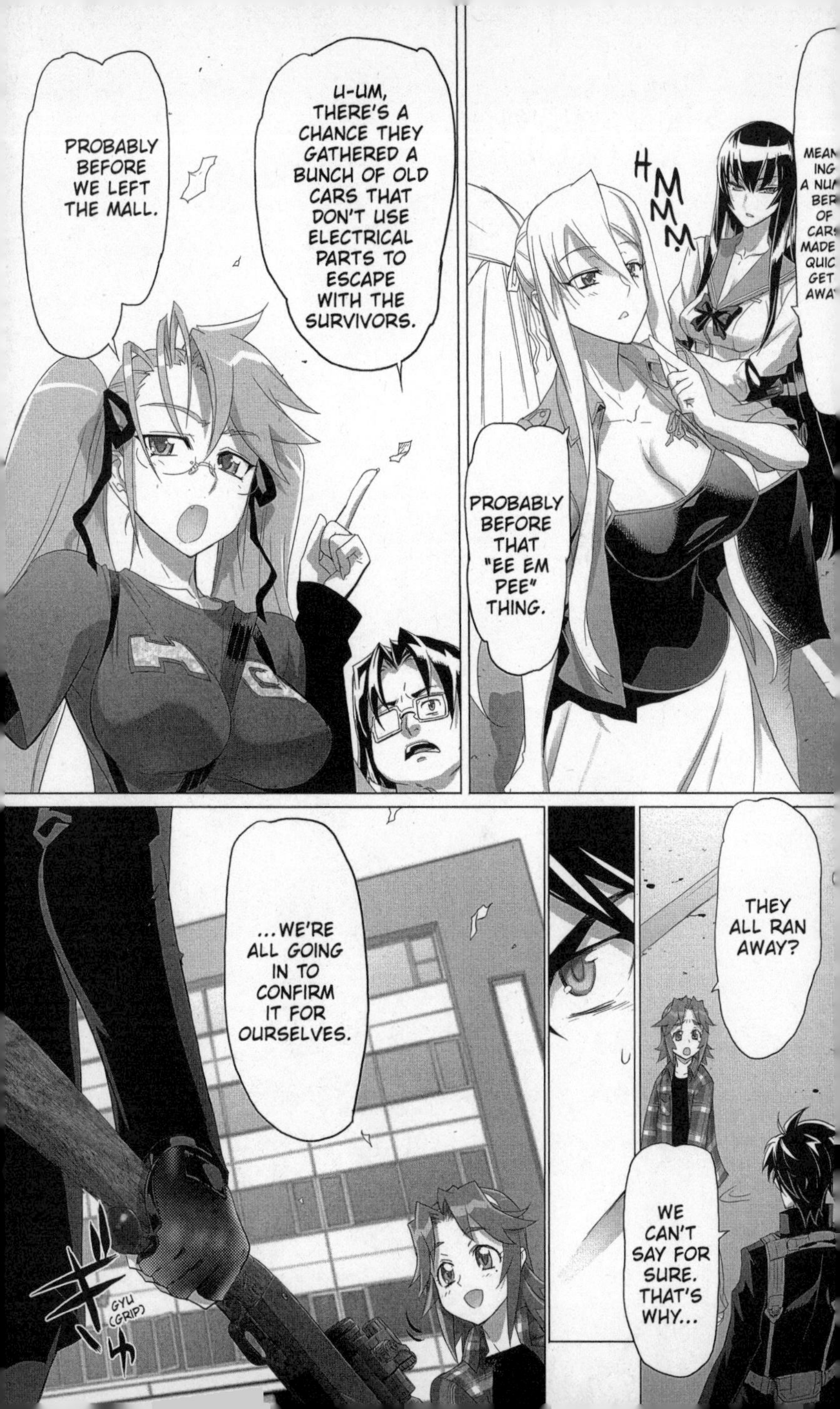
MEAN ING A NUM BER OF CARS MADE QUIC GET AWA
HMMM
PROBABLY BEFORE THAT "EE EM PEE" THING.
U-UM, THERE'S A CHANCE THEY GATHERED A BUNCH OF OLD CARS THAT DON'T USE ELECTRICAL PARTS TO ESCAPE WITH THE SURVIVORS.
PROBABLY BEFORE WE LEFT THE MALL.
THEY ALL RAN AWAY?
WE CAN'T SAY FOR SURE. THAT'S WHY...
...WE'RE ALL GOING IN TO CONFIRM IT FOR OURSELVES.
GYU (GRIP)

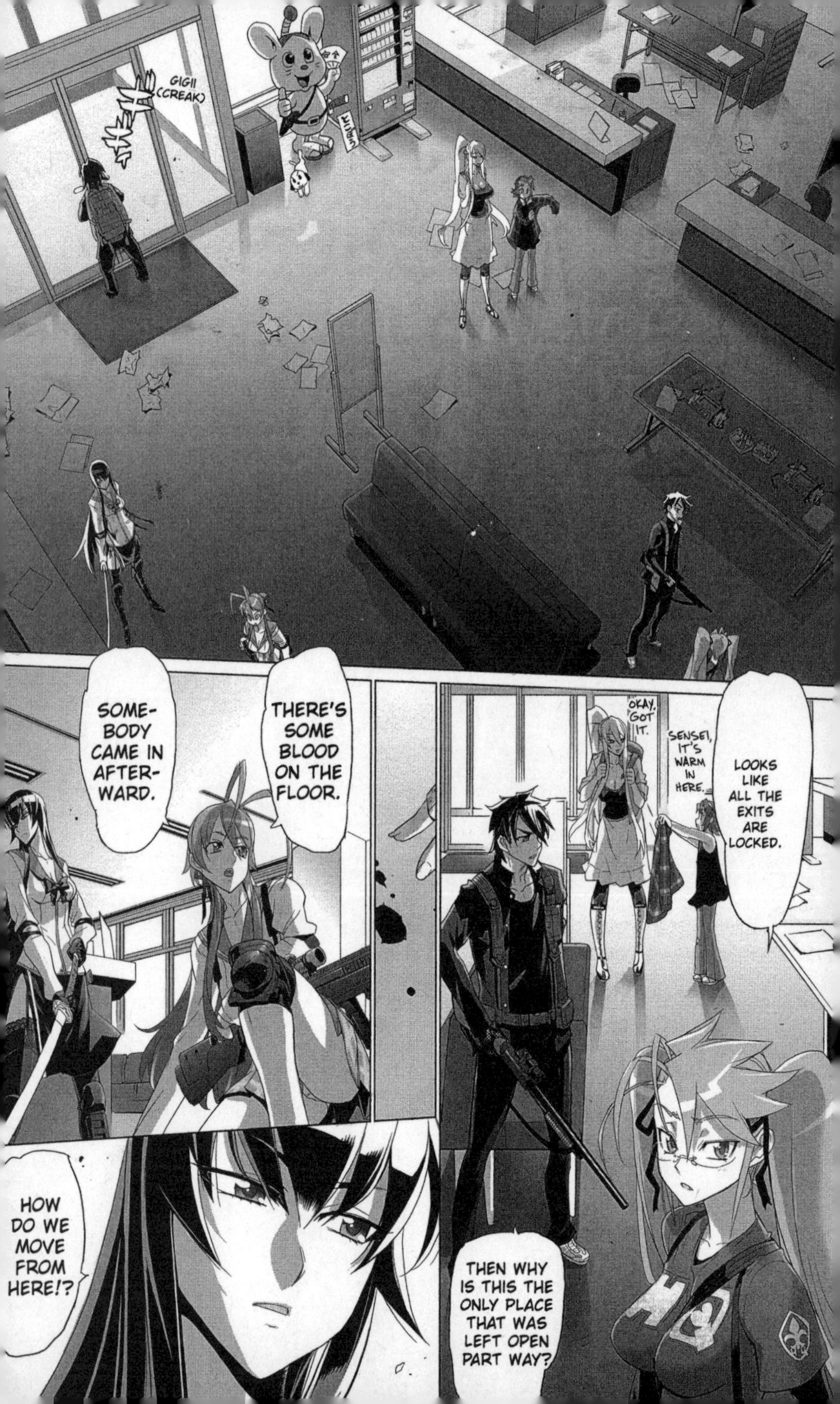

GIGII (CREAK)
LOOKS LIKE ALL THE EXITS ARE LOCKED.
SENSEI, IT'S WARM IN HERE.
OKAY. GOT IT.
THEN WHY IS THIS THE ONLY PLACE THAT WAS LEFT OPEN PART WAY?
THERE'S SOME BLOOD ON THE FLOOR.
SOME-BODY CAME IN AFTER-WARD.
HOW DO WE MOVE FROM HERE!?

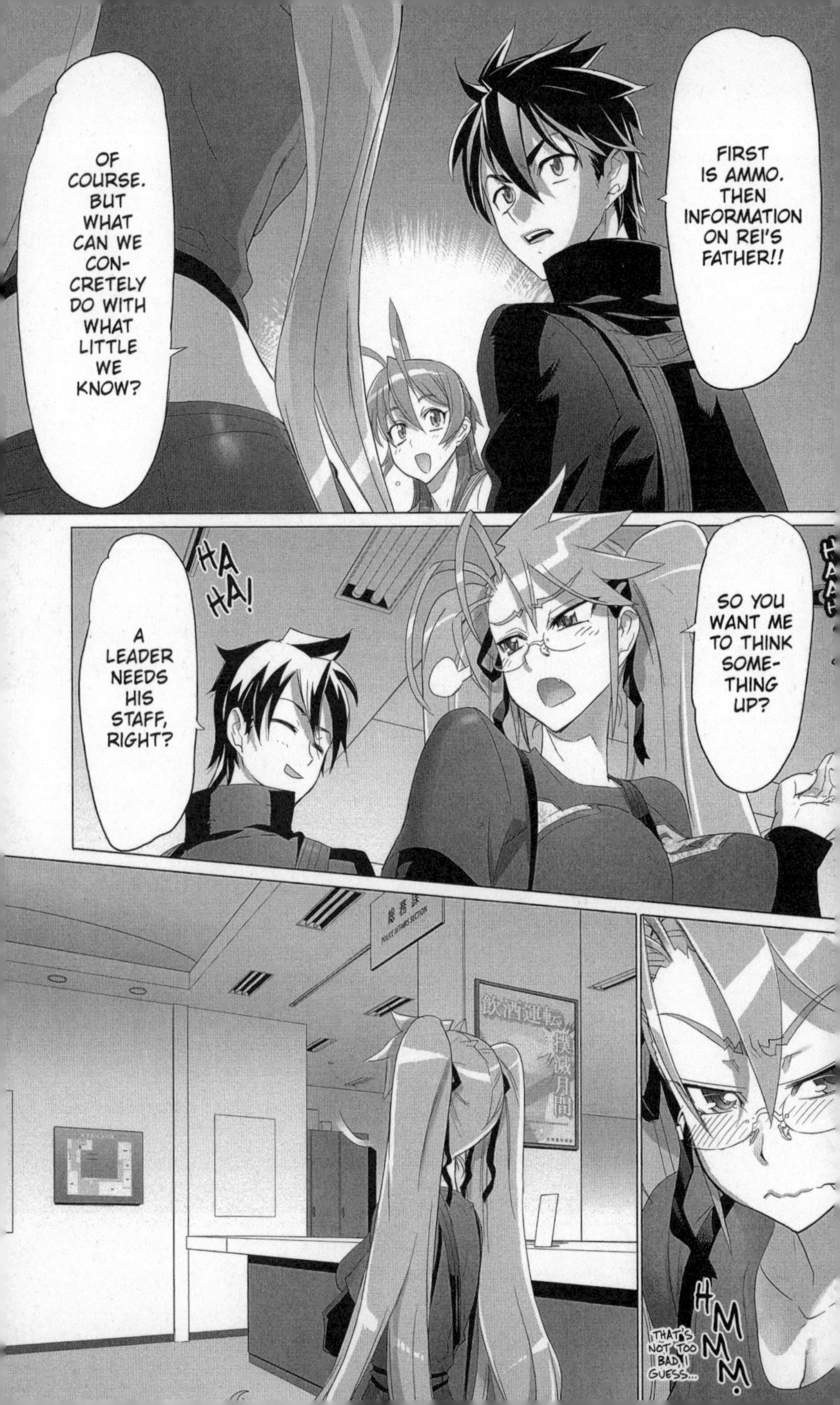
FIRST IS AMMO. THEN INFORMATION ON REI'S FATHER!!
OF COURSE. BUT WHAT CAN WE CON-CRETELY DO WITH WHAT LITTLE WE KNOW?
SO YOU WANT ME TO THINK SOME-THING UP?
HA HA!
A LEADER NEEDS HIS STAFF, RIGHT?
HMMM.
THAT'S NOT TOO BAD, I GUESS...
総務課
POLICE AFFAIRS SECTION
飲酒運転撲滅月間

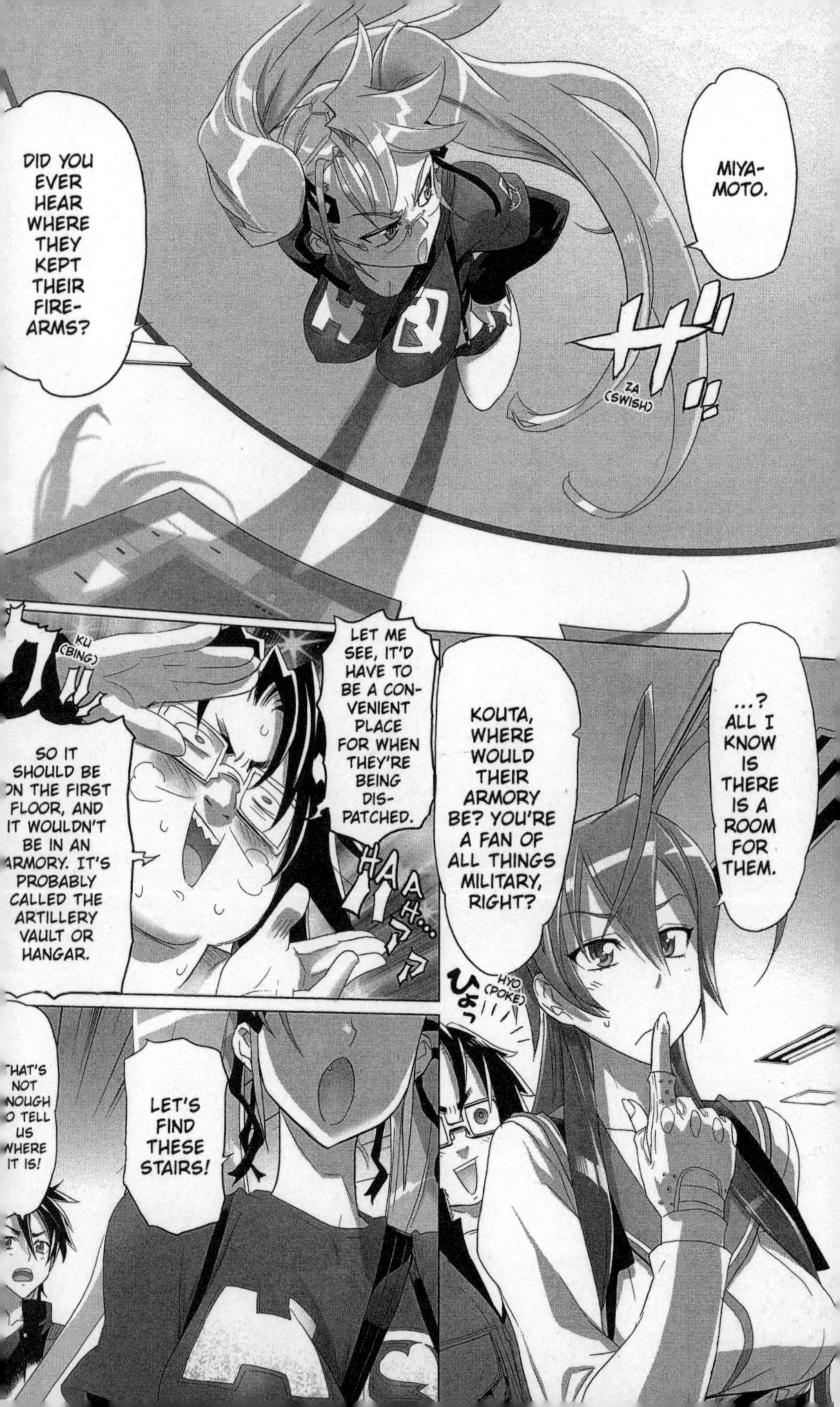
MIYA-MOTO.
ZA (SWISH)
DID YOU EVER HEAR WHERE THEY KEPT THEIR FIRE-ARMS?
...? ALL I KNOW IS THERE IS A ROOM FOR THEM.
KOUTA, WHERE WOULD THEIR ARMORY BE? YOU'RE A FAN OF ALL THINGS MILITARY, RIGHT?
HYO (POKE)
LET ME SEE, IT'D HAVE TO BE A CON-VENIENT PLACE FOR WHEN THEY'RE BEING DIS-PATCHED.
KU (BING)
HAAAH...
SO IT SHOULD BE N THE FIRST FLOOR, AND T WOULDN'T BE IN AN RMORY. IT'S PROBABLY CALLED THE ARTILLERY VAULT OR HANGAR.
LET'S FIND THESE STAIRS!
HAT'S NOT NOUGH O TELL US WHERE IT IS!

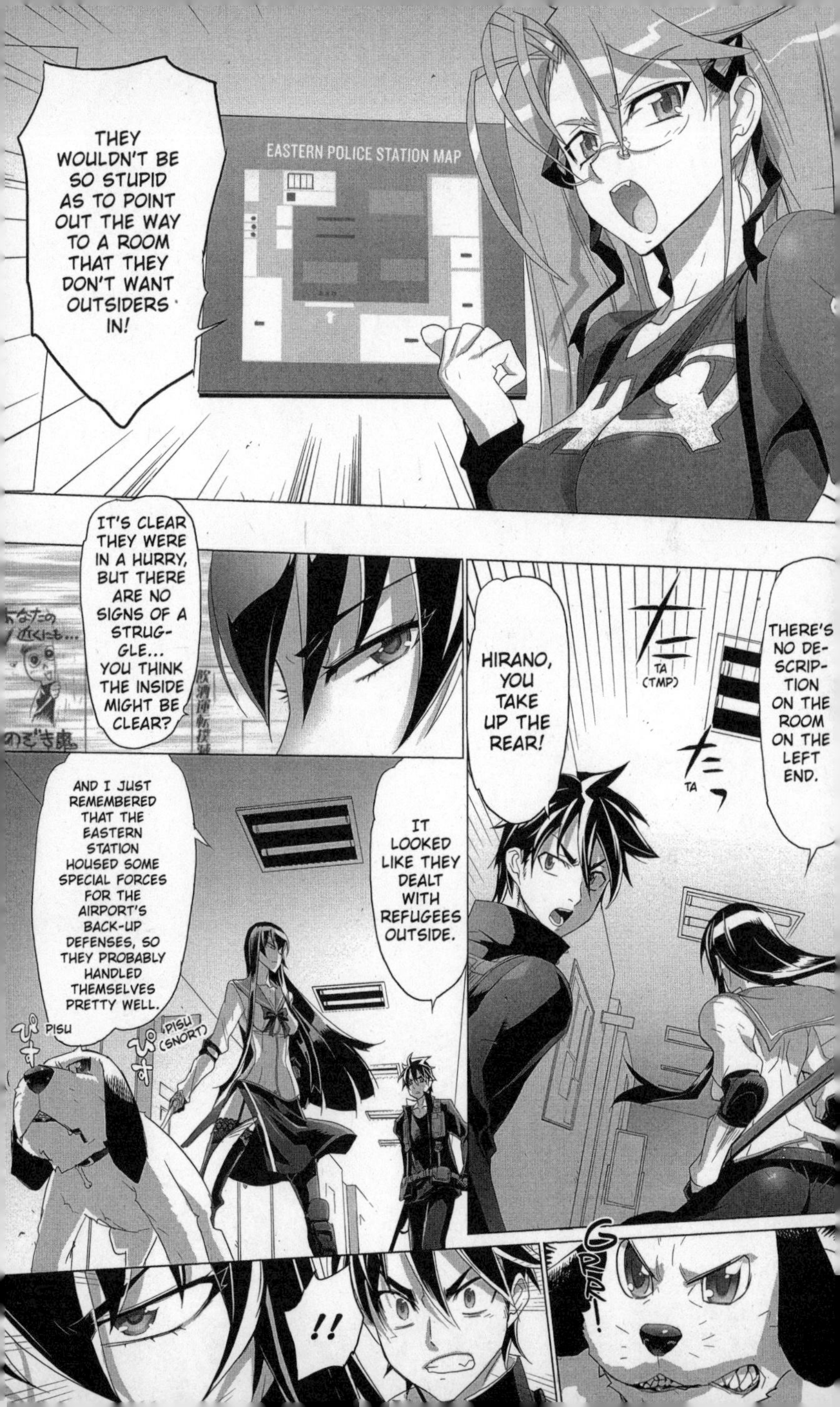
EASTERN POLICE STATION MAP
THEY WOULDN'T BE SO STUPID AS TO POINT OUT THE WAY TO A ROOM THAT THEY DON'T WANT OUTSIDERS IN!
THERE'S NO DESCRIPTION ON THE ROOM ON THE LEFT END.
TA (TMP)
TA
HIRANO, YOU TAKE UP THE REAR!
IT'S CLEAR THEY WERE IN A HURRY, BUT THERE ARE NO SIGNS OF A STRUGGLE... YOU THINK THE INSIDE MIGHT BE CLEAR?
IT LOOKED LIKE THEY DEALT WITH REFUGEES OUTSIDE.
AND I JUST REMEMBERED THAT THE EASTERN STATION HOUSED SOME SPECIAL FORCES FOR THE AIRPORT'S BACK-UP DEFENSES, SO THEY PROBABLY HANDLED THEMSELVES PRETTY WELL.
ぴす
PISU (SNORT)
ぴす
PISU
GRRR!
!!

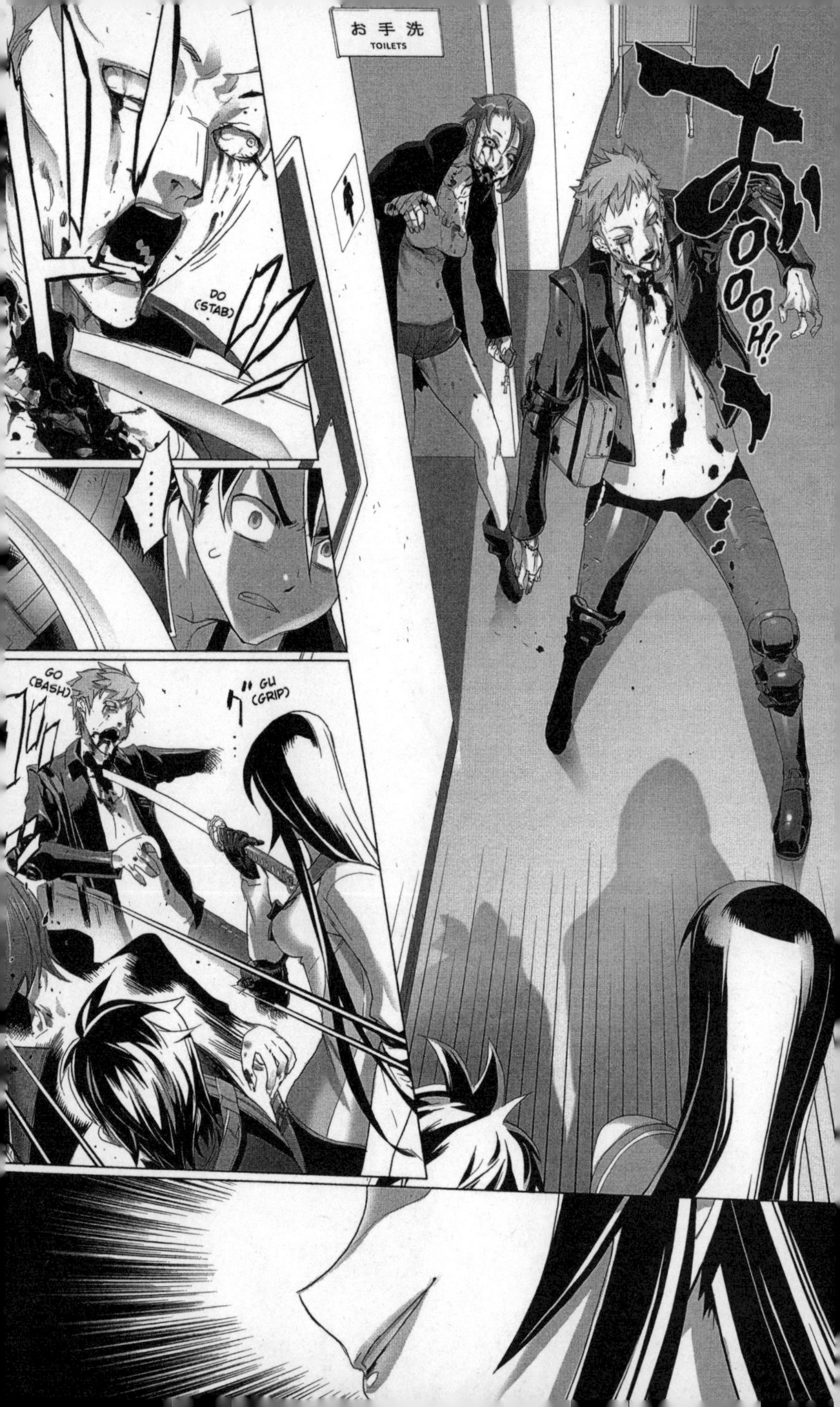
お手洗
TOILETS
OOOH!
DO (STAB)
GO (BASH)
GU (GRIP)

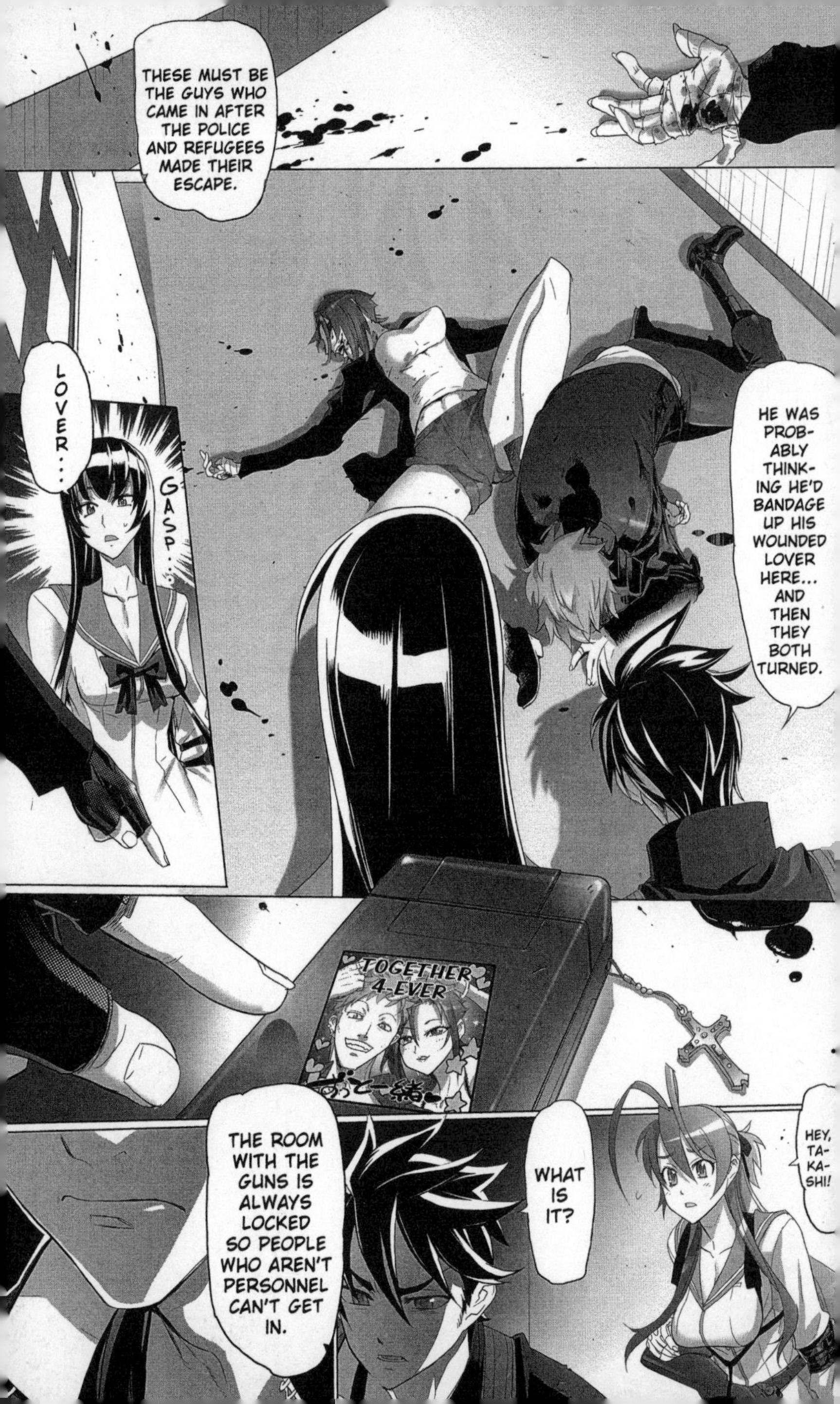
THESE MUST BE THE GUYS WHO CAME IN AFTER THE POLICE AND REFUGEES MADE THEIR ESCAPE.
HE WAS PROB-ABLY THINK-ING HE'D BANDAGE UP HIS WOUNDED LOVER HERE... AND THEN THEY BOTH TURNED.
LOVER...
GASP...
TOGETHER 4-EVER
ずっと一緒
HEY, TA-KA-SHI!
WHAT IS IT?
THE ROOM WITH THE GUNS IS ALWAYS LOCKED SO PEOPLE WHO AREN'T PERSONNEL CAN'T GET IN.

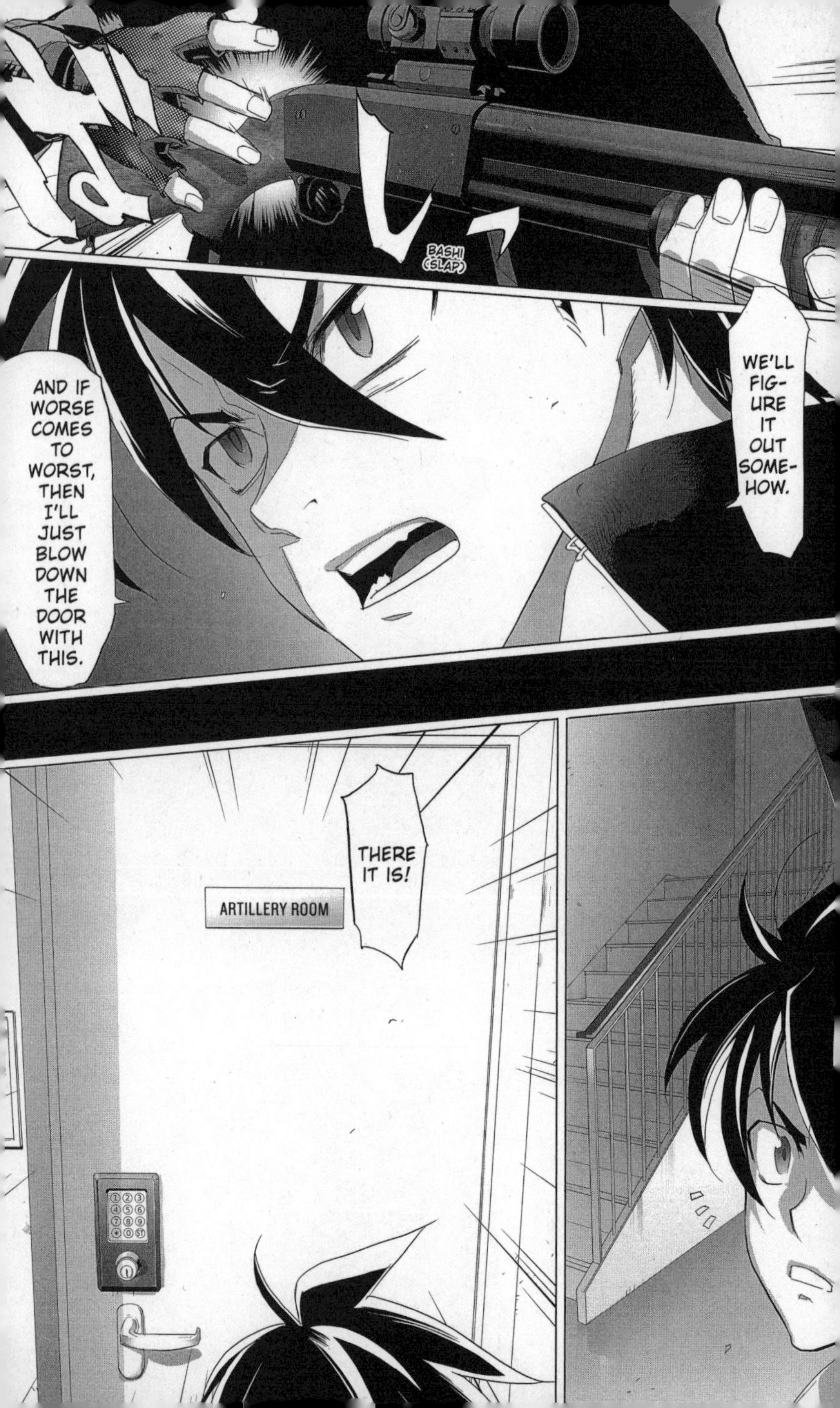
BASHI (SLAP)
WE'LL FIGURE IT OUT SOMEHOW.
AND IF WORSE COMES TO WORST, THEN I'LL JUST BLOW DOWN THE DOOR WITH THIS.
THERE IT IS!
ARTILLERY ROOM

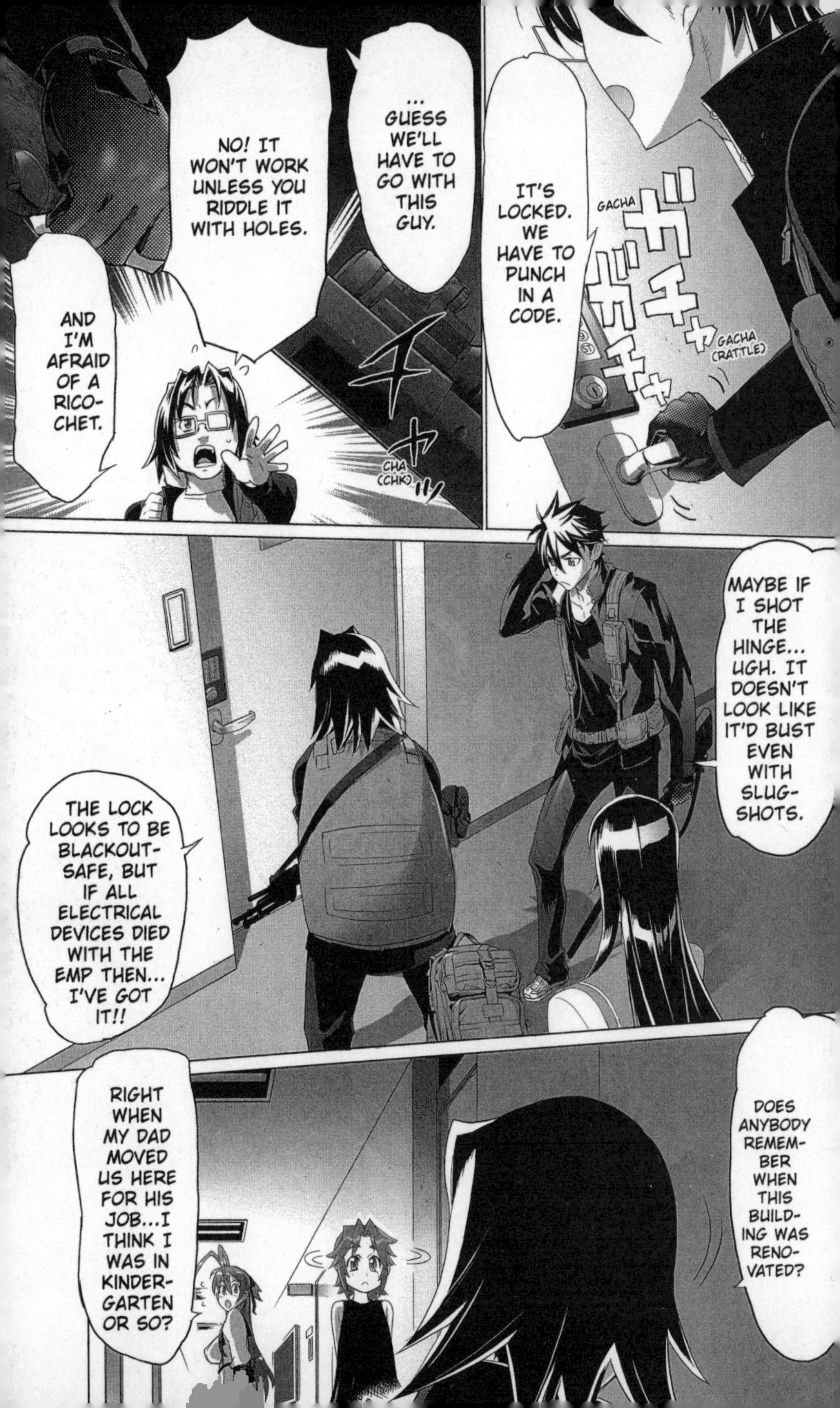
IT'S LOCKED. WE HAVE TO PUNCH IN A CODE.
GACHA
GACHA (RATTLE)
... GUESS WE'LL HAVE TO GO WITH THIS GUY.
NO! IT WON'T WORK UNLESS YOU RIDDLE IT WITH HOLES.
CHA (CHK)
AND I'M AFRAID OF A RICO-CHET.
MAYBE IF I SHOT THE HINGE... UGH. IT DOESN'T LOOK LIKE IT'D BUST EVEN WITH SLUG-SHOTS.
THE LOCK LOOKS TO BE BLACKOUT-SAFE, BUT IF ALL ELECTRICAL DEVICES DIED WITH THE EMP THEN... I'VE GOT IT!!
DOES ANYBODY REMEM-BER WHEN THIS BUILD-ING WAS RENO-VATED?
RIGHT WHEN MY DAD MOVED US HERE FOR HIS JOB...I THINK I WAS IN KINDER-GARTEN OR SO?

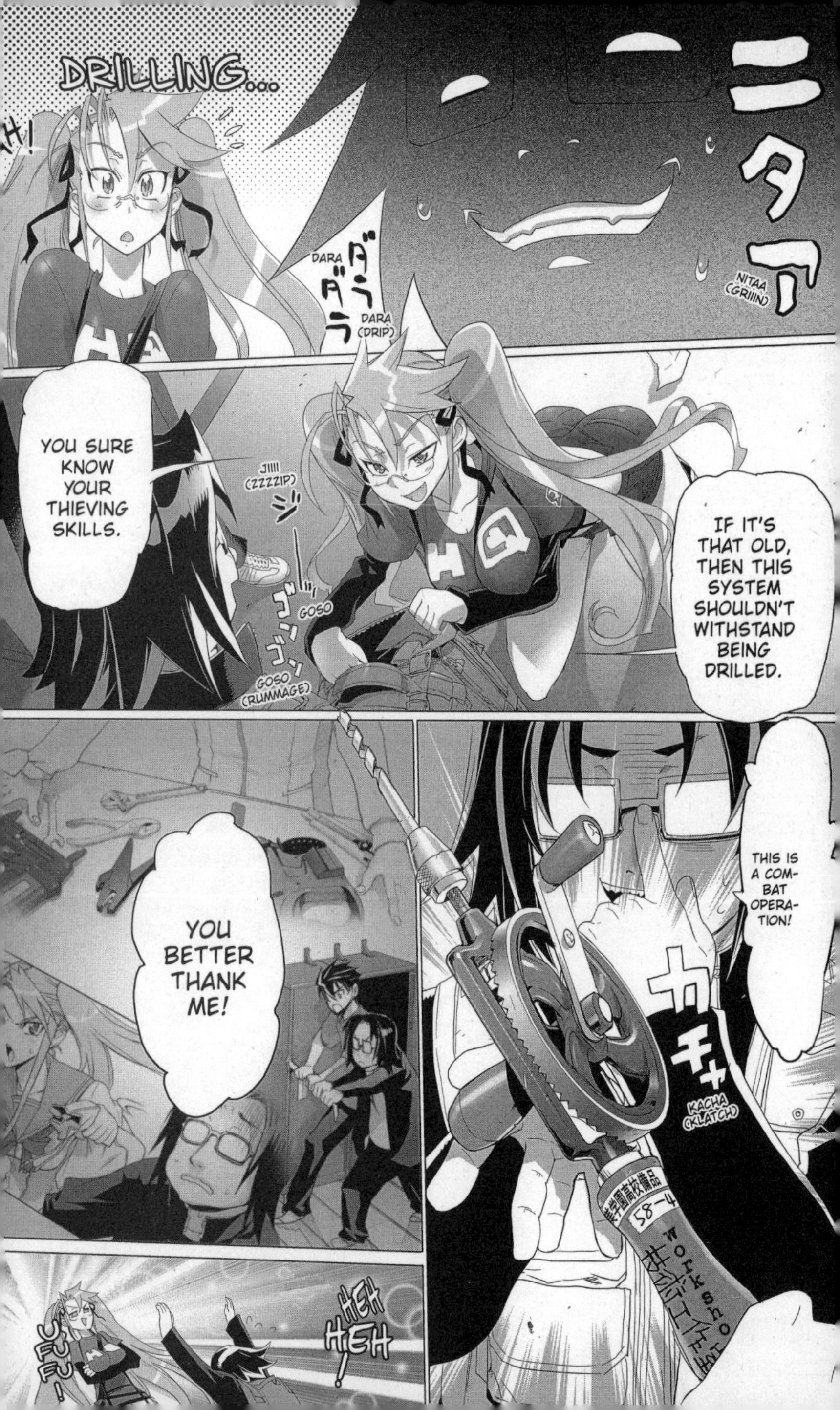
ニタア
NITAA (GRIIIN)
ダラダラ
DARA DARA (DRIP)
DRILLING...
H!
IF IT'S THAT OLD, THEN THIS SYSTEM SHOULDN'T WITHSTAND BEING DRILLED.
ジ
JIIII (ZZZZIP)
YOU SURE KNOW YOUR THIEVING SKILLS.
ゴソゴソ
GOSO GOSO (RUMMAGE)
THIS IS A COMBAT OPERATION!
カチャ
KACHA (KLATCH)
58-4
workshop
YOU BETTER THANK ME!
HEH HEH!
UFUFUFU!

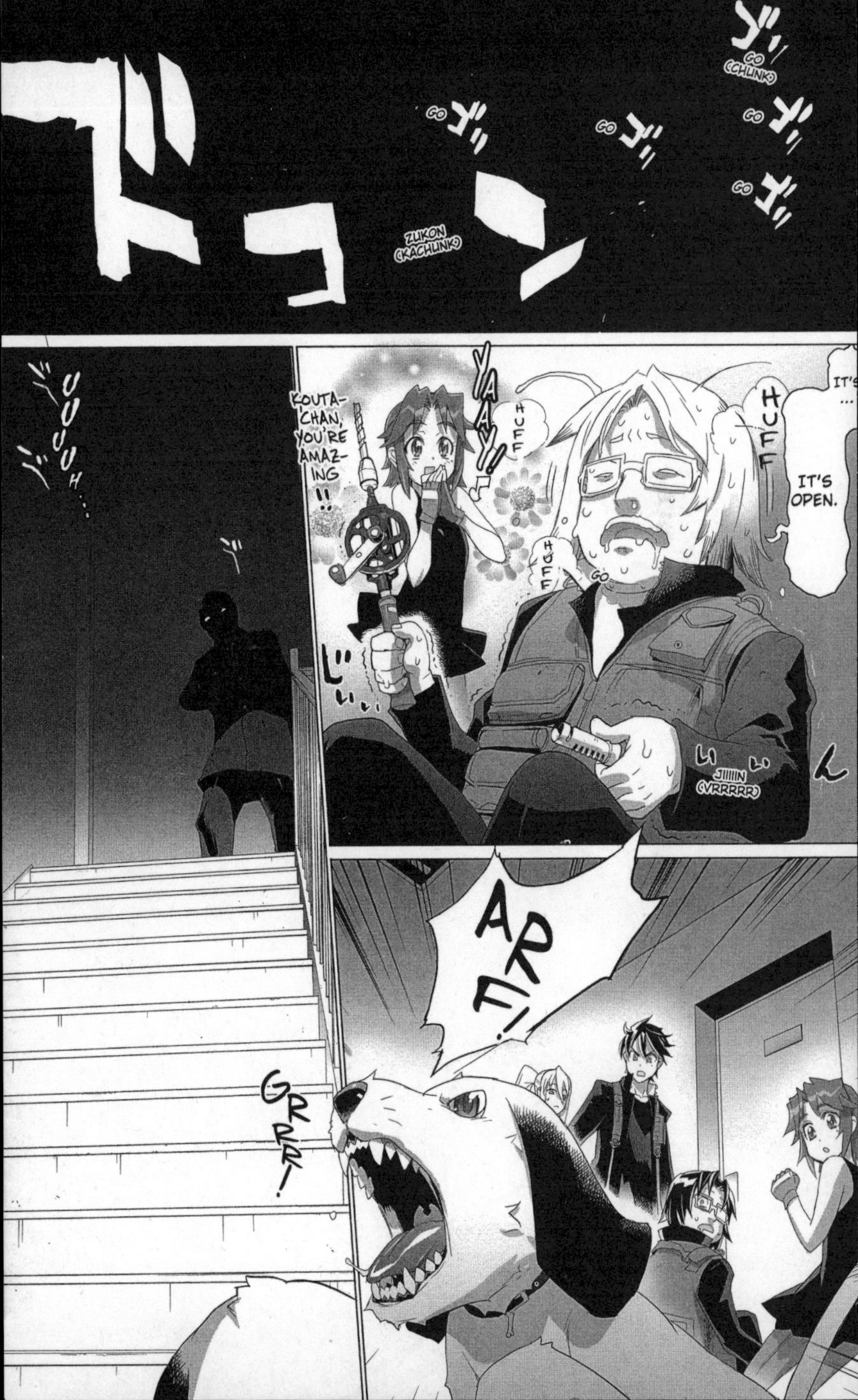
GO (CHUNK)
GO
GO
GO
GO
ZUKON (KACHUNK)
IT'S ...
HUFF
IT'S OPEN.
YAAAY!
KOUTA-CHAN, YOU'RE AMAZING!!
HUFF
HUFF
GO
JIIIIN (VRRRRR)
ARF!
GRRR!
UUUUUH...

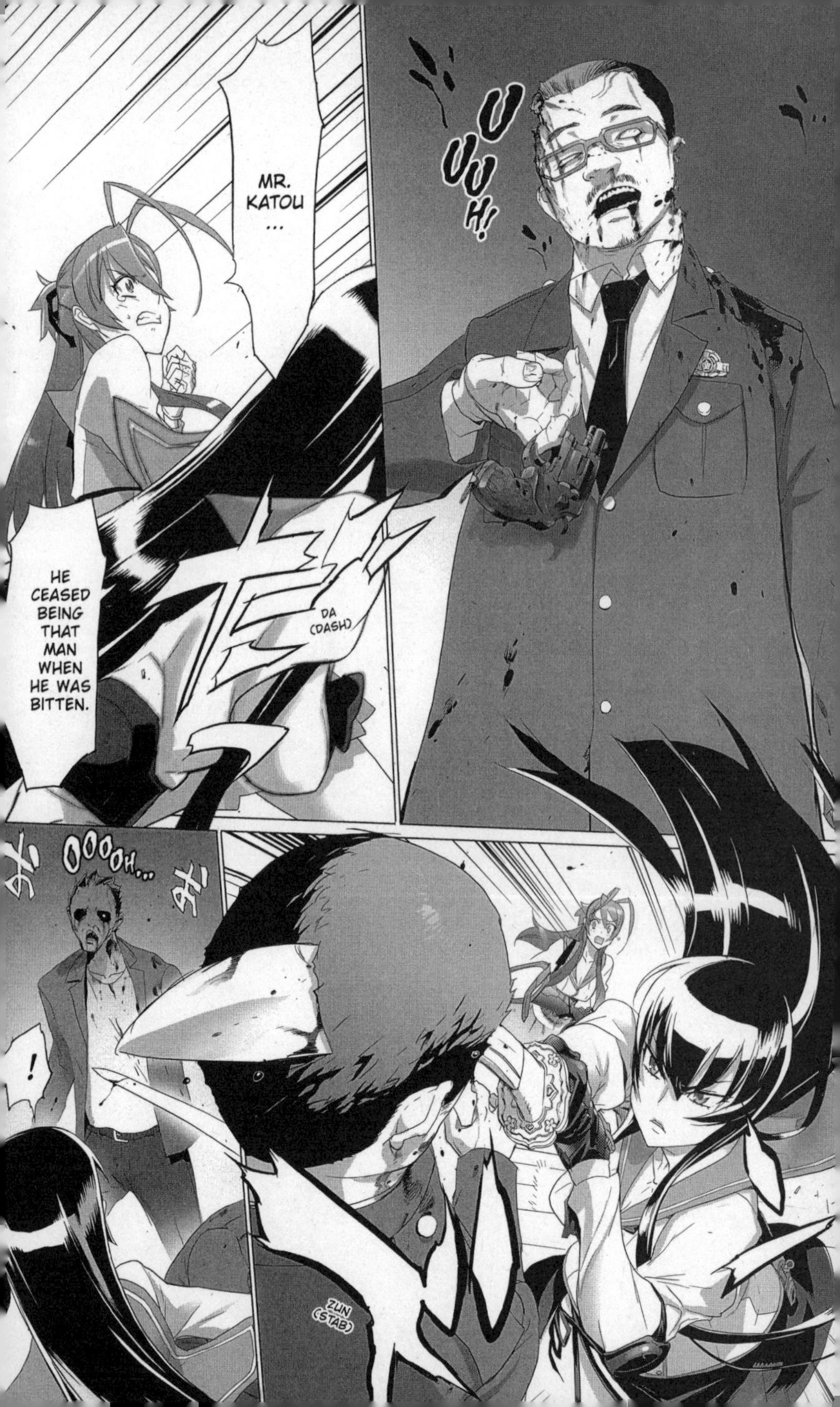
UUUH!
MR. KATOU ...
HE CEASED BEING THAT MAN WHEN HE WAS BITTEN.
DA (DASH)
OOOOH...
!
ZUN (STAB)

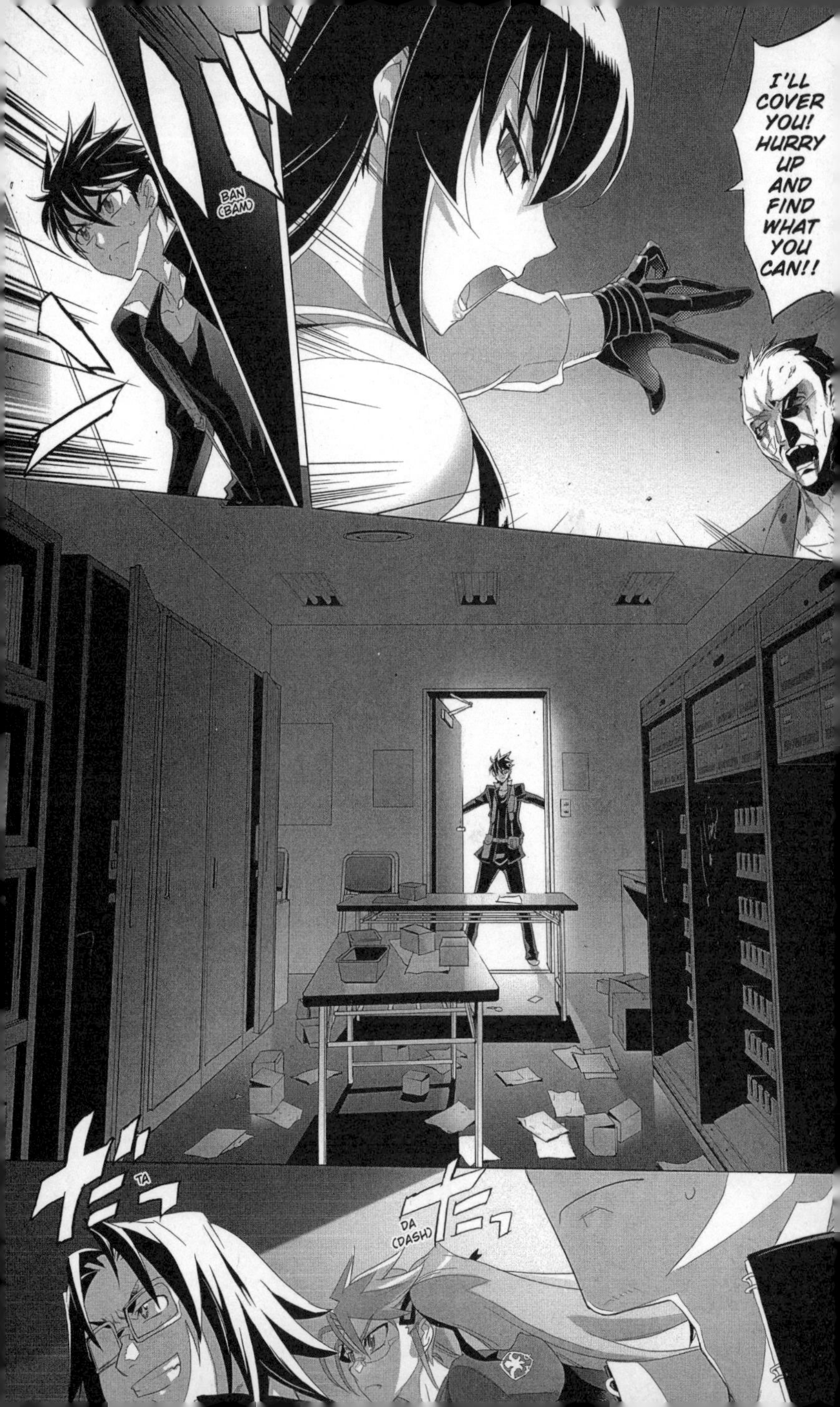
I'LL COVER YOU! HURRY UP AND FIND WHAT YOU CAN!!
BAN (BAM)
DA (DASH)
TA

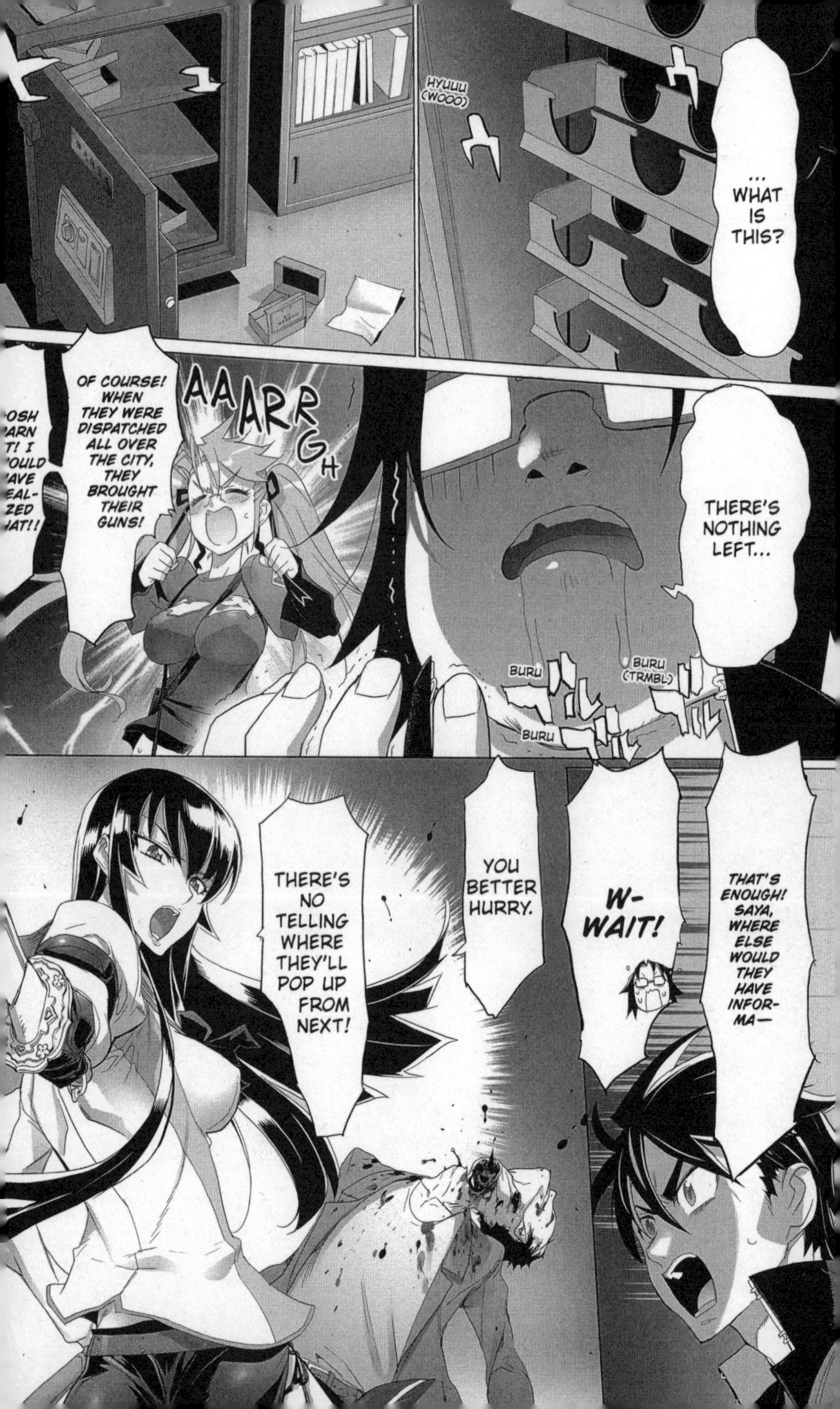
... WHAT IS THIS?
HYUUU (WOOO)
THERE'S NOTHING LEFT...
BURU
BURU (TRMBL)
BURU
AAARRGH
OF COURSE! WHEN THEY WERE DISPATCHED ALL OVER THE CITY, THEY BROUGHT THEIR GUNS!
THAT'S ENOUGH! SAYA, WHERE ELSE WOULD THEY HAVE INFORMA—
W-WAIT!
YOU BETTER HURRY.
THERE'S NO TELLING WHERE THEY'LL POP UP FROM NEXT!

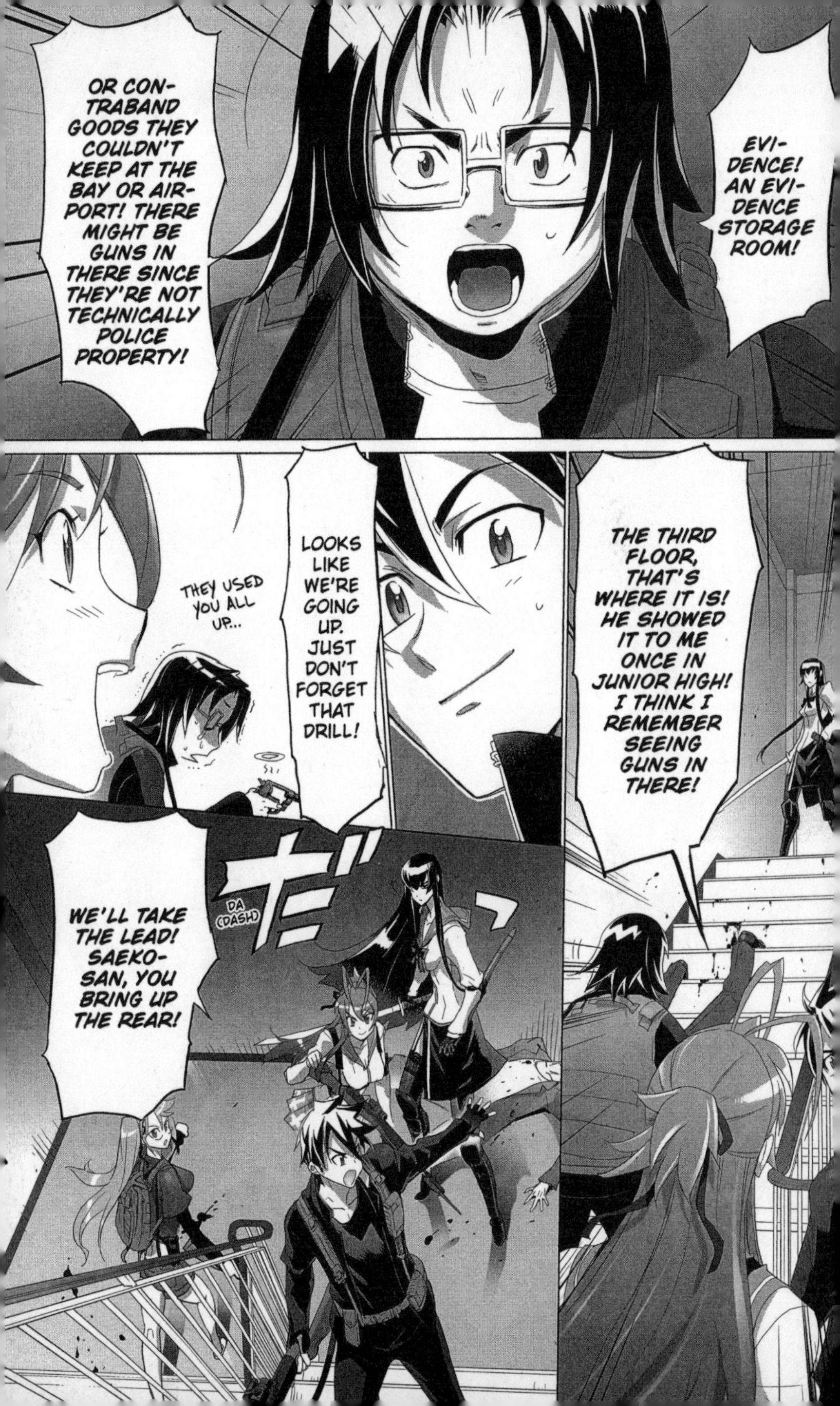
EVIDENCE! AN EVIDENCE STORAGE ROOM!
OR CONTRABAND GOODS THEY COULDN'T KEEP AT THE BAY OR AIRPORT! THERE MIGHT BE GUNS IN THERE SINCE THEY'RE NOT TECHNICALLY POLICE PROPERTY!
THE THIRD FLOOR, THAT'S WHERE IT IS! HE SHOWED IT TO ME ONCE IN JUNIOR HIGH! I THINK I REMEMBER SEEING GUNS IN THERE!
LOOKS LIKE WE'RE GOING UP. JUST DON'T FORGET THAT DRILL!
THEY USED YOU ALL UP...
DA (DASH)
WE'LL TAKE THE LEAD! SAEKO-SAN, YOU BRING UP THE REAR!

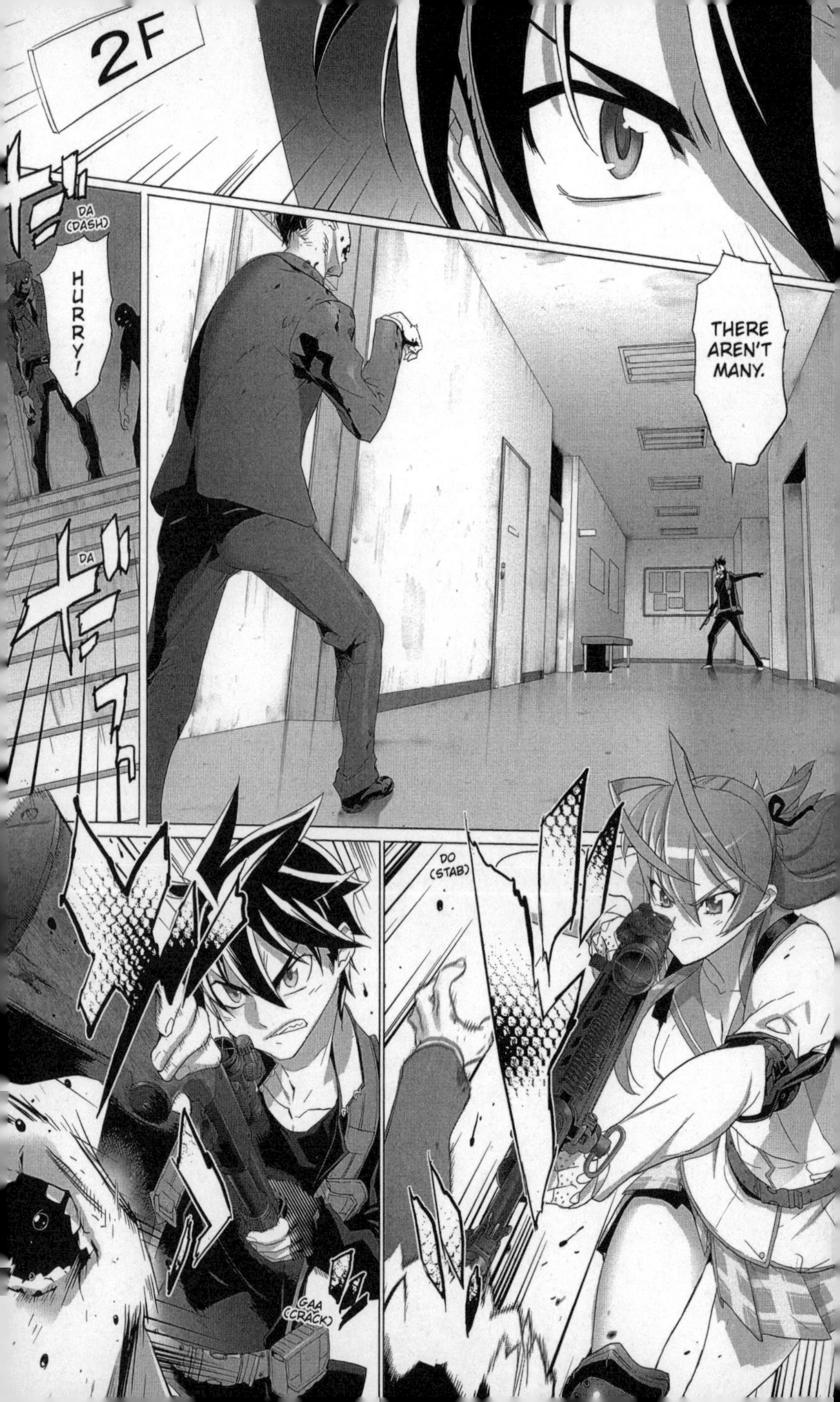
2F
THERE AREN'T MANY.
DA (DASH)
HURRY!
DA
DO (STAB)
GAA (CRACK)

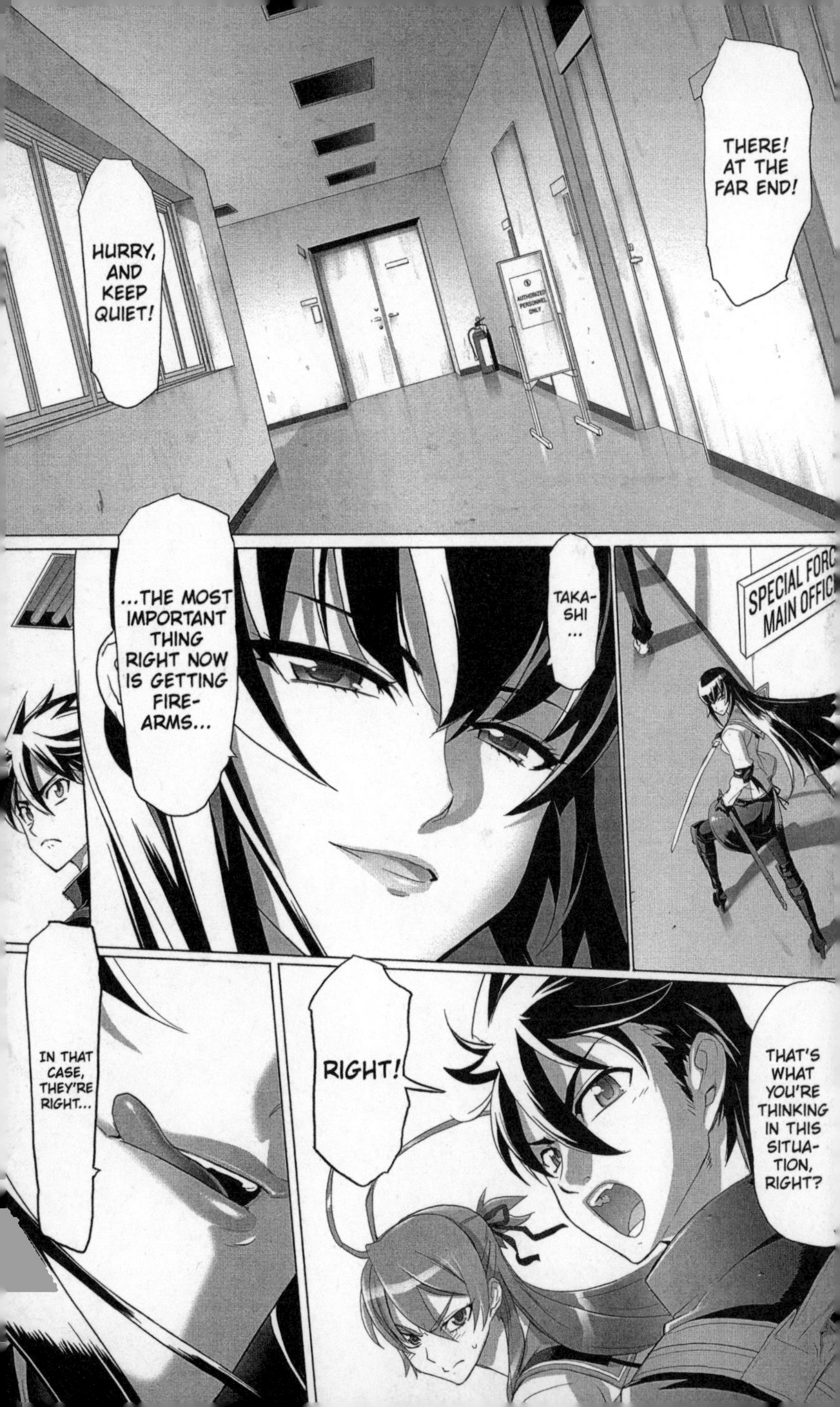
THERE! AT THE FAR END!
AUTHORIZED PERSONNEL ONLY
HURRY, AND KEEP QUIET!
SPECIAL FORC
MAIN OFFIC
TAKA-SHI ...
...THE MOST IMPORTANT THING RIGHT NOW IS GETTING FIRE-ARMS...
THAT'S WHAT YOU'RE THINKING IN THIS SITUA-TION, RIGHT?
RIGHT!
IN THAT CASE, THEY'RE RIGHT...

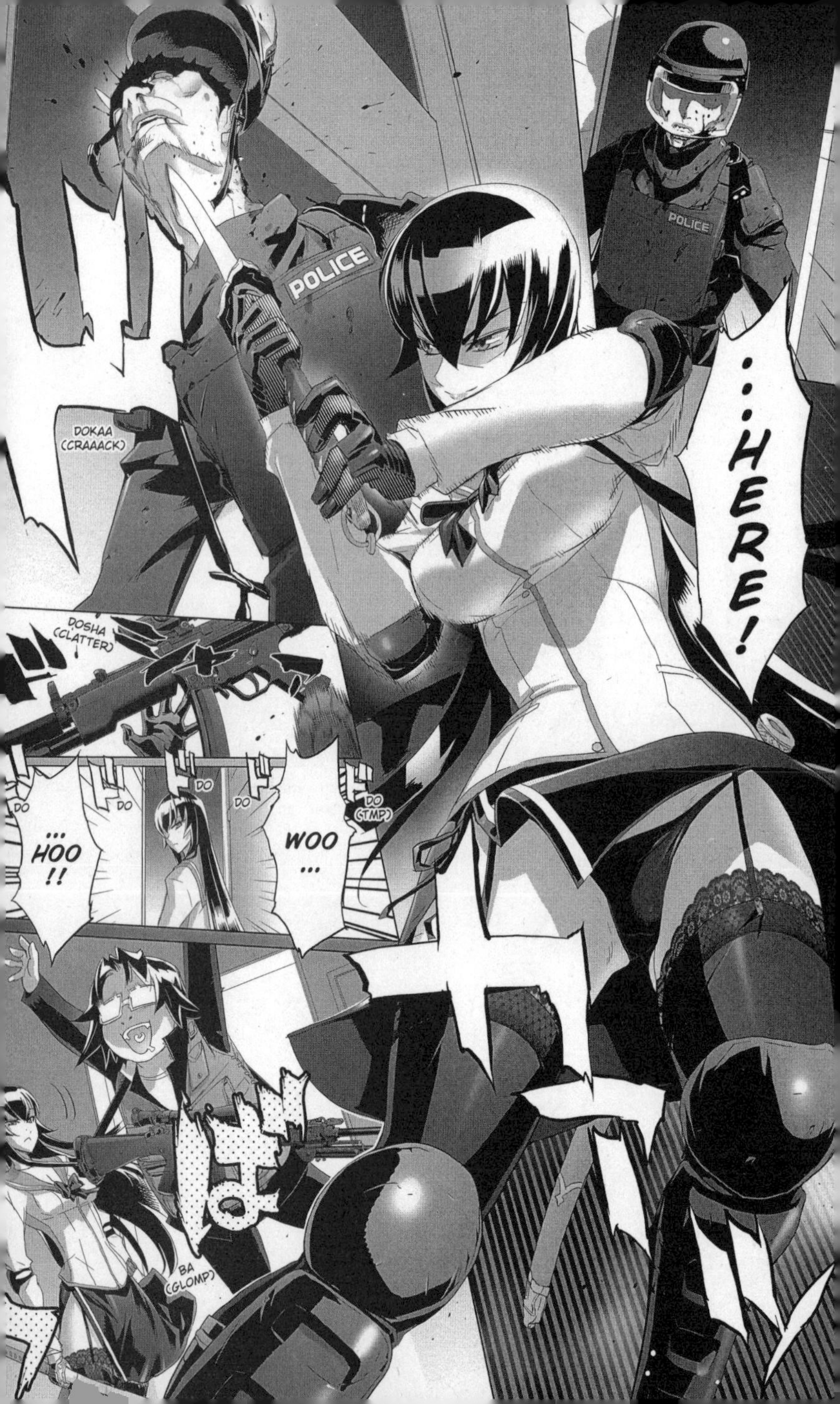

...HERE!
DOKAA (CRAAACK)
DOSHA (CLATTER)
DO (TMP)
WOO ...
DO
DO
DO
... HÖO !!
DO
BA (GLOMP)

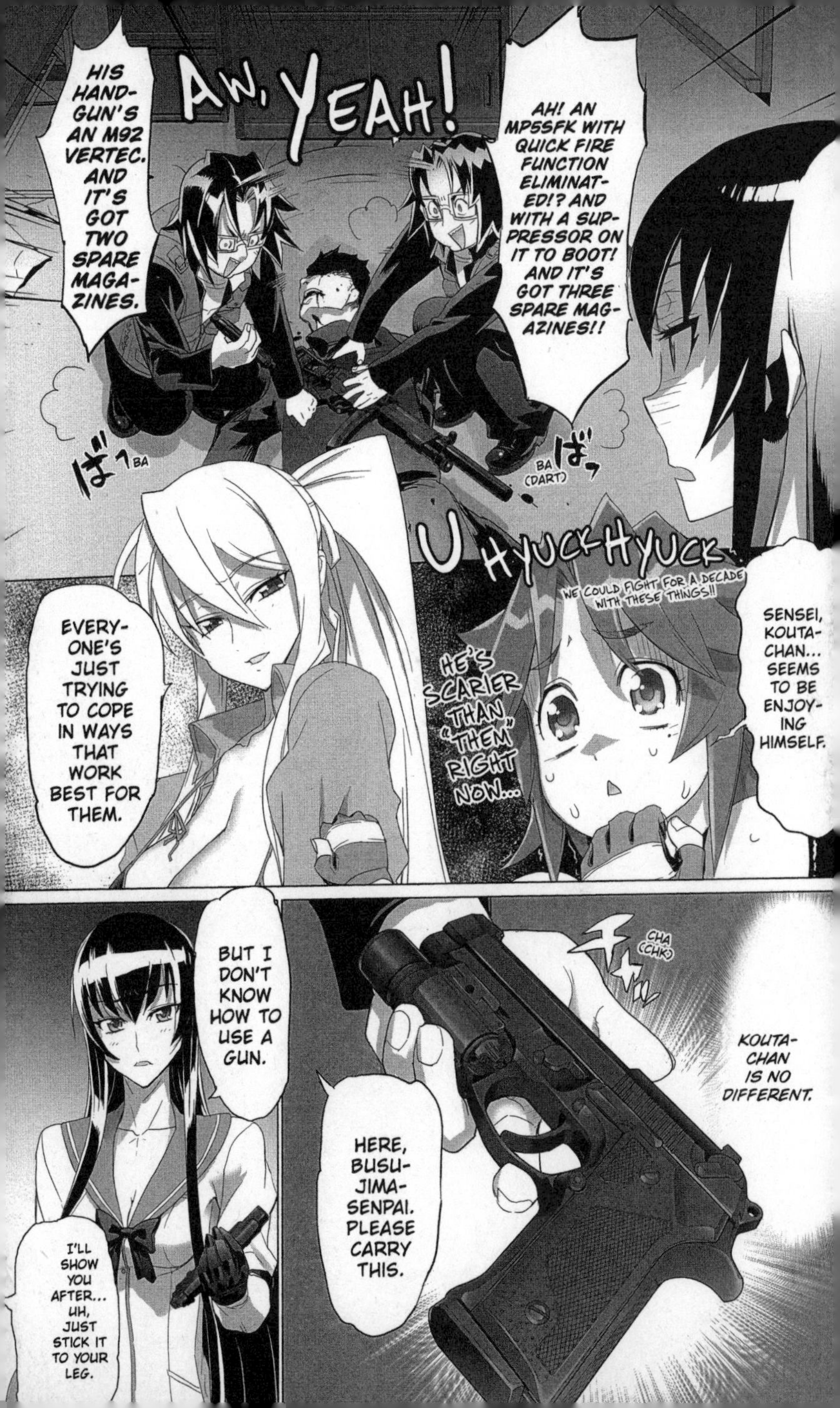

AH! AN MP5SFK WITH QUICK FIRE FUNCTION ELIMINATED!? AND WITH A SUPPRESSOR ON IT TO BOOT! AND IT'S GOT THREE SPARE MAGAZINES!!
AW, YEAH!
HIS HANDGUN'S AN M92 VERTEC. AND IT'S GOT TWO SPARE MAGAZINES.
ばっ BA (DART)
ばっ BA
SENSEI, KOUTA-CHAN... SEEMS TO BE ENJOYING HIMSELF.
U HYUCK HYUCK
WE COULD FIGHT FOR A DECADE WITH THESE THINGS!!
HE'S SCARIER THAN "THEM" RIGHT NOW...
EVERYONE'S JUST TRYING TO COPE IN WAYS THAT WORK BEST FOR THEM.
KOUTA-CHAN IS NO DIFFERENT.
CHA (CHK)
HERE, BUSUJIMA-SENPAI. PLEASE CARRY THIS.
BUT I DON'T KNOW HOW TO USE A GUN.
I'LL SHOW YOU AFTER... UH, JUST STICK IT TO YOUR LEG.

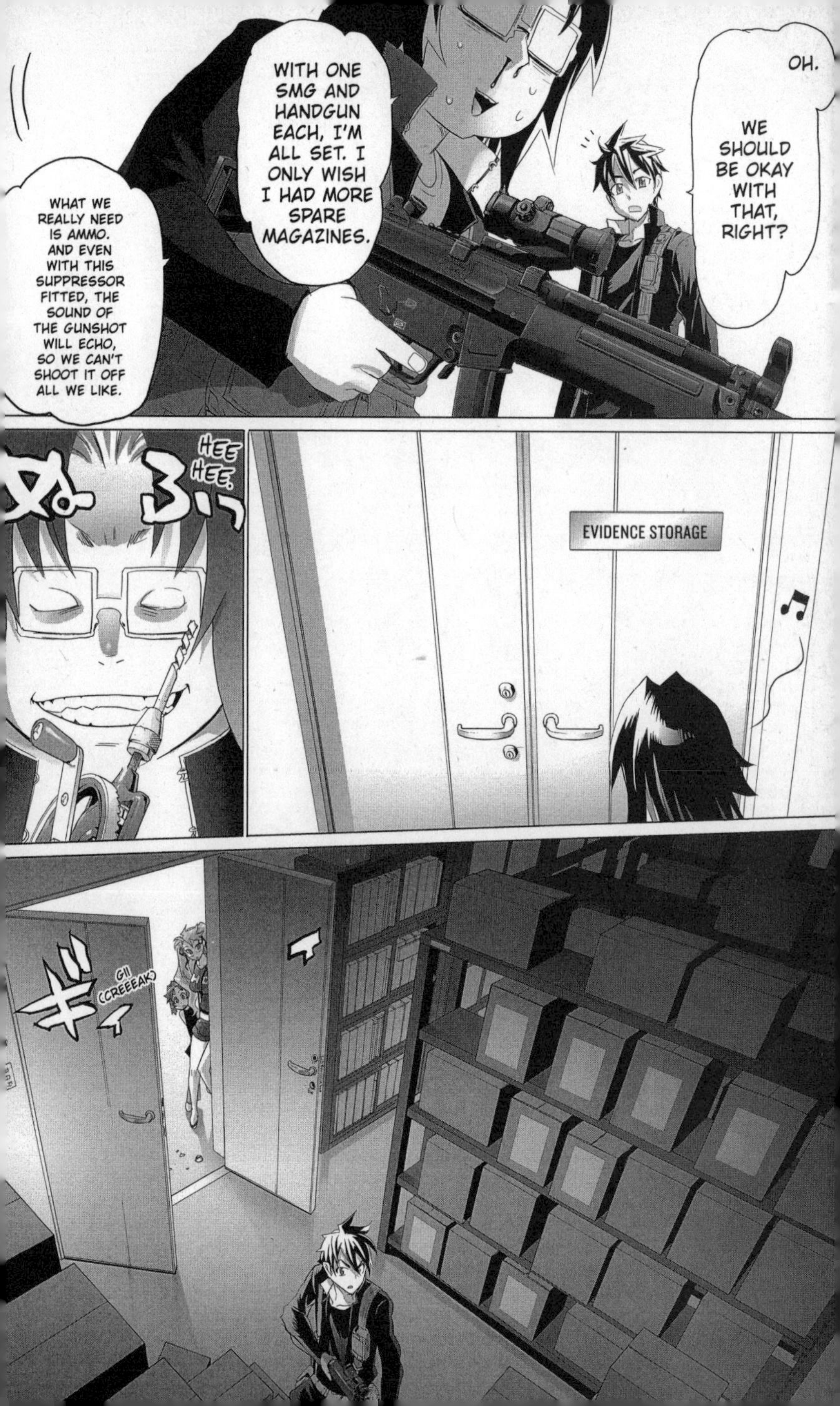
OH.
WE SHOULD BE OKAY WITH THAT, RIGHT?
WITH ONE SMG AND HANDGUN EACH, I'M ALL SET. I ONLY WISH I HAD MORE SPARE MAGAZINES.
WHAT WE REALLY NEED IS AMMO. AND EVEN WITH THIS SUPPRESSOR FITTED, THE SOUND OF THE GUNSHOT WILL ECHO, SO WE CAN'T SHOOT IT OFF ALL WE LIKE.
EVIDENCE STORAGE
HEE HEE.
GII (CREEEAK)

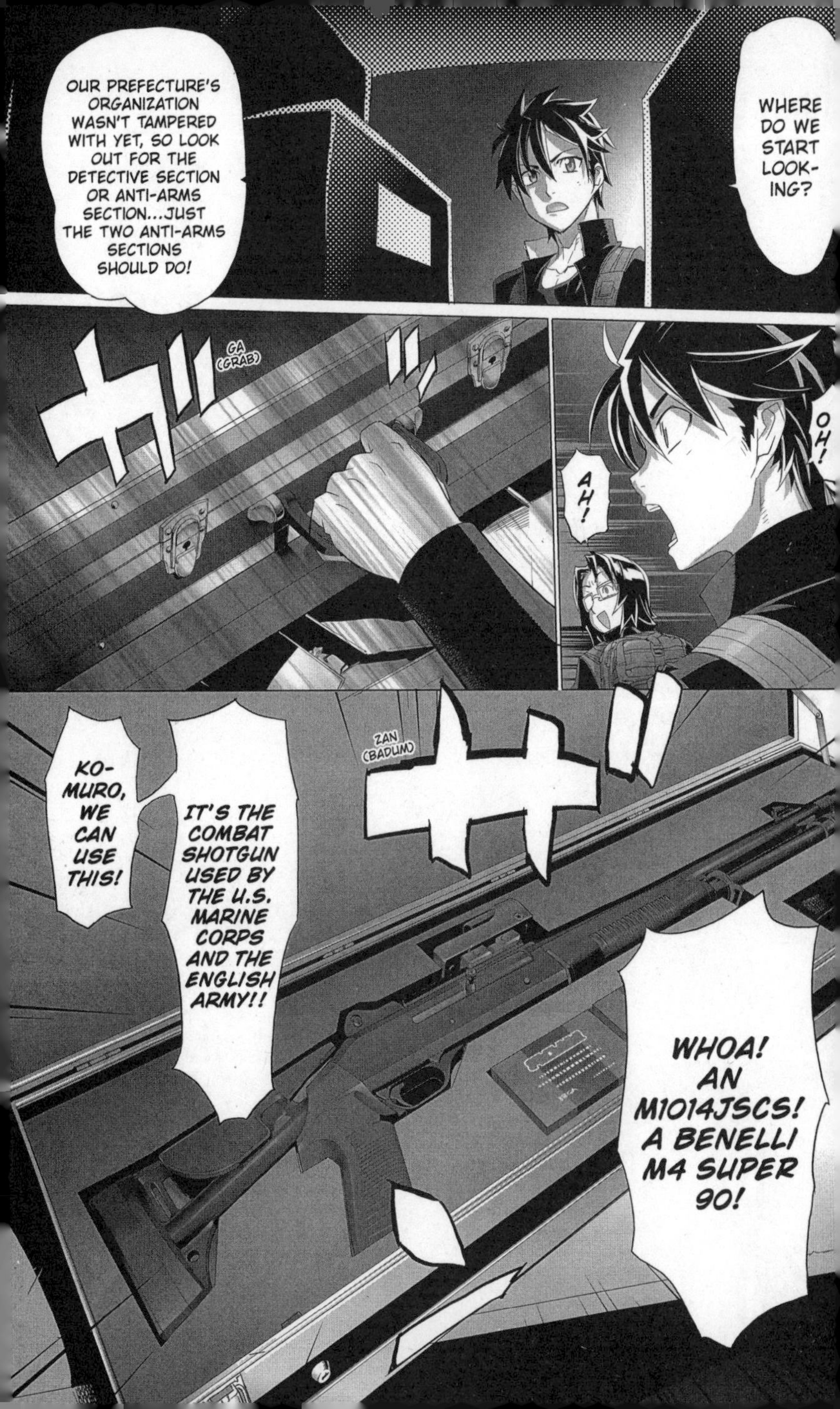
WHERE DO WE START LOOKING?
OUR PREFECTURE'S ORGANIZATION WASN'T TAMPERED WITH YET, SO LOOK OUT FOR THE DETECTIVE SECTION OR ANTI-ARMS SECTION...JUST THE TWO ANTI-ARMS SECTIONS SHOULD DO!
OH!
AH!
GA (GRAB)
WHOA! AN M1014JSCS! A BENELLI M4 SUPER 90!
ZAN (BADUM)
IT'S THE COMBAT SHOTGUN USED BY THE U.S. MARINE CORPS AND THE ENGLISH ARMY!!
KOMURO, WE CAN USE THIS!

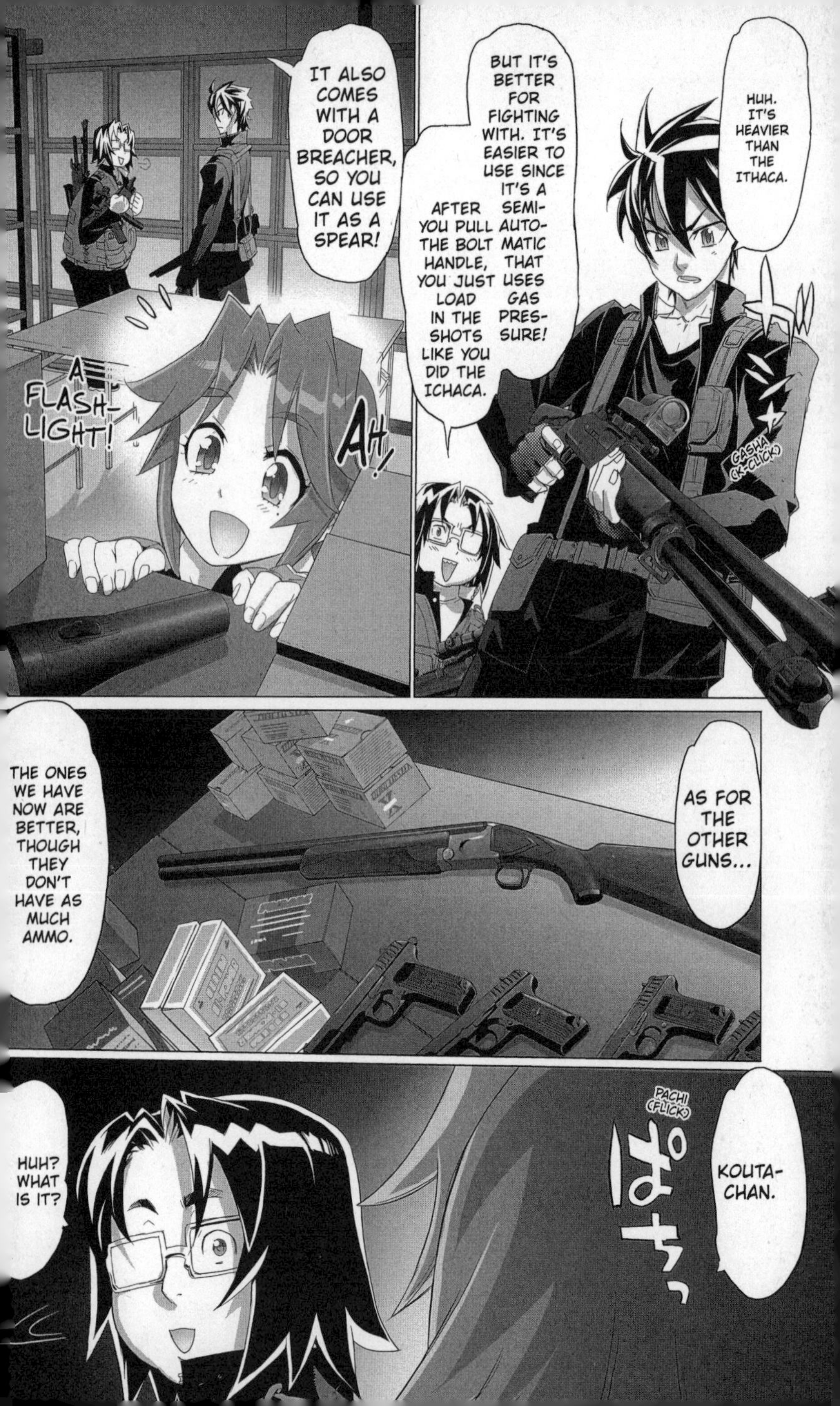
HUH. IT'S HEAVIER THAN THE ITHACA.
GASHA (K-CLICK)
BUT IT'S BETTER FOR FIGHTING WITH. IT'S EASIER TO USE SINCE IT'S A SEMI-AUTOMATIC THAT USES GAS PRESSURE!
AFTER YOU PULL THE BOLT HANDLE, YOU JUST LOAD IN THE SHOTS LIKE YOU DID THE ICHACA.
IT ALSO COMES WITH A DOOR BREACHER, SO YOU CAN USE IT AS A SPEAR!
AH!
A FLASH-LIGHT!
AS FOR THE OTHER GUNS...
THE ONES WE HAVE NOW ARE BETTER, THOUGH THEY DON'T HAVE AS MUCH AMMO.
KOUTA-CHAN.
PACHI (FLICK)
ぱちっ
HUH? WHAT IS IT?

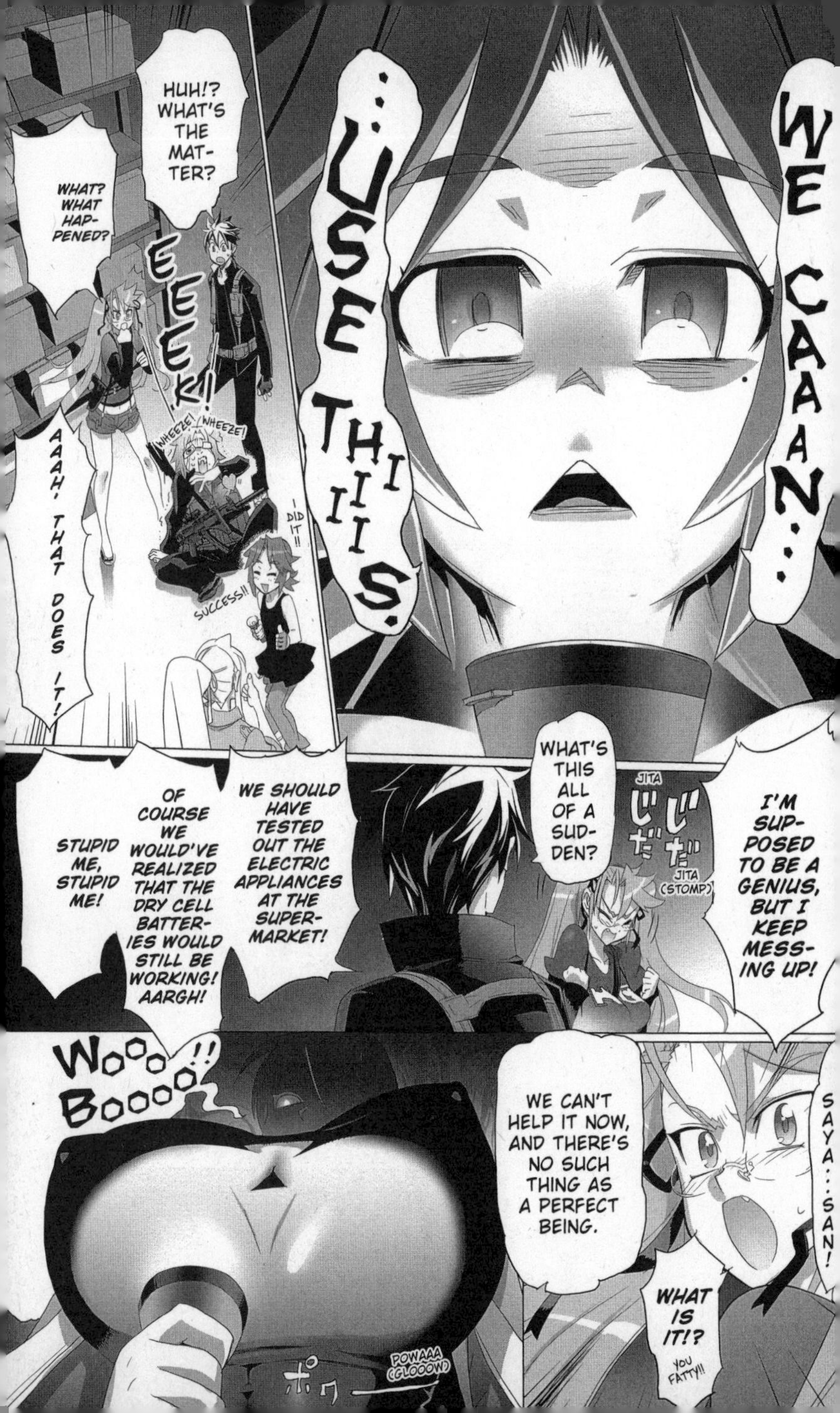

WE CAAAN...
...USE THIIIIS.
HUH!? WHAT'S THE MATTER?
WHAT? WHAT HAPPENED?
EEEK!
WHEEZE! WHEEZE!
I DID IT!!
SUCCESS!!
AAAH! THAT DOES IT!
I'M SUPPOSED TO BE A GENIUS, BUT I KEEP MESSING UP!
JITA じだ じだ JITA (STOMP)
WHAT'S THIS ALL OF A SUDDEN?
WE SHOULD HAVE TESTED OUT THE ELECTRIC APPLIANCES AT THE SUPERMARKET!
OF COURSE WE WOULD'VE REALIZED THAT THE DRY CELL BATTERIES WOULD STILL BE WORKING! AARGH!
STUPID ME, STUPID ME!
SAYA...SAN!
WE CAN'T HELP IT NOW, AND THERE'S NO SUCH THING AS A PERFECT BEING.
WHAT IS IT!?
YOU FATTY!!
WOOO!! BOOOO
POWAAA (GLOOOW)

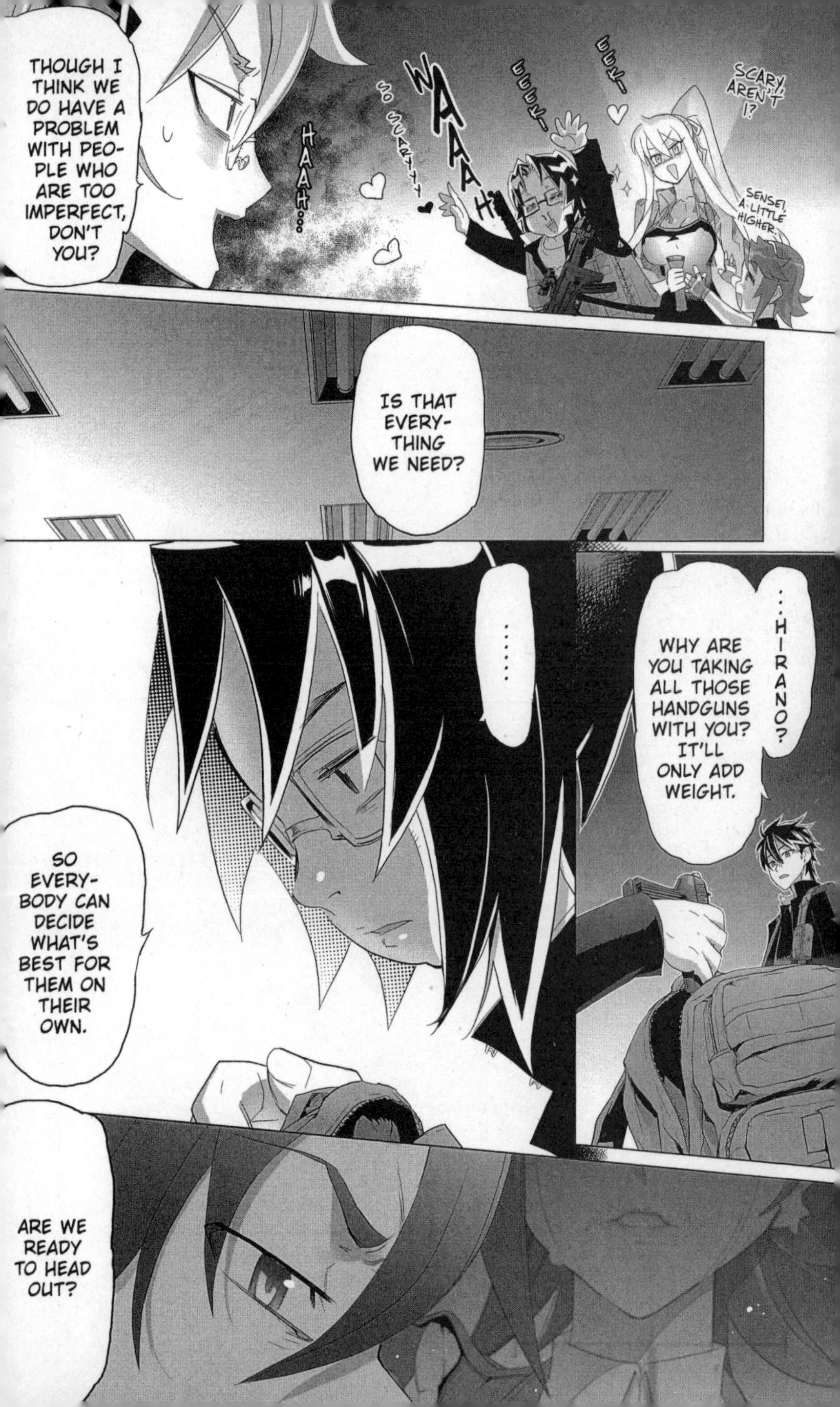
SCARY, AREN'T I?
SENSEI, A LITTLE HIGHER.
EEK!
EEEK!
WAAAAH
SO SCARYYYY
HAAAH...
THOUGH I THINK WE DO HAVE A PROBLEM WITH PEOPLE WHO ARE TOO IMPERFECT, DON'T YOU?
IS THAT EVERYTHING WE NEED?
...HIRANO?
WHY ARE YOU TAKING ALL THOSE HANDGUNS WITH YOU? IT'LL ONLY ADD WEIGHT.
......
SO EVERYBODY CAN DECIDE WHAT'S BEST FOR THEM ON THEIR OWN.
ARE WE READY TO HEAD OUT?

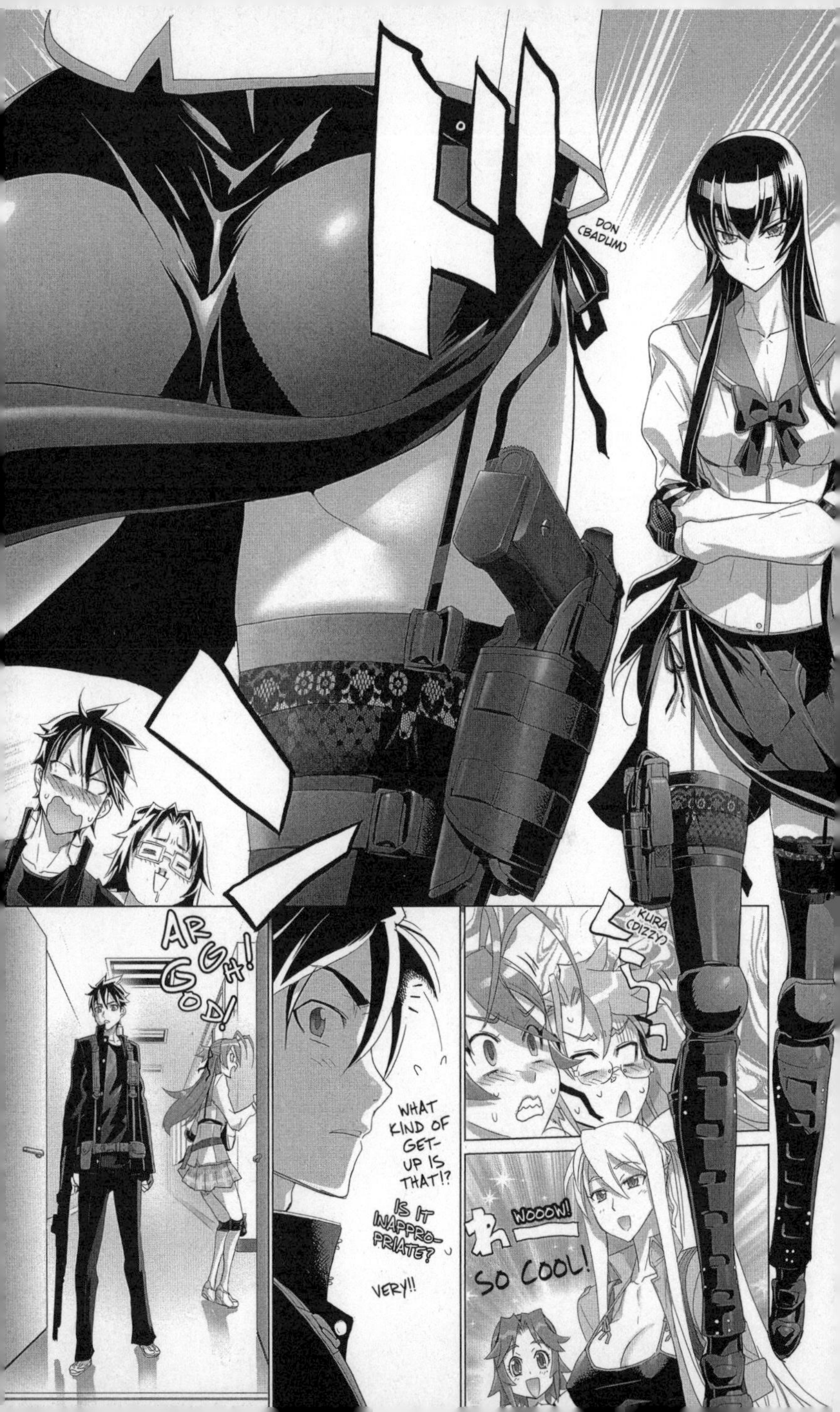
DON (BADUM)
ARGH! GOD!
WHAT KIND OF GET-UP IS THAT!?
IS IT INAPPROPRIATE?
VERY!!
KURA (DIZZY)
WOOOW!
SO COOL!

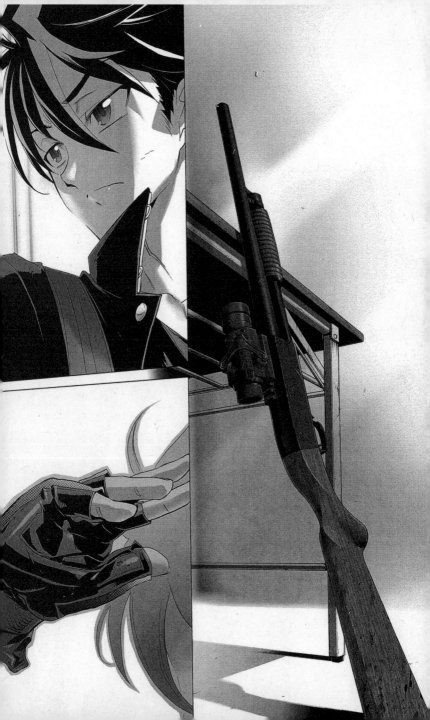

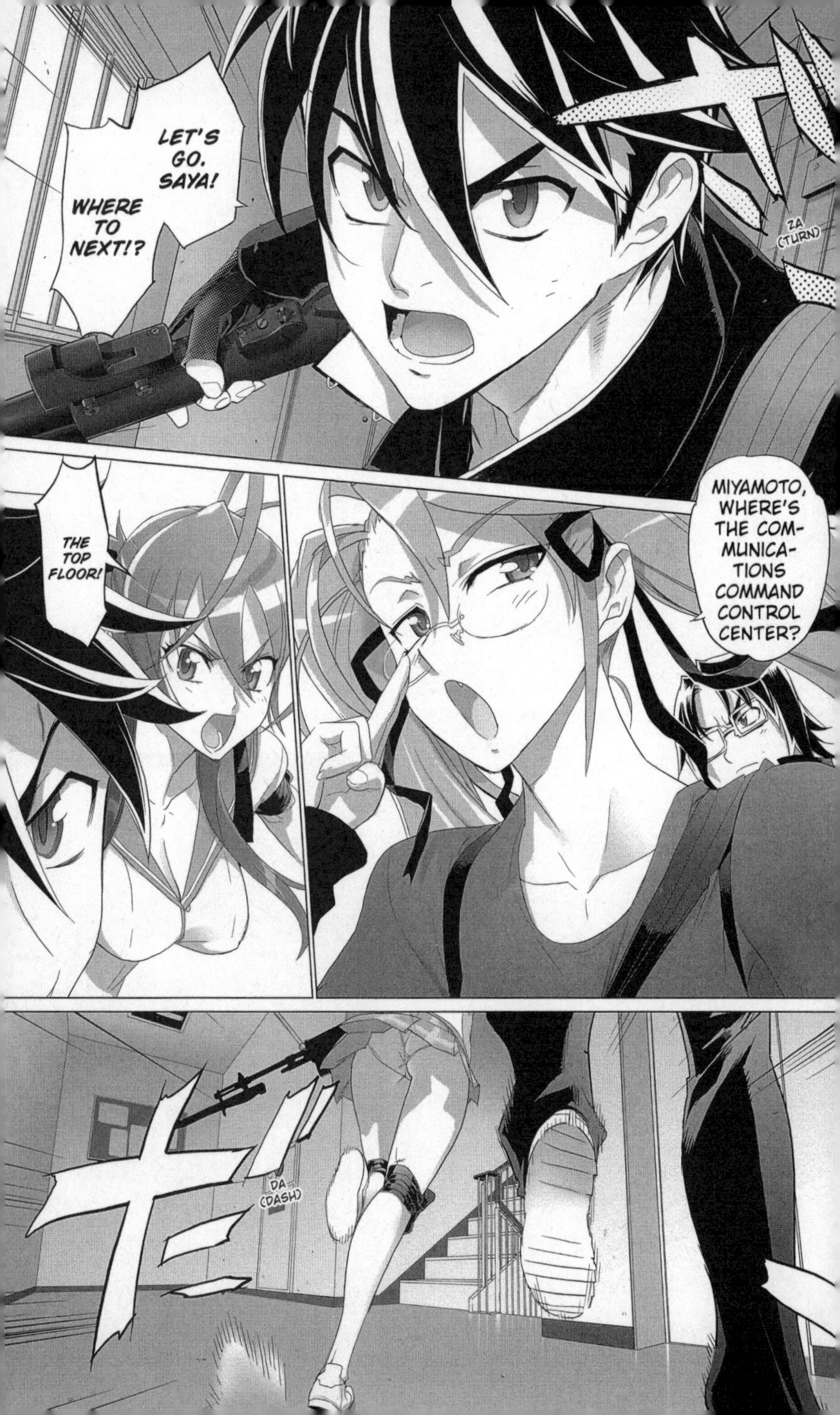
LET'S GO. SAYA!
WHERE TO NEXT!?
ZA (TURN)
MIYAMOTO, WHERE'S THE COM-MUNICA-TIONS COMMAND CONTROL CENTER?
THE TOP FLOOR!
DA (DASH)

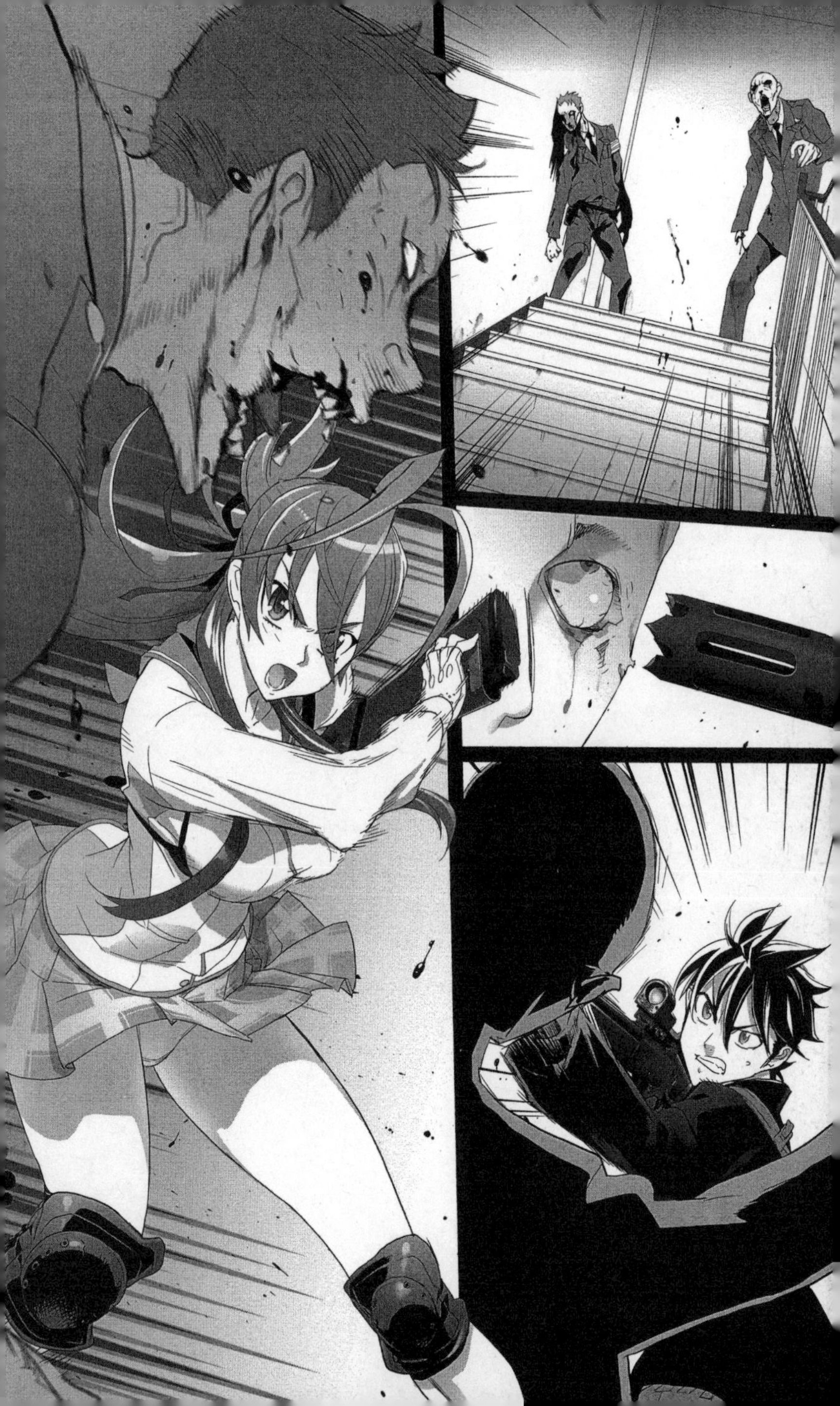

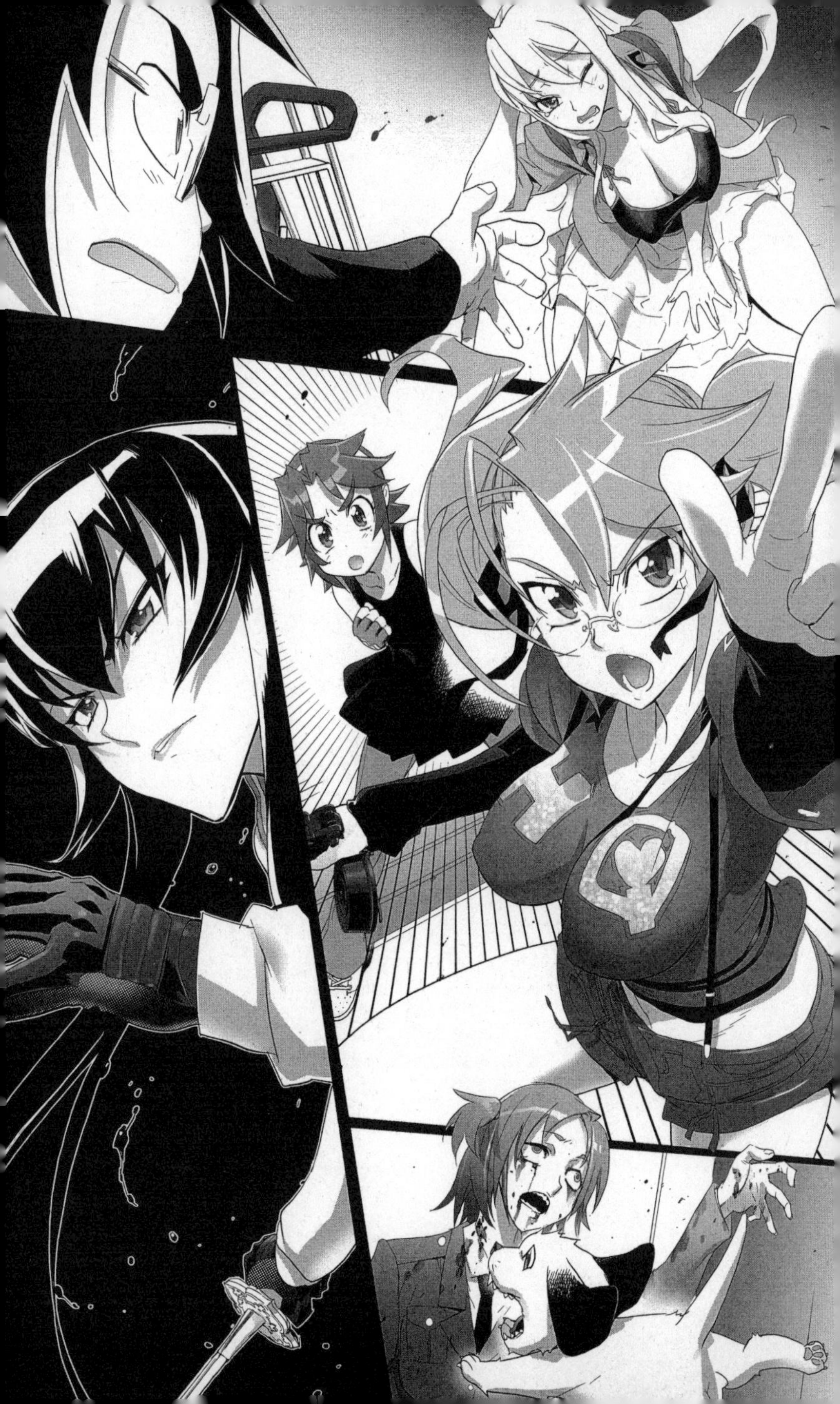

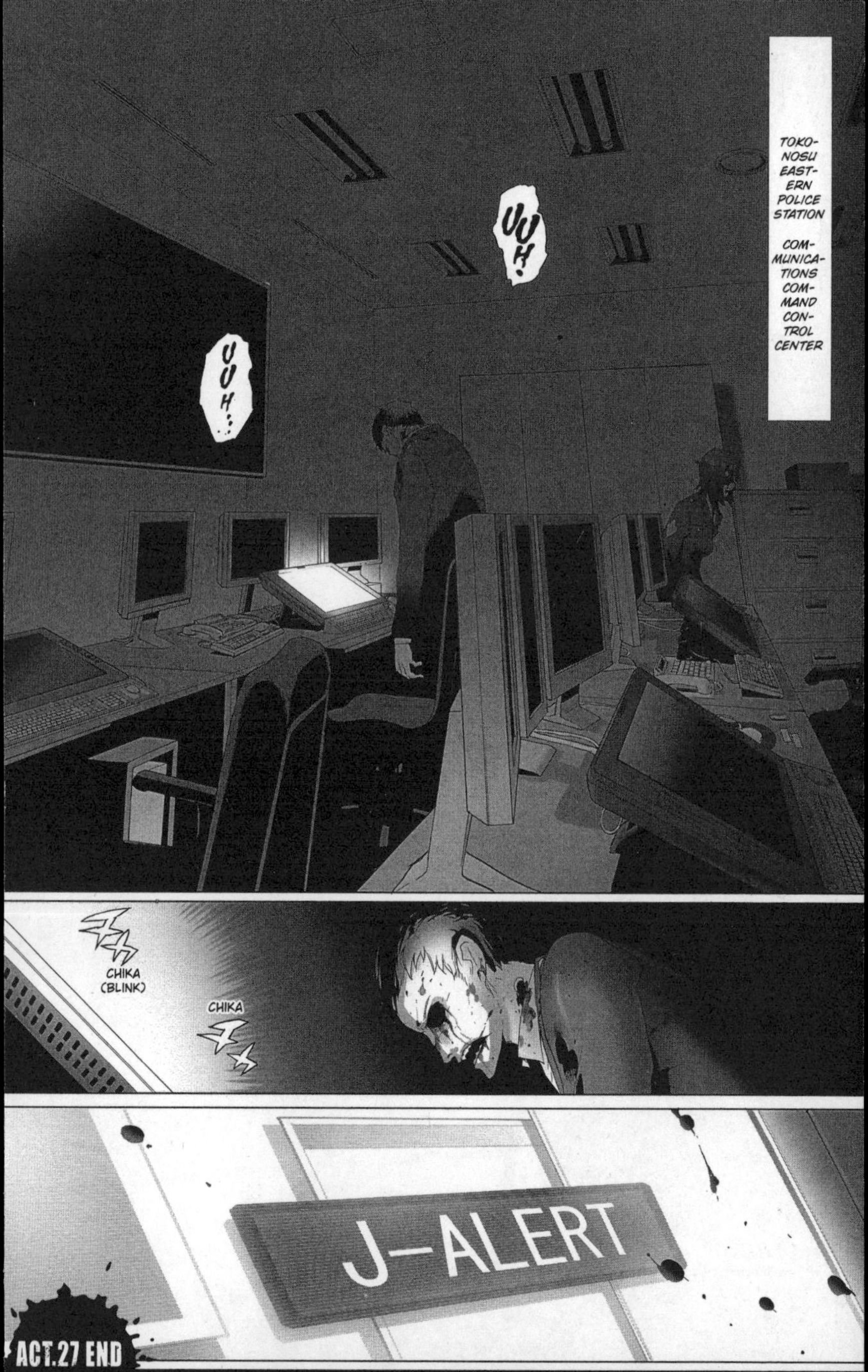
TOKONOSU EASTERN POLICE STATION
COMMUNICATIONS COMMAND CONTROL CENTER
UUH!
UUH...
CHIKA (BLINK)
CHIKA
J-ALERT
ACT.27 END

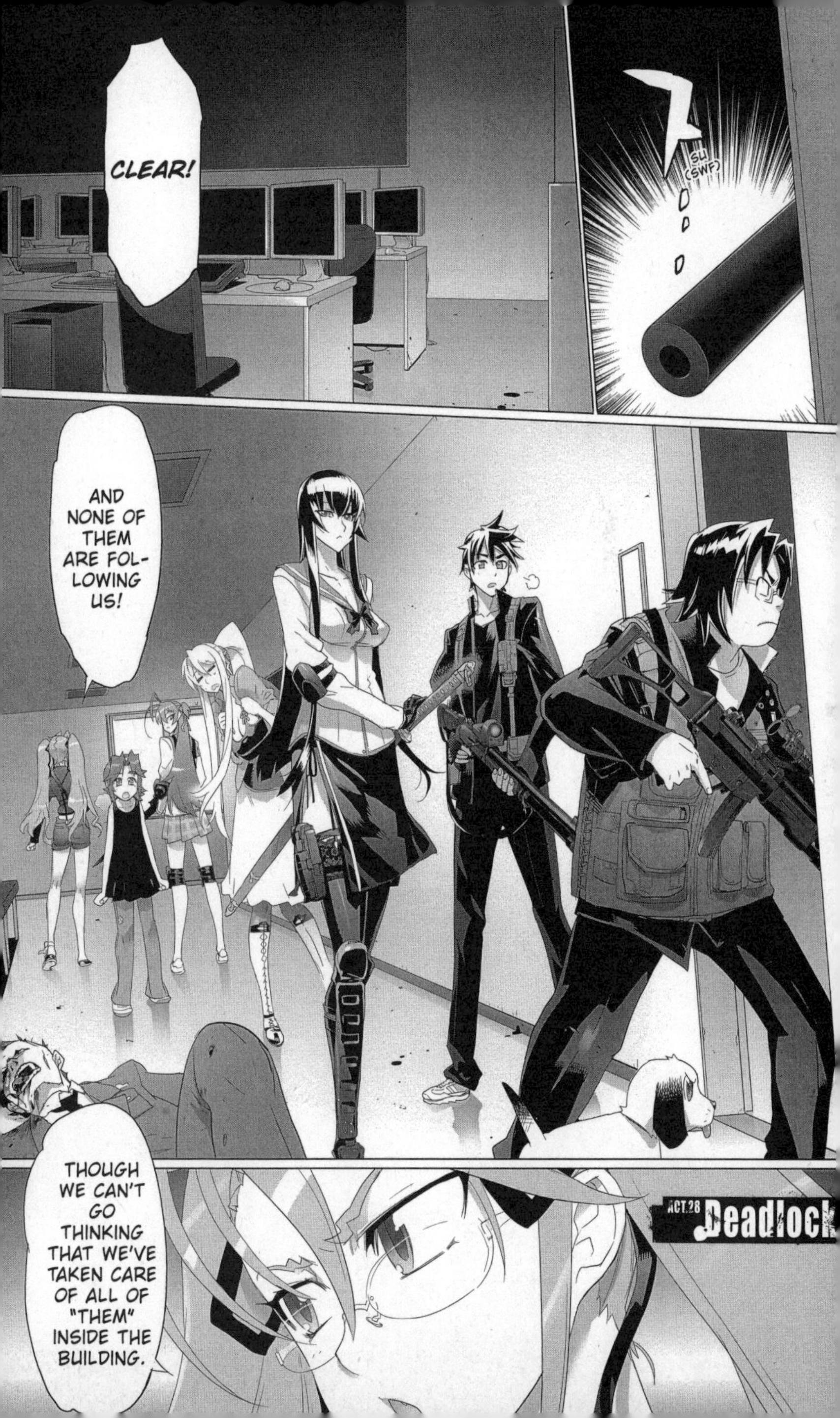
SU (SWF)
CLEAR!
AND NONE OF THEM ARE FOL-LOWING US!
ACT.28 Deadlock
THOUGH WE CAN'T GO THINKING THAT WE'VE TAKEN CARE OF ALL OF "THEM" INSIDE THE BUILDING.

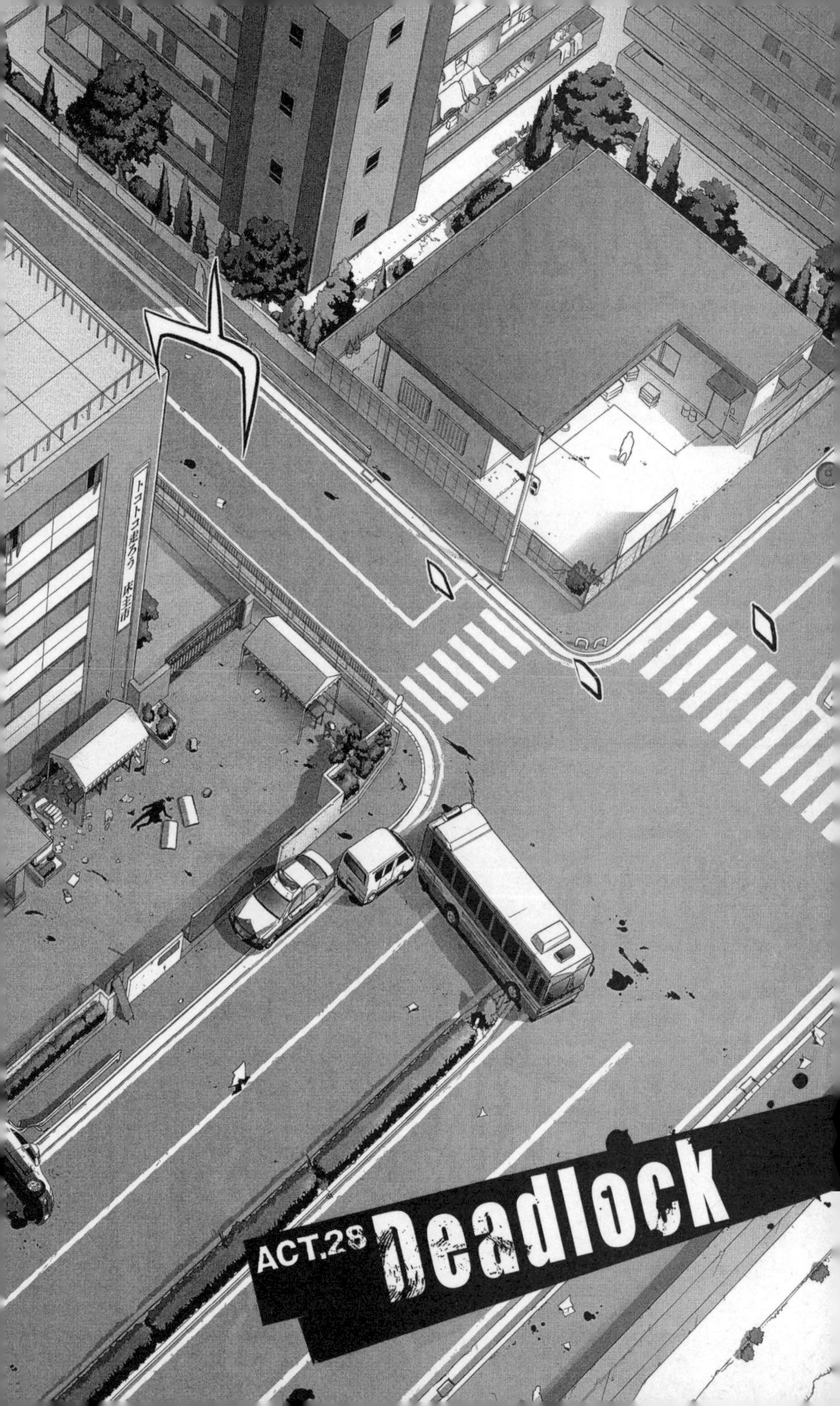

トコトコ走ろう　床主市
ACT.28 Deadlock

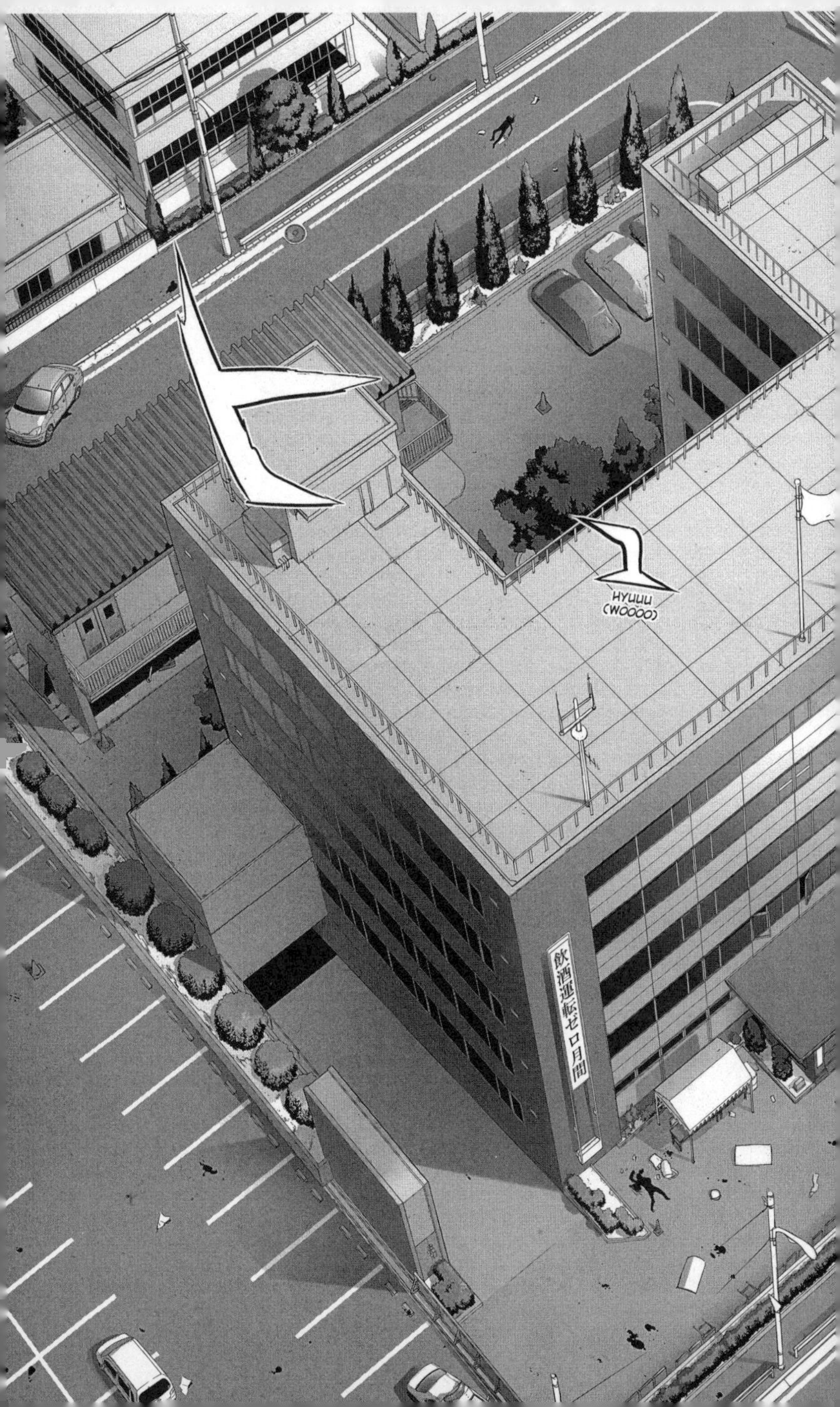
HYUUU
(WOOOO)
飲酒運転ゼロ月間

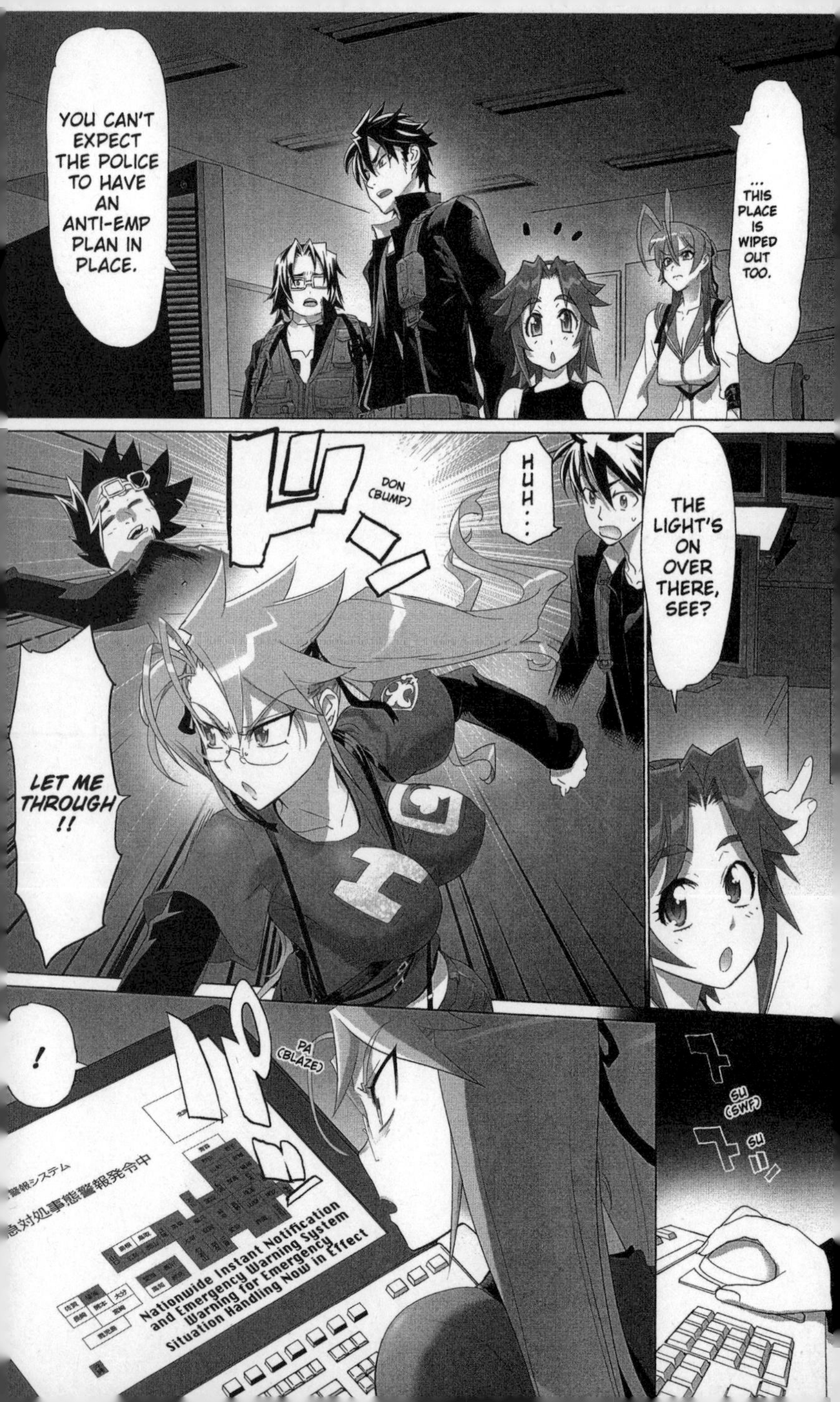

...
THIS PLACE IS WIPED OUT TOO.
YOU CAN'T EXPECT THE POLICE TO HAVE AN ANTI-EMP PLAN IN PLACE.
THE LIGHT'S ON OVER THERE, SEE?
HUH...
DON (BUMP)
LET ME THROUGH!!
SU (SWP)
SU
!
PA (BLAZE)
警報システム
急対処事態警報発令中
Nationwide Instant Notification and Emergency Warning System
Warning for Emergency Situation Handling Now in Effect

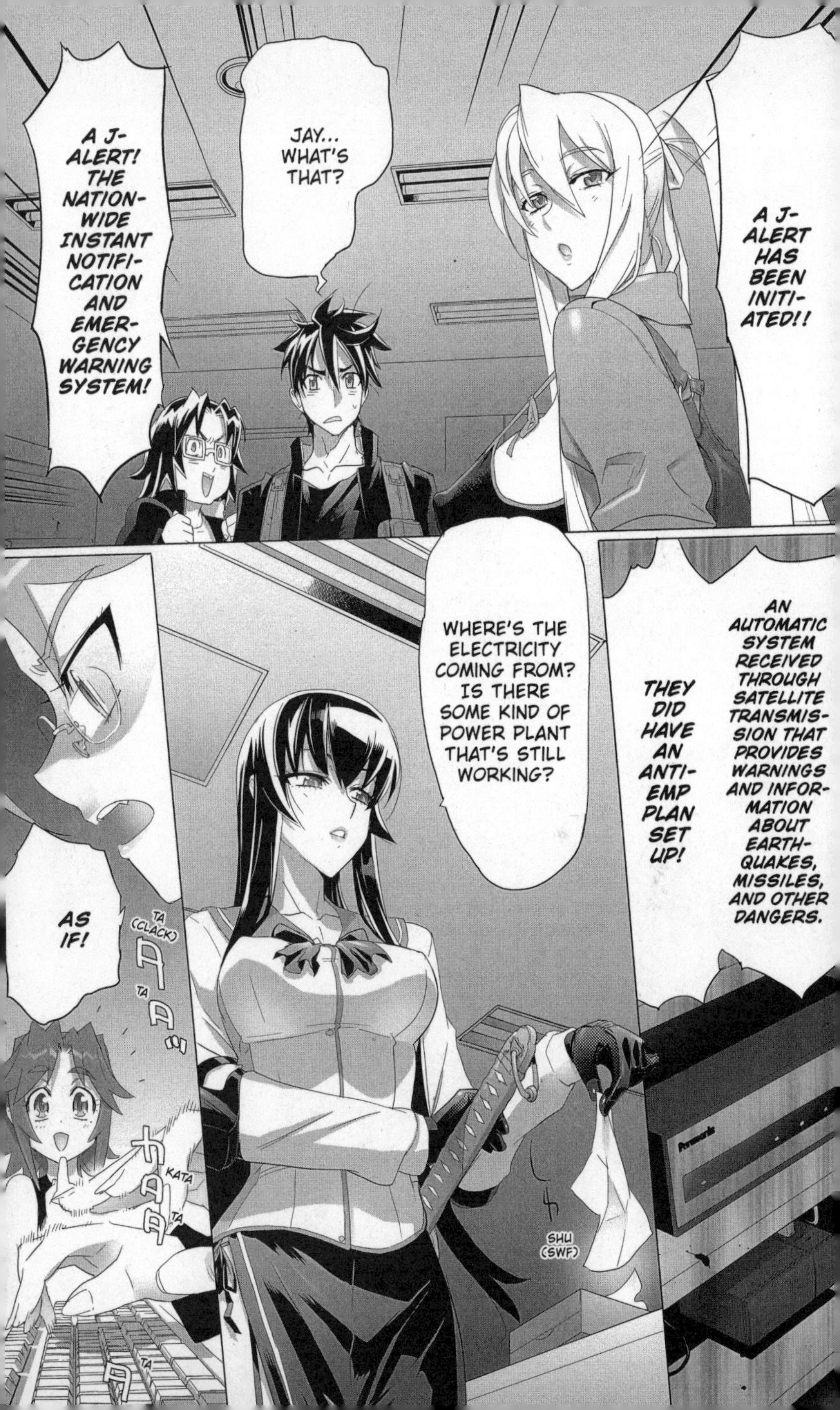
A J-ALERT HAS BEEN INITIATED!!
JAY... WHAT'S THAT?
A J-ALERT! THE NATION-WIDE INSTANT NOTIFICATION AND EMERGENCY WARNING SYSTEM!
AN AUTOMATIC SYSTEM RECEIVED THROUGH SATELLITE TRANSMISSION THAT PROVIDES WARNINGS AND INFORMATION ABOUT EARTHQUAKES, MISSILES, AND OTHER DANGERS.
THEY DID HAVE AN ANTI-EMP PLAN SET UP!
WHERE'S THE ELECTRICITY COMING FROM? IS THERE SOME KIND OF POWER PLANT THAT'S STILL WORKING?
SHU (SWF)
AS IF!
TA (CLACK)
TA
KATA
TA
TA

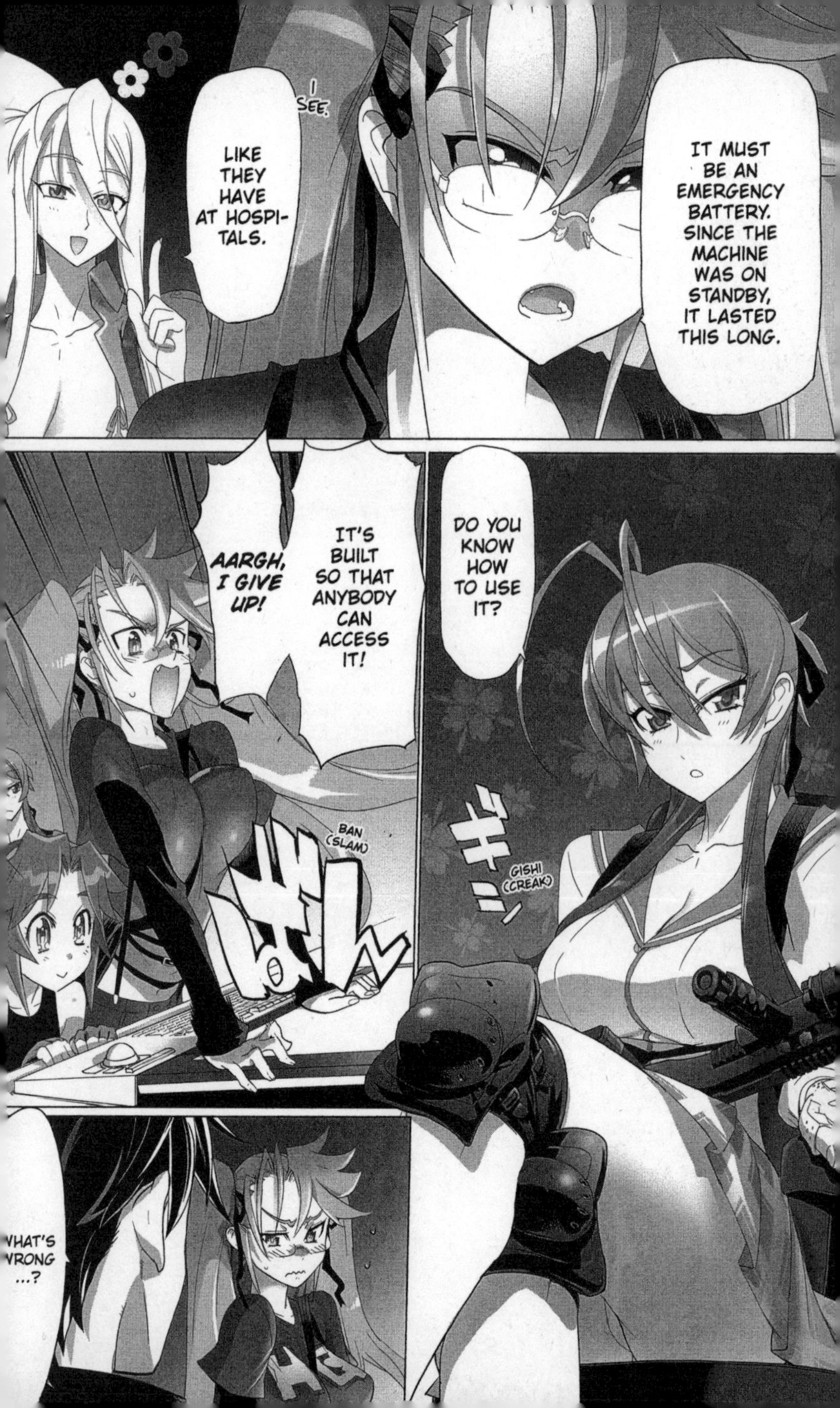

IT MUST BE AN EMERGENCY BATTERY. SINCE THE MACHINE WAS ON STANDBY, IT LASTED THIS LONG.
I SEE.
LIKE THEY HAVE AT HOSPITALS.
DO YOU KNOW HOW TO USE IT?
GISHI (CREAK)
IT'S BUILT SO THAT ANYBODY CAN ACCESS IT!
AARGH, I GIVE UP!
BAN (SLAM)
WHAT'S WRONG ...?

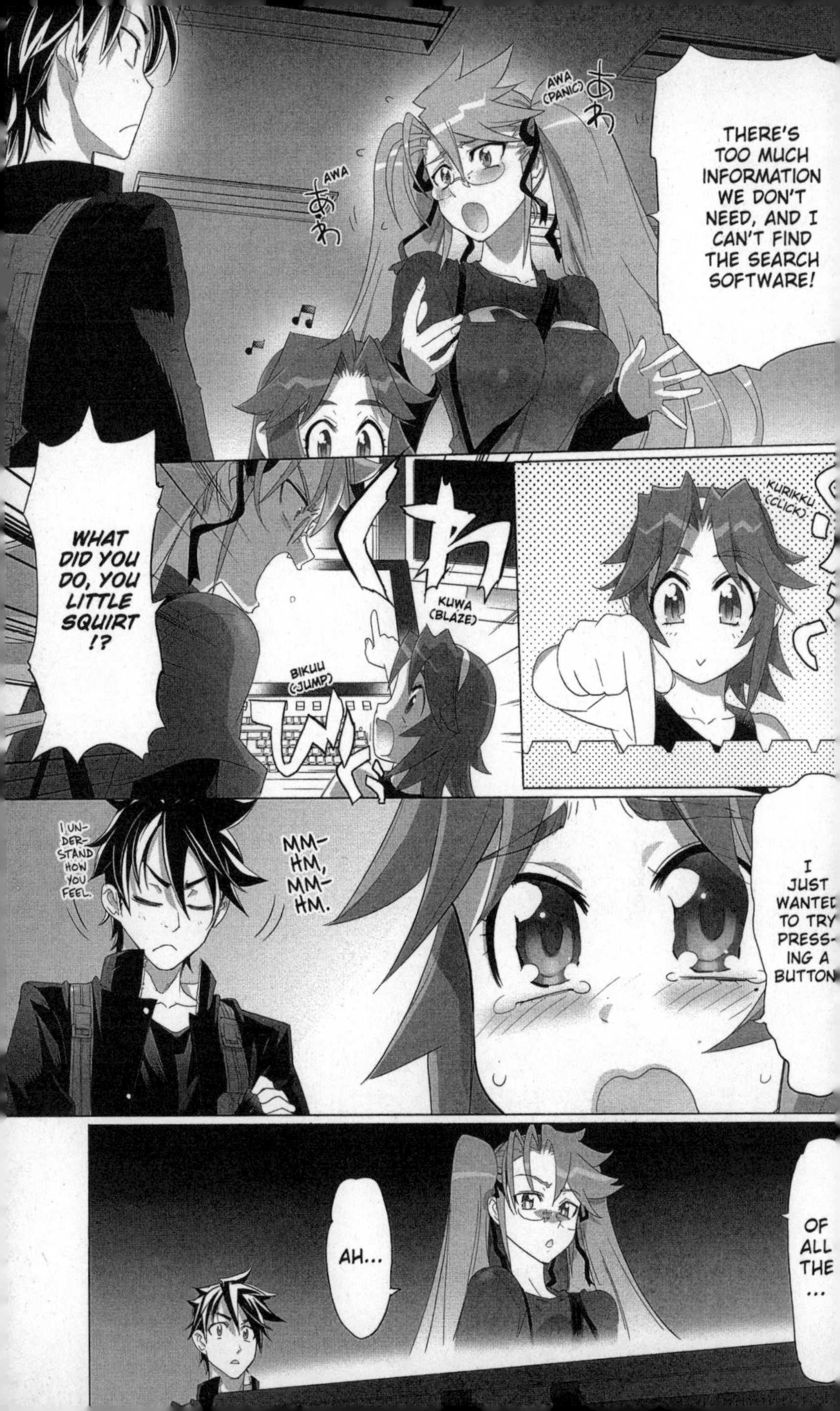
THERE'S TOO MUCH INFORMATION WE DON'T NEED, AND I CAN'T FIND THE SEARCH SOFTWARE!
AWA (PANIC)
あわ
AWA
あわ
KURIKKU (CLICK)
KUWA (BLAZE)
BIKUU (JUMP)
WHAT DID YOU DO, YOU LITTLE SQUIRT!?
I JUST WANTED TO TRY PRESS-ING A BUTTON
MM-HM, MM-HM.
I UN-DER-STAND HOW YOU FEEL.
OF ALL THE ...
AH...

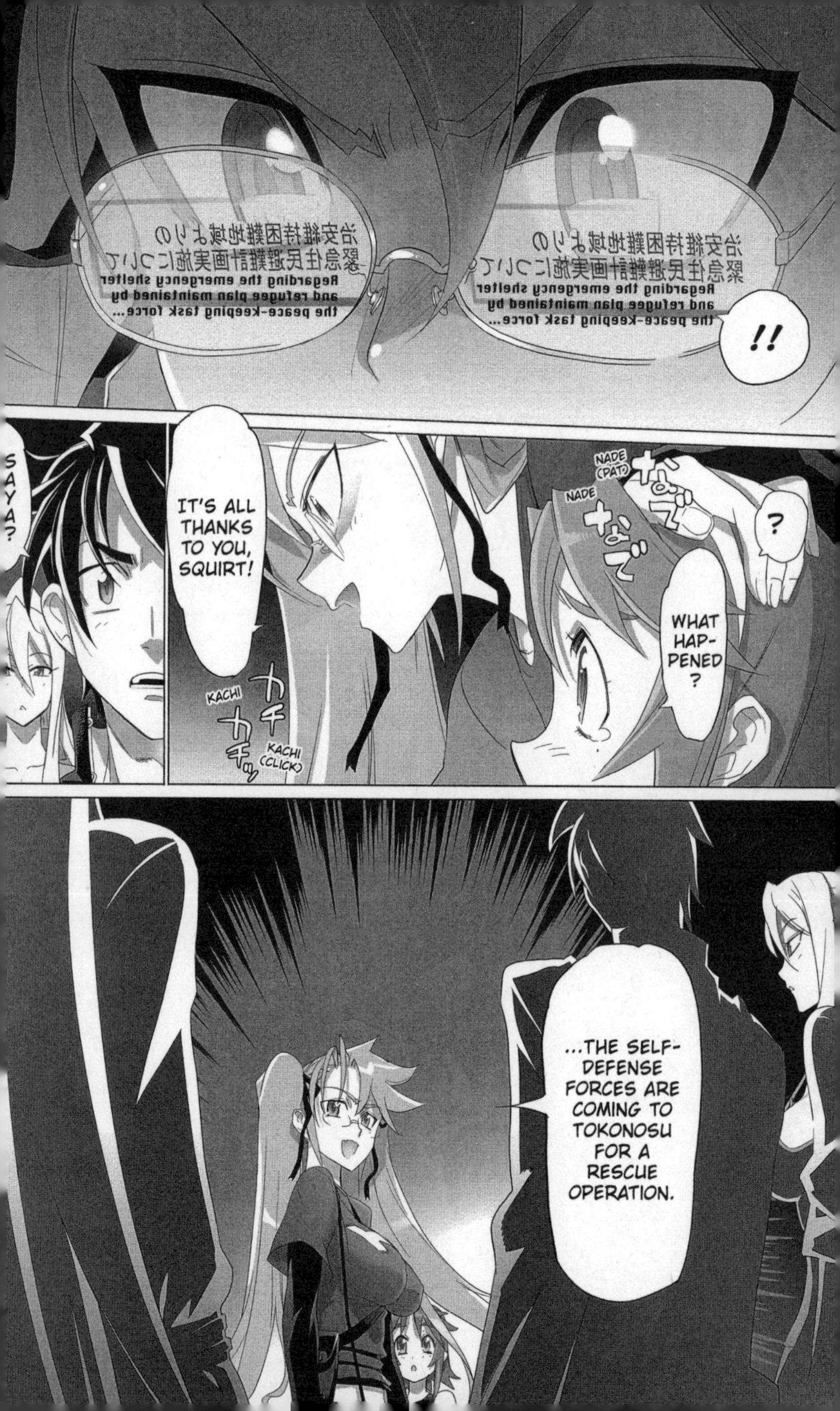
治安維持困難地域よりの
緊急住民避難計画実施について
Regarding the emergency shelter and refugee plan maintained by the peace-keeping task force...
治安維持困難地域よりの
緊急住民避難計画実施について
Regarding the emergency shelter and refugee plan maintained by the peace-keeping task force...
!!
NADE (PAT) なで
NADE なで
?
WHAT HAP-PENED?
IT'S ALL THANKS TO YOU, SQUIRT!
KACHI カチ
KACHI (CLICK) カチッ
SAYA?
...THE SELF-DEFENSE FORCES ARE COMING TO TOKONOSU FOR A RESCUE OPERATION.

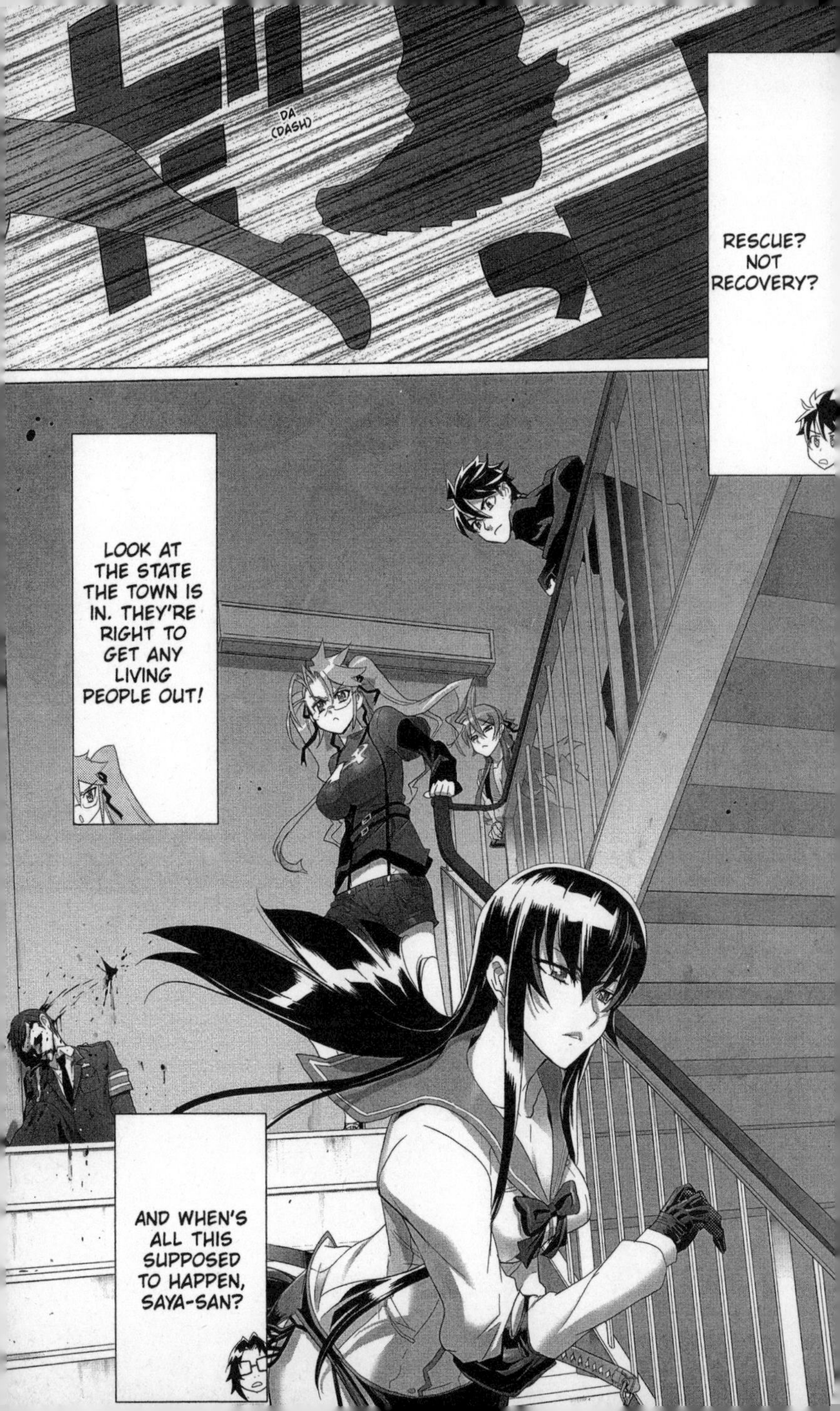
RESCUE? NOT RECOVERY?
DA (DASH)
LOOK AT THE STATE THE TOWN IS IN. THEY'RE RIGHT TO GET ANY LIVING PEOPLE OUT!
AND WHEN'S ALL THIS SUPPOSED TO HAPPEN, SAYA-SAN?

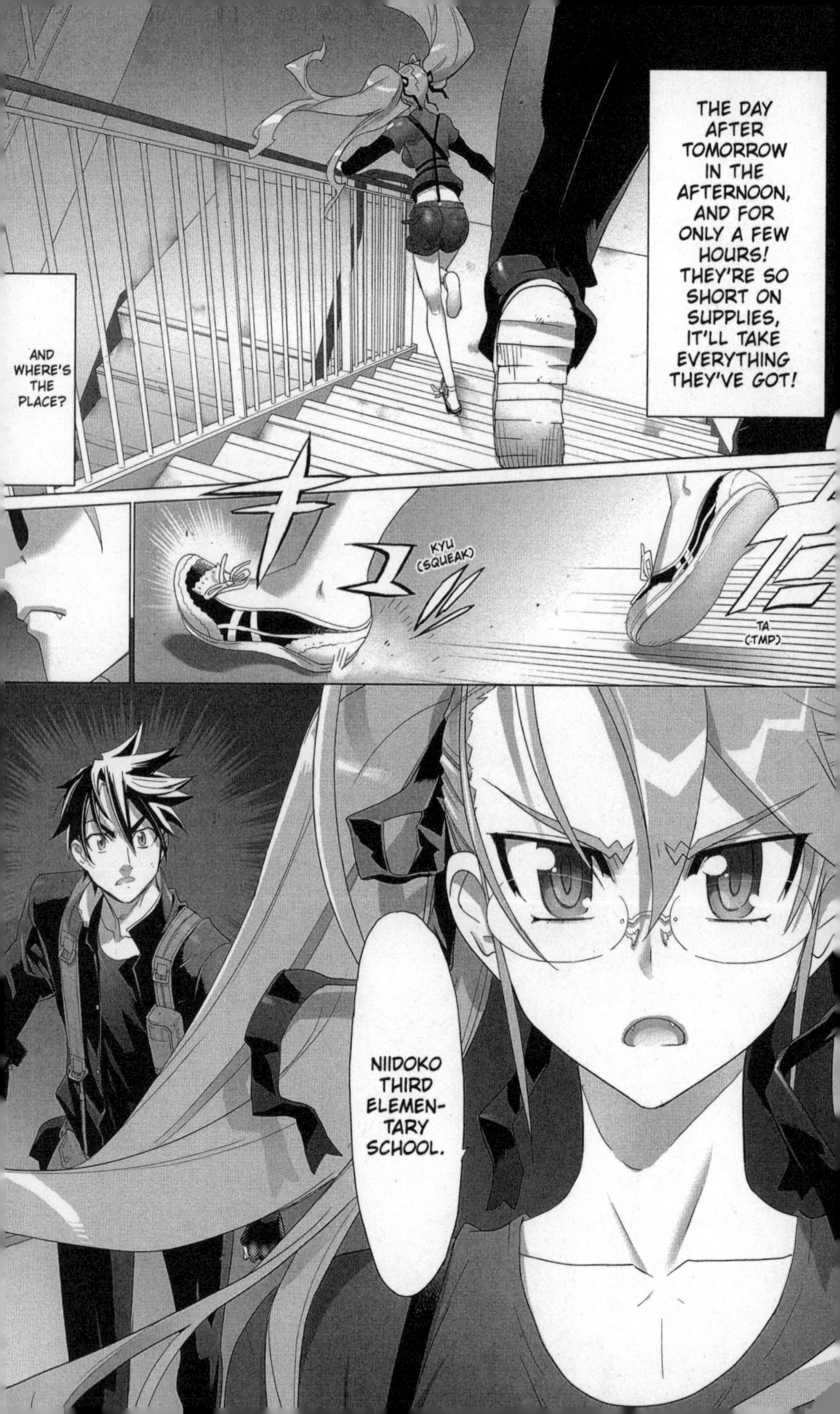
THE DAY AFTER TOMORROW IN THE AFTERNOON, AND FOR ONLY A FEW HOURS! THEY'RE SO SHORT ON SUPPLIES, IT'LL TAKE EVERYTHING THEY'VE GOT!
AND WHERE'S THE PLACE?
KYU (SQUEAK)
TA (TMP)
NIIDOKO THIRD ELEMENTARY SCHOOL.

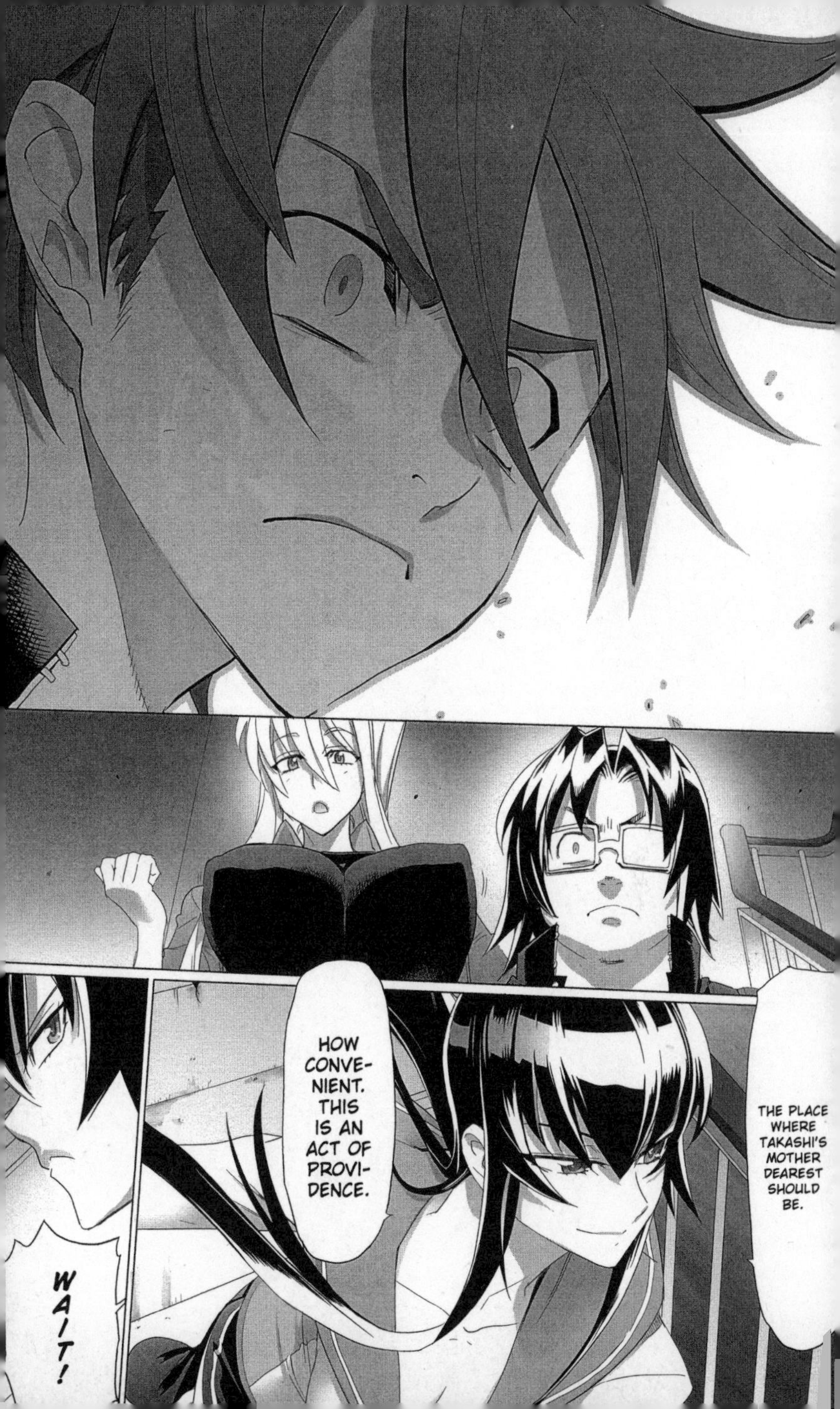
THE PLACE WHERE TAKASHI'S MOTHER DEAREST SHOULD BE.
HOW CONVE-NIENT. THIS IS AN ACT OF PROVI-DENCE.
WAIT!

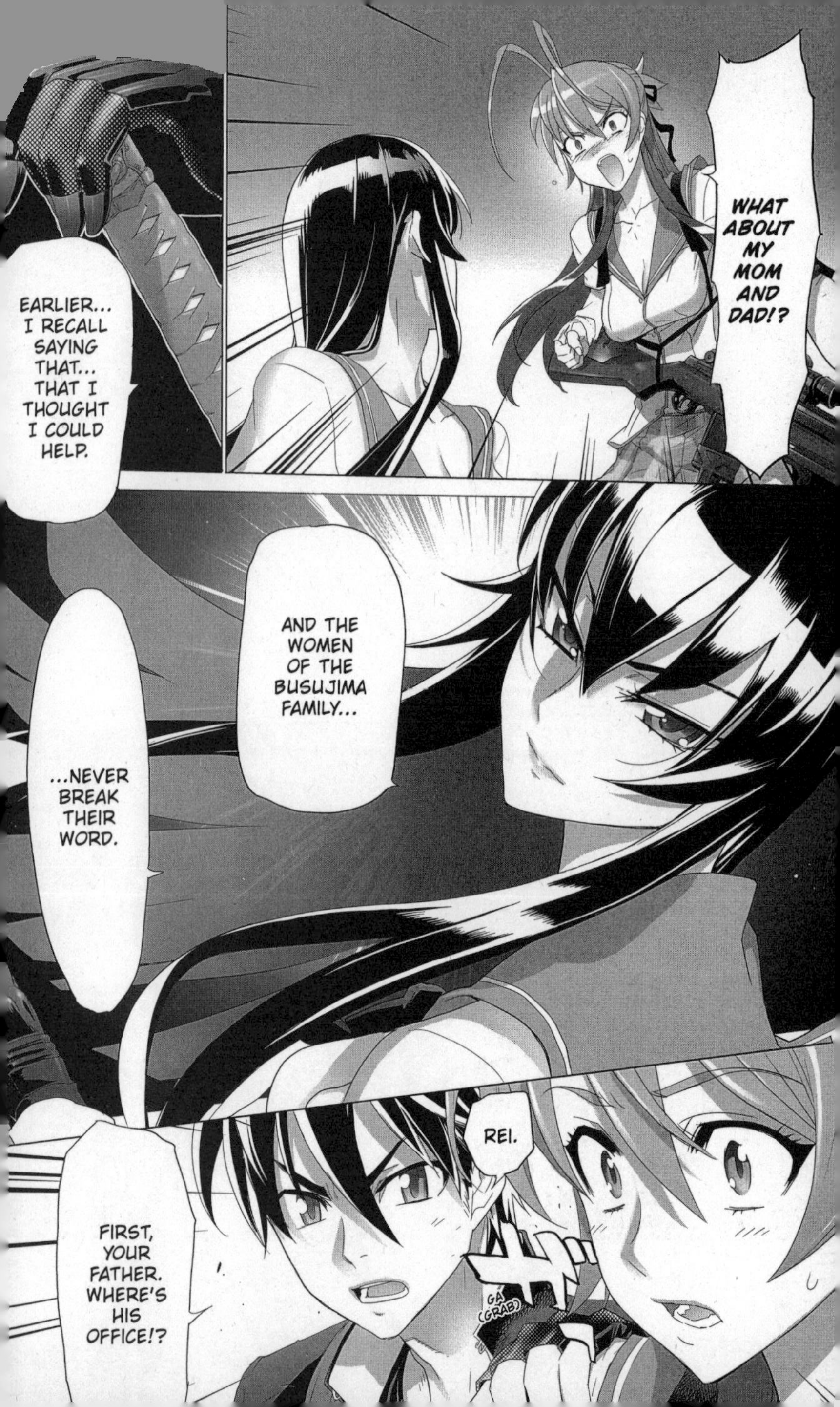
WHAT ABOUT MY MOM AND DAD!?
EARLIER... I RECALL SAYING THAT... THAT I THOUGHT I COULD HELP.
AND THE WOMEN OF THE BUSUJIMA FAMILY...
...NEVER BREAK THEIR WORD.
REI.
GA (GRAB)
FIRST, YOUR FATHER. WHERE'S HIS OFFICE!?

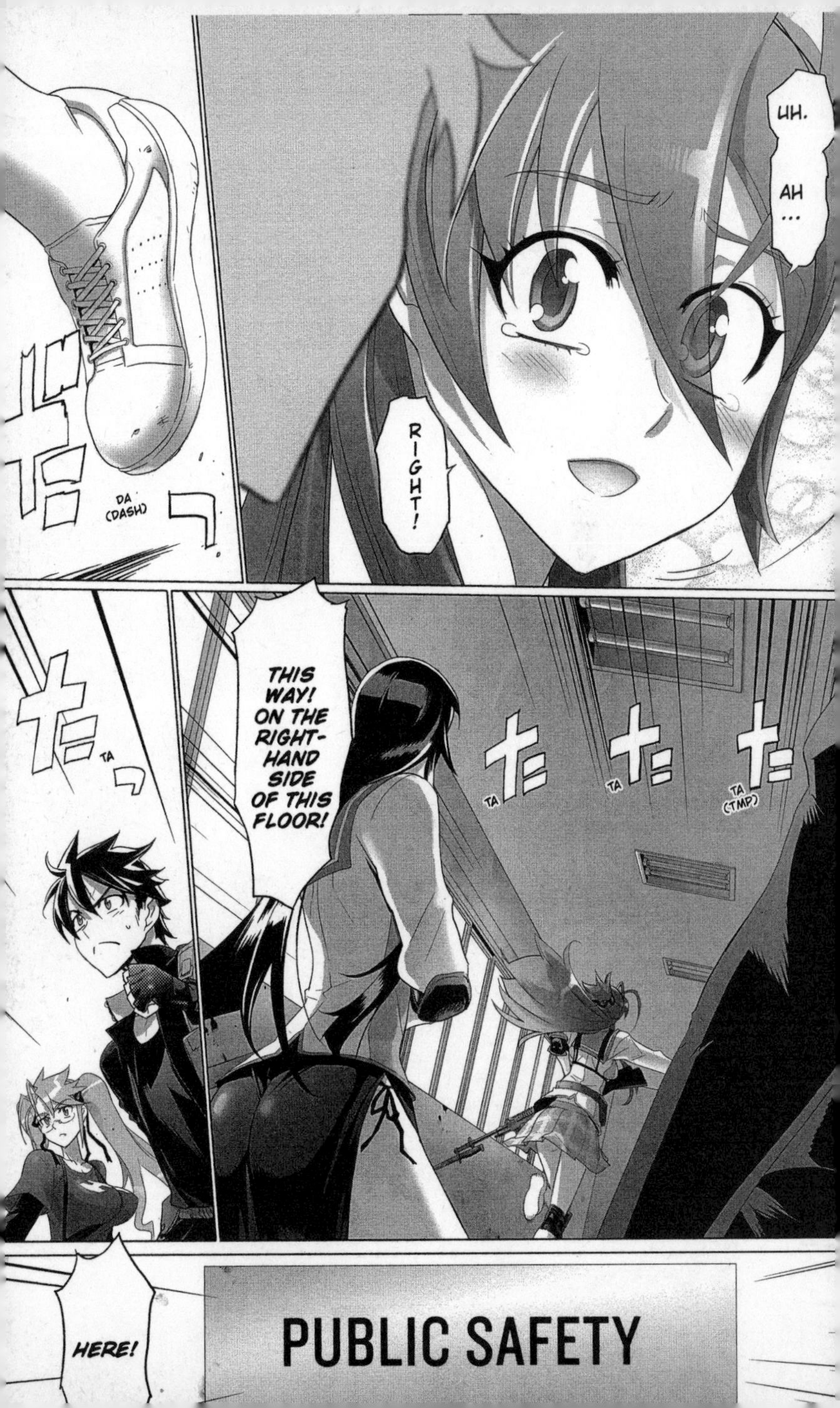
UH.
AH ...
RIGHT!
DA (DASH)
THIS WAY! ON THE RIGHT-HAND SIDE OF THIS FLOOR!
TA (TMP)
TA
TA
TA
PUBLIC SAFETY
HERE!

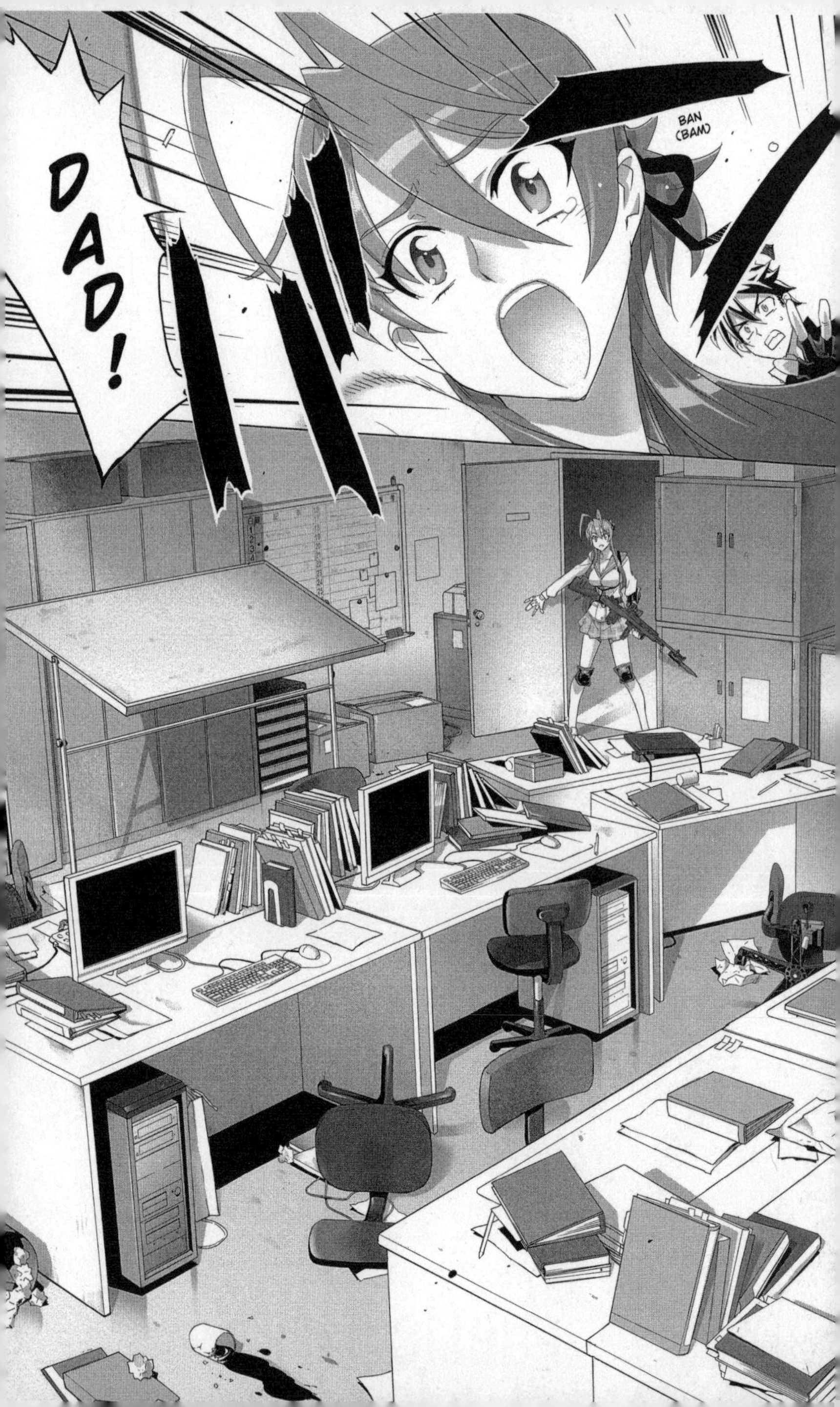
BAN
(BAM)
DAD!

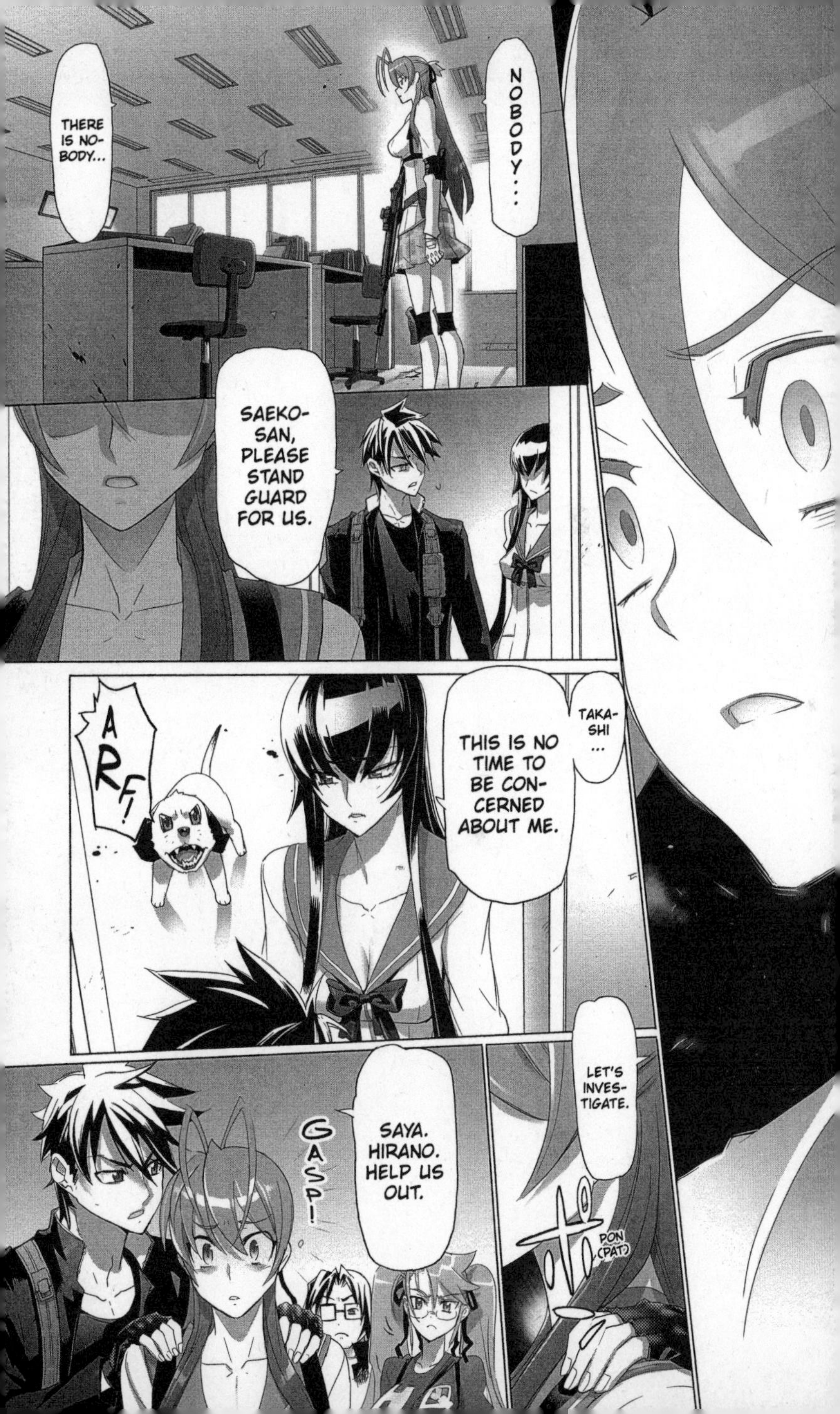
NOBODY...
THERE IS NOBODY...
SAEKO-SAN, PLEASE STAND GUARD FOR US.
TAKASHI...
THIS IS NO TIME TO BE CONCERNED ABOUT ME.
ARF!
LET'S INVESTIGATE.
PON (PAT)
SAYA. HIRANO. HELP US OUT.
GASP!

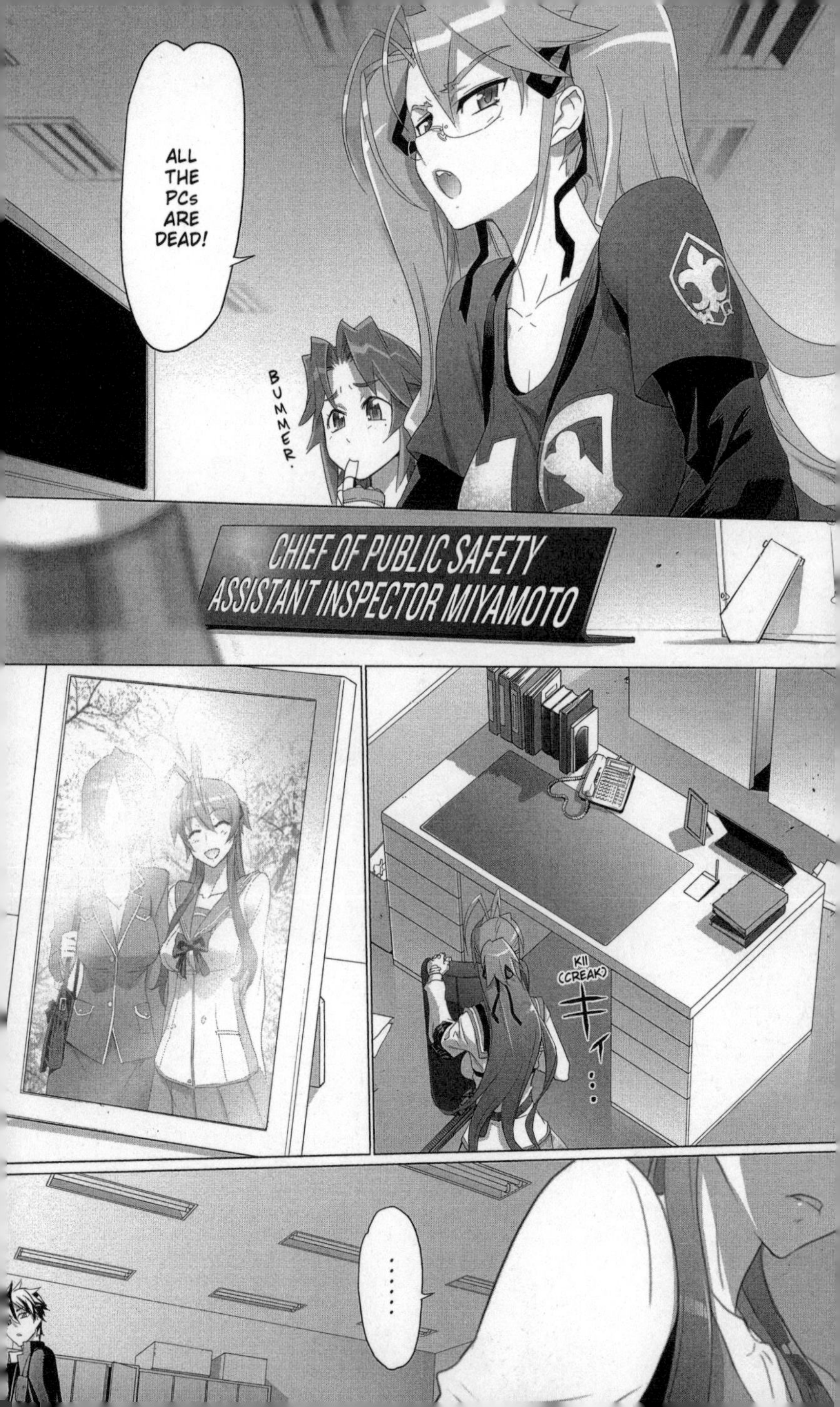
ALL THE PCs ARE DEAD!
BUMMER.
CHIEF OF PUBLIC SAFETY
ASSISTANT INSPECTOR MIYAMOTO
KII (CREAK)
キイ…
……

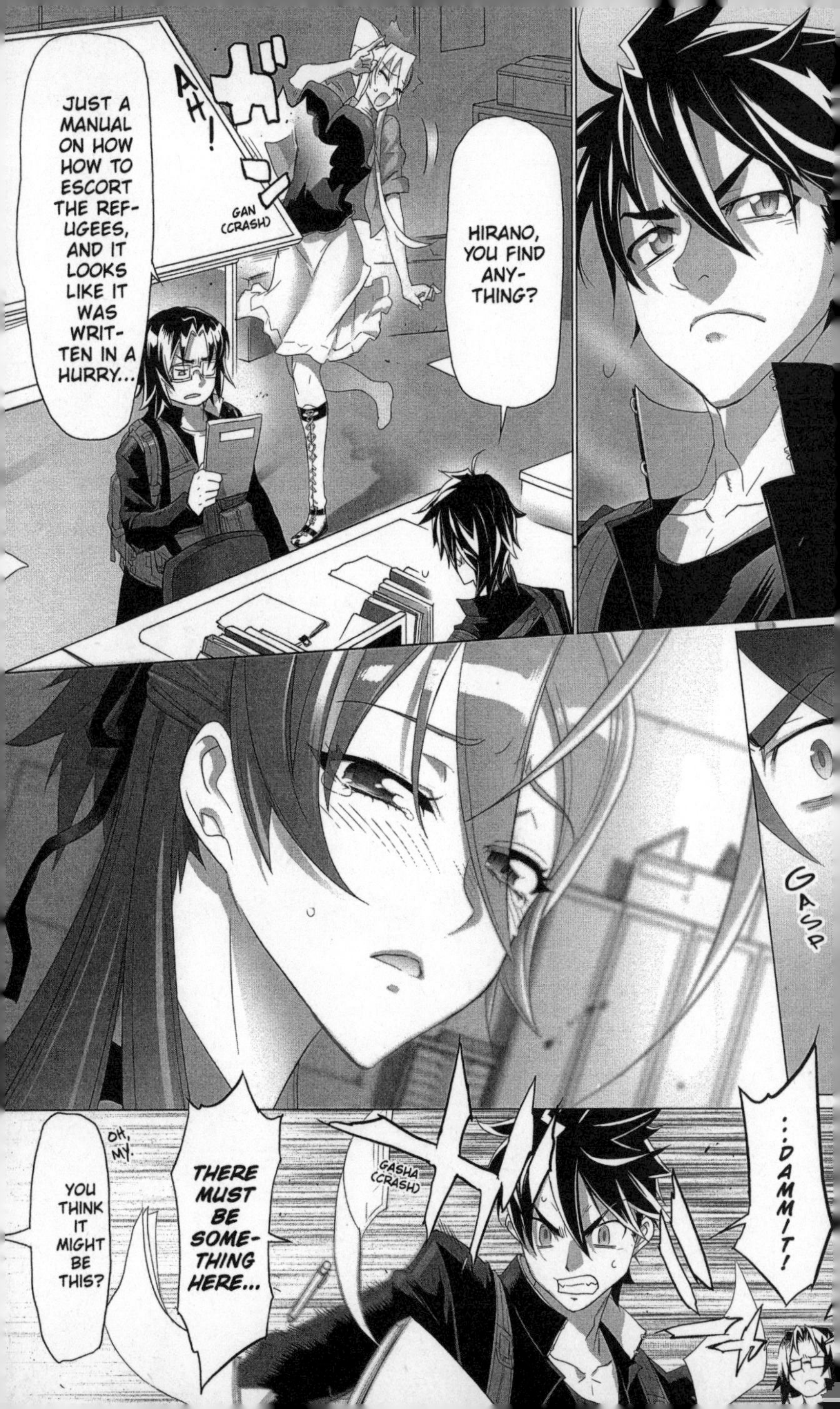
HIRANO, YOU FIND ANY-THING?
AH!
GAN (CRASH)
JUST A MANUAL ON HOW HOW TO ESCORT THE REF-UGEES, AND IT LOOKS LIKE IT WAS WRIT-TEN IN A HURRY...
GASP
...DAMMIT!
GASHA (CRASH)
THERE MUST BE SOME-THING HERE...
OH, MY.
YOU THINK IT MIGHT BE THIS?

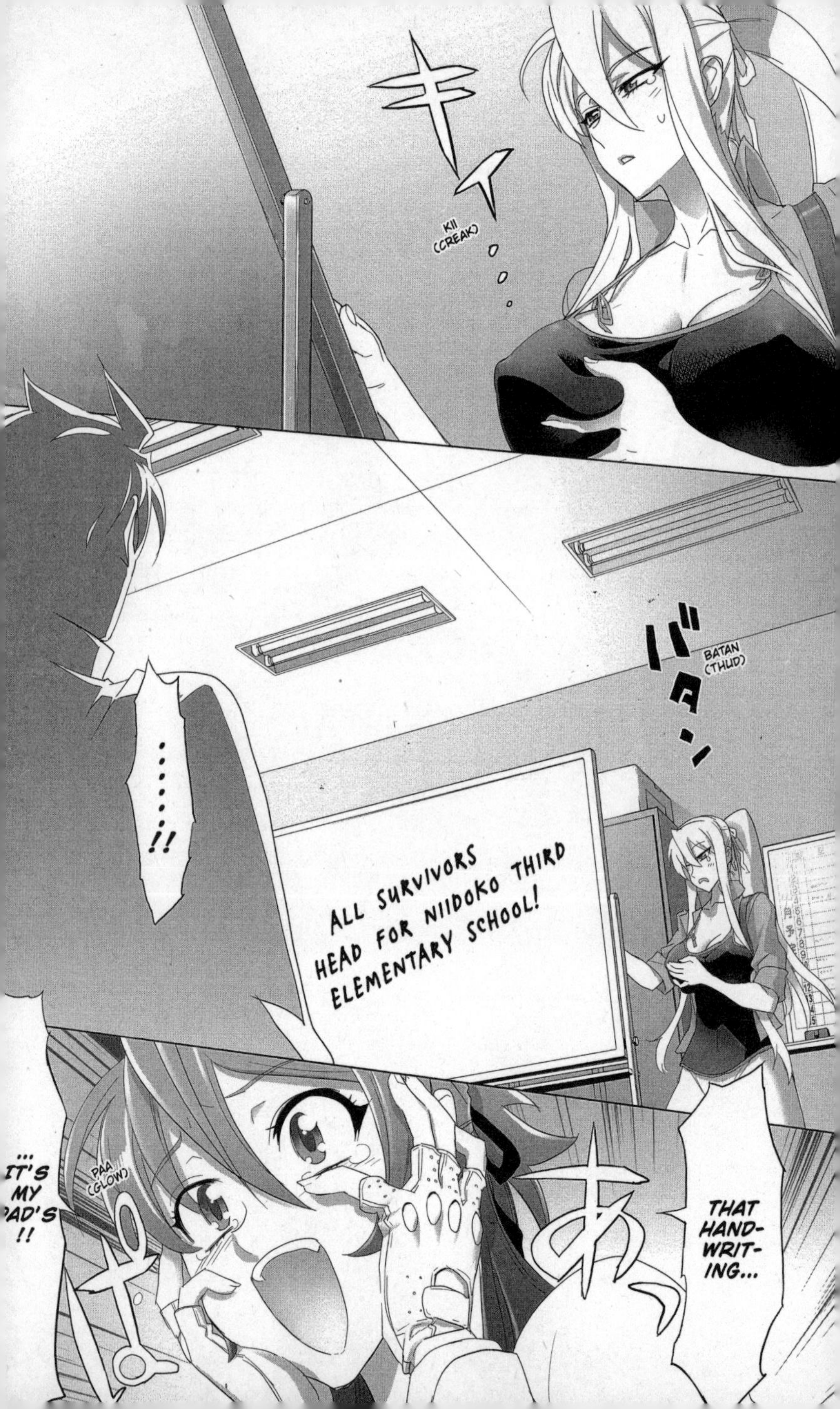
キイ
KII (CREAK)
バタン
BATAN (THUD)
......!!
ALL SURVIVORS HEAD FOR NIIDOKO THIRD ELEMENTARY SCHOOL!
THAT HAND-WRIT-ING...
あ
PAA (GLOW)
... IT'S MY AD'S !!

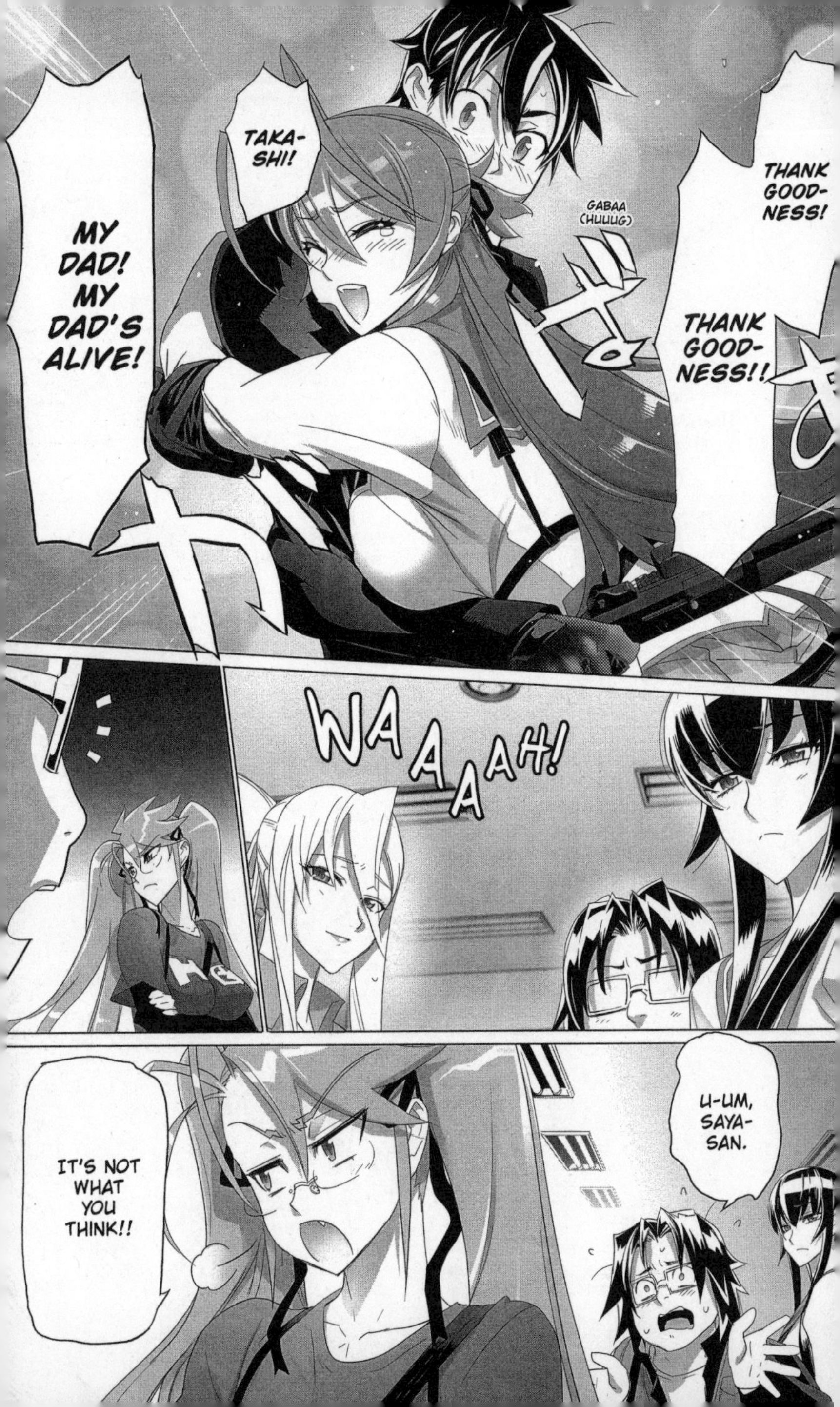
THANK GOODNESS!
GABAA (HUUUG)
TAKA-SHI!
THANK GOODNESS!!
MY DAD! MY DAD'S ALIVE!
WAAAAH!
U-UM, SAYA-SAN.
IT'S NOT WHAT YOU THINK!!

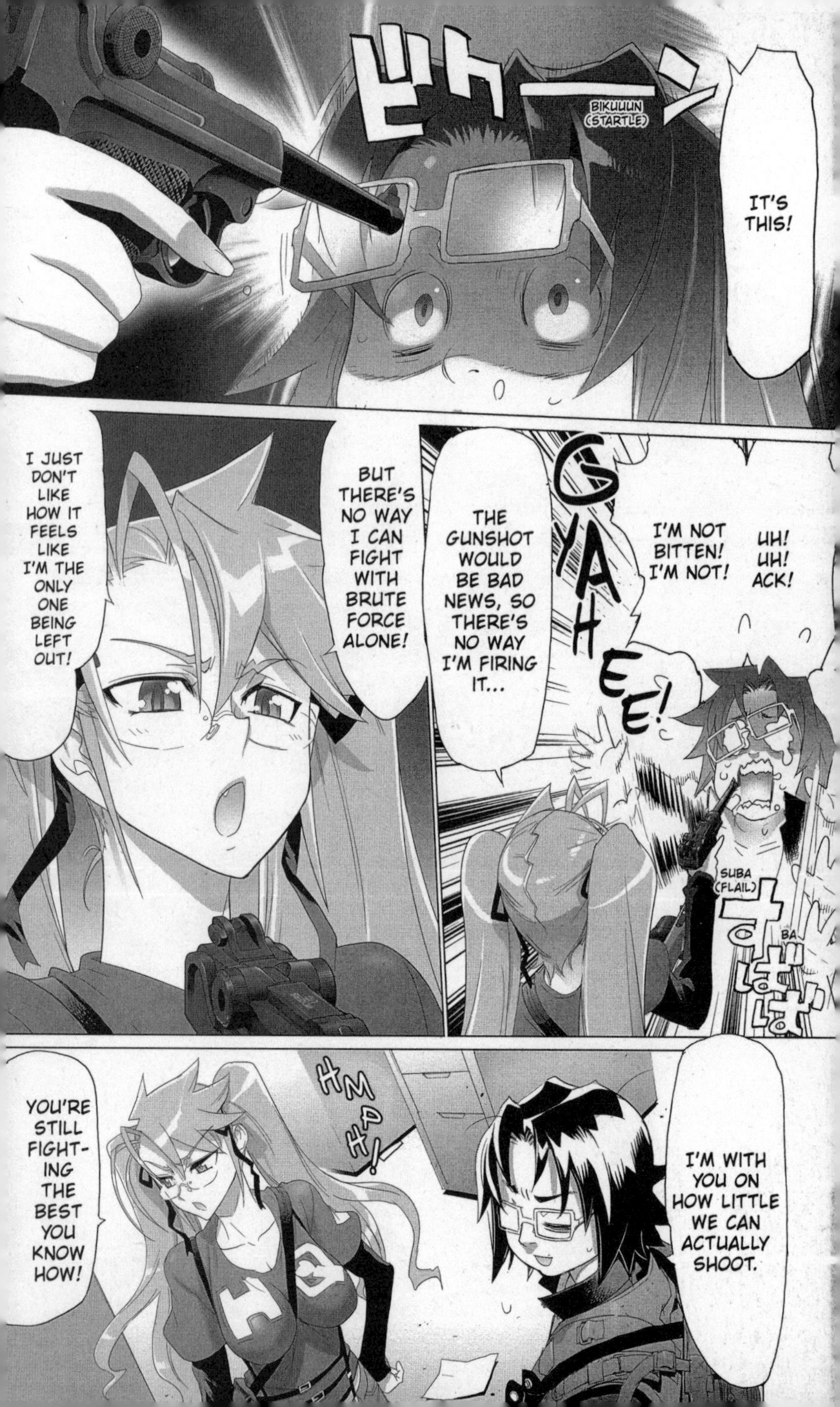

BIKUUUN (STARTLE)
IT'S THIS!
UH! UH! ACK!
I'M NOT BITTEN! I'M NOT!
SUBA (FLAIL)
BA
GYAHEE!
THE GUNSHOT WOULD BE BAD NEWS, SO THERE'S NO WAY I'M FIRING IT...
BUT THERE'S NO WAY I CAN FIGHT WITH BRUTE FORCE ALONE!
I JUST DON'T LIKE HOW IT FEELS LIKE I'M THE ONLY ONE BEING LEFT OUT!
I'M WITH YOU ON HOW LITTLE WE CAN ACTUALLY SHOOT.
HMPH!
YOU'RE STILL FIGHT-ING THE BEST YOU KNOW HOW!

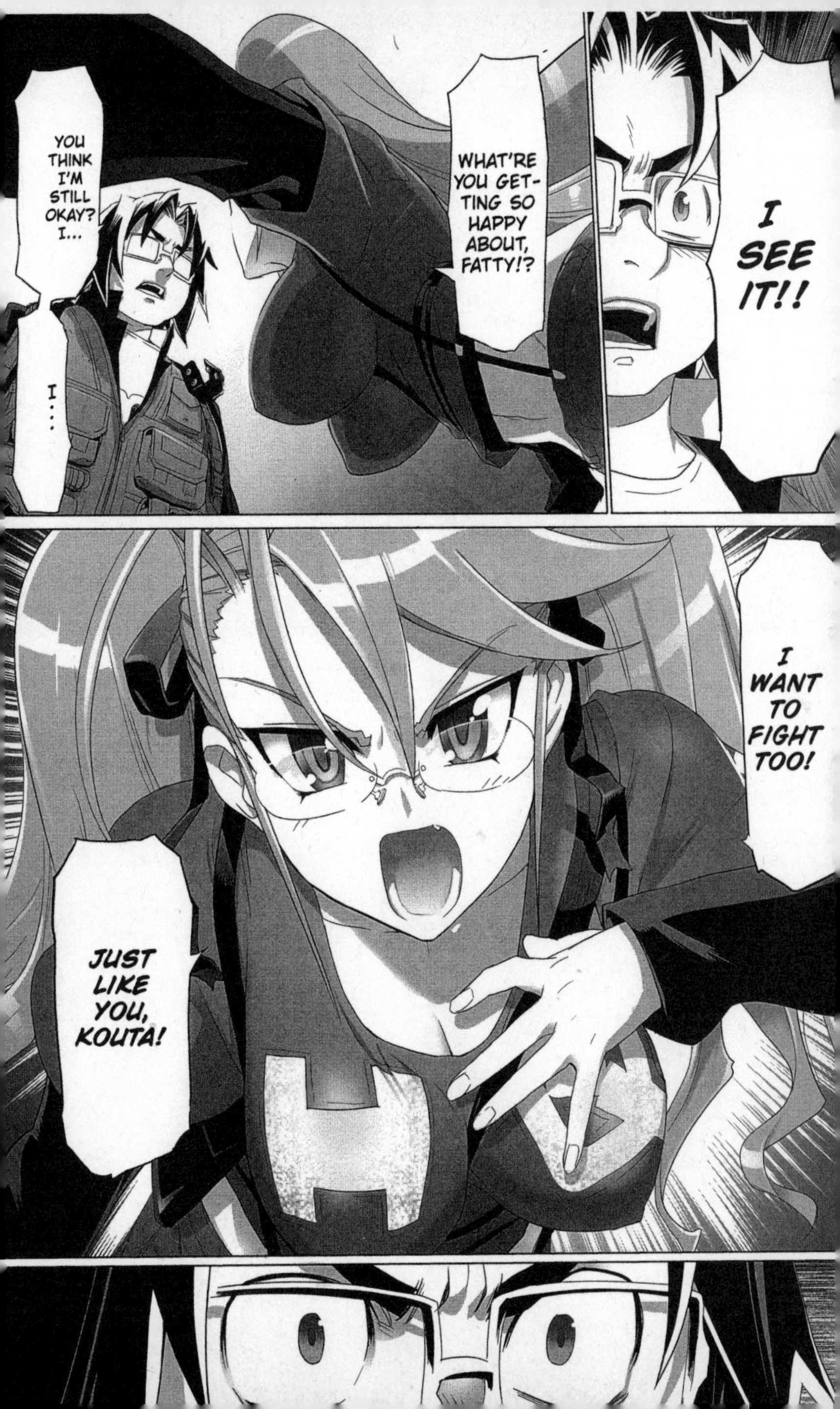

I SEE IT!!
WHAT'RE YOU GET-TING SO HAPPY ABOUT, FATTY!?
YOU THINK I'M STILL OKAY? I...
I...
I WANT TO FIGHT TOO!
JUST LIKE YOU, KOUTA!

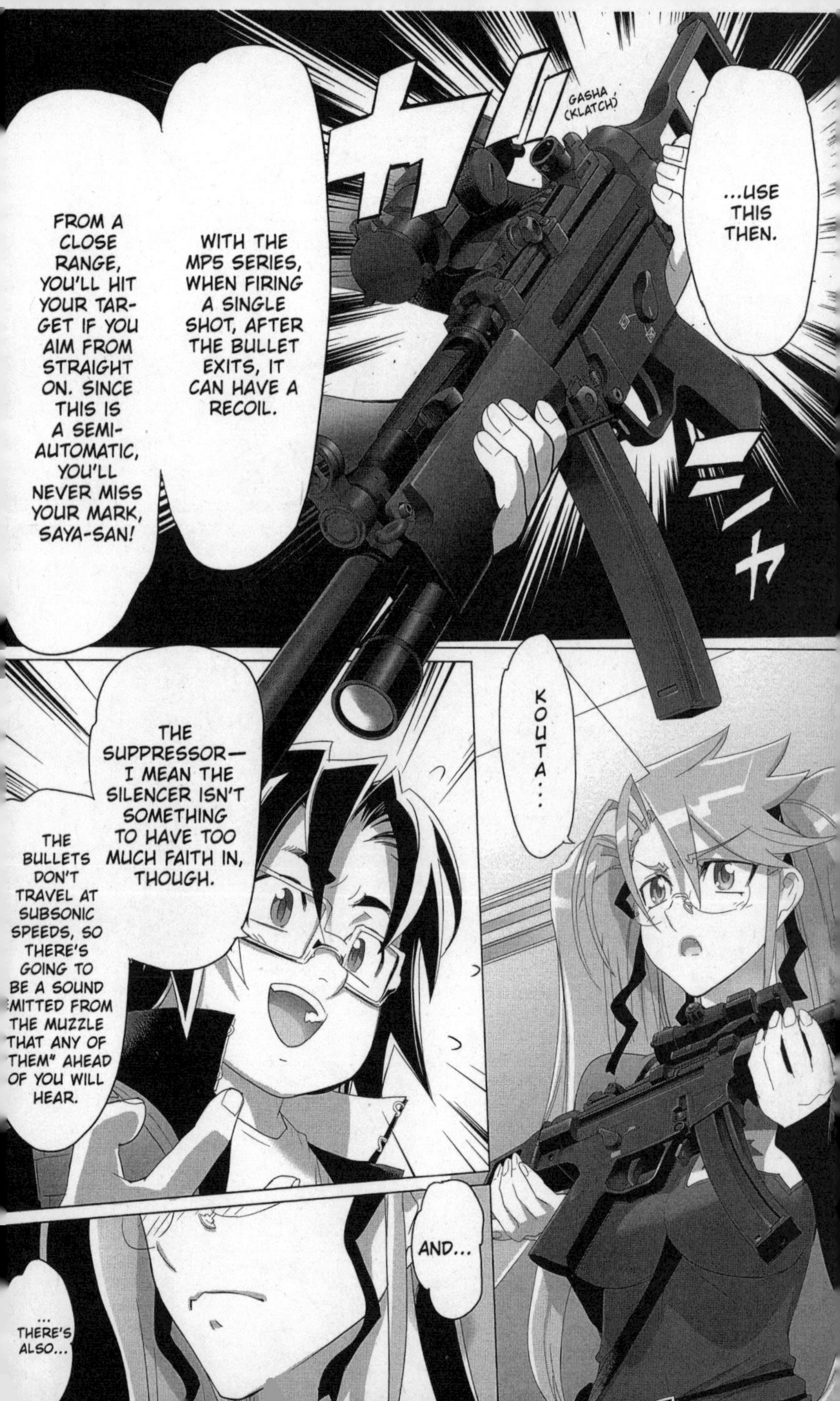
...USE THIS THEN.
GASHA (KLATCH)
WITH THE MP5 SERIES, WHEN FIRING A SINGLE SHOT, AFTER THE BULLET EXITS, IT CAN HAVE A RECOIL.
FROM A CLOSE RANGE, YOU'LL HIT YOUR TARGET IF YOU AIM FROM STRAIGHT ON. SINCE THIS IS A SEMI-AUTOMATIC, YOU'LL NEVER MISS YOUR MARK, SAYA-SAN!
KOUTA...
THE SUPPRESSOR— I MEAN THE SILENCER ISN'T SOMETHING TO HAVE TOO MUCH FAITH IN, THOUGH.
THE BULLETS DON'T TRAVEL AT SUBSONIC SPEEDS, SO THERE'S GOING TO BE A SOUND EMITTED FROM THE MUZZLE THAT ANY OF THEM" AHEAD OF YOU WILL HEAR.
AND...
...THERE'S ALSO...

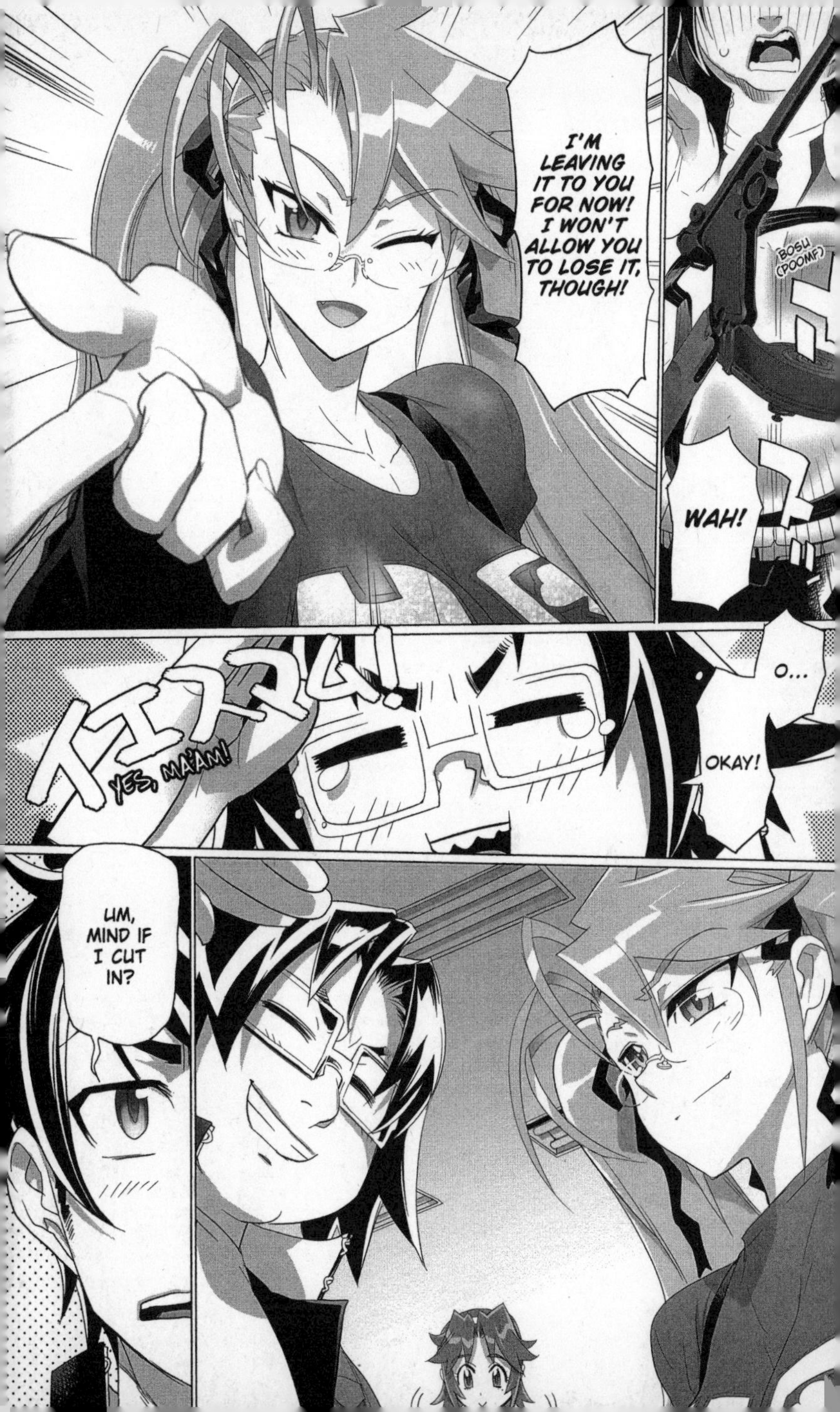
BOSU (POOMF)
WAH!
I'M LEAVING IT TO YOU FOR NOW! I WON'T ALLOW YOU TO LOSE IT, THOUGH!
O... OKAY!
YES, MA'AM!
UM, MIND IF I CUT IN?

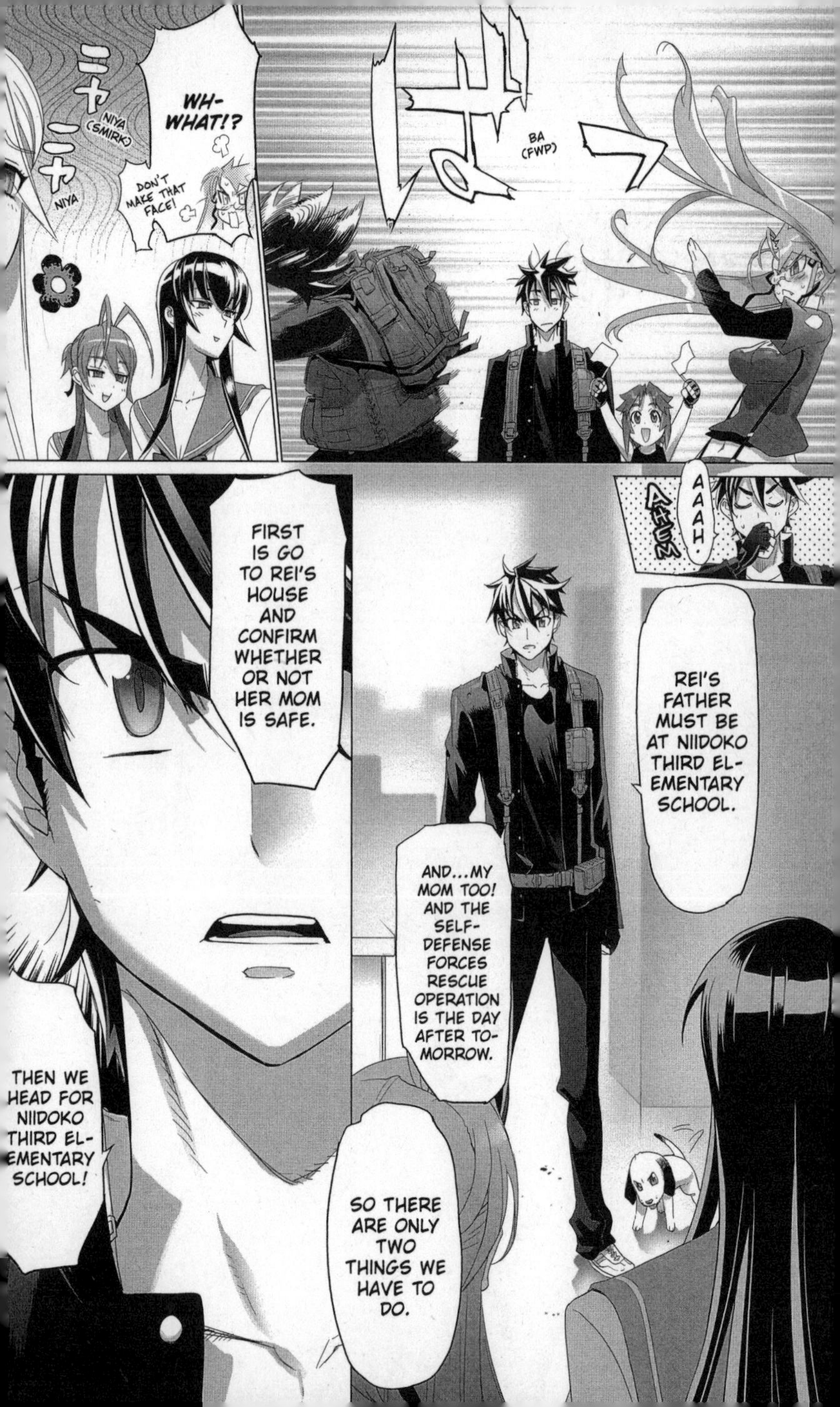
BA (FWP)
WH-WHAT!?
NIYA (SMIRK)
DON'T MAKE THAT FACE!
NIYA
AHEM
AAAH.
REI'S FATHER MUST BE AT NIIDOKO THIRD EL-EMENTARY SCHOOL.
AND...MY MOM TOO! AND THE SELF-DEFENSE FORCES RESCUE OPERATION IS THE DAY AFTER TO-MORROW.
SO THERE ARE ONLY TWO THINGS WE HAVE TO DO.
FIRST IS GO TO REI'S HOUSE AND CONFIRM WHETHER OR NOT HER MOM IS SAFE.
THEN WE HEAD FOR NIIDOKO THIRD EL-EMENTARY SCHOOL!

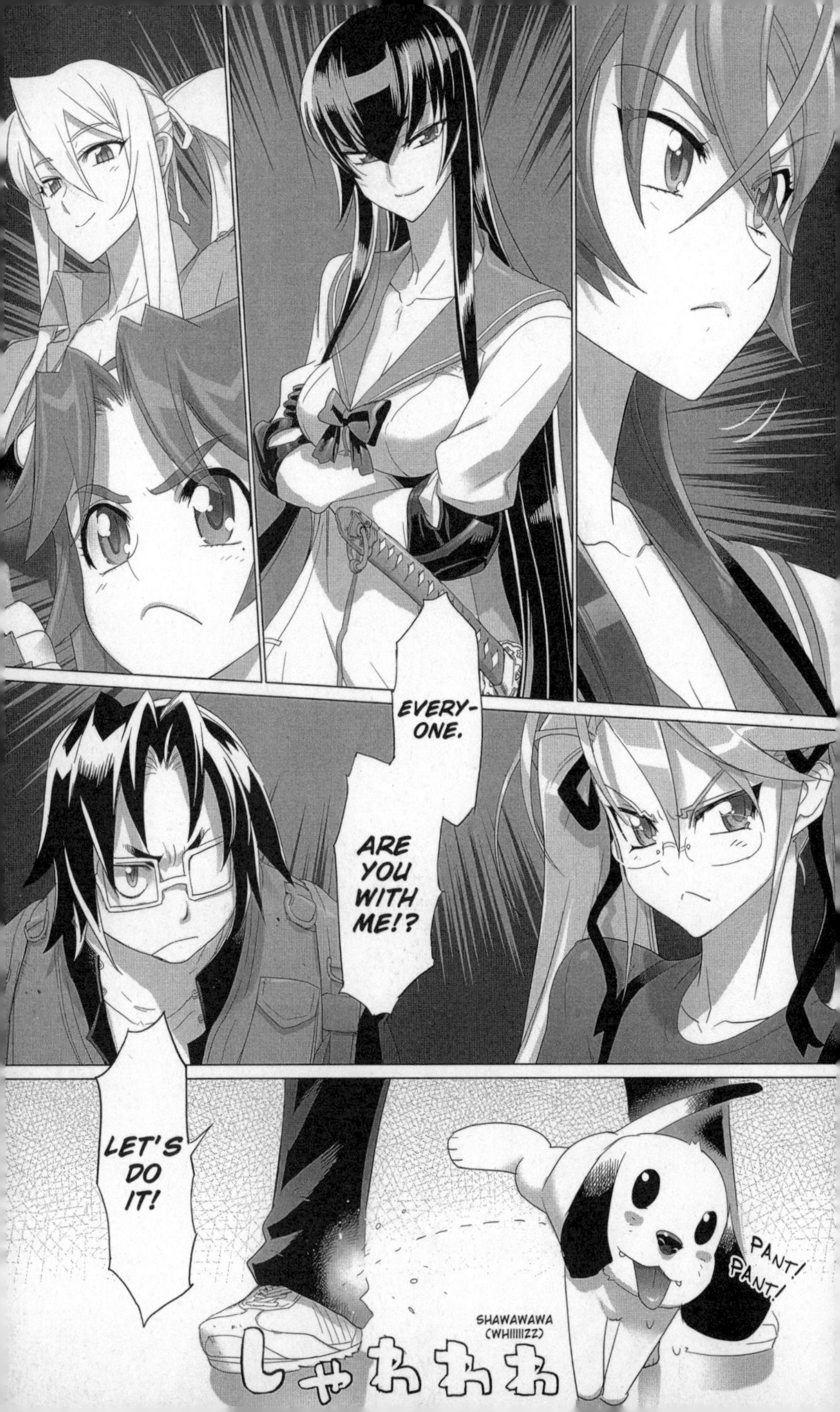
EVERY-ONE.
ARE YOU WITH ME!?
LET'S DO IT!
PANT! PANT!
しゃわわわ
SHAWAWAWA (WHIIIIIIZZ)

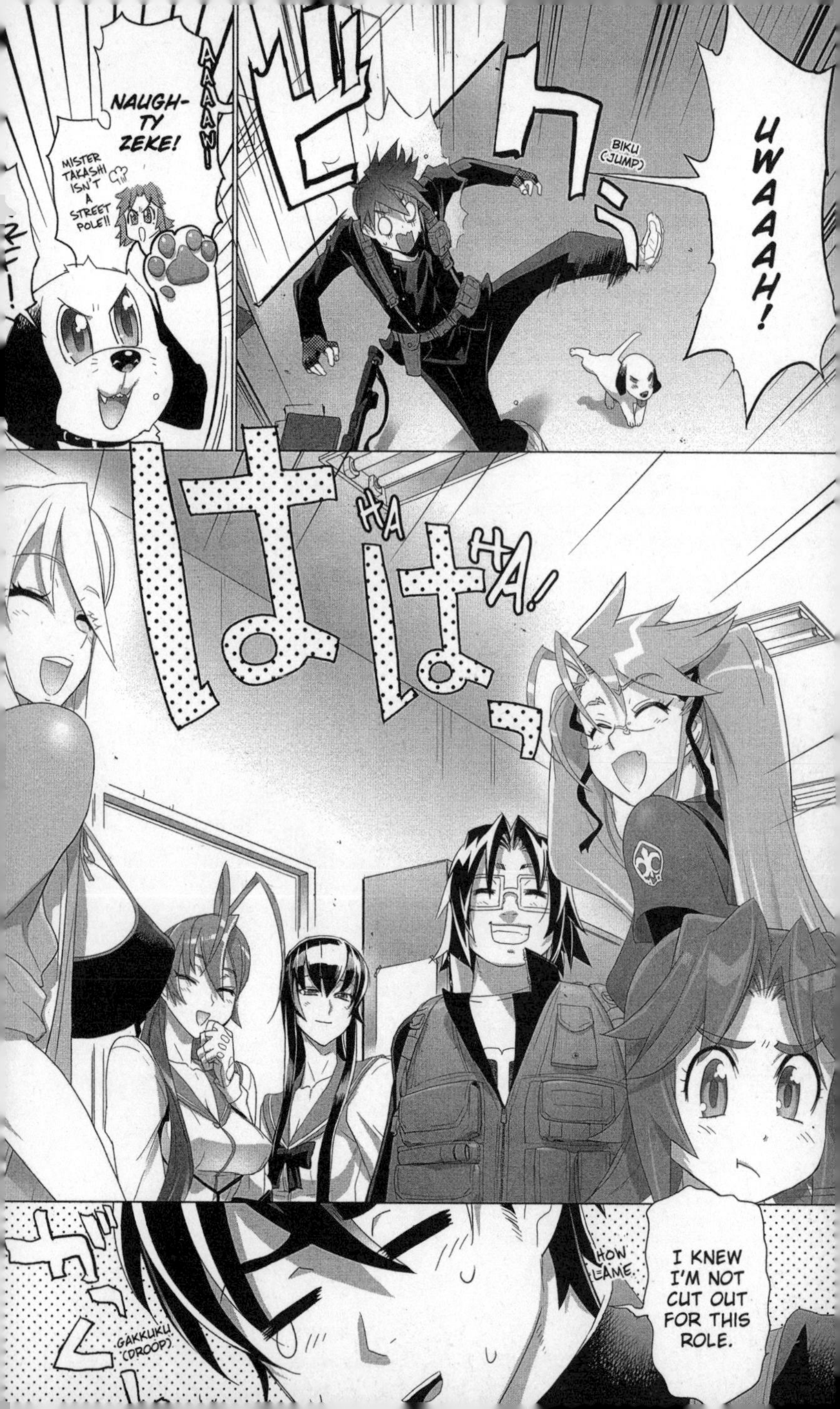
UWAAAAH!
BIKU (JUMP)
AAAAAW!
NAUGH-TY ZEKE!
MISTER TAKASHI ISN'T A STREET POLE!!
HA HA HA!
I KNEW I'M NOT CUT OUT FOR THIS ROLE.
HOW LAME.
GAKKUKU (DROOP)

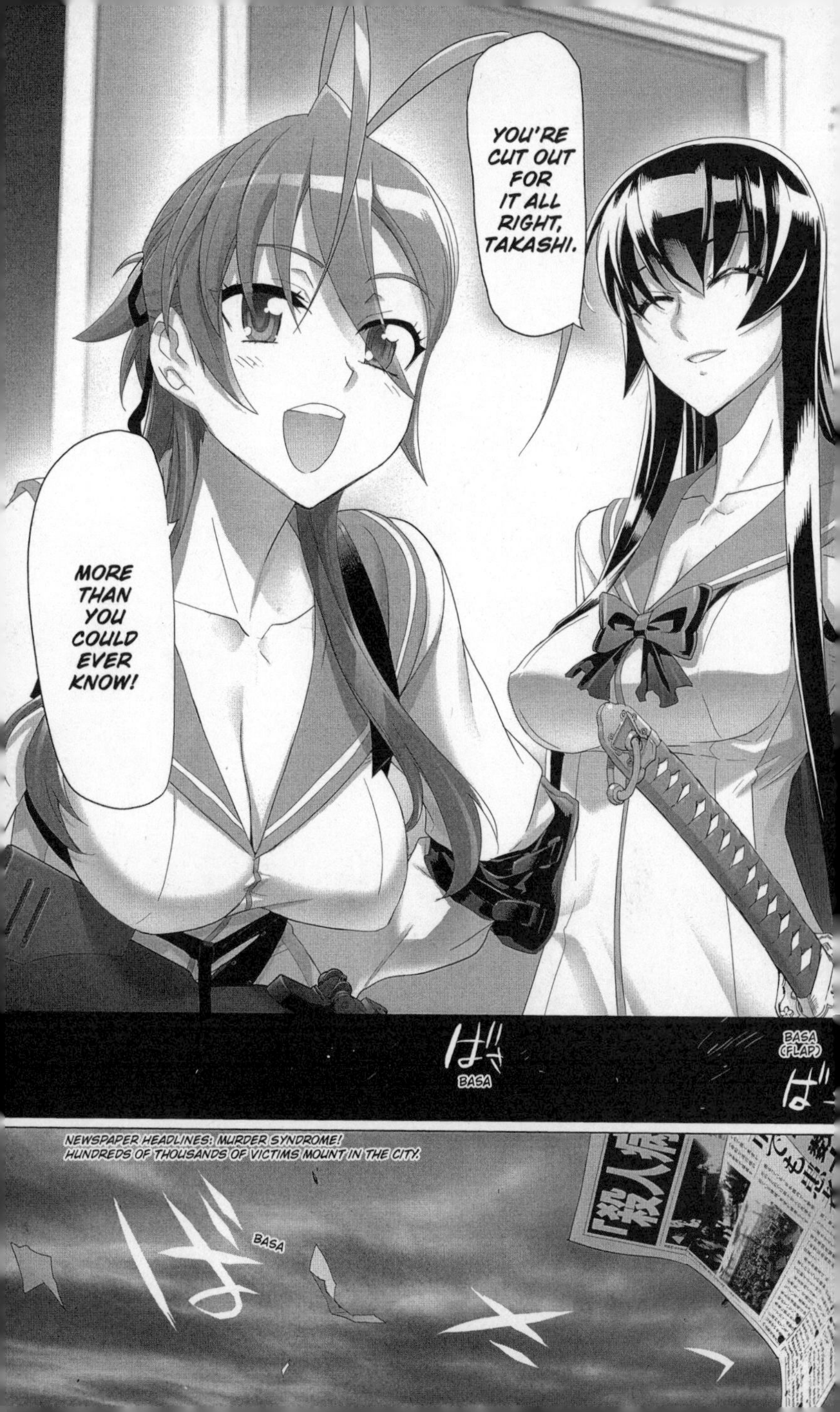
YOU'RE CUT OUT FOR IT ALL RIGHT, TAKASHI.
MORE THAN YOU COULD EVER KNOW!
BASA (FLAP)
BASA
NEWSPAPER HEADLINES: MURDER SYNDROME! HUNDREDS OF THOUSANDS OF VICTIMS MOUNT IN THE CITY.
BASA

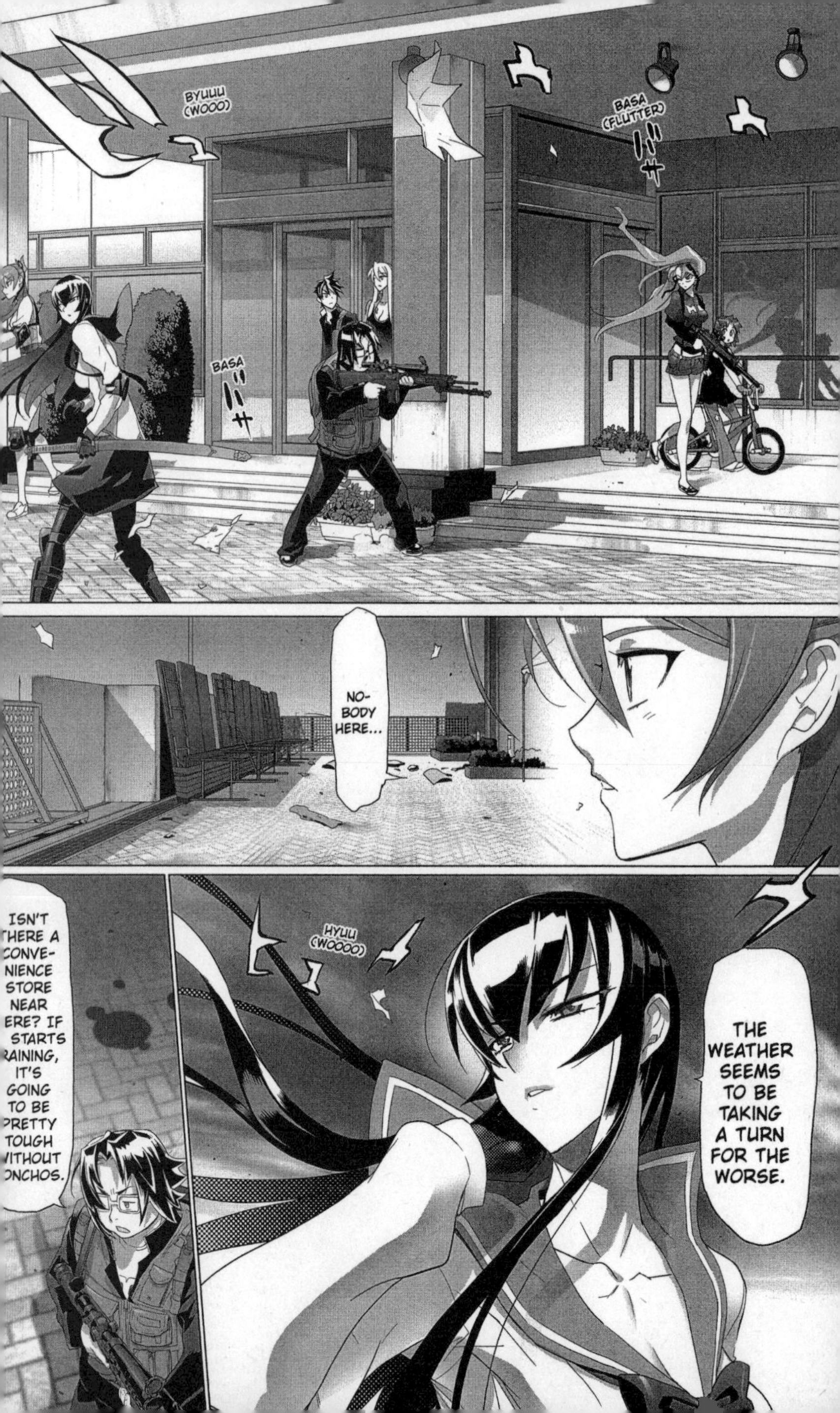
BASA (FLUTTER)
BYUUU (WOOO)
BASA
NO-BODY HERE...
THE WEATHER SEEMS TO BE TAKING A TURN FOR THE WORSE.
HYUU (WOOOO)
ISN'T THERE A CONVE-NIENCE STORE NEAR ERE? IF STARTS RAINING, IT'S GOING TO BE PRETTY TOUGH WITHOUT ONCHOS.

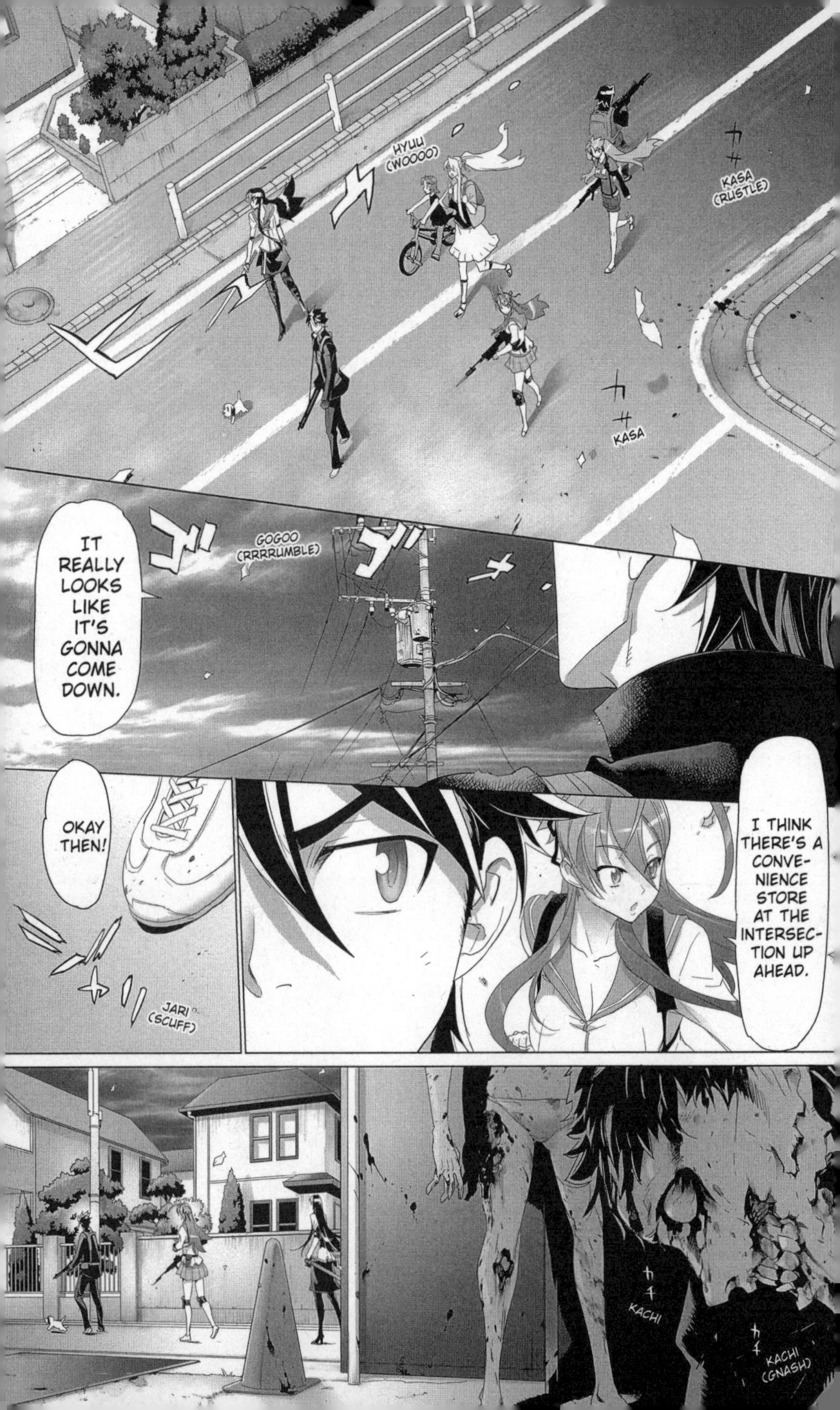
KASA (RUSTLE)
HYUU (WOOOO)
KASA
GOGOO (RRRRUMBLE)
IT REALLY LOOKS LIKE IT'S GONNA COME DOWN.
I THINK THERE'S A CONVE-NIENCE STORE AT THE INTERSEC-TION UP AHEAD.
OKAY THEN!
JARI (SCUFF)
KACHI
KACHI (GNASH)

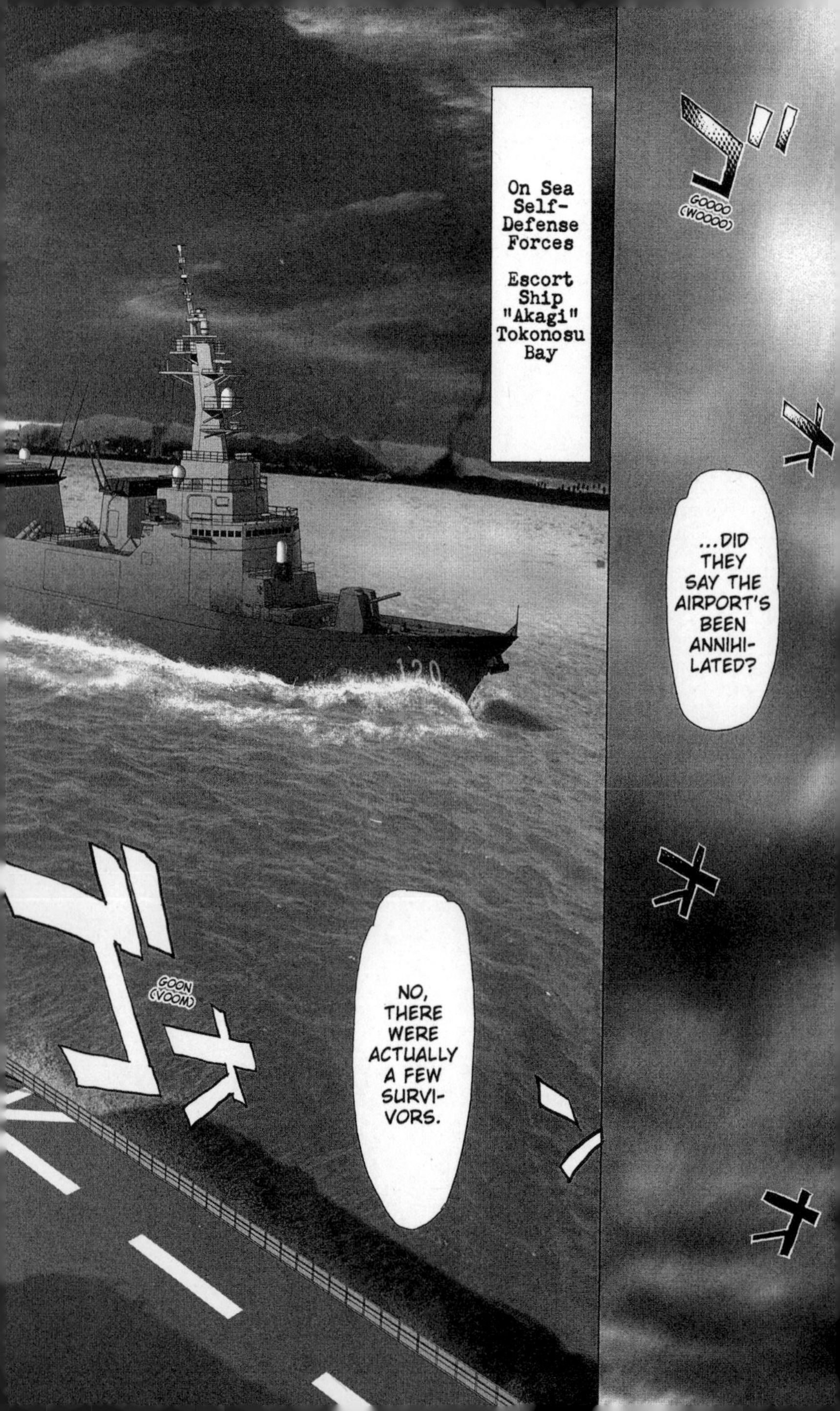
GOOOO (WOOOO)
...DID THEY SAY THE AIRPORT'S BEEN ANNIHILATED?
On Sea Self-Defense Forces
Escort Ship "Akagi" Tokonosu Bay
GOON (VOOM)
NO, THERE WERE ACTUALLY A FEW SURVIVORS.

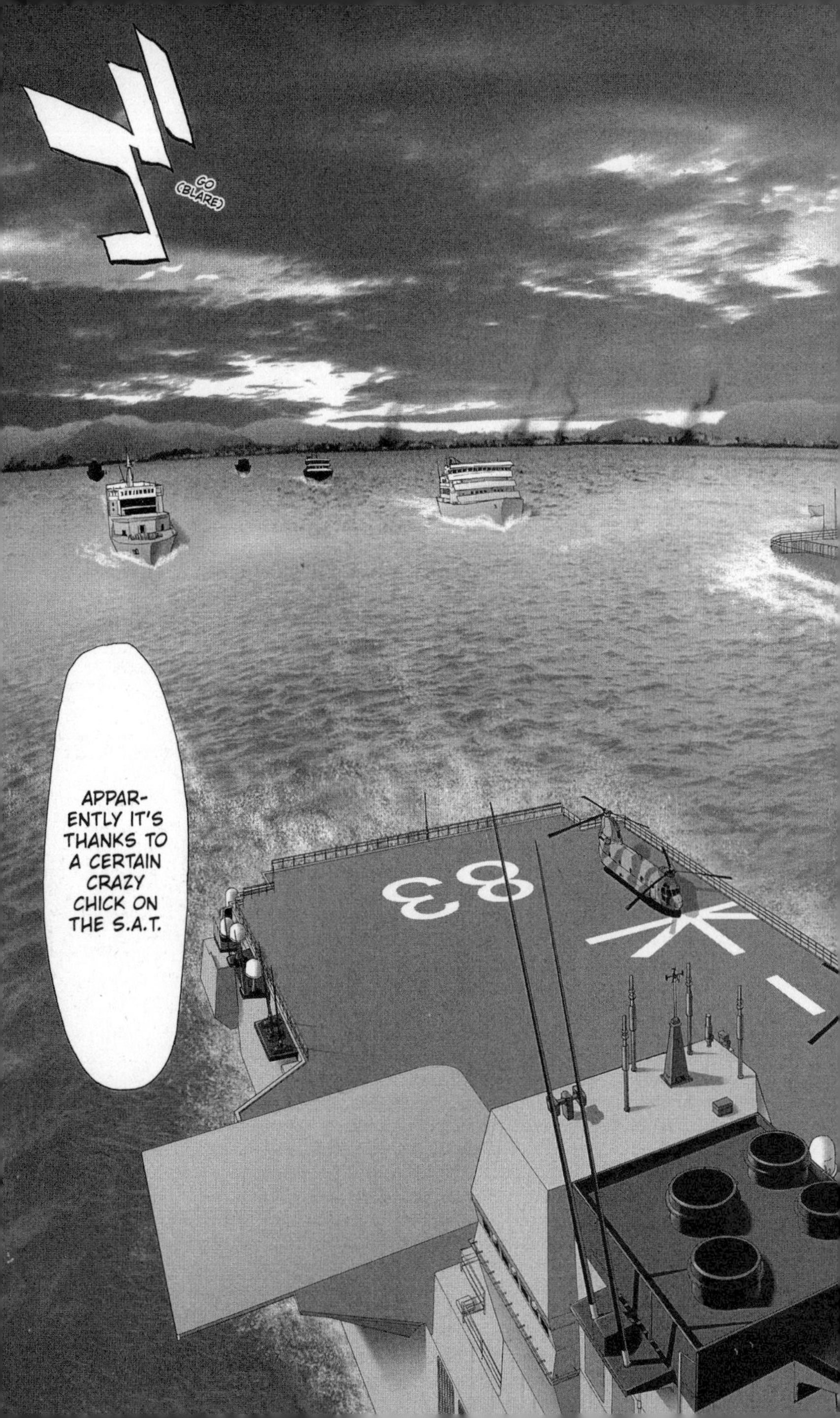
ゴ
GO (BLARE)
APPARENTLY IT'S THANKS TO A CERTAIN CRAZY CHICK ON THE S.A.T.
83

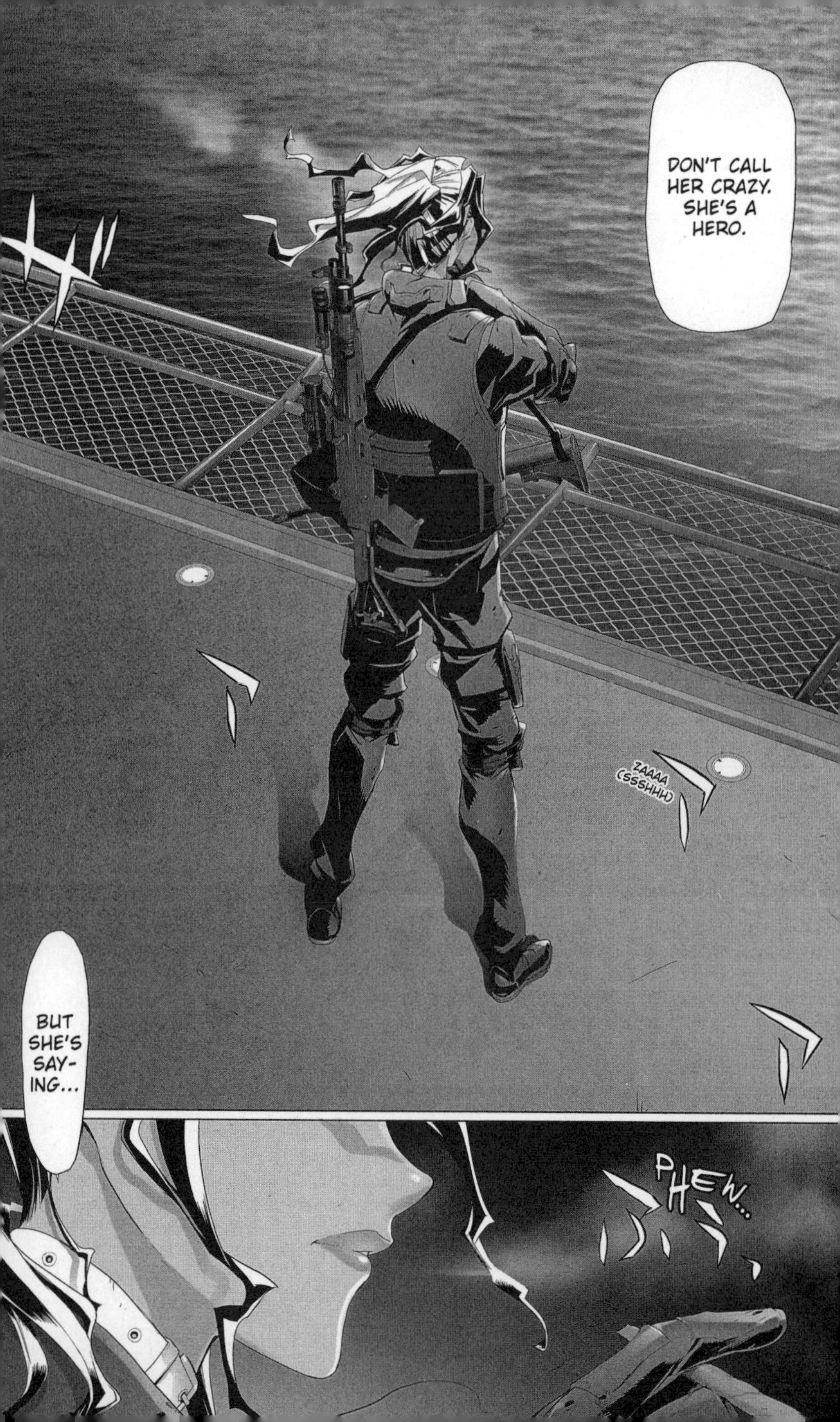
DON'T CALL HER CRAZY. SHE'S A HERO.
ZAAAA (SSSHHH)
BUT SHE'S SAY-ING...
PHEW...

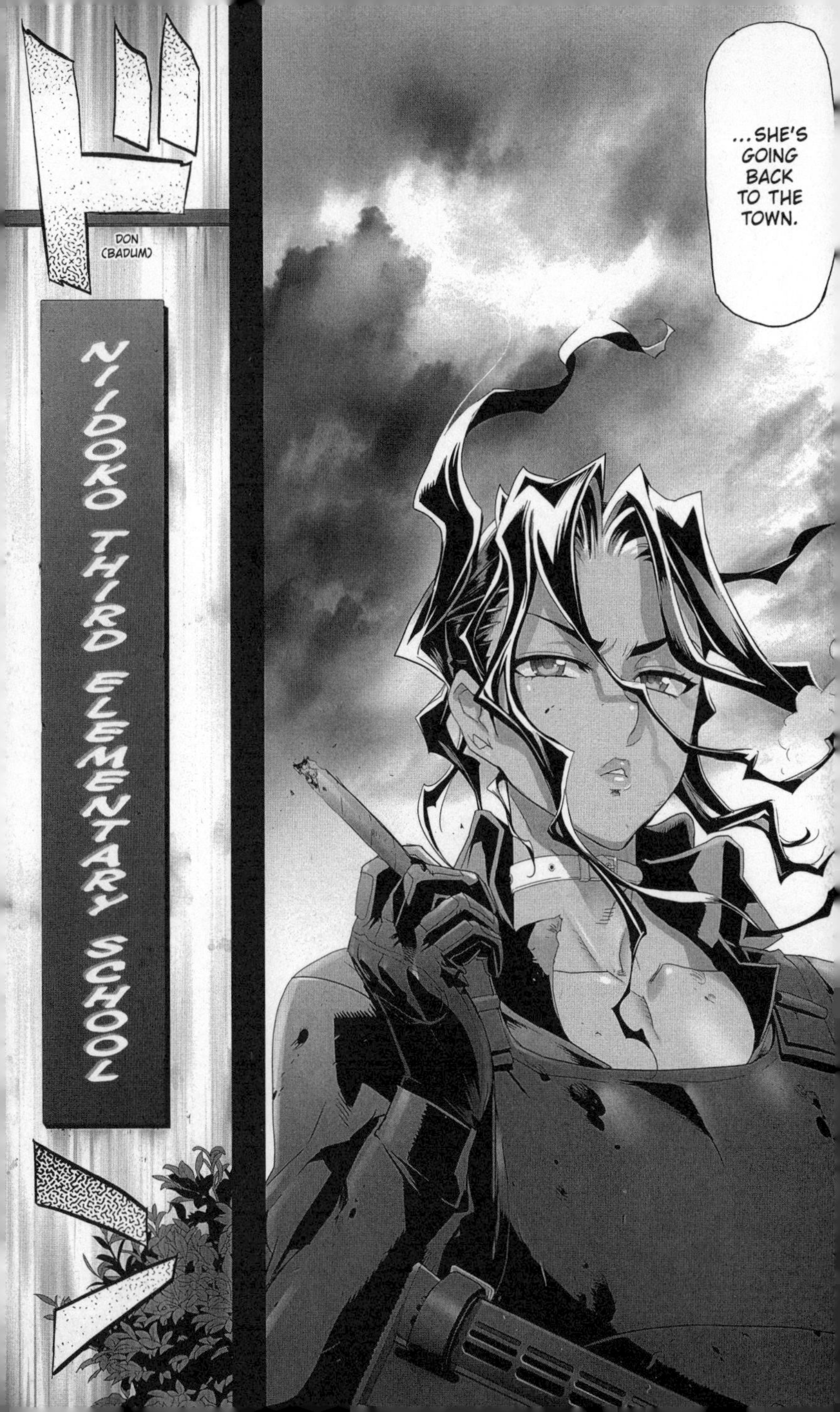
...SHE'S GOING BACK TO THE TOWN.
DON (BADUM)
NIIDOKO THIRD ELEMENTARY SCHOOL

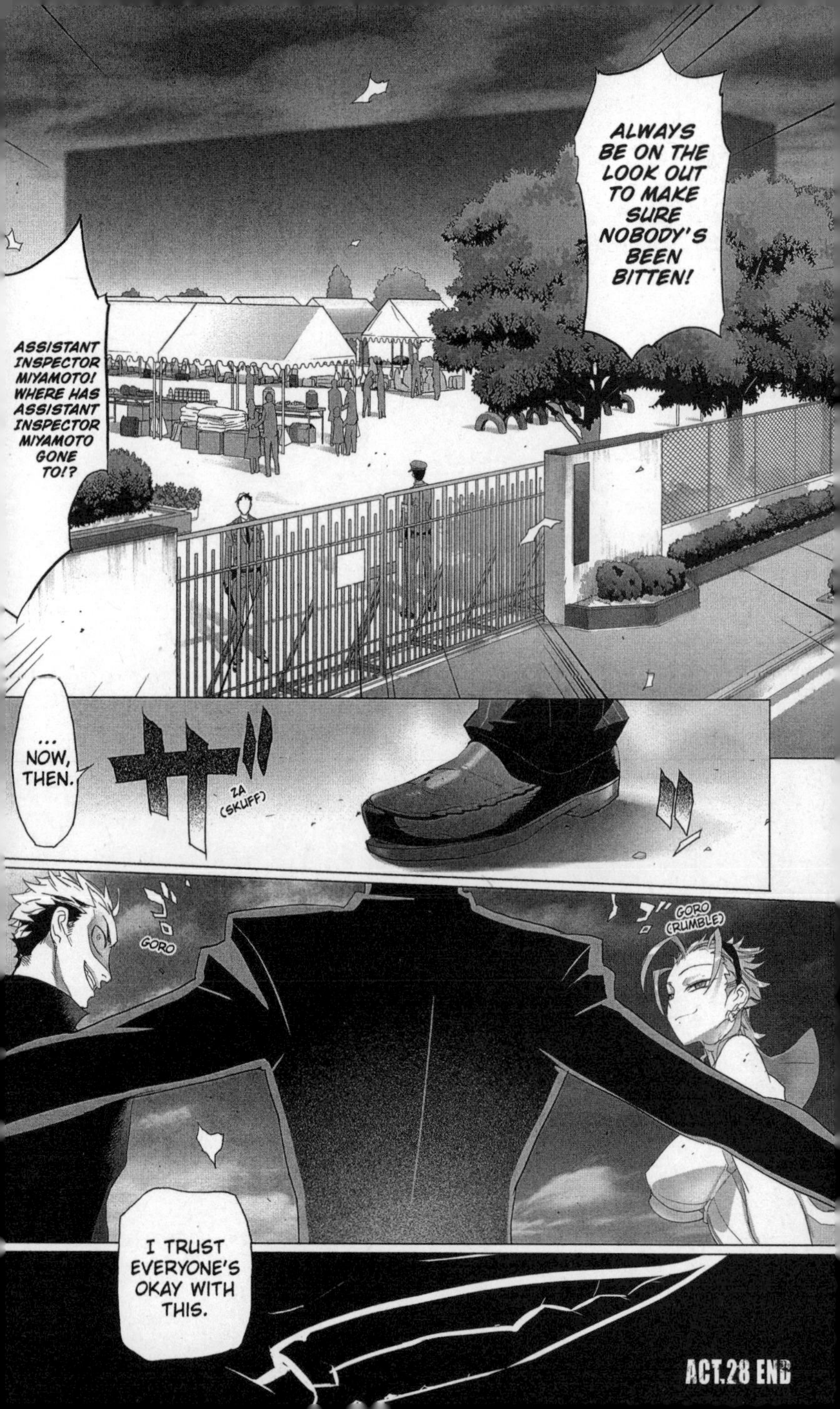
ALWAYS BE ON THE LOOK OUT TO MAKE SURE NOBODY'S BEEN BITTEN!
ASSISTANT INSPECTOR MIYAMOTO! WHERE HAS ASSISTANT INSPECTOR MIYAMOTO GONE TO!?
ZA (SKUFF)
... NOW, THEN.
GORO (RUMBLE)
GORO
I TRUST EVERYONE'S OKAY WITH THIS.
ACT.28 END

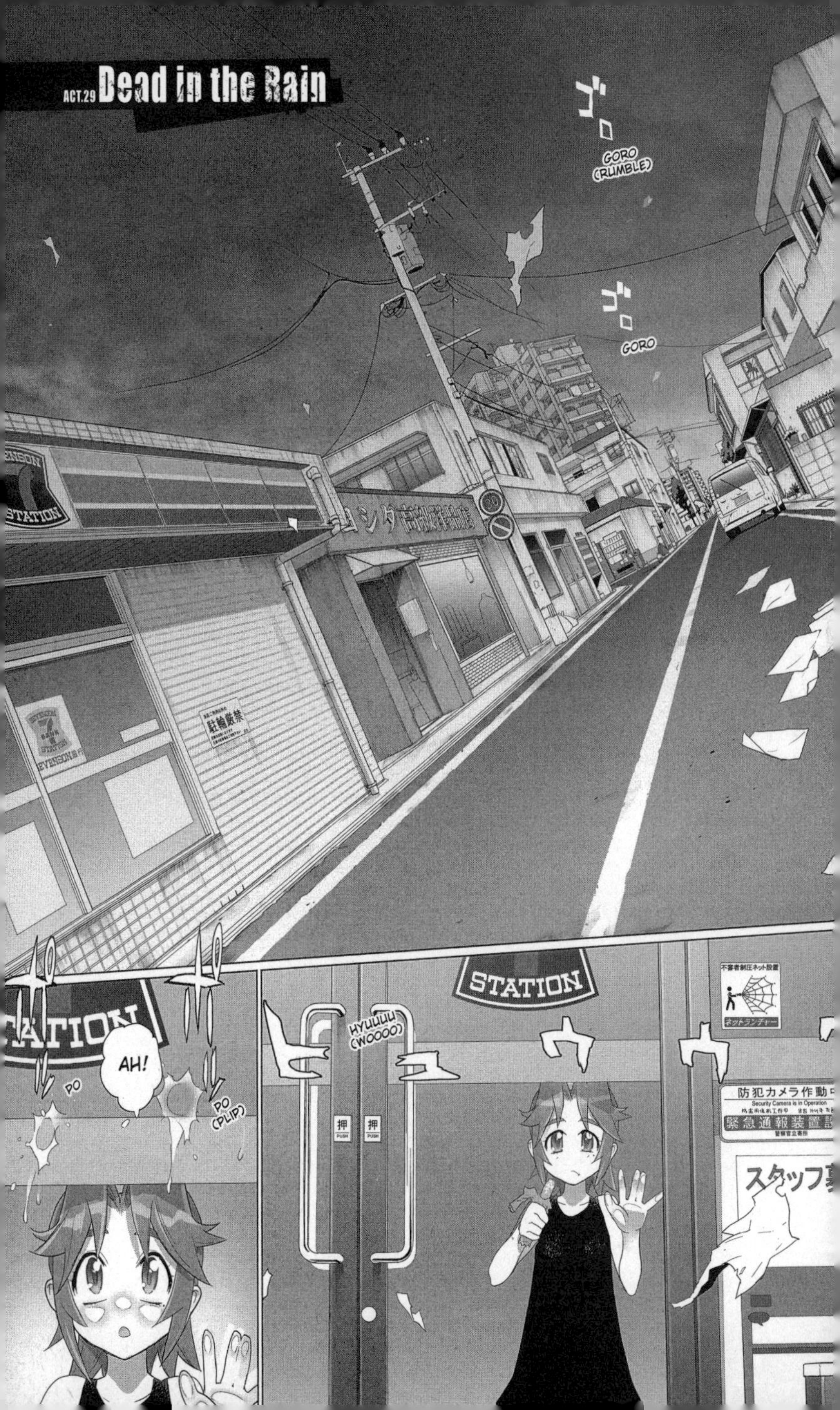
ACT.29 Dead in the Rain
ゴロ
GORO (RUMBLE)
ゴロ
GORO
STATION
駐輪厳禁
STATION
不審者制圧ネット設置
ネットランチャー
防犯カメラ作動中
Security Camera is in Operation
緊急通報装置設
スタッフ募
ヒュウウウ
HYUUUU (WOOOO)
押 PUSH
押 PUSH
STATION
AH!
ポ
PO
ポ
PO (PLIP)

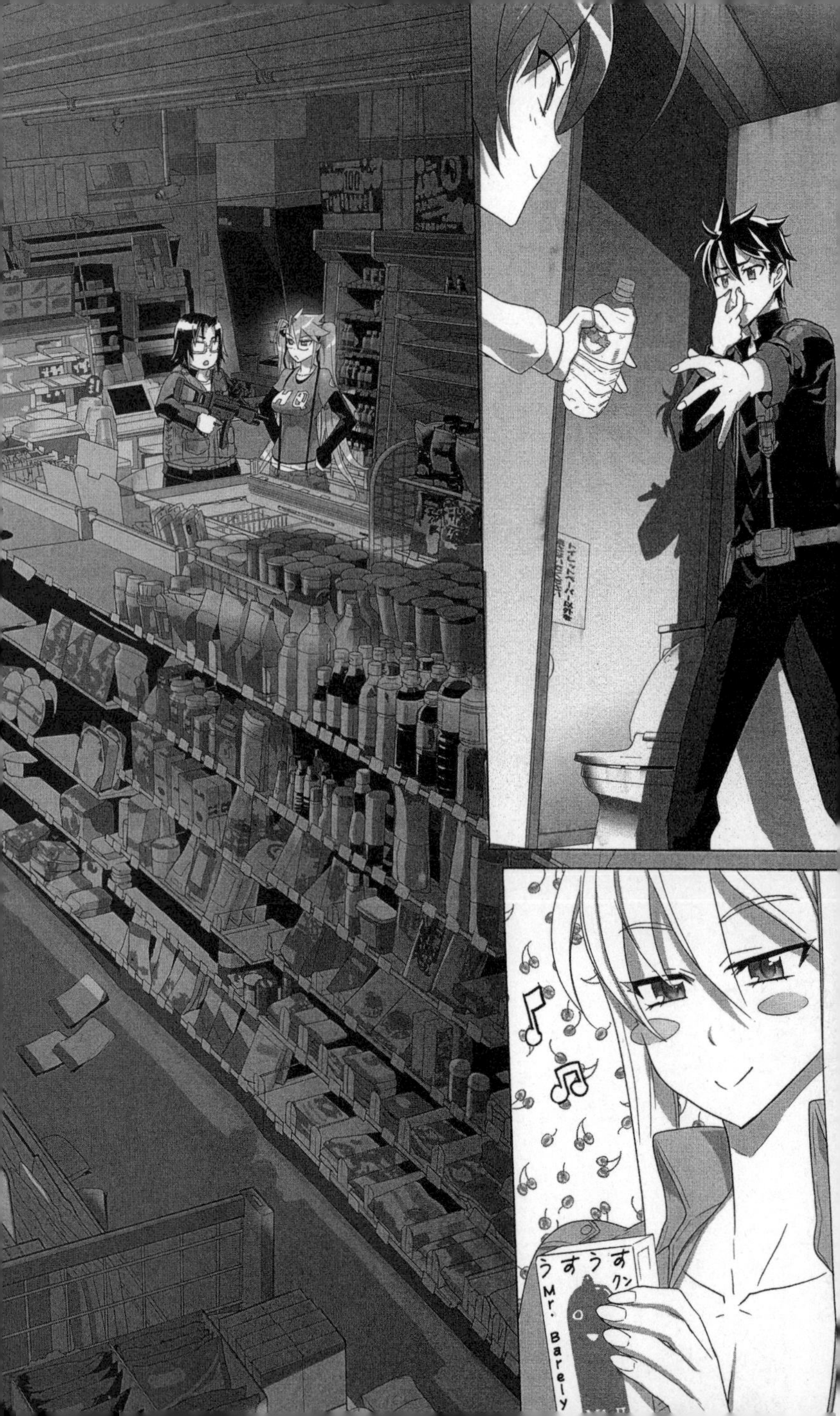
トイレットペーパー以外を
うすうすクン
Mr. Barely

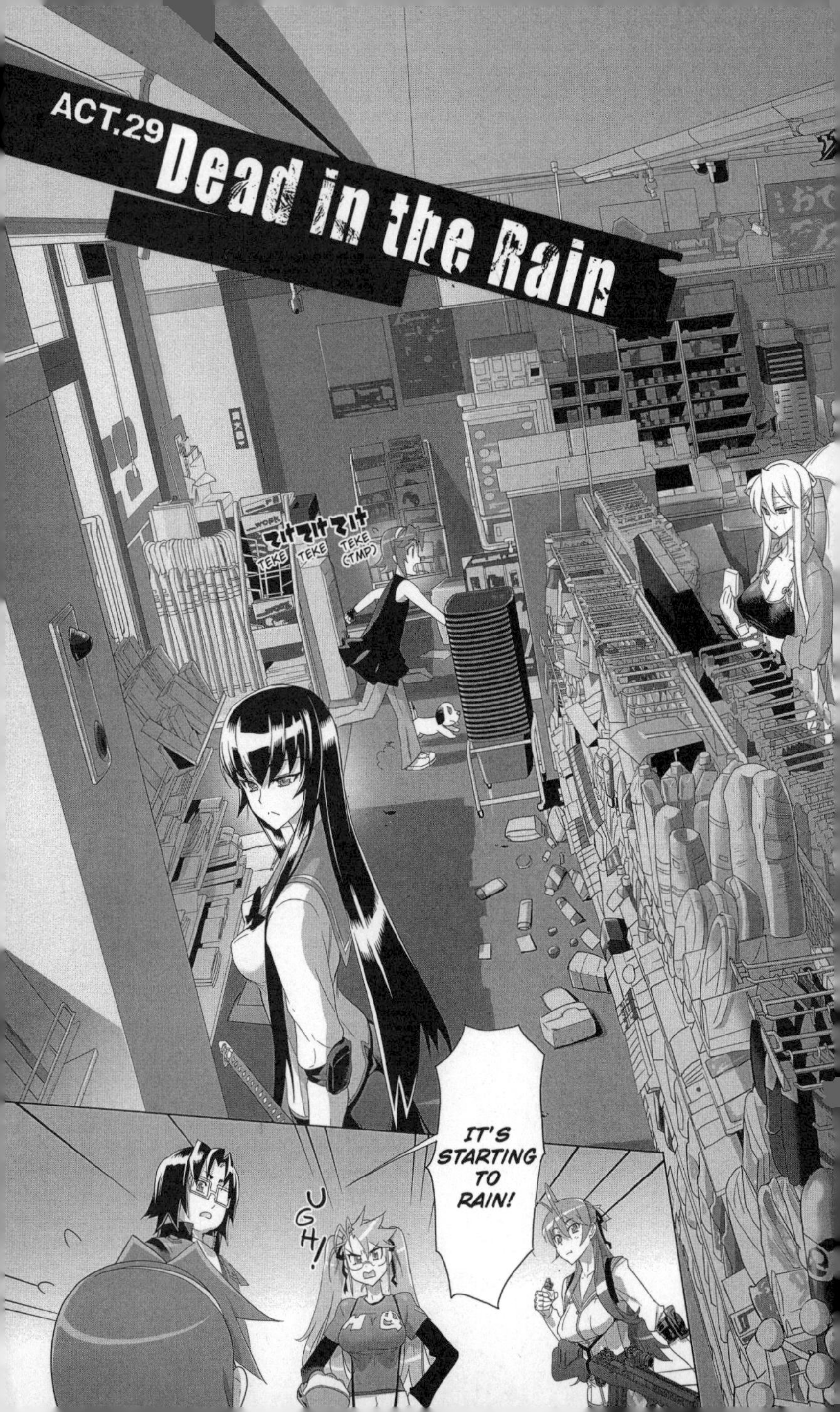
ACT.29 Dead in the Rain
てけてけてけ
TEKE TEKE TEKE (TMP)
IT'S STARTING TO RAIN!
UGH!

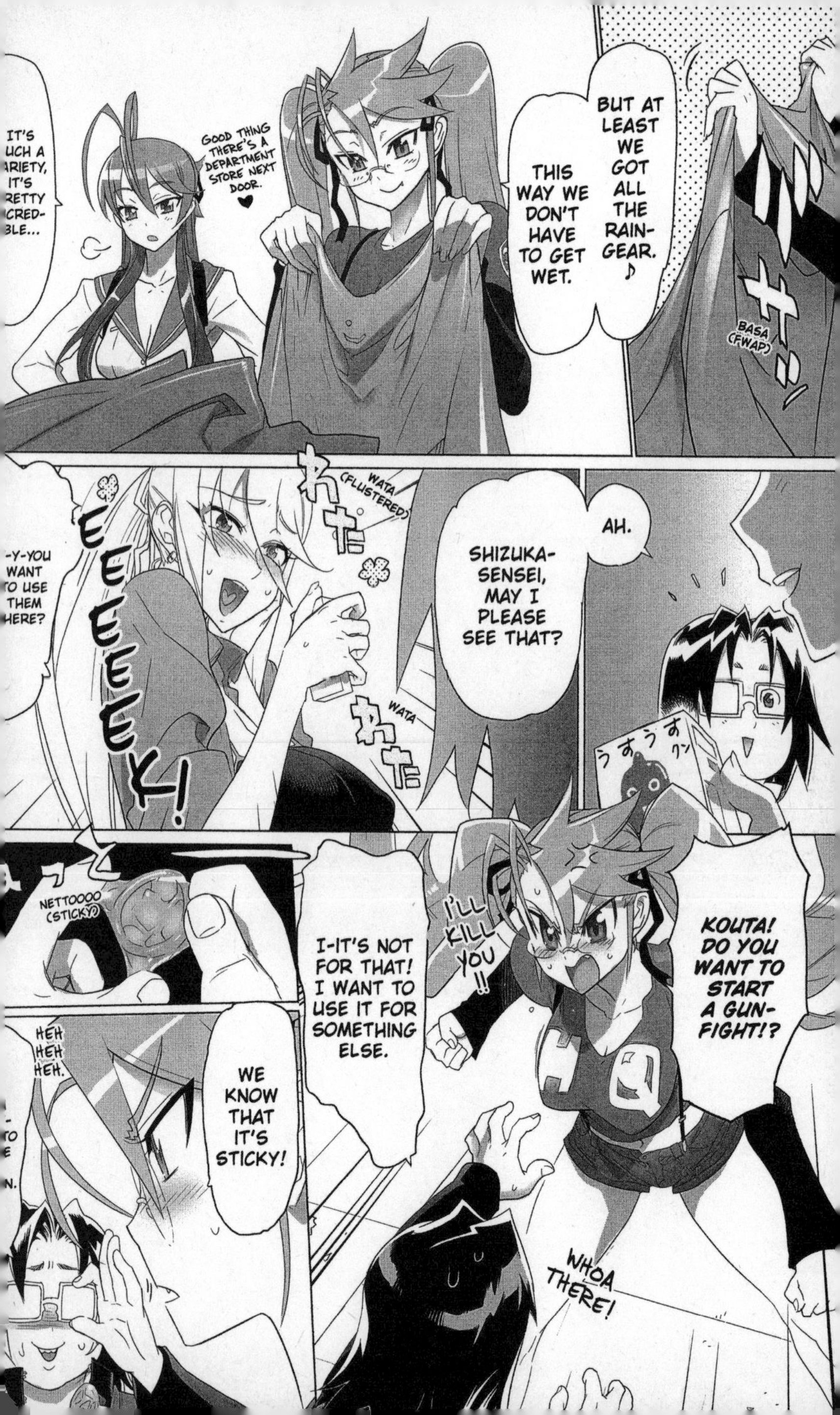
BASA (FWAP)
BUT AT LEAST WE GOT ALL THE RAIN-GEAR. ♪
THIS WAY WE DON'T HAVE TO GET WET.
GOOD THING THERE'S A DEPARTMENT STORE NEXT DOOR. ♥
IT'S UCH A ARIETY, IT'S RETTY CRED- BLE...
AH.
SHIZUKA-SENSEI, MAY I PLEASE SEE THAT?
WATA (FLUSTERED)
WATA
EEEEEEK!
-Y-YOU WANT TO USE THEM HERE?
KOUTA! DO YOU WANT TO START A GUN-FIGHT!?
I'LL KILL YOU!!
WHOA THERE!
NETTOOOO (STICKY)
I-IT'S NOT FOR THAT! I WANT TO USE IT FOR SOMETHING ELSE.
WE KNOW THAT IT'S STICKY!
HEH HEH HEH.

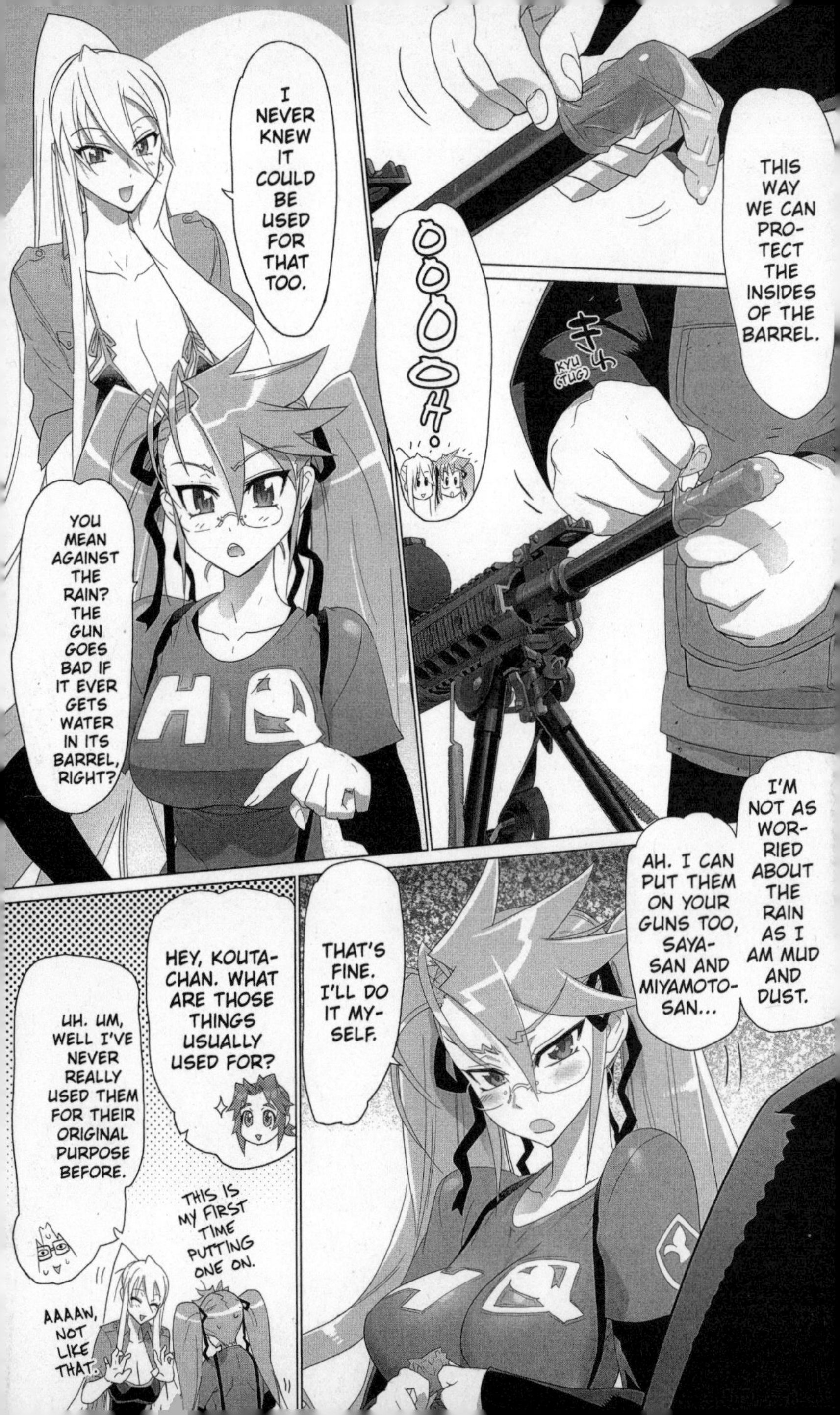
THIS WAY WE CAN PROTECT THE INSIDES OF THE BARREL.
OOOOH!
KYU (TUG)
I NEVER KNEW IT COULD BE USED FOR THAT TOO.
YOU MEAN AGAINST THE RAIN? THE GUN GOES BAD IF IT EVER GETS WATER IN ITS BARREL, RIGHT?
I'M NOT AS WORRIED ABOUT THE RAIN AS I AM MUD AND DUST.
AH. I CAN PUT THEM ON YOUR GUNS TOO, SAYA-SAN AND MIYAMOTO-SAN...
THAT'S FINE. I'LL DO IT MYSELF.
HEY, KOUTA-CHAN. WHAT ARE THOSE THINGS USUALLY USED FOR?
UH. UM, WELL I'VE NEVER REALLY USED THEM FOR THEIR ORIGINAL PURPOSE BEFORE.
THIS IS MY FIRST TIME PUTTING ONE ON.
AAAAW, NOT LIKE THAT.

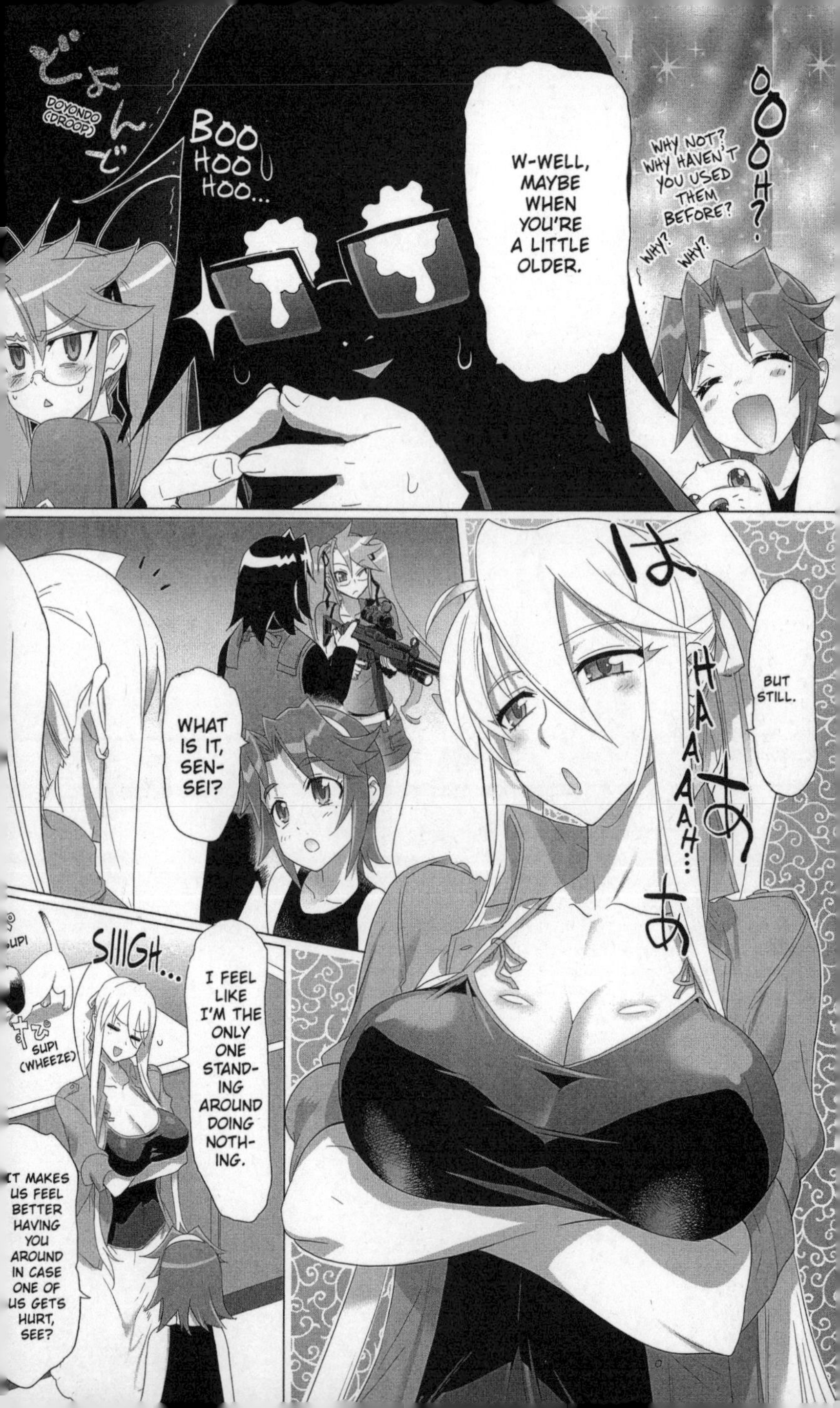

O O O H?
WHY NOT? WHY HAVEN'T YOU USED THEM BEFORE?
WHY? WHY?
W-WELL, MAYBE WHEN YOU'RE A LITTLE OLDER.
BOO HOO HOO...
どよんど
DOYONDO (DROOP)
はあああ
HAAAAAH...
BUT STILL.
WHAT IS IT, SEN-SEI?
I FEEL LIKE I'M THE ONLY ONE STANDING AROUND DOING NOTHING.
SIIIGH...
すぴ
SUPI (WHEEZE)
IT MAKES US FEEL BETTER HAVING YOU AROUND IN CASE ONE OF US GETS HURT, SEE?

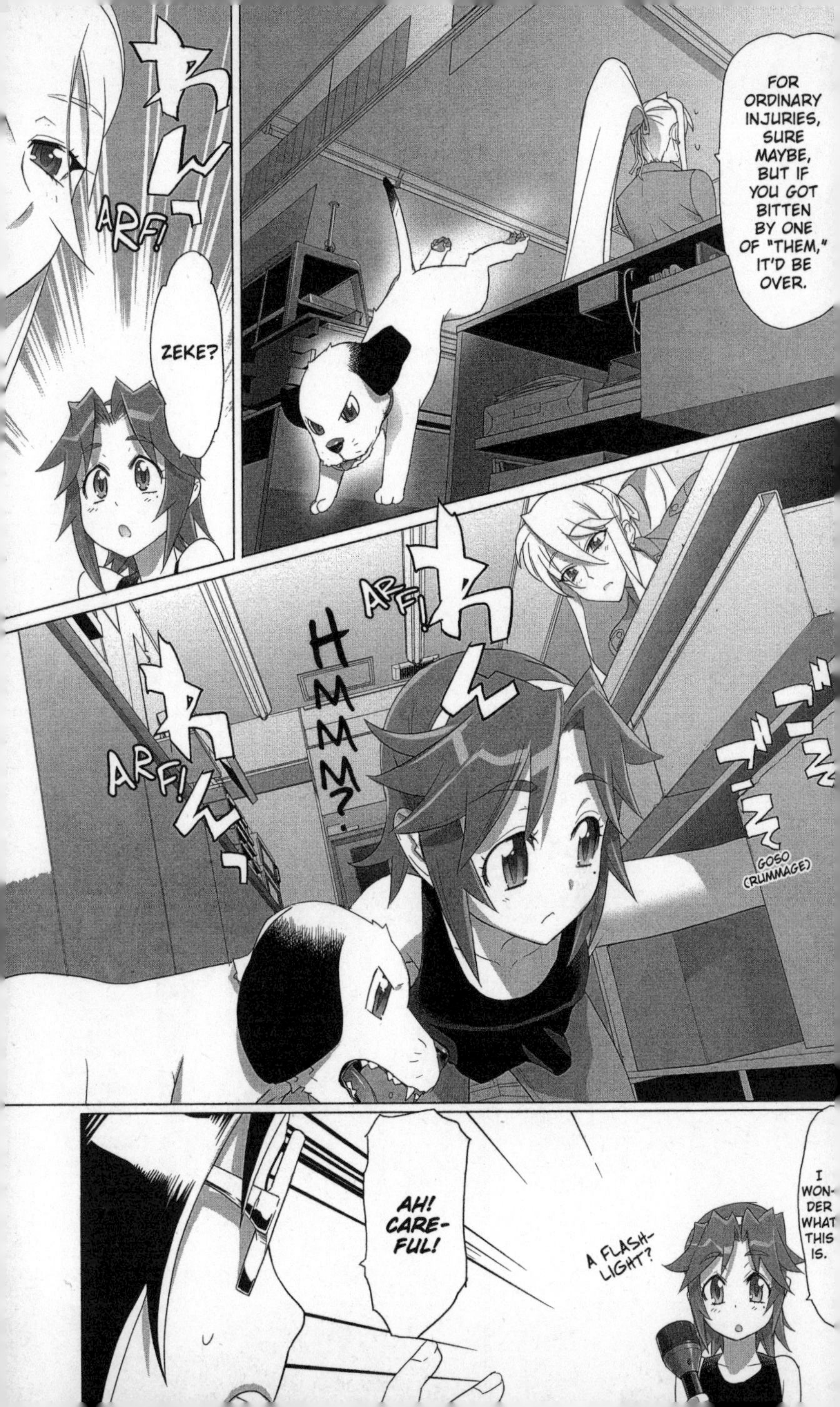

FOR ORDINARY INJURIES, SURE MAYBE, BUT IF YOU GOT BITTEN BY ONE OF "THEM," IT'D BE OVER.
わん
ARF!
ZEKE?
ゴソゴソ
GOSO (RUMMAGE)
わん
ARF!
HMMM?
わん
ARF!
I WONDER WHAT THIS IS.
A FLASH-LIGHT?
AH! CARE-FUL!

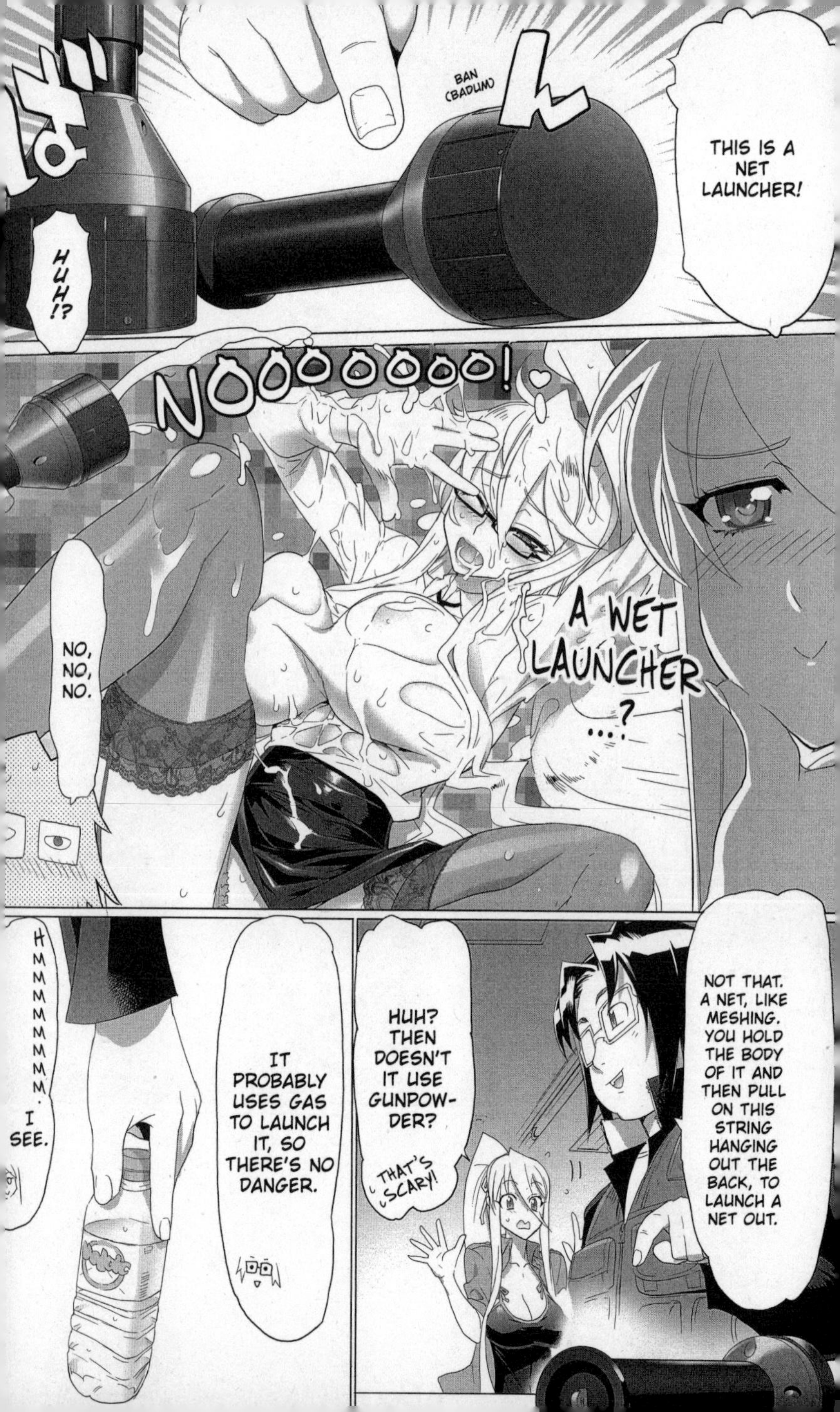
THIS IS A NET LAUNCHER!
BAN (BADUM)
ばん
HUH!?
A WET LAUNCHER ...?
NOOOOOOO!
NO, NO, NO.
NOT THAT. A NET, LIKE MESHING. YOU HOLD THE BODY OF IT AND THEN PULL ON THIS STRING HANGING OUT THE BACK, TO LAUNCH A NET OUT.
HUH? THEN DOESN'T IT USE GUNPOW-DER?
THAT'S SCARY!
IT PROBABLY USES GAS TO LAUNCH IT, SO THERE'S NO DANGER.
HMMMMMMMMMM. I SEE.

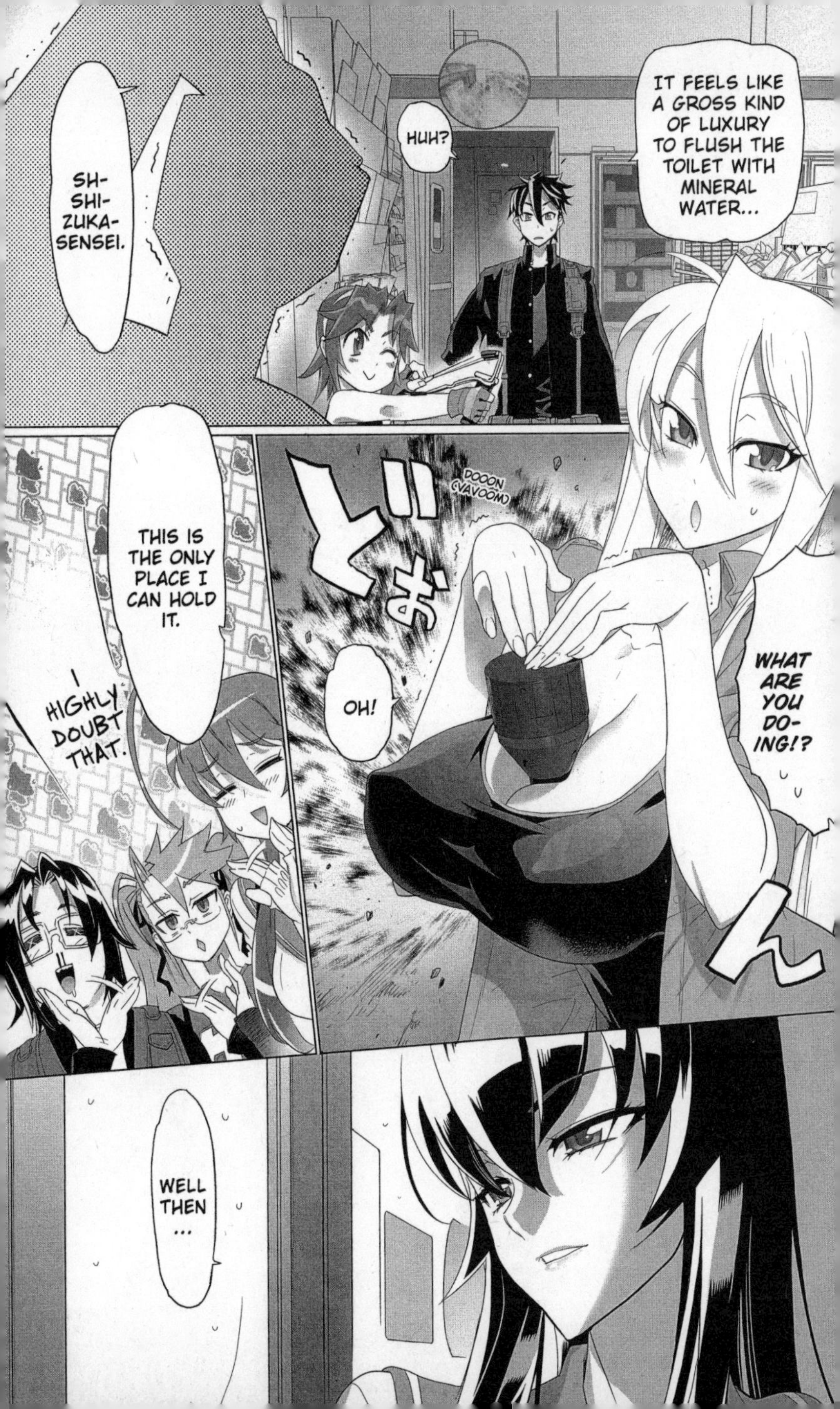
IT FEELS LIKE A GROSS KIND OF LUXURY TO FLUSH THE TOILET WITH MINERAL WATER...
HUH?
SH-SHI-ZUKA-SENSEI.
WHAT ARE YOU DO-ING!?
どぉん
DOOON (VAVOOM)
OH!
THIS IS THE ONLY PLACE I CAN HOLD IT.
I HIGHLY DOUBT THAT.
WELL THEN...

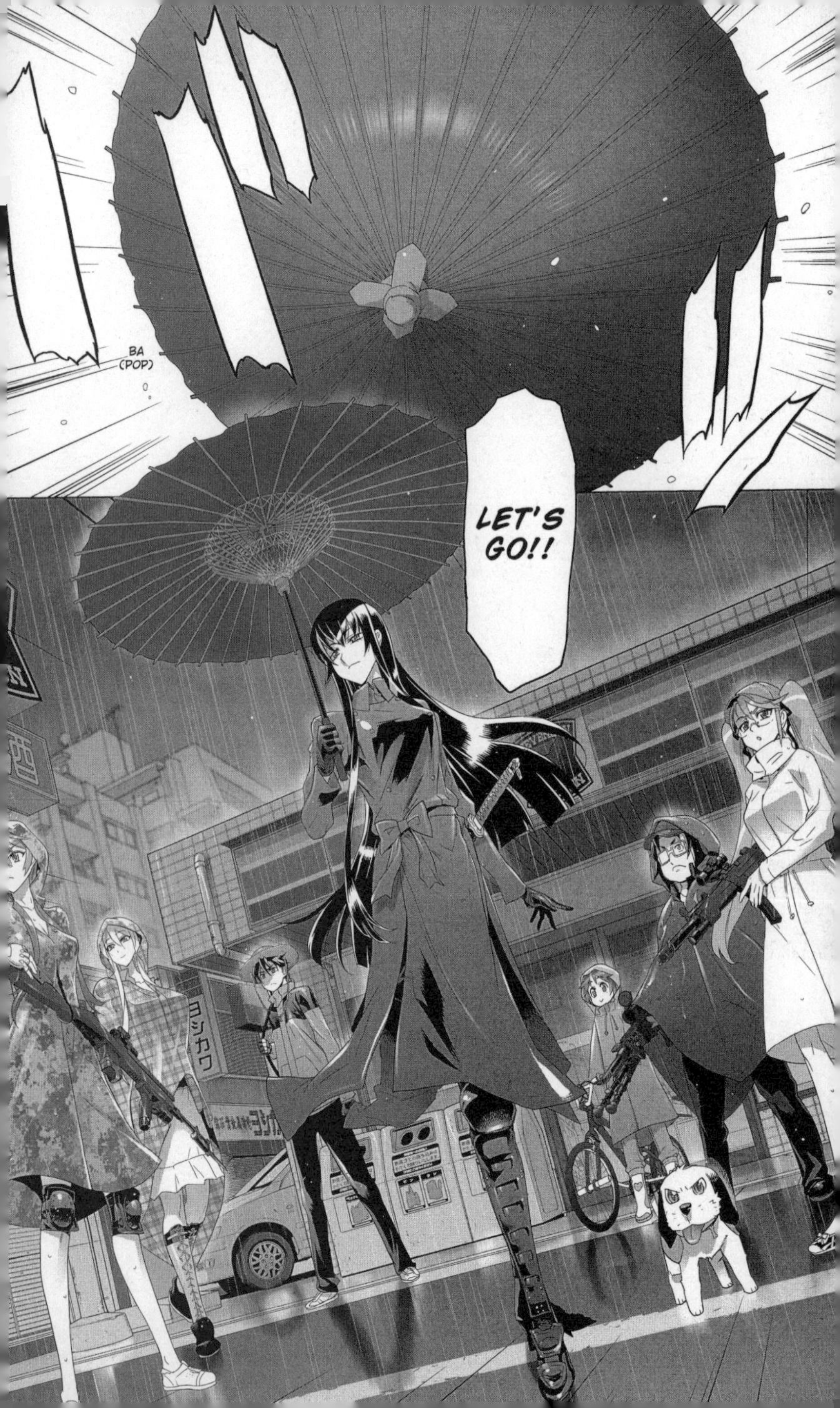
BA
(POP)
LET'S GO!!

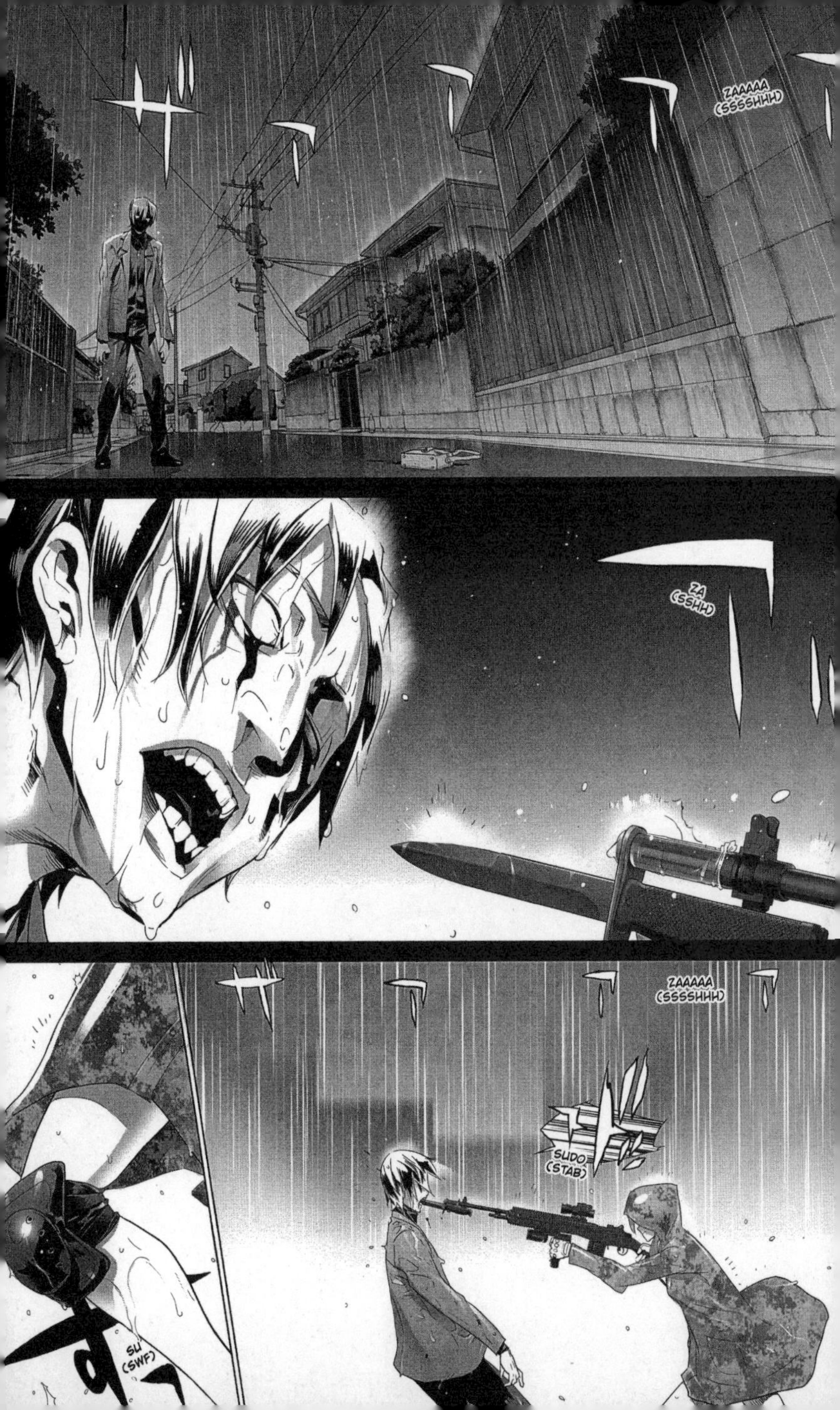
ZAAAAA
(SSSSHHH)
ZA
(SSHH)
ZAAAAA
(SSSSHHH)
SUDO
(STAB)
SU
(SWF)

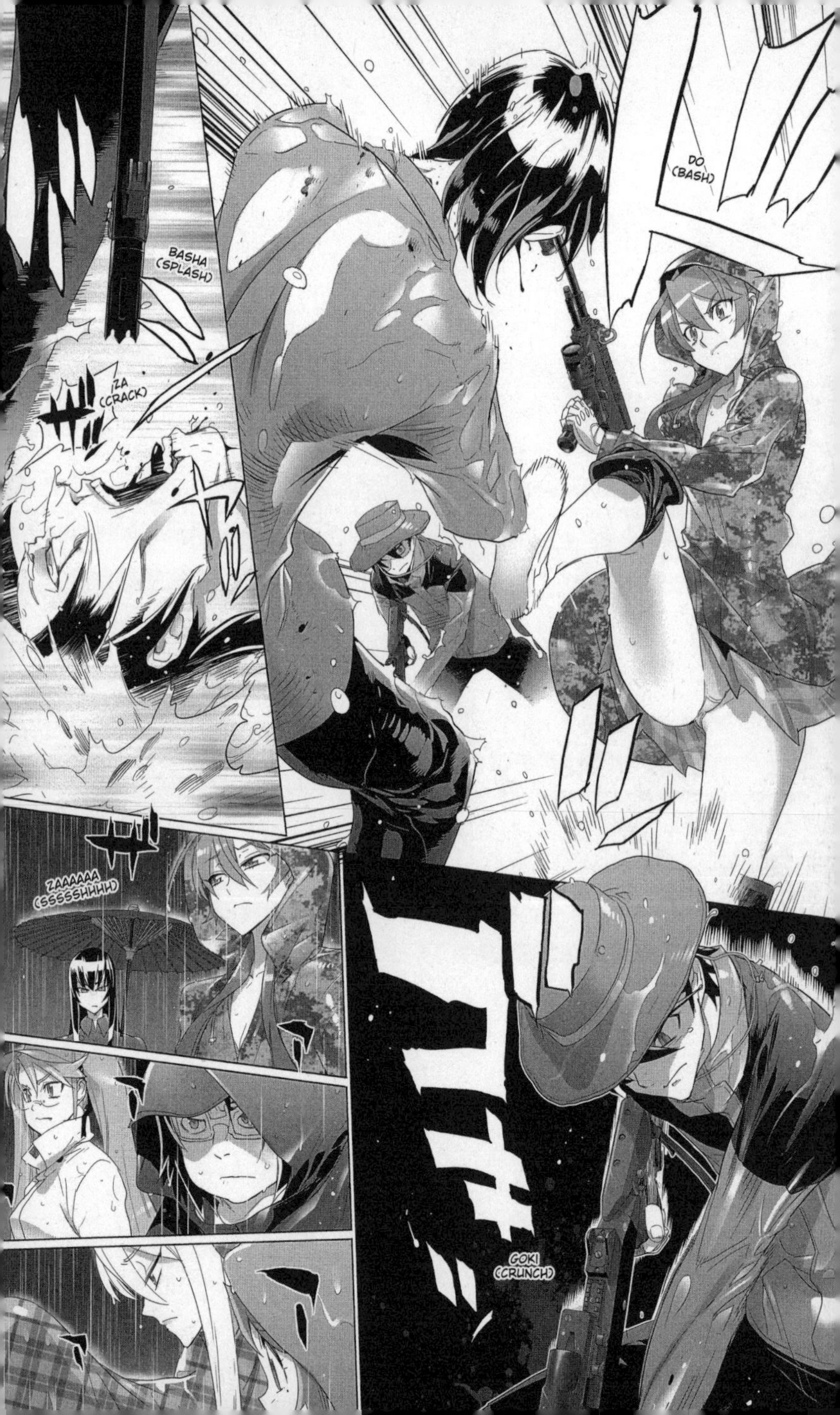
DO (BASH)
BASHA (SPLASH)
ZA (CRACK)
GOKI (CRUNCH)
ZAAAAAA (SSSSSHHHH)

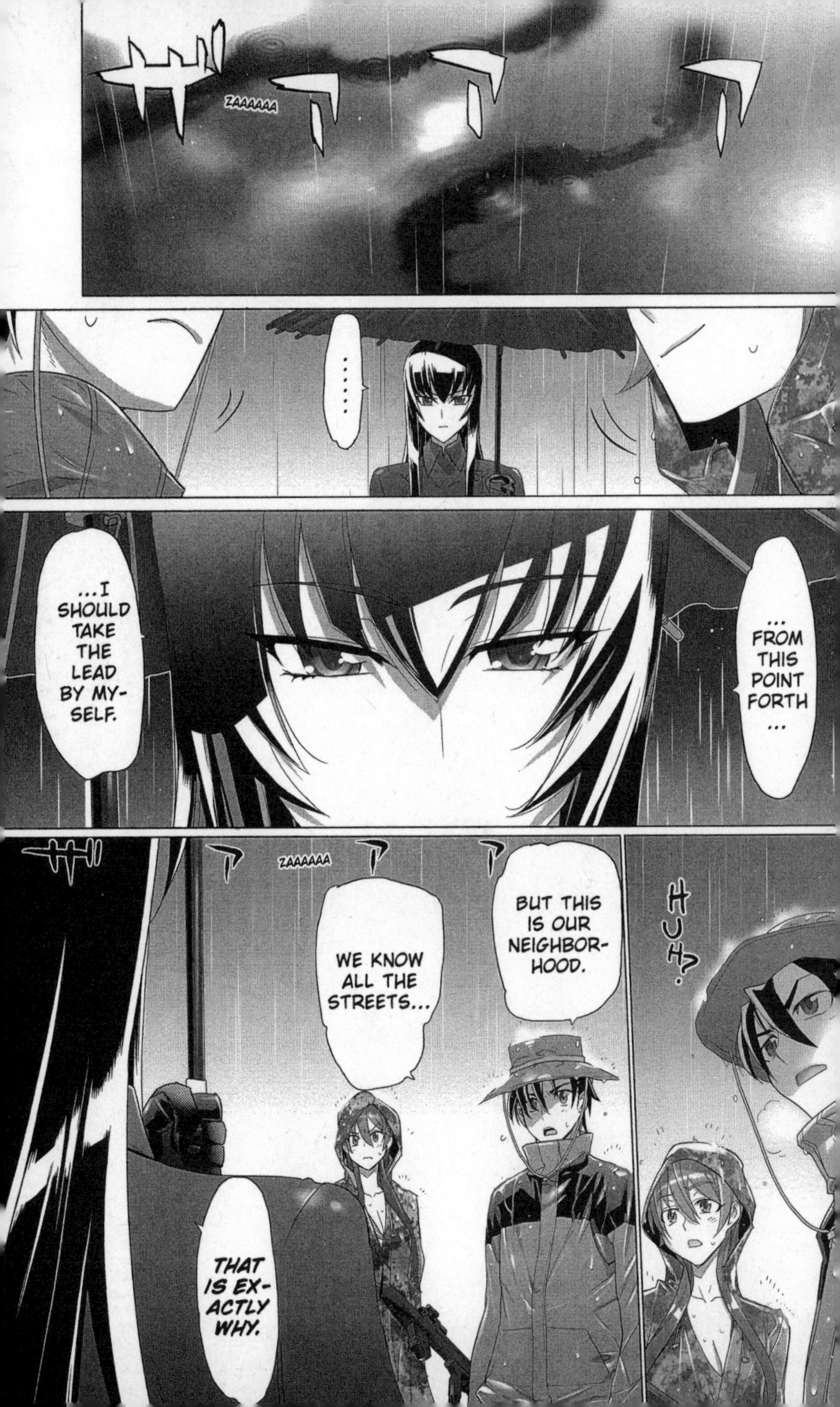
ZAAAAAA
......
...FROM THIS POINT FORTH...
...I SHOULD TAKE THE LEAD BY MY-SELF.
HUH?
ZAAAAAA
BUT THIS IS OUR NEIGHBOR-HOOD.
WE KNOW ALL THE STREETS...
THAT IS EX-ACTLY WHY.

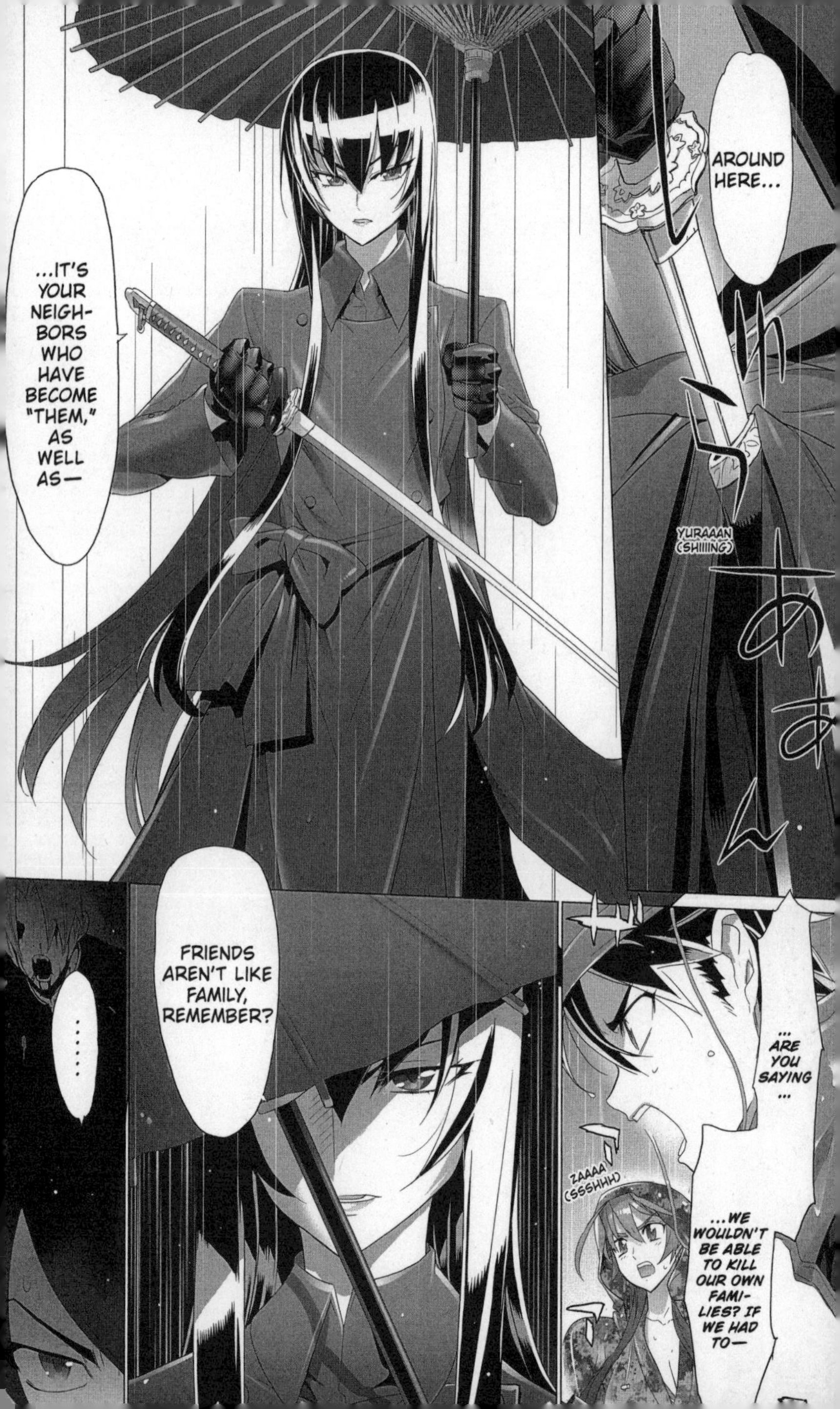
AROUND HERE...
YURAAAN (SHIIIING)
...IT'S YOUR NEIGHBORS WHO HAVE BECOME "THEM," AS WELL AS—
... ARE YOU SAYING ...
ZAAAA (SSSHHH)
...WE WOULDN'T BE ABLE TO KILL OUR OWN FAMILIES? IF WE HAD TO—
FRIENDS AREN'T LIKE FAMILY, REMEMBER?
......

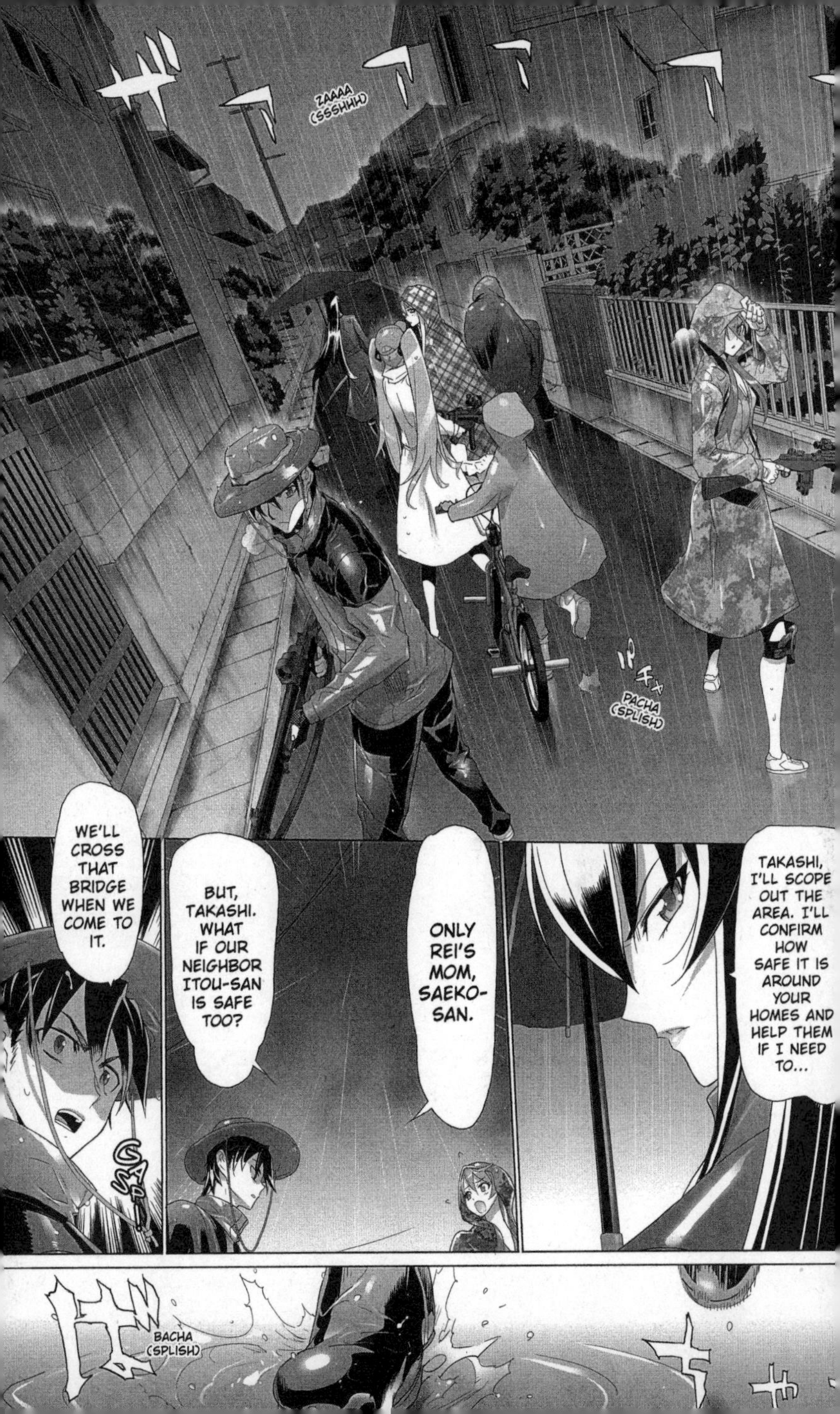
ZAAAA (SSSHHH)
PACHA (SPLISH)
TAKASHI, I'LL SCOPE OUT THE AREA. I'LL CONFIRM HOW SAFE IT IS AROUND YOUR HOMES AND HELP THEM IF I NEED TO...
ONLY REI'S MOM, SAEKO-SAN.
BUT, TAKASHI. WHAT IF OUR NEIGHBOR ITOU-SAN IS SAFE TOO?
WE'LL CROSS THAT BRIDGE WHEN WE COME TO IT.
GASP
BACHA (SPLISH)

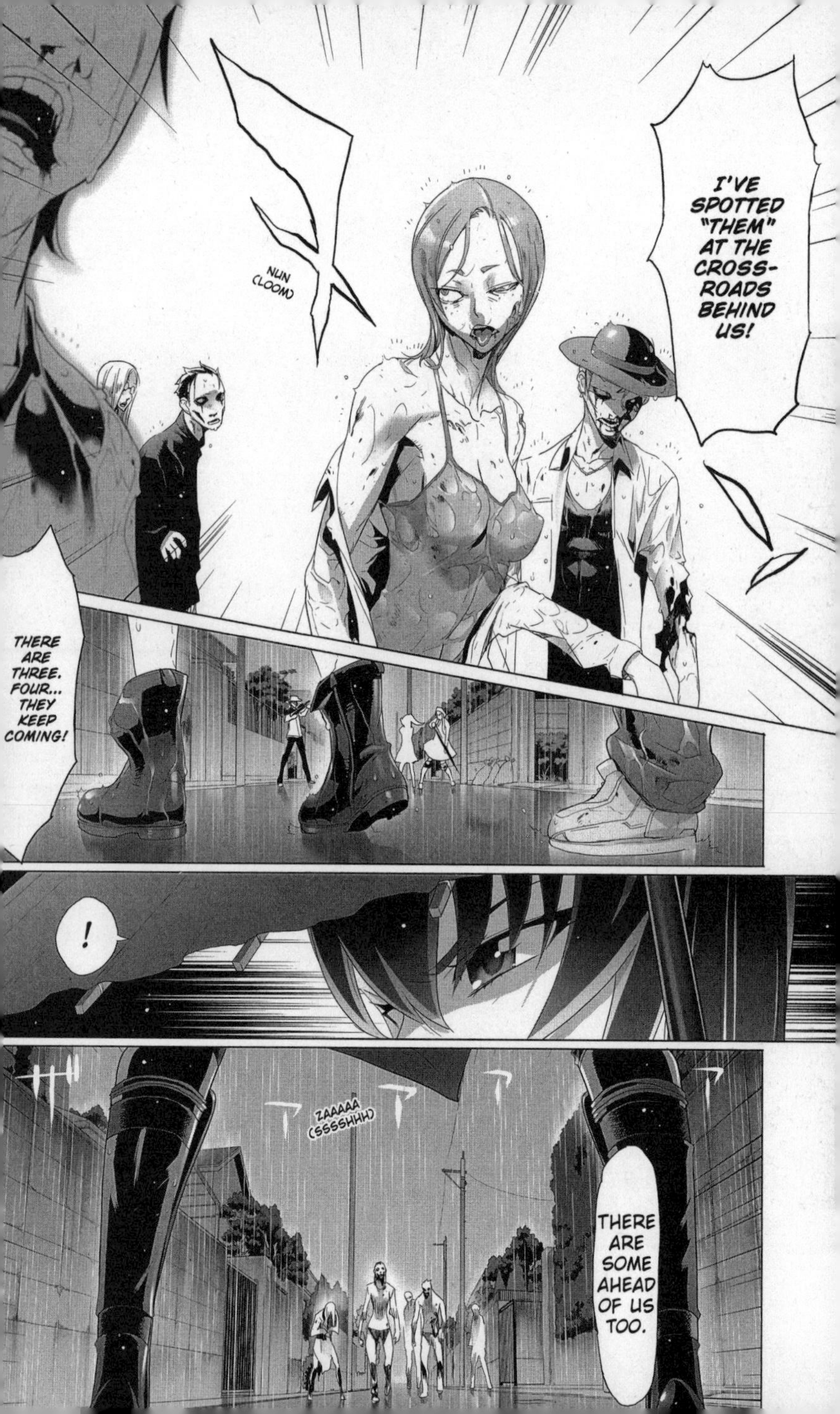

I'VE SPOTTED "THEM" AT THE CROSS-ROADS BEHIND US!
NUN (LOOM)
THERE ARE THREE. FOUR... THEY KEEP COMING!
!
ZAAAAA (SSSSHHH)
THERE ARE SOME AHEAD OF US TOO.

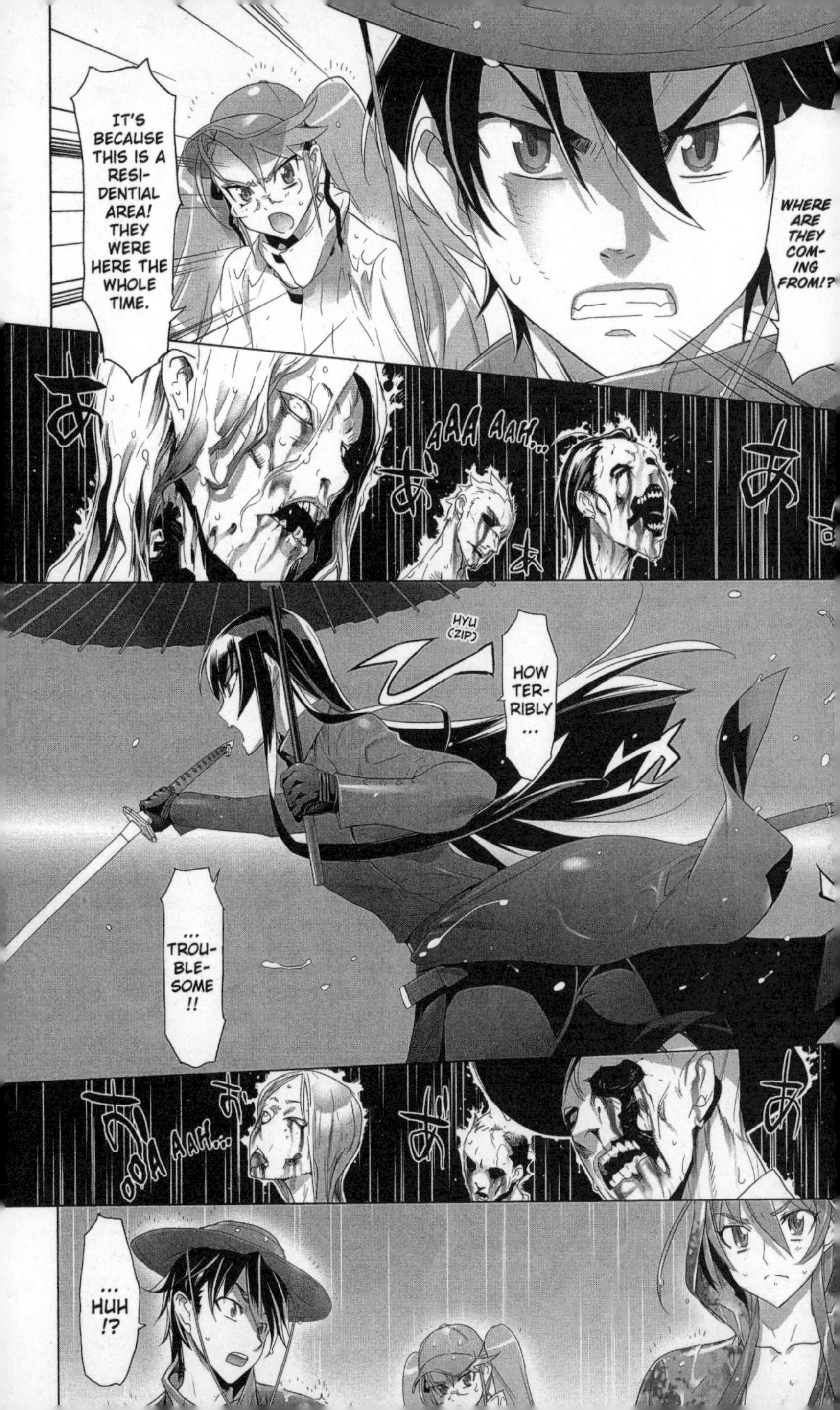
WHERE ARE THEY COMING FROM!?
IT'S BECAUSE THIS IS A RESIDENTIAL AREA! THEY WERE HERE THE WHOLE TIME.
AAA AAH...
HYU (ZIP)
HOW TERRIBLY ...
... TROUBLESOME !!
OOA AAH...
... HUH !?

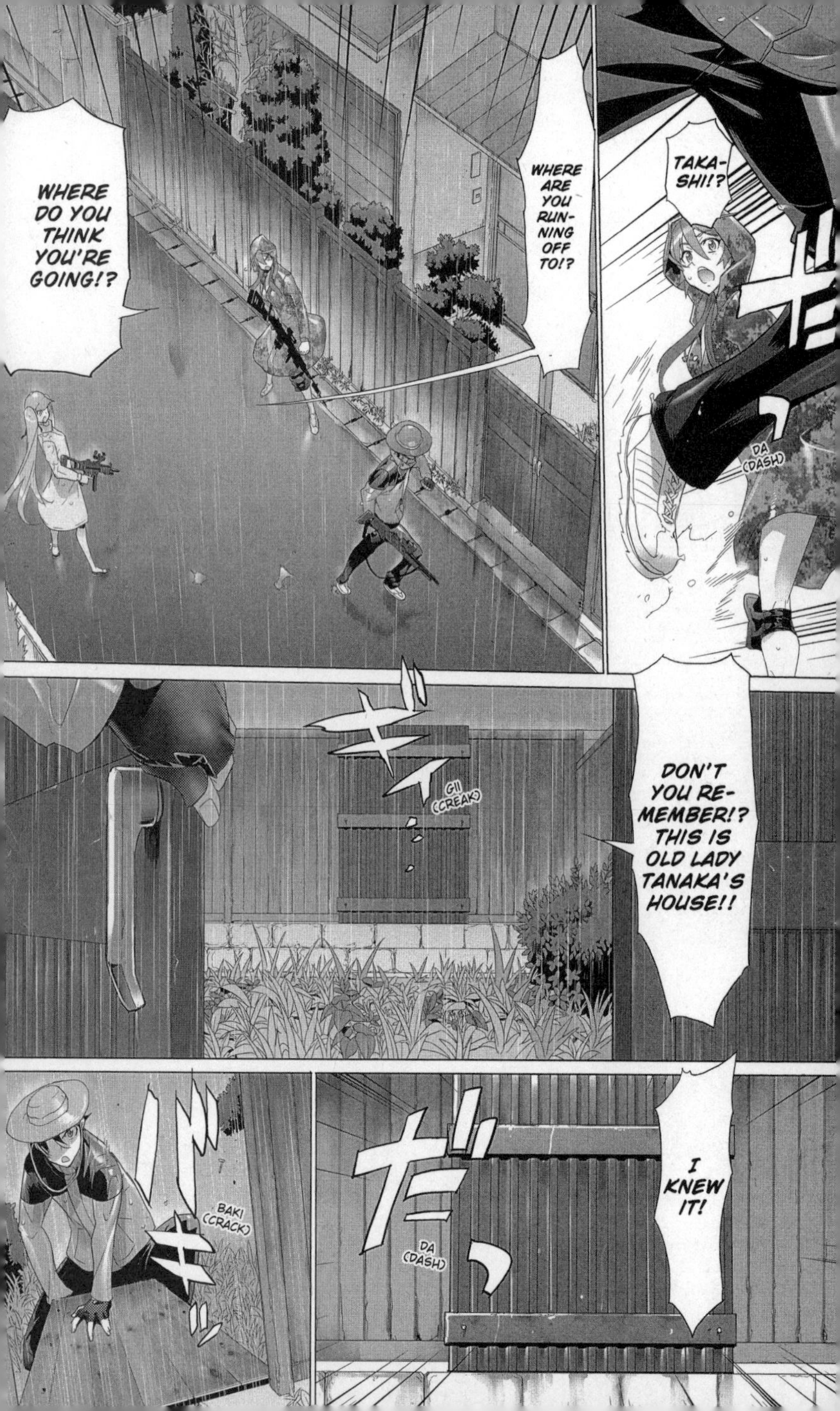
TAKASHI!?
DA (DASH)
WHERE ARE YOU RUNNING OFF TO!?
WHERE DO YOU THINK YOU'RE GOING!?
DON'T YOU REMEMBER!? THIS IS OLD LADY TANAKA'S HOUSE!!
GII (CREAK)
I KNEW IT!
DA (DASH)
BAKI (CRACK)

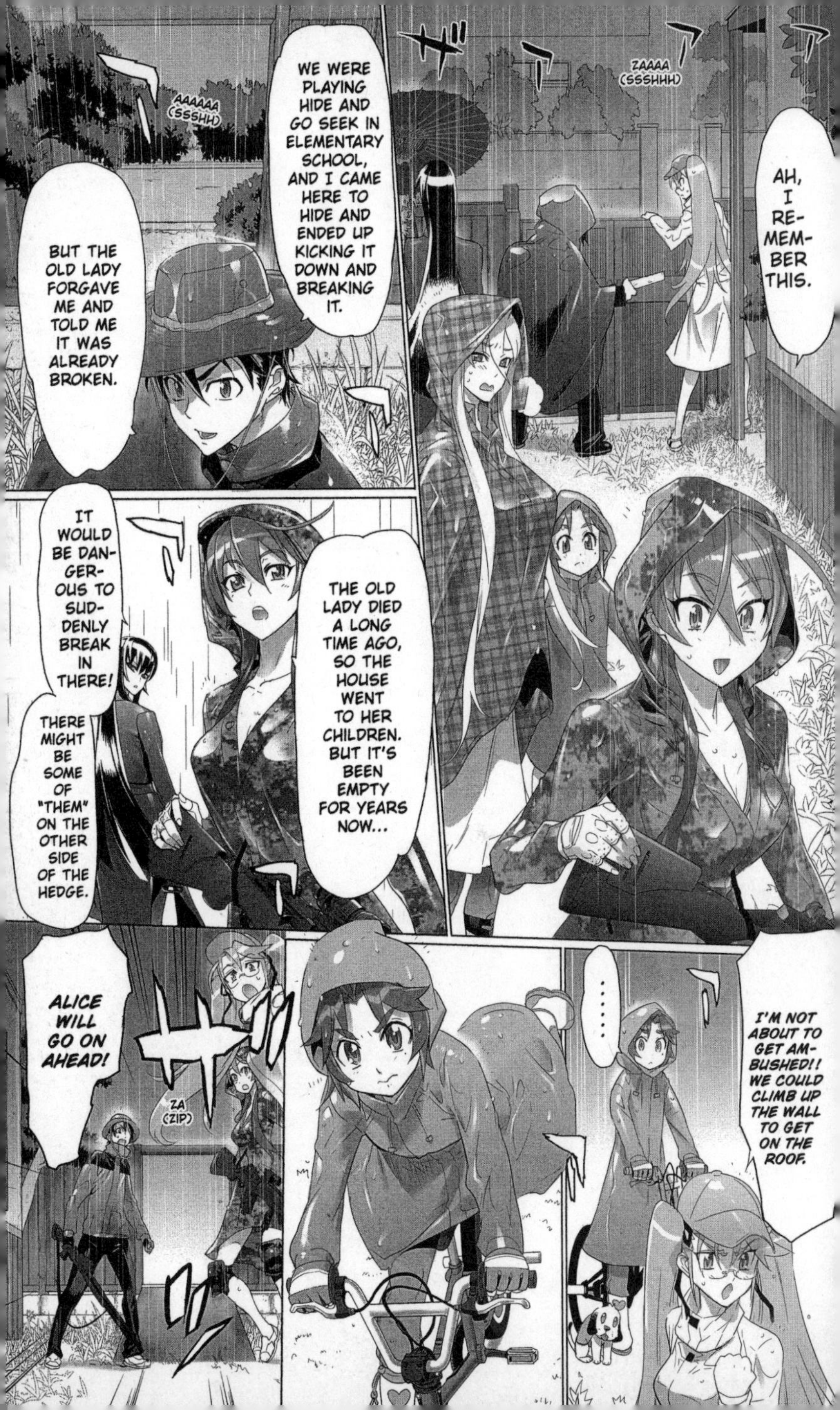
ZAAAA (SSSHHH)
AH, I RE-MEM-BER THIS.
AAAAAA (SSSHH)
WE WERE PLAYING HIDE AND GO SEEK IN ELEMENTARY SCHOOL, AND I CAME HERE TO HIDE AND ENDED UP KICKING IT DOWN AND BREAKING IT.
BUT THE OLD LADY FORGAVE ME AND TOLD ME IT WAS ALREADY BROKEN.
THE OLD LADY DIED A LONG TIME AGO, SO THE HOUSE WENT TO HER CHILDREN. BUT IT'S BEEN EMPTY FOR YEARS NOW...
IT WOULD BE DAN-GER-OUS TO SUD-DENLY BREAK IN THERE!
THERE MIGHT BE SOME OF "THEM" ON THE OTHER SIDE OF THE HEDGE.
I'M NOT ABOUT TO GET AM-BUSHED!! WE COULD CLIMB UP THE WALL TO GET ON THE ROOF.
......
ALICE WILL GO ON AHEAD!
ZA (ZIP)

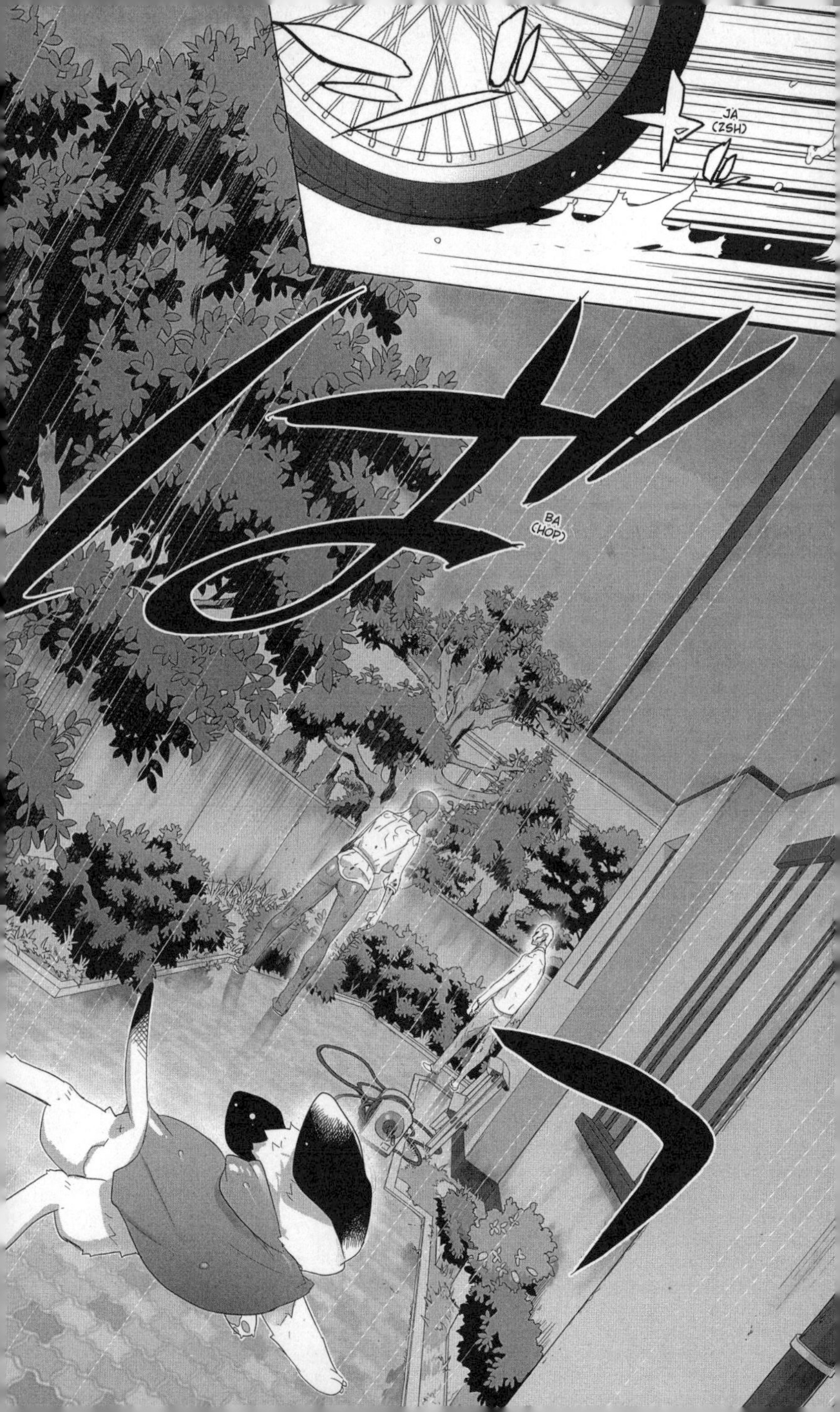

JÀ
(ZSH)
BA
(HOP)

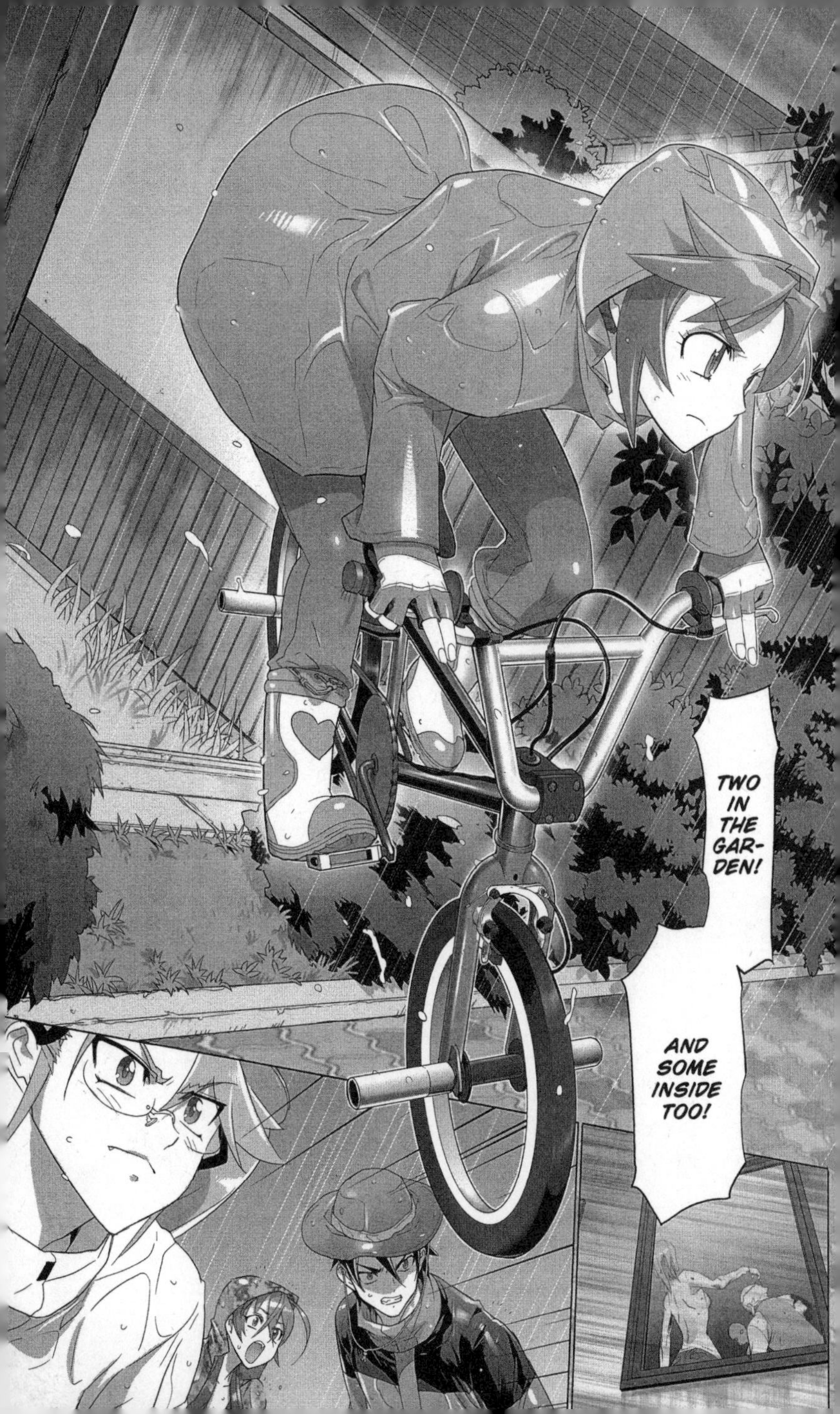
TWO IN THE GAR-DEN!
AND SOME INSIDE TOO!

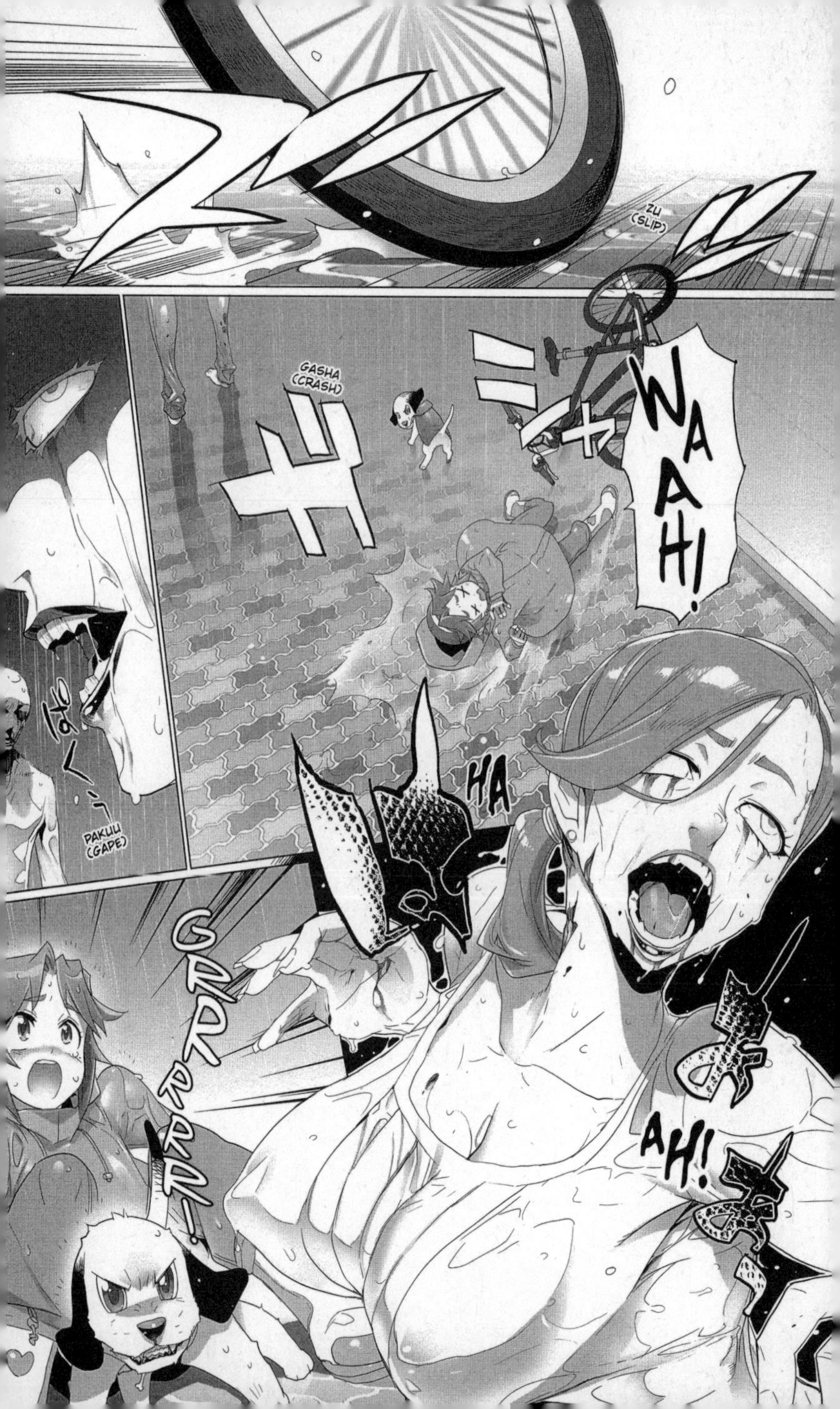

ZU (SLIP)
WAAH!
GASHA (CRASH)
PAKUU (GAPE)
HA
AH!
GRRRRRR!

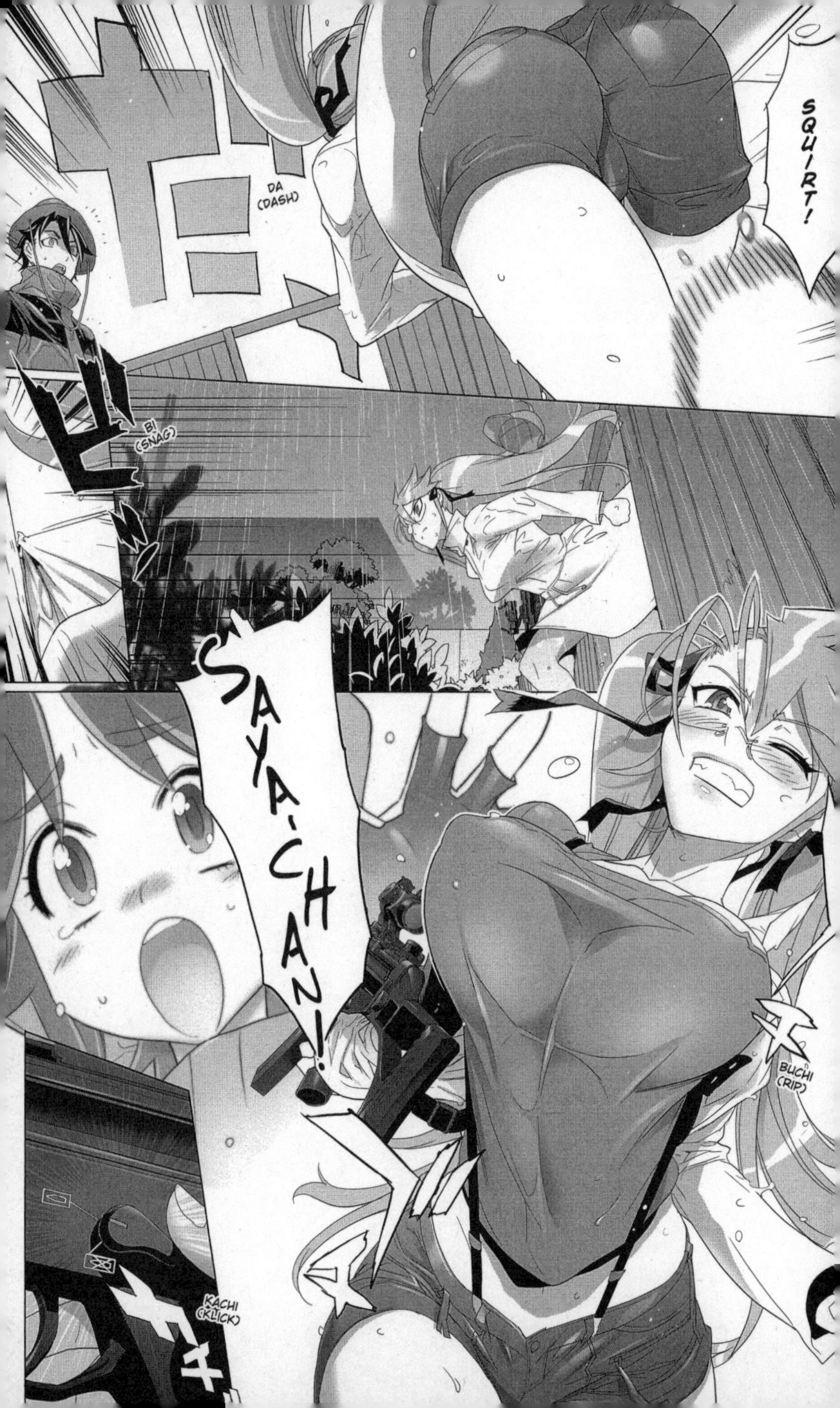
SQUIRT!
DA (DASH)
BI (SNAG)
BUCHI (RIP)
SAYA-CHAN!
KACHI (KLICK)

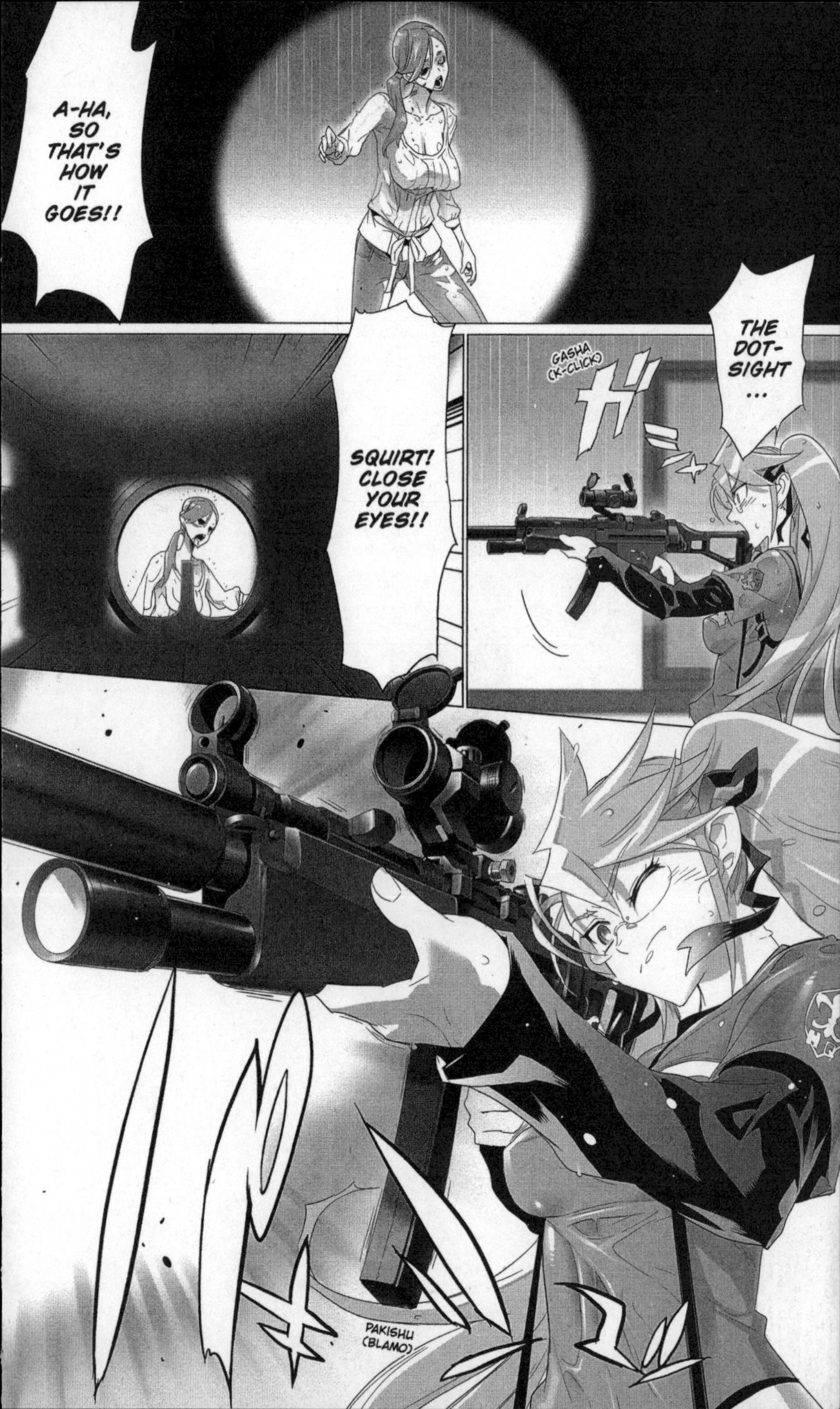

A-HA, SO THAT'S HOW IT GOES!!
GASHA (K-CLICK)
THE DOT-SIGHT...
SQUIRT! CLOSE YOUR EYES!!
PAKISHU (BLAMO)

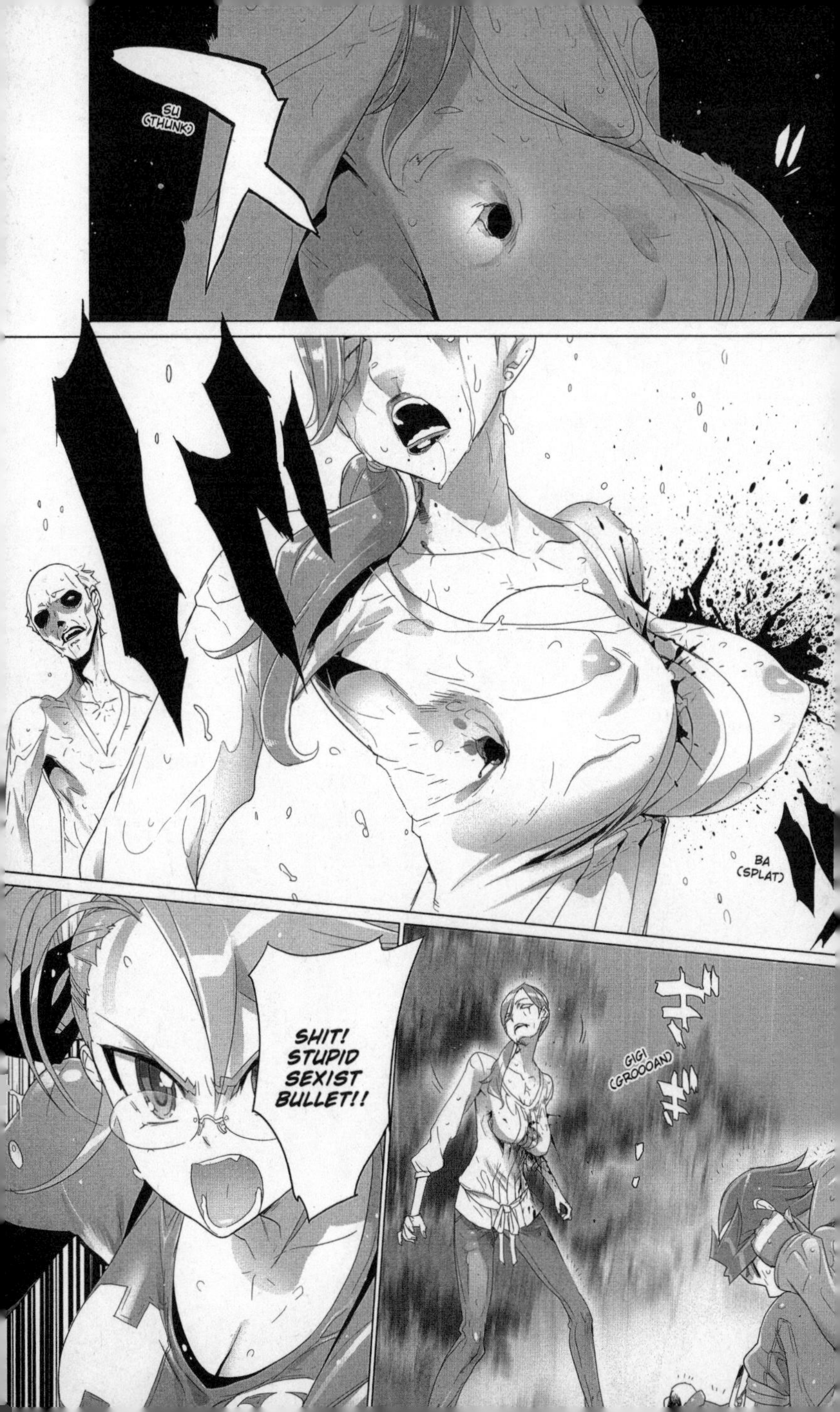
SU
(THUNK)
BA
(SPLAT)
GIGI
(GROOOAN)
SHIT!
STUPID
SEXIST
BULLET!!

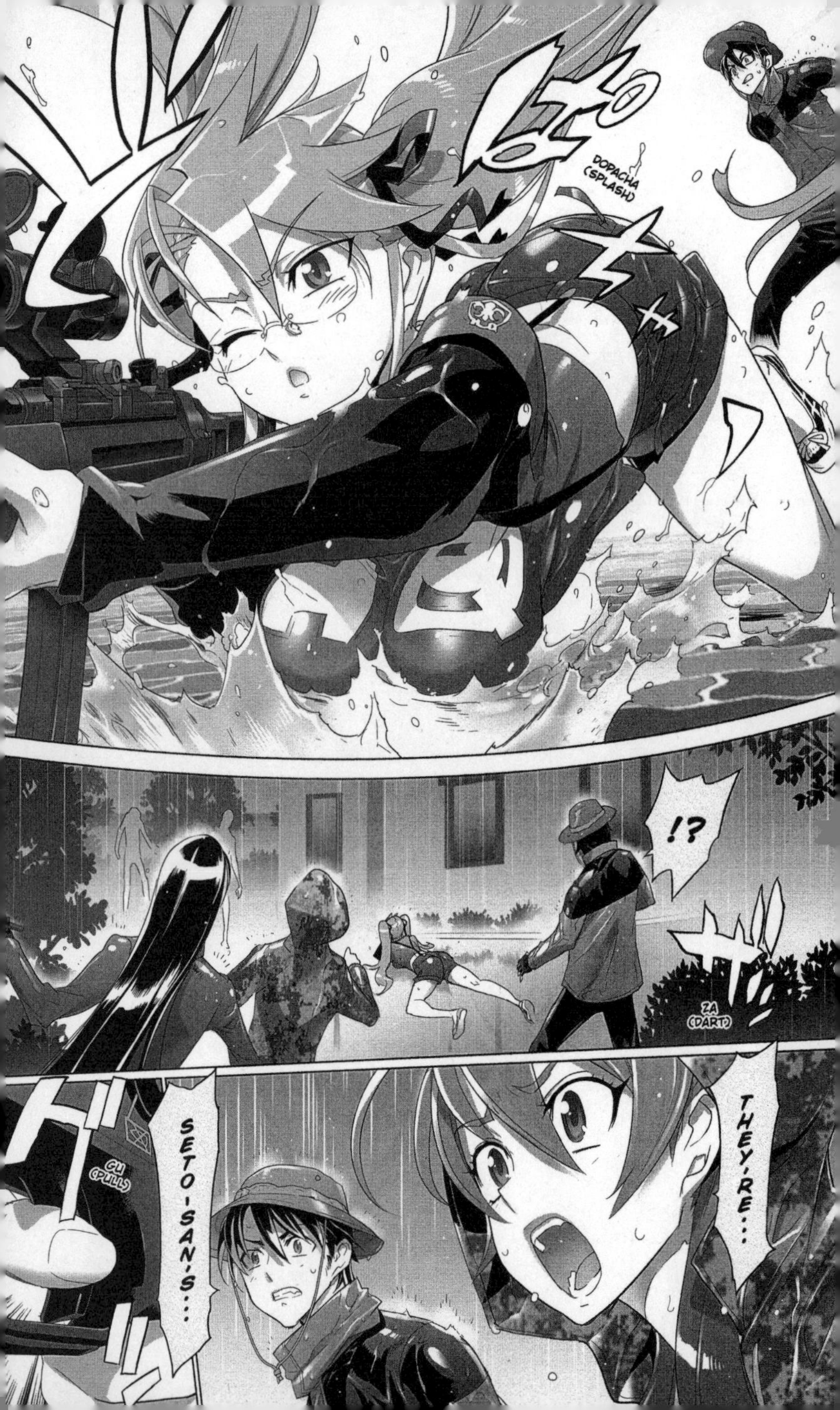
DOPACHA (SPLASH)
!?
ZA (DART)
THEY'RE...
SETO-SAN'S...
GU (PULL)

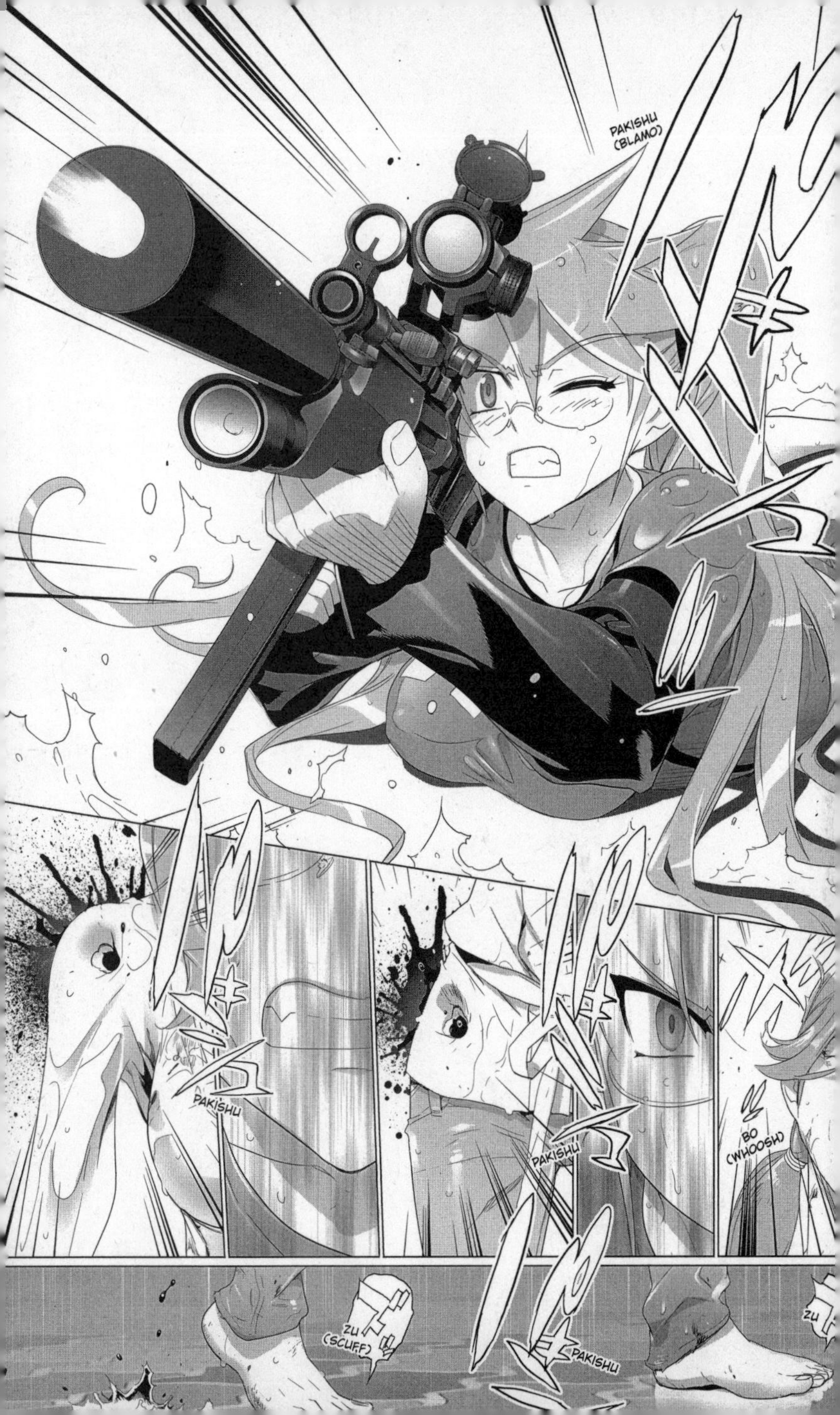
PAKISHU (BLAMO)
BO (WHOOSH)
PAKISHU
PAKISHU
ZU
PAKISHU
ZU (SCUFF)

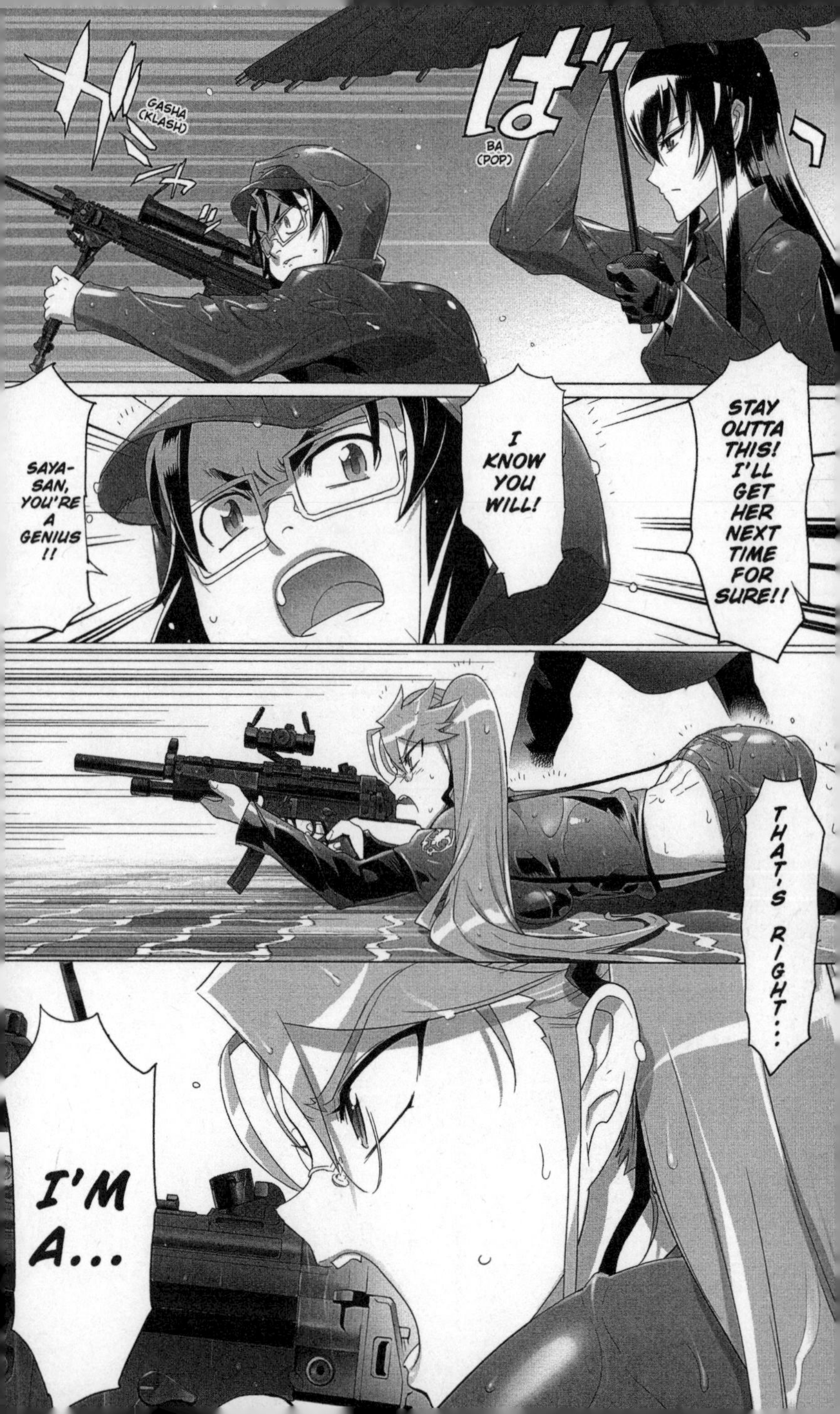

ば
BA (POP)
ガシャ
GASHA (KLASH)
STAY OUTTA THIS! I'LL GET HER NEXT TIME FOR SURE!!
I KNOW YOU WILL!
SAYA-SAN, YOU'RE A GENIUS!!
THAT'S RIGHT...
I'M A...

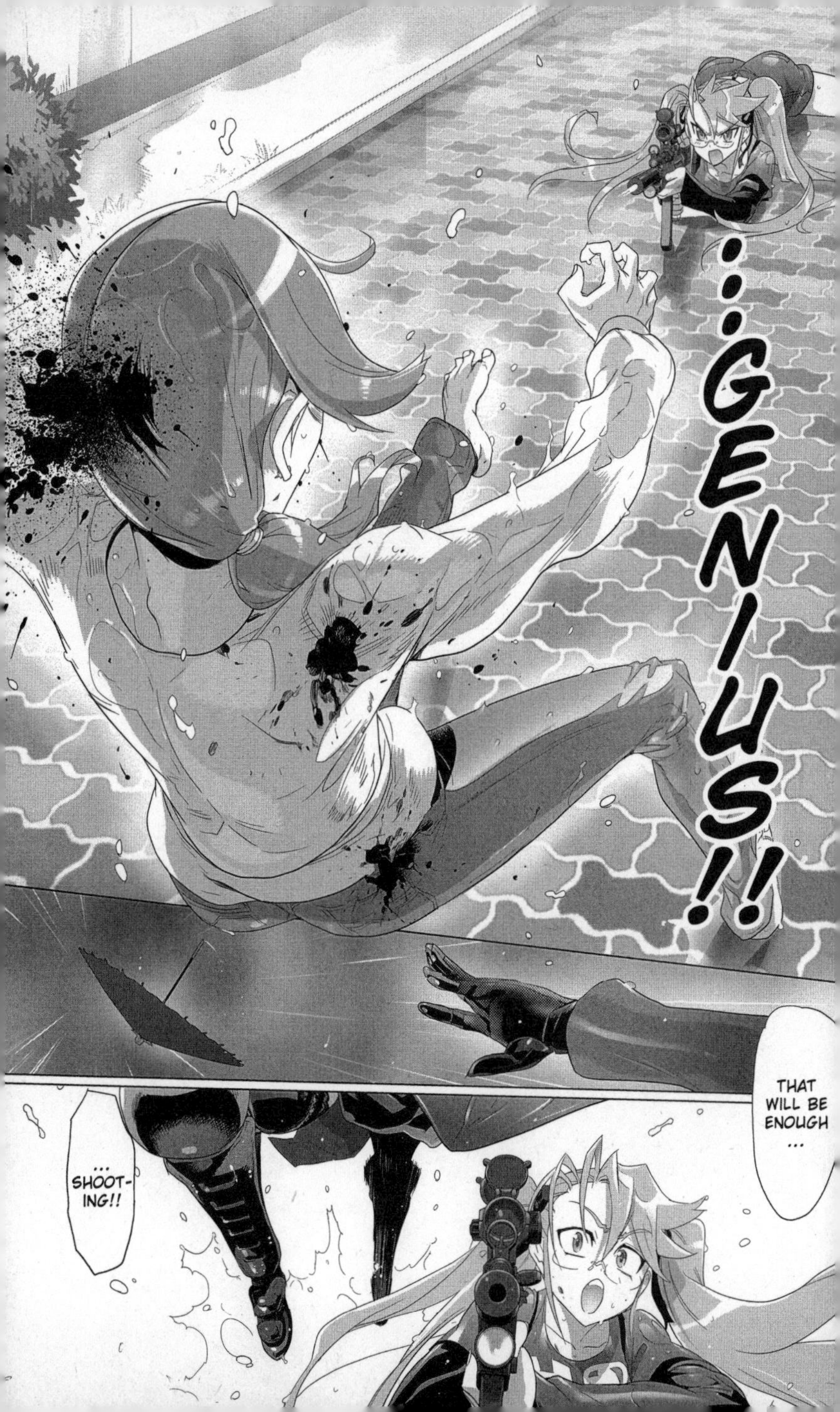
...GENIUS!!
THAT WILL BE ENOUGH ...
... SHOOT-ING!!

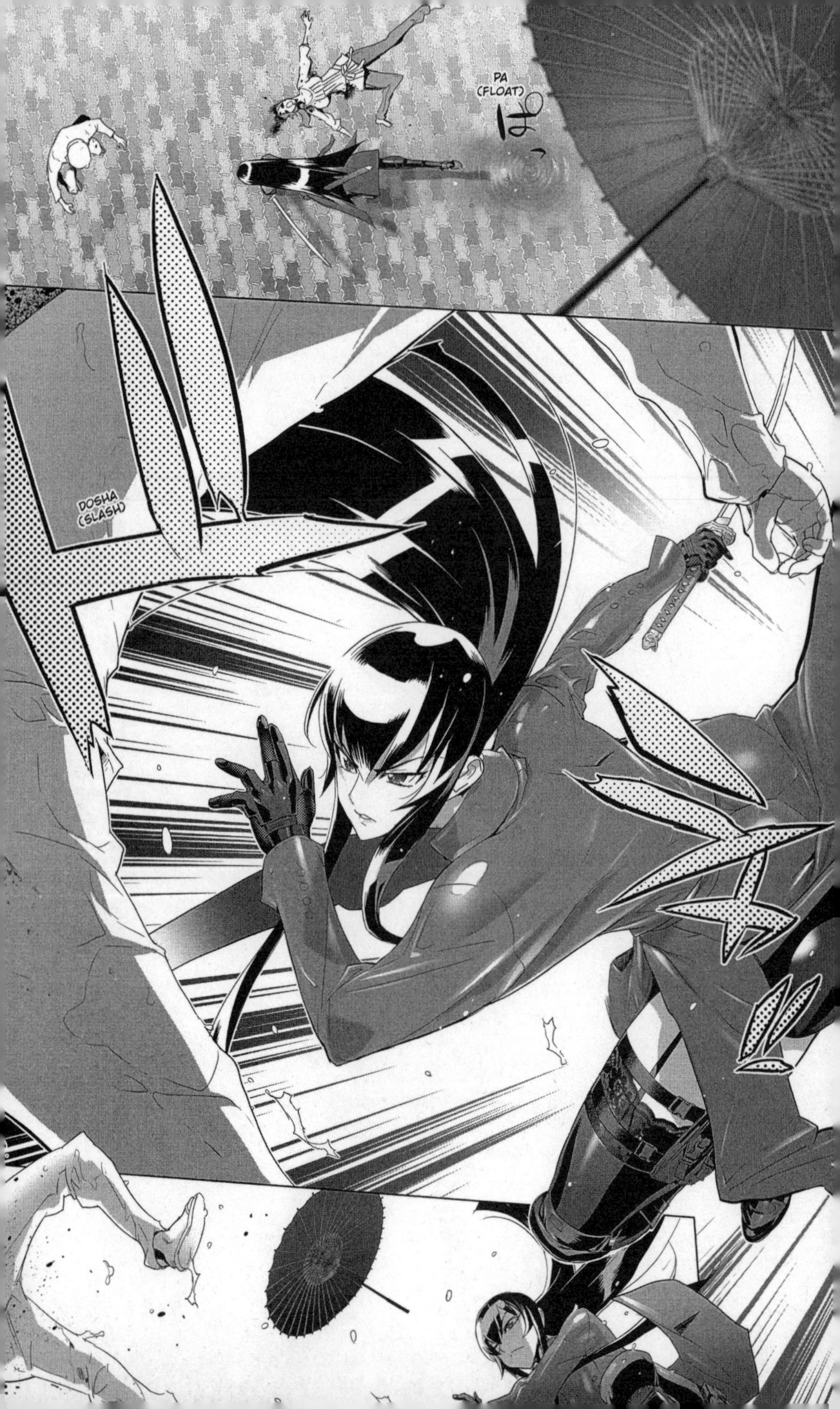
PA
(FLOAT)
ぱっ
DOSHA
(SLASH)

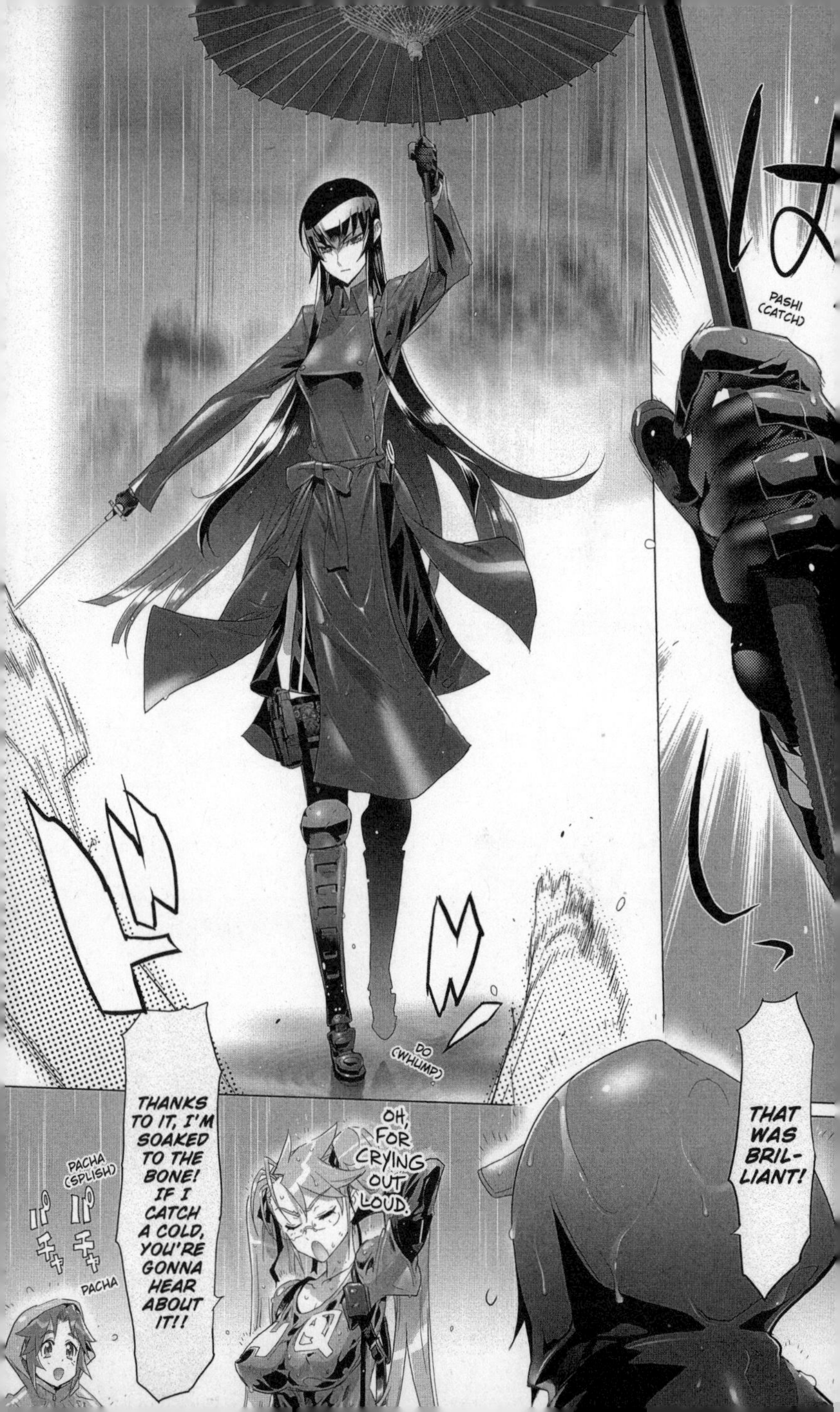
PASHI (CATCH)
DO (WHUMP)
THAT WAS BRIL-LIANT!
OH, FOR CRYING OUT LOUD.
THANKS TO IT, I'M SOAKED TO THE BONE! IF I CATCH A COLD, YOU'RE GONNA HEAR ABOUT IT!!
PACHA (SPLISH)
パチャ
パチャ
PACHA

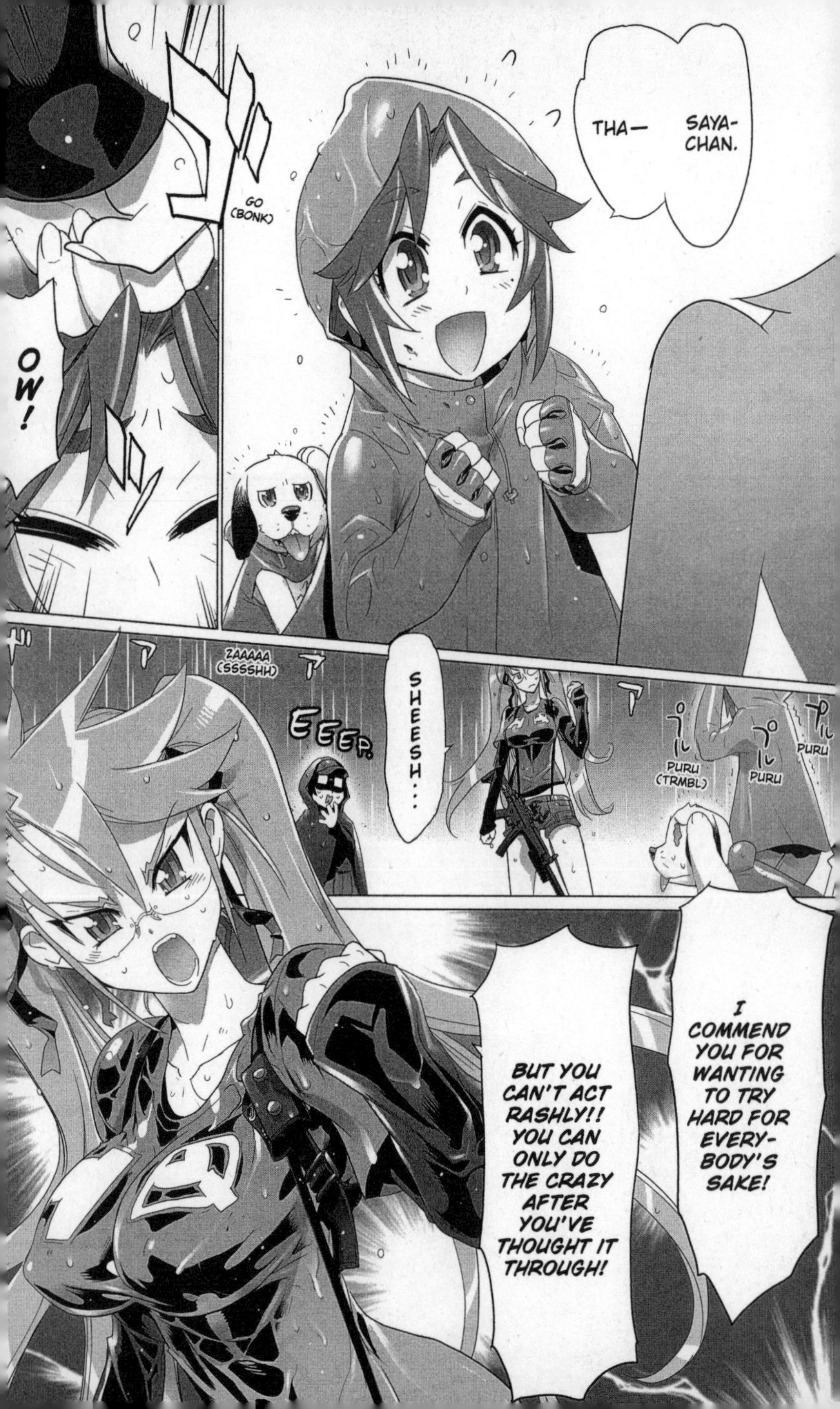

SAYA-CHAN.
THA—
GO (BONK)
OW!
PURU
PURU
PURU (TRMBL)
SHEESH...
EEEP.
ZAAAAA (SSSSHH)
I COMMEND YOU FOR WANTING TO TRY HARD FOR EVERY-BODY'S SAKE!
BUT YOU CAN'T ACT RASHLY!! YOU CAN ONLY DO THE CRAZY AFTER YOU'VE THOUGHT IT THROUGH!

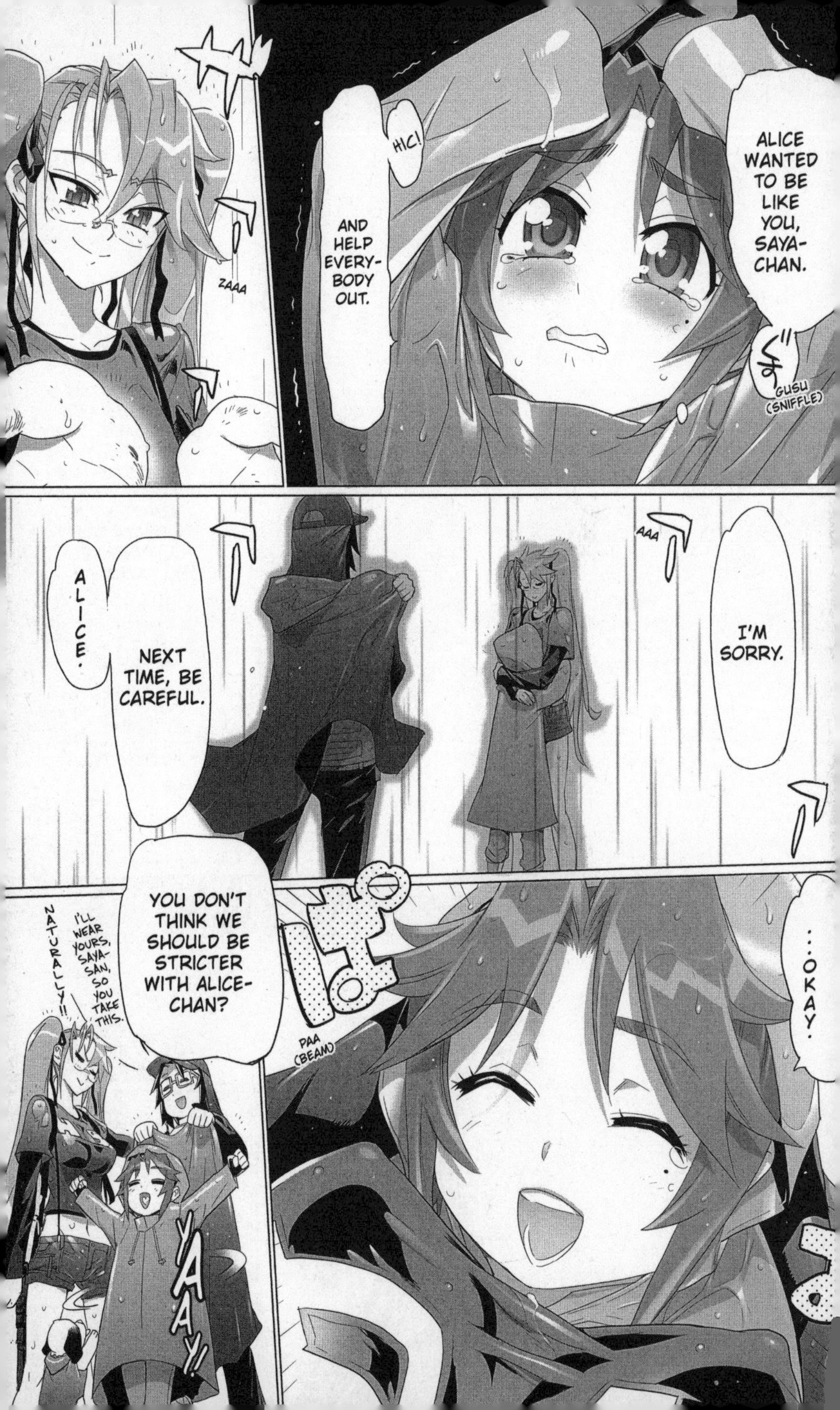
ALICE WANTED TO BE LIKE YOU, SAYA-CHAN.
HIC!
AND HELP EVERY-BODY OUT.
GUSU (SNIFFLE)
ZAAA
I'M SORRY.
AAA
ALICE.
NEXT TIME, BE CAREFUL.
...OKAY.
PAA (BEAM)
YOU DON'T THINK WE SHOULD BE STRICTER WITH ALICE-CHAN?
I'LL WEAR YOURS, SAYA-SAN, SO YOU TAKE THIS.
NATURALLY!!
YAAAY!

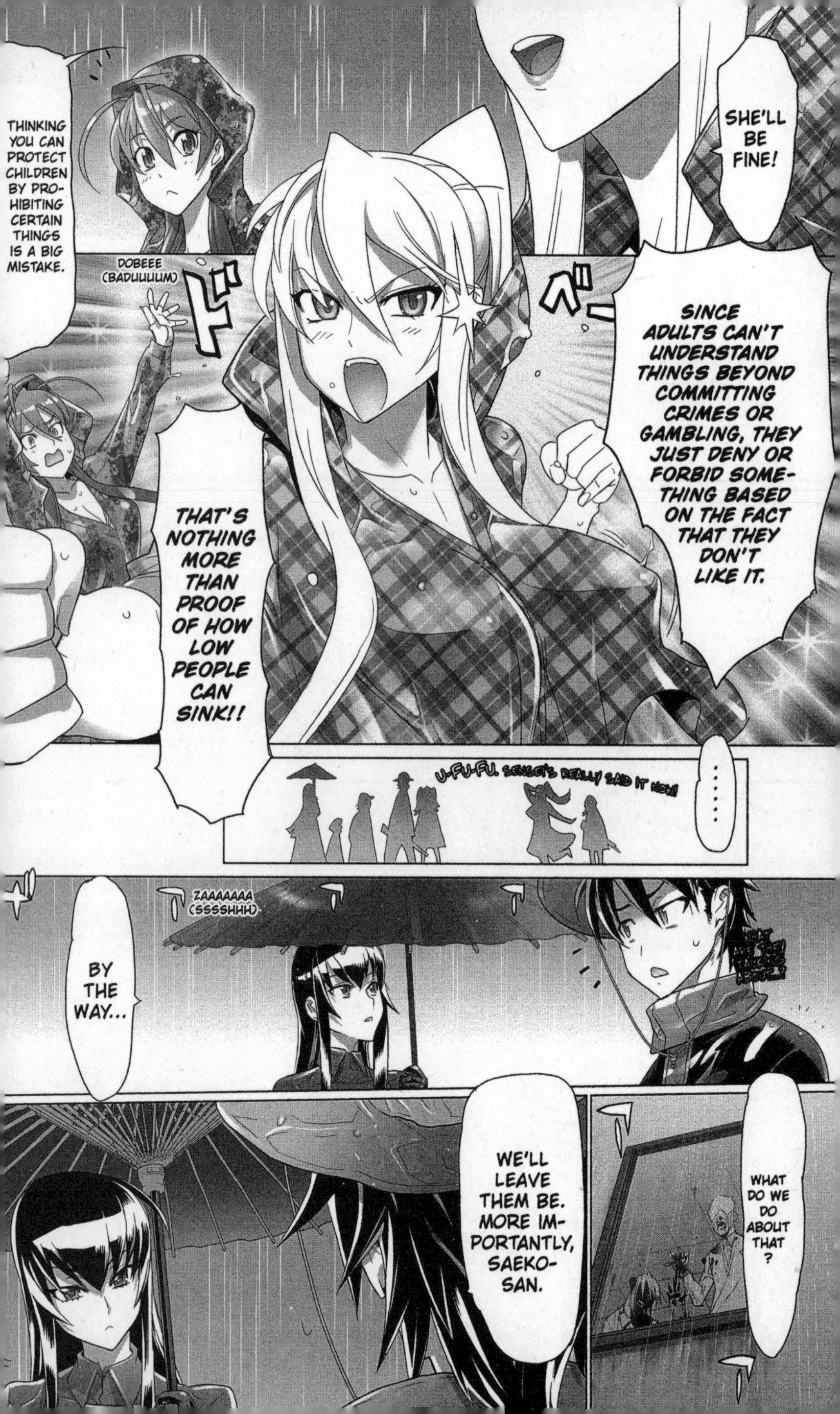
SHE'LL BE FINE!
THINKING YOU CAN PROTECT CHILDREN BY PROHIBITING CERTAIN THINGS IS A BIG MISTAKE.
SINCE ADULTS CAN'T UNDERSTAND THINGS BEYOND COMMITTING CRIMES OR GAMBLING, THEY JUST DENY OR FORBID SOMETHING BASED ON THE FACT THAT THEY DON'T LIKE IT.
THAT'S NOTHING MORE THAN PROOF OF HOW LOW PEOPLE CAN SINK!!
DOBEEE (BADUUUUM)
......
U-FU-FU. SENSEI'S REALLY SAID IT NOW!
WHAT ARE THEY TALKING ABOUT...?
ZAAAAAAA (SSSSHHH)
BY THE WAY...
WHAT DO WE DO ABOUT THAT?
WE'LL LEAVE THEM BE. MORE IMPORTANTLY, SAEKO-SAN.

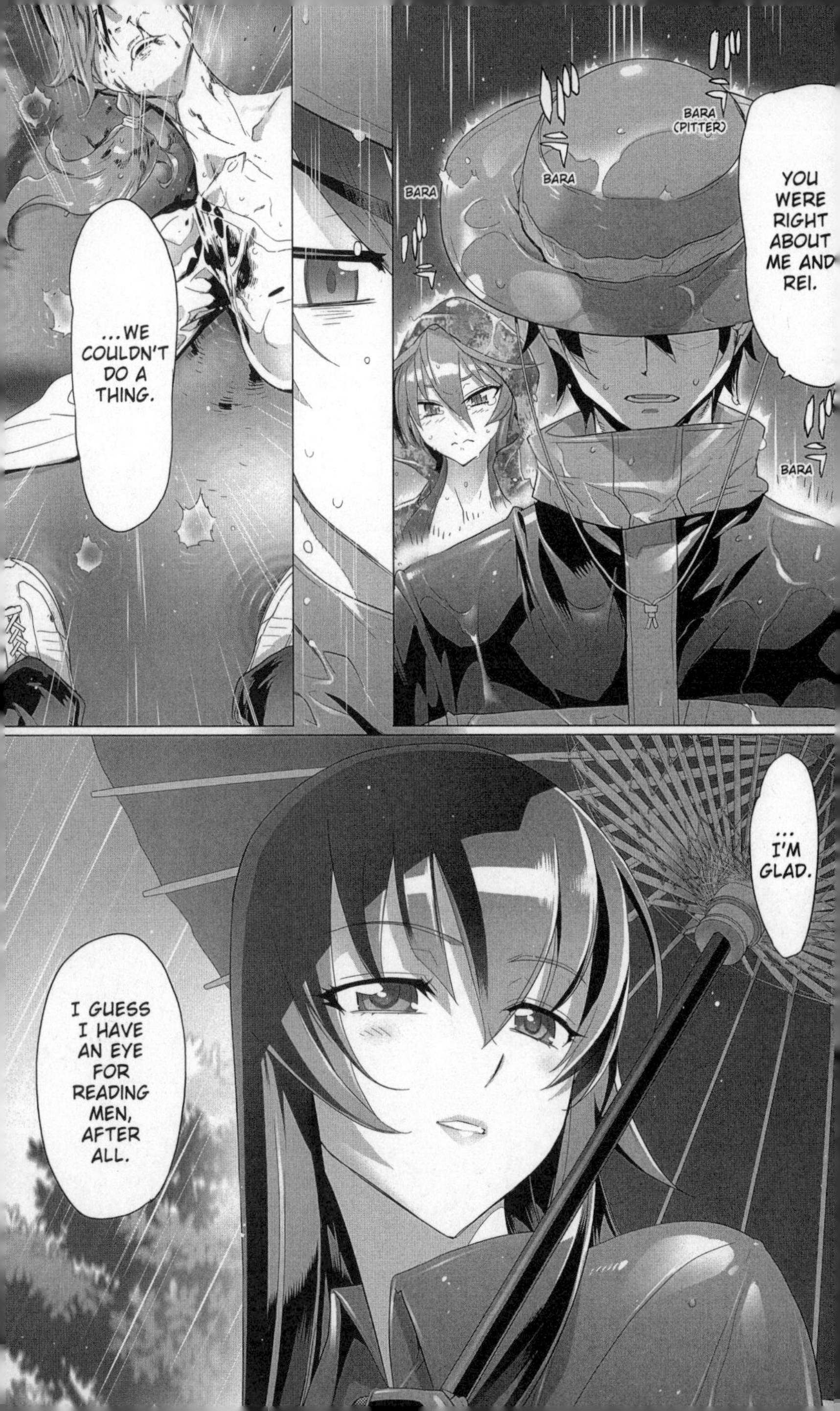
YOU WERE RIGHT ABOUT ME AND REI.
BARA (PITTER)
BARA
BARA
BARA
...WE COULDN'T DO A THING.
... I'M GLAD.
I GUESS I HAVE AN EYE FOR READING MEN, AFTER ALL.

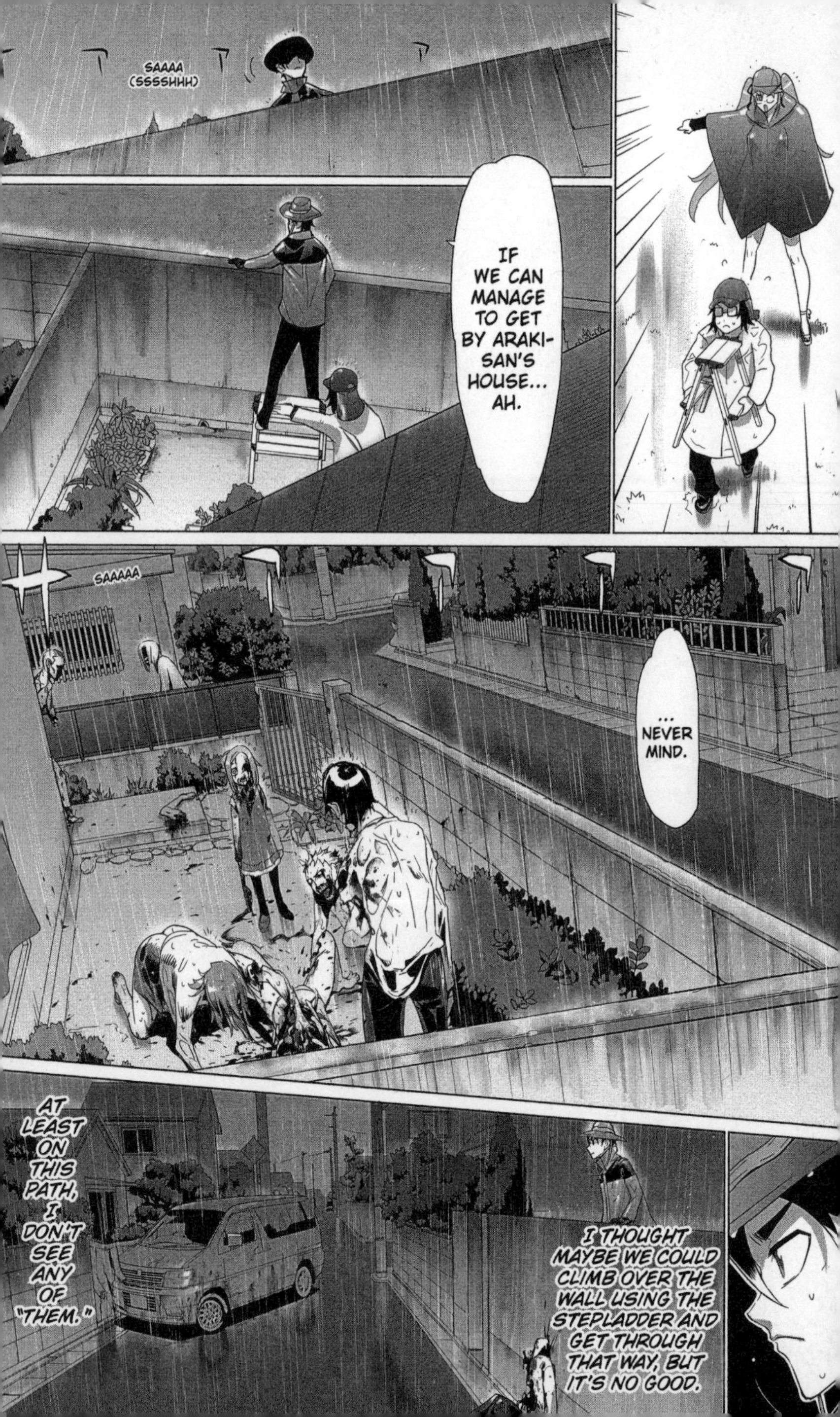
SAAAA (SSSSHHH)
IF WE CAN MANAGE TO GET BY ARAKI-SAN'S HOUSE... AH.
SAAAAA
... NEVER MIND.
I THOUGHT MAYBE WE COULD CLIMB OVER THE WALL USING THE STEPLADDER AND GET THROUGH THAT WAY, BUT IT'S NO GOOD.
AT LEAST ON THIS PATH, I DON'T SEE ANY OF "THEM."

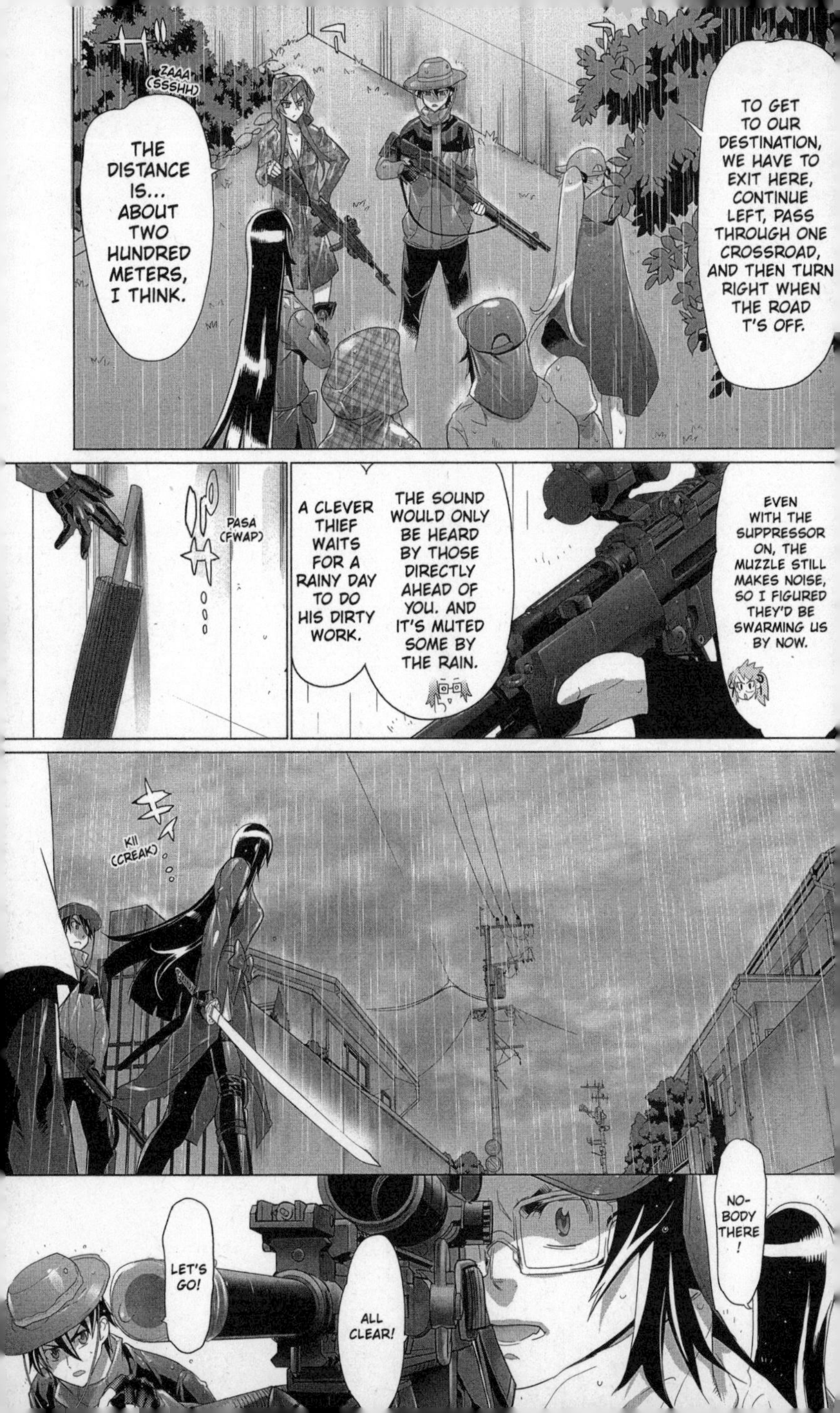
TO GET TO OUR DESTINATION, WE HAVE TO EXIT HERE, CONTINUE LEFT, PASS THROUGH ONE CROSSROAD, AND THEN TURN RIGHT WHEN THE ROAD T'S OFF.
ZAAA (SSSHH)
THE DISTANCE IS... ABOUT TWO HUNDRED METERS, I THINK.
EVEN WITH THE SUPPRESSOR ON, THE MUZZLE STILL MAKES NOISE, SO I FIGURED THEY'D BE SWARMING US BY NOW.
THE SOUND WOULD ONLY BE HEARD BY THOSE DIRECTLY AHEAD OF YOU. AND IT'S MUTED SOME BY THE RAIN.
A CLEVER THIEF WAITS FOR A RAINY DAY TO DO HIS DIRTY WORK.
PASA (FWAP)
KII (CREAK)
NO-BODY THERE!
ALL CLEAR!
LET'S GO!

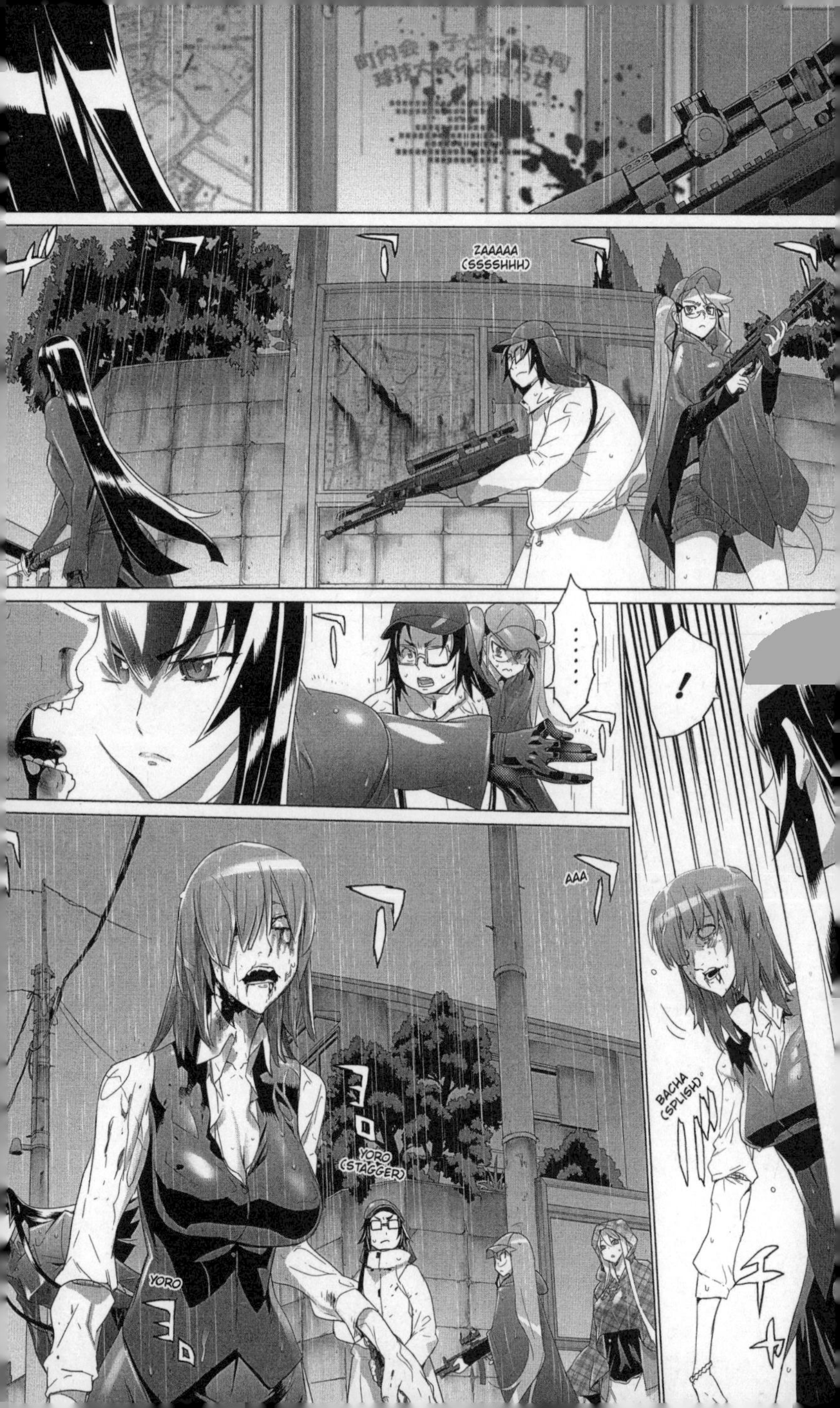
ZAAAAA (SSSSHHH)
!
BACHA (SPLISH)
......
AAA
YORO (STAGGER)
YORO

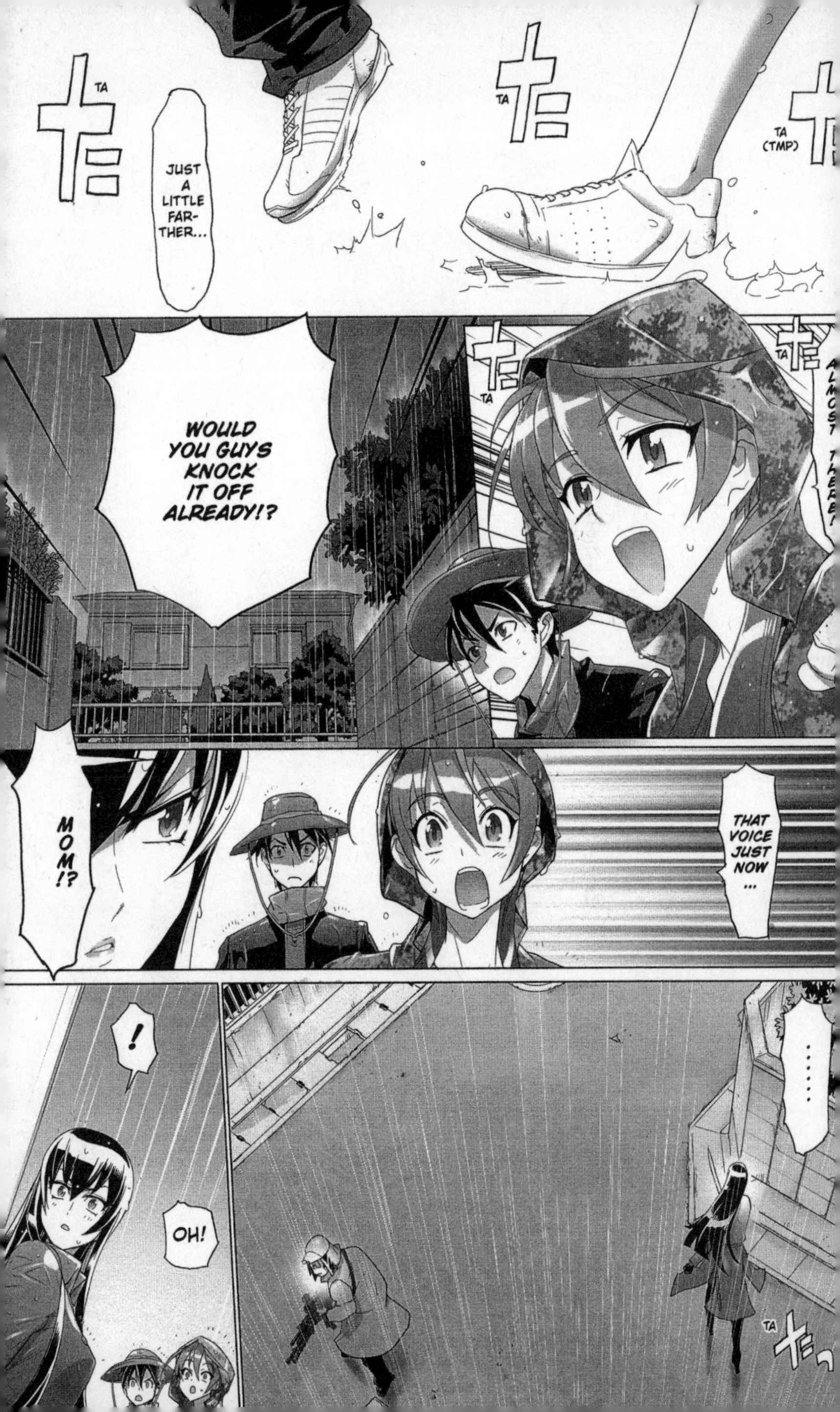
TA (TMP)
TA
JUST A LITTLE FAR-THER...
TA
TA
ALMOST THERE!
TA
WOULD YOU GUYS KNOCK IT OFF ALREADY!?
THAT VOICE JUST NOW...
MOM!?
......
TA
!
OH!

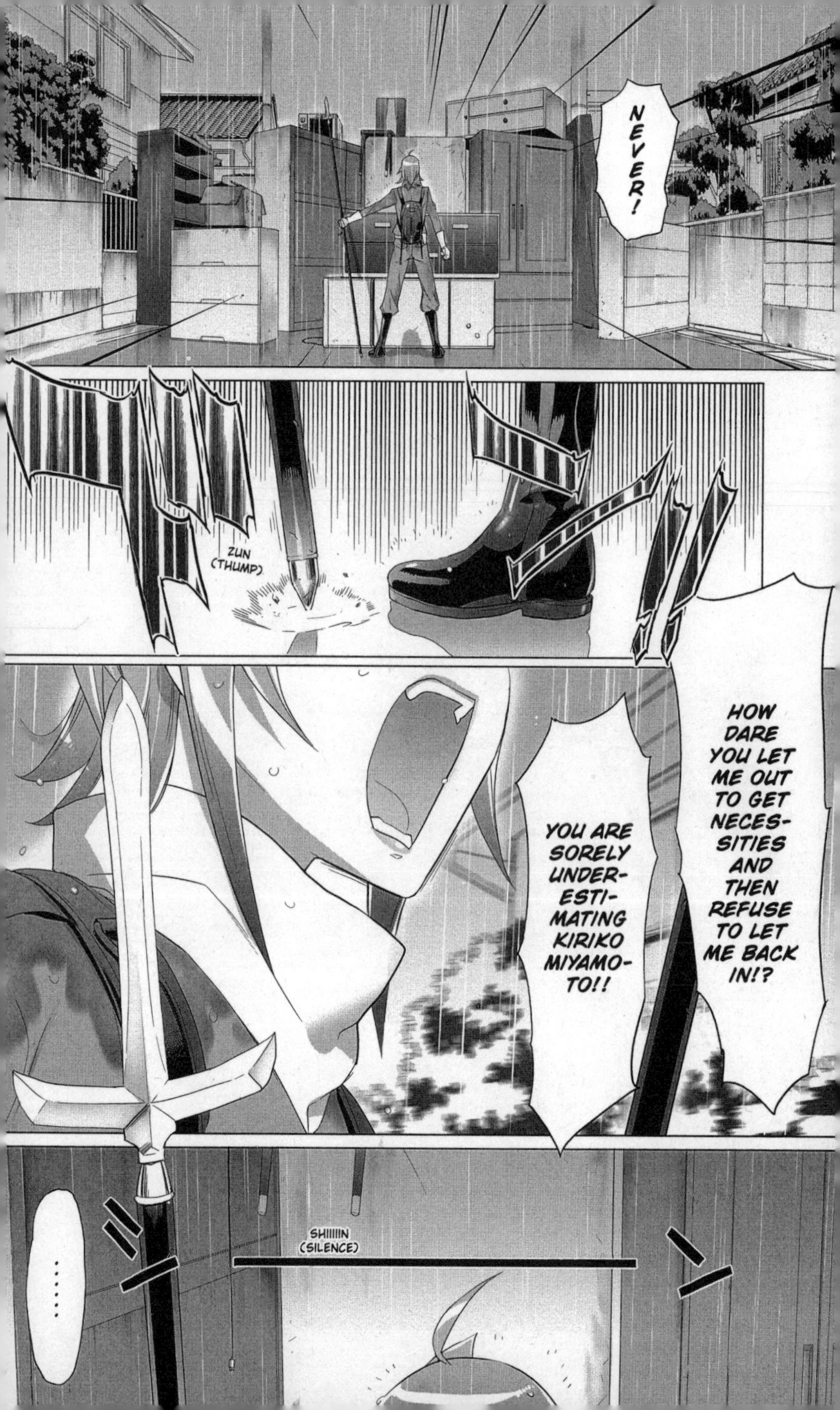
NEVER!
ZUN (THUMP)
HOW DARE YOU LET ME OUT TO GET NECES-SITIES AND THEN REFUSE TO LET ME BACK IN!?
YOU ARE SORELY UNDER-ESTI-MATING KIRIKO MIYAMO-TO!!
SHIIIIIN (SILENCE)
......

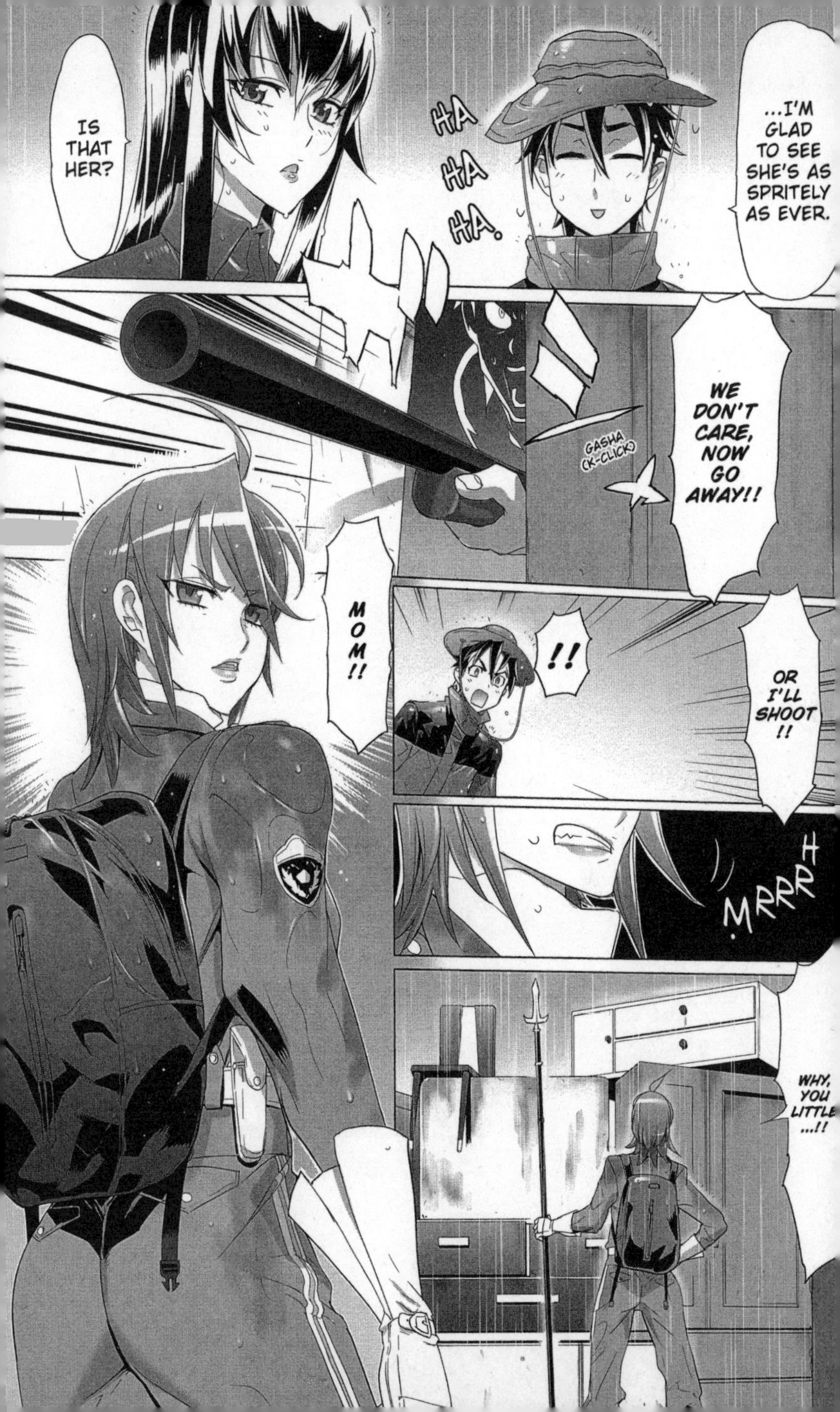

...I'M GLAD TO SEE SHE'S AS SPRITELY AS EVER.
HA HA HA.
IS THAT HER?
WE DON'T CARE, NOW GO AWAY!!
GASHA (K-CLICK)
OR I'LL SHOOT!!
!!
MRRRH
WHY, YOU LITTLE...!!
MOM!!

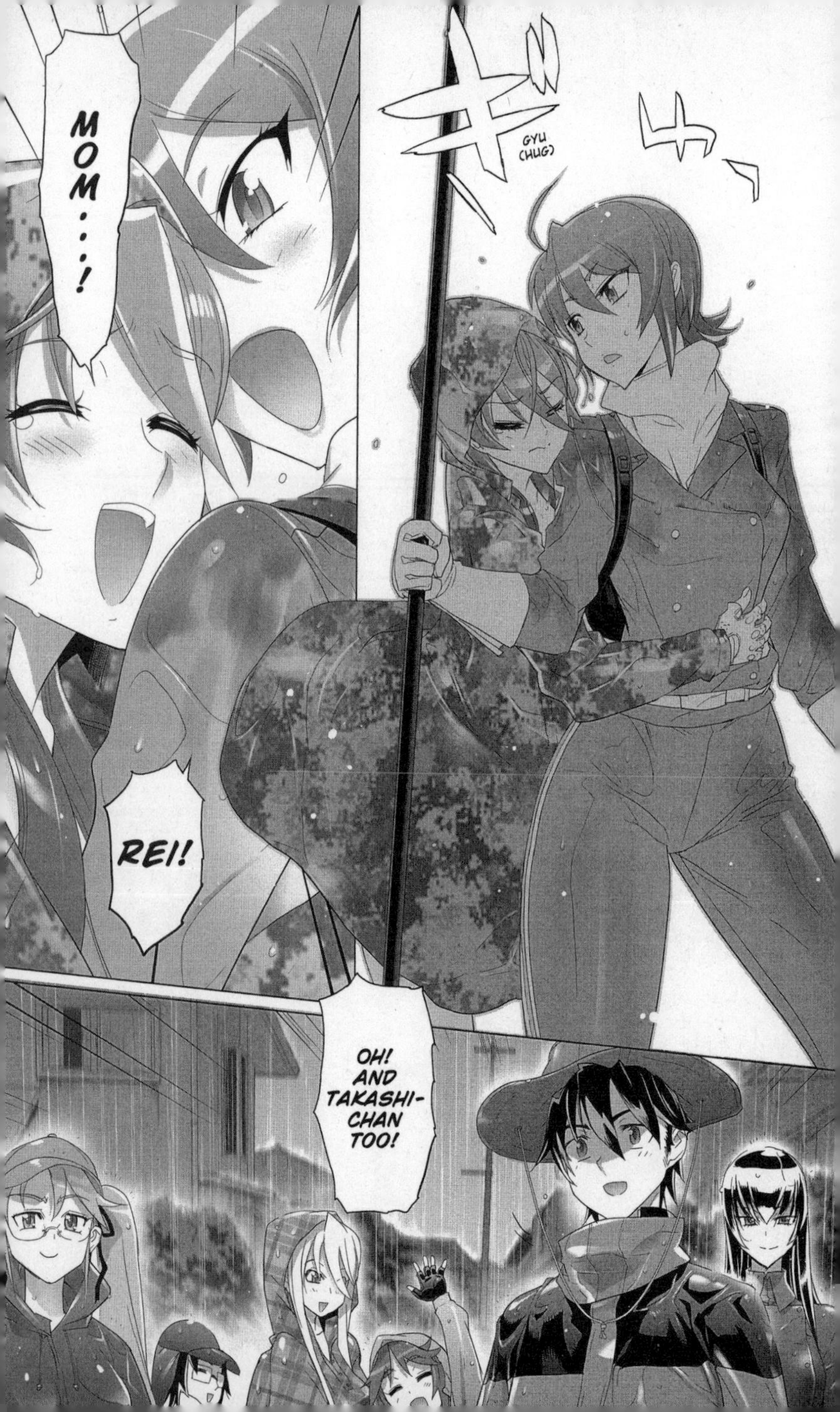
GYU (HUG)
MOM...!
REI!
OH! AND TAKASHI-CHAN TOO!

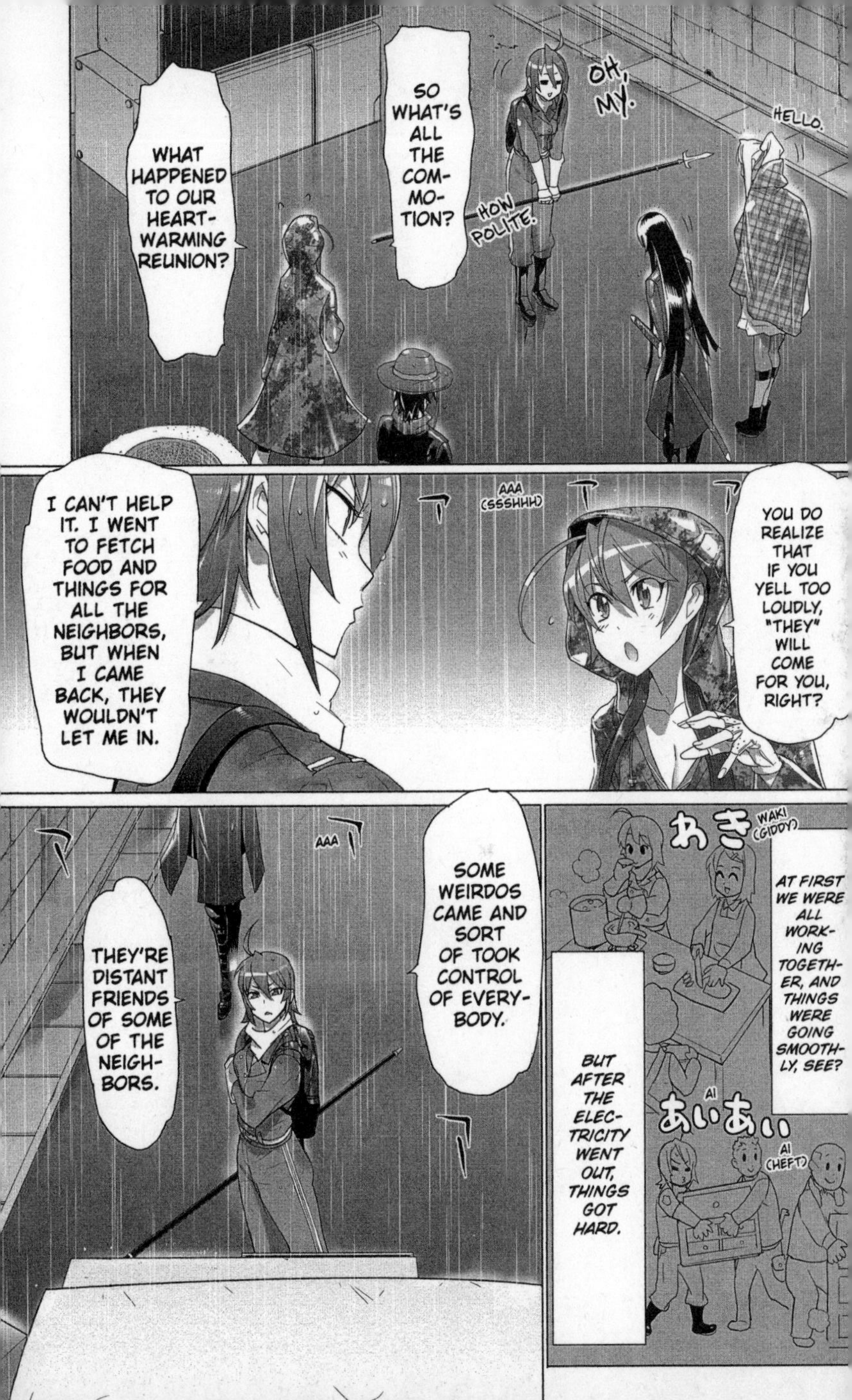
HELLO.
OH, MY.
SO WHAT'S ALL THE COMMOTION?
HOW POLITE.
WHAT HAPPENED TO OUR HEARTWARMING REUNION?
YOU DO REALIZE THAT IF YOU YELL TOO LOUDLY, "THEY" WILL COME FOR YOU, RIGHT?
AAA (SSSHHH)
I CAN'T HELP IT. I WENT TO FETCH FOOD AND THINGS FOR ALL THE NEIGHBORS, BUT WHEN I CAME BACK, THEY WOULDN'T LET ME IN.
わき
WAKI (GIDDY)
AT FIRST WE WERE ALL WORKING TOGETHER, AND THINGS WERE GOING SMOOTHLY, SEE?
あいあい
AI
AI (HEFT)
BUT AFTER THE ELECTRICITY WENT OUT, THINGS GOT HARD.
AAA
SOME WEIRDOS CAME AND SORT OF TOOK CONTROL OF EVERYBODY.
THEY'RE DISTANT FRIENDS OF SOME OF THE NEIGHBORS.

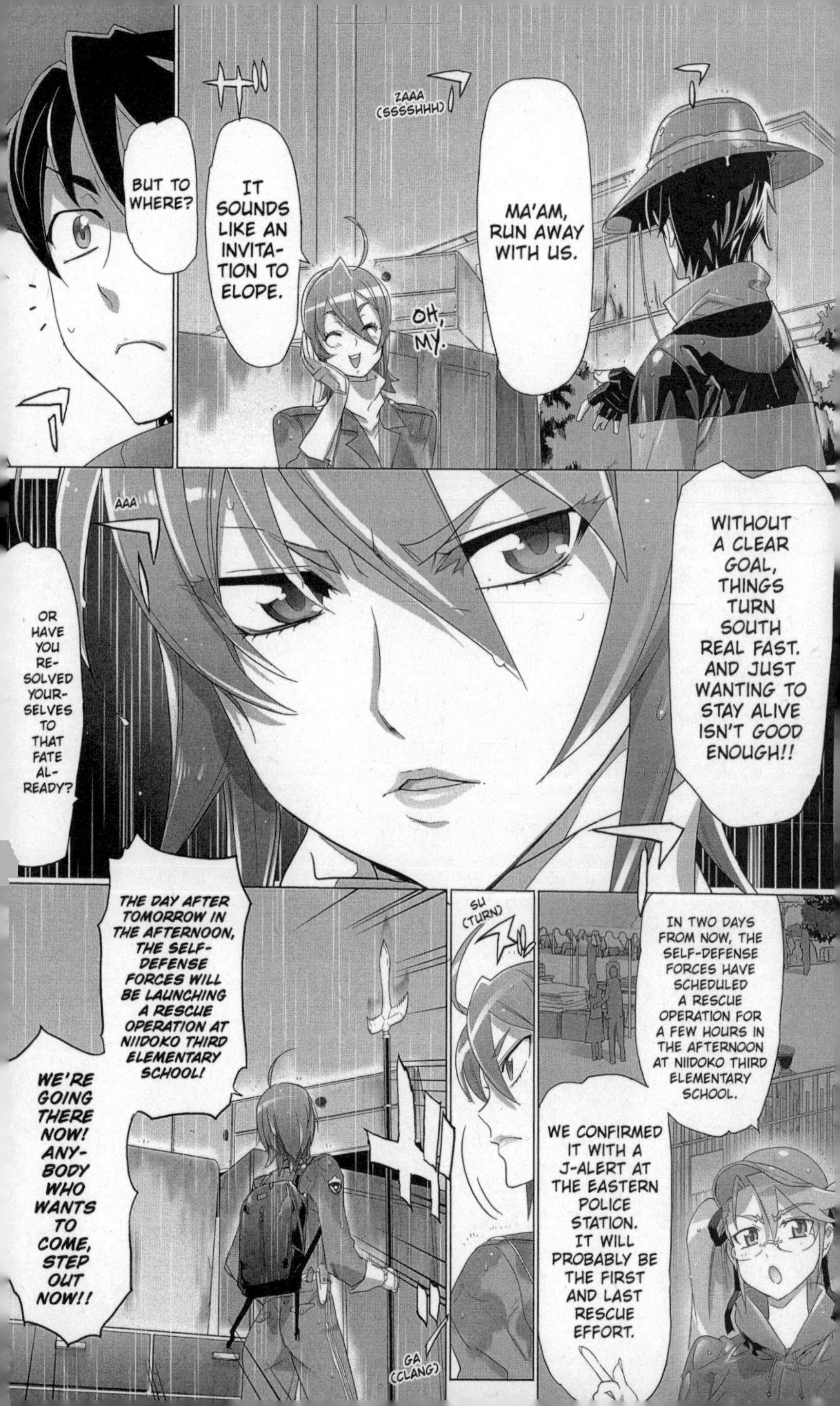
ZAAA (SSSSHHH)
MA'AM, RUN AWAY WITH US.
OH, MY.
IT SOUNDS LIKE AN INVITATION TO ELOPE.
BUT TO WHERE?
WITHOUT A CLEAR GOAL, THINGS TURN SOUTH REAL FAST. AND JUST WANTING TO STAY ALIVE ISN'T GOOD ENOUGH!!
AAA
OR HAVE YOU RESOLVED YOURSELVES TO THAT FATE ALREADY?
IN TWO DAYS FROM NOW, THE SELF-DEFENSE FORCES HAVE SCHEDULED A RESCUE OPERATION FOR A FEW HOURS IN THE AFTERNOON AT NIIDOKO THIRD ELEMENTARY SCHOOL.
WE CONFIRMED IT WITH A J-ALERT AT THE EASTERN POLICE STATION. IT WILL PROBABLY BE THE FIRST AND LAST RESCUE EFFORT.
SU (TURN)
THE DAY AFTER TOMORROW IN THE AFTERNOON, THE SELF-DEFENSE FORCES WILL BE LAUNCHING A RESCUE OPERATION AT NIIDOKO THIRD ELEMENTARY SCHOOL!
WE'RE GOING THERE NOW! ANYBODY WHO WANTS TO COME, STEP OUT NOW!!
GA (CLANG)

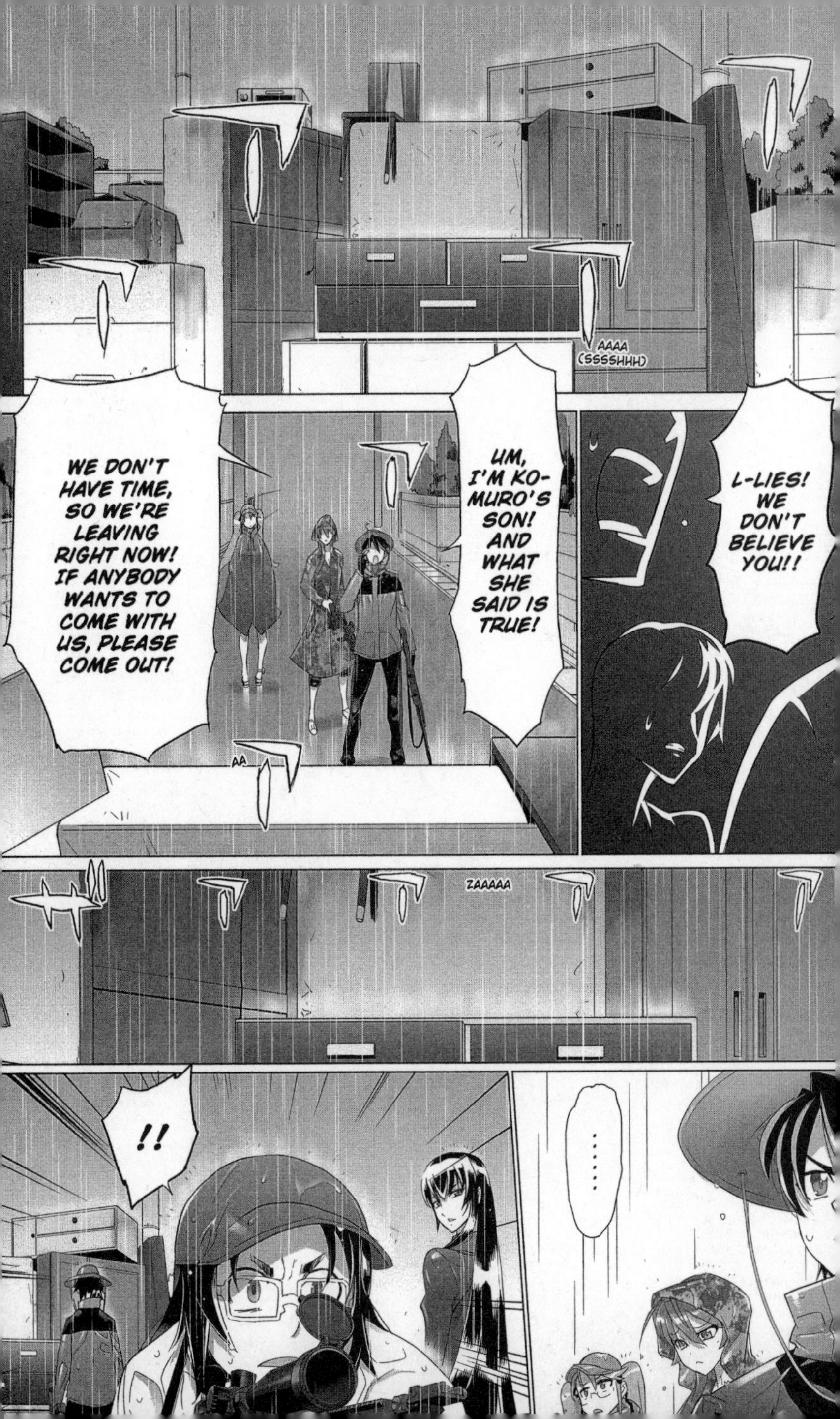
AAAA
(SSSSHHH)
L-LIES! WE DON'T BELIEVE YOU!!
UM, I'M KO-MURO'S SON! AND WHAT SHE SAID IS TRUE!
WE DON'T HAVE TIME, SO WE'RE LEAVING RIGHT NOW! IF ANYBODY WANTS TO COME WITH US, PLEASE COME OUT!
AA
ZAAAAA
......
!!

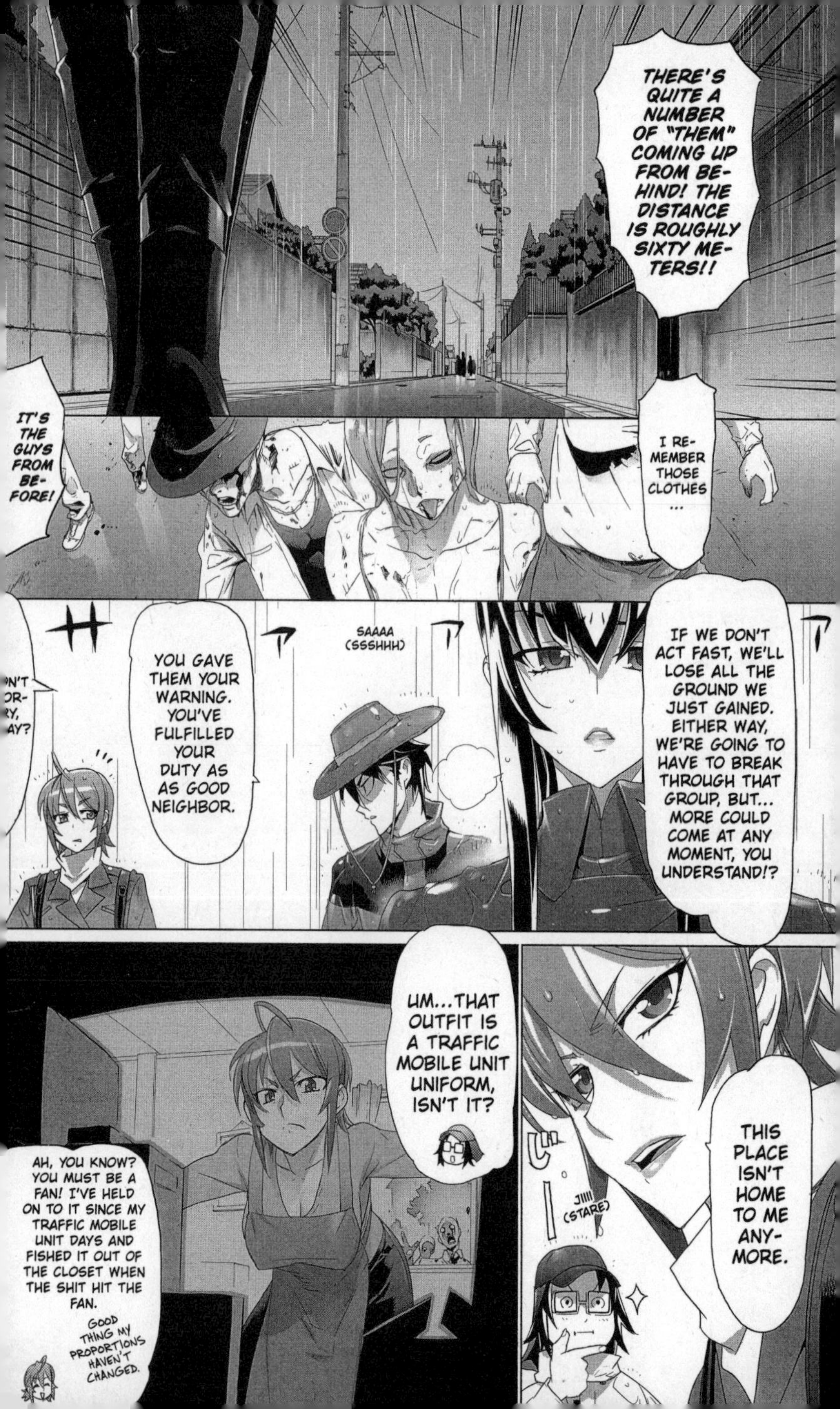
THERE'S QUITE A NUMBER OF "THEM" COMING UP FROM BE-HIND! THE DISTANCE IS ROUGHLY SIXTY ME-TERS!!
I RE-MEMBER THOSE CLOTHES...
IT'S THE GUYS FROM BE-FORE!
IF WE DON'T ACT FAST, WE'LL LOSE ALL THE GROUND WE JUST GAINED. EITHER WAY, WE'RE GOING TO HAVE TO BREAK THROUGH THAT GROUP, BUT... MORE COULD COME AT ANY MOMENT, YOU UNDERSTAND!?
SAAAA (SSSHHH)
YOU GAVE THEM YOUR WARNING. YOU'VE FULFILLED YOUR DUTY AS AS GOOD NEIGHBOR.
THIS PLACE ISN'T HOME TO ME ANY-MORE.
JIIII (STARE)
UM...THAT OUTFIT IS A TRAFFIC MOBILE UNIT UNIFORM, ISN'T IT?
AH, YOU KNOW? YOU MUST BE A FAN! I'VE HELD ON TO IT SINCE MY TRAFFIC MOBILE UNIT DAYS AND FISHED IT OUT OF THE CLOSET WHEN THE SHIT HIT THE FAN.
GOOD THING MY PROPORTIONS HAVEN'T CHANGED.

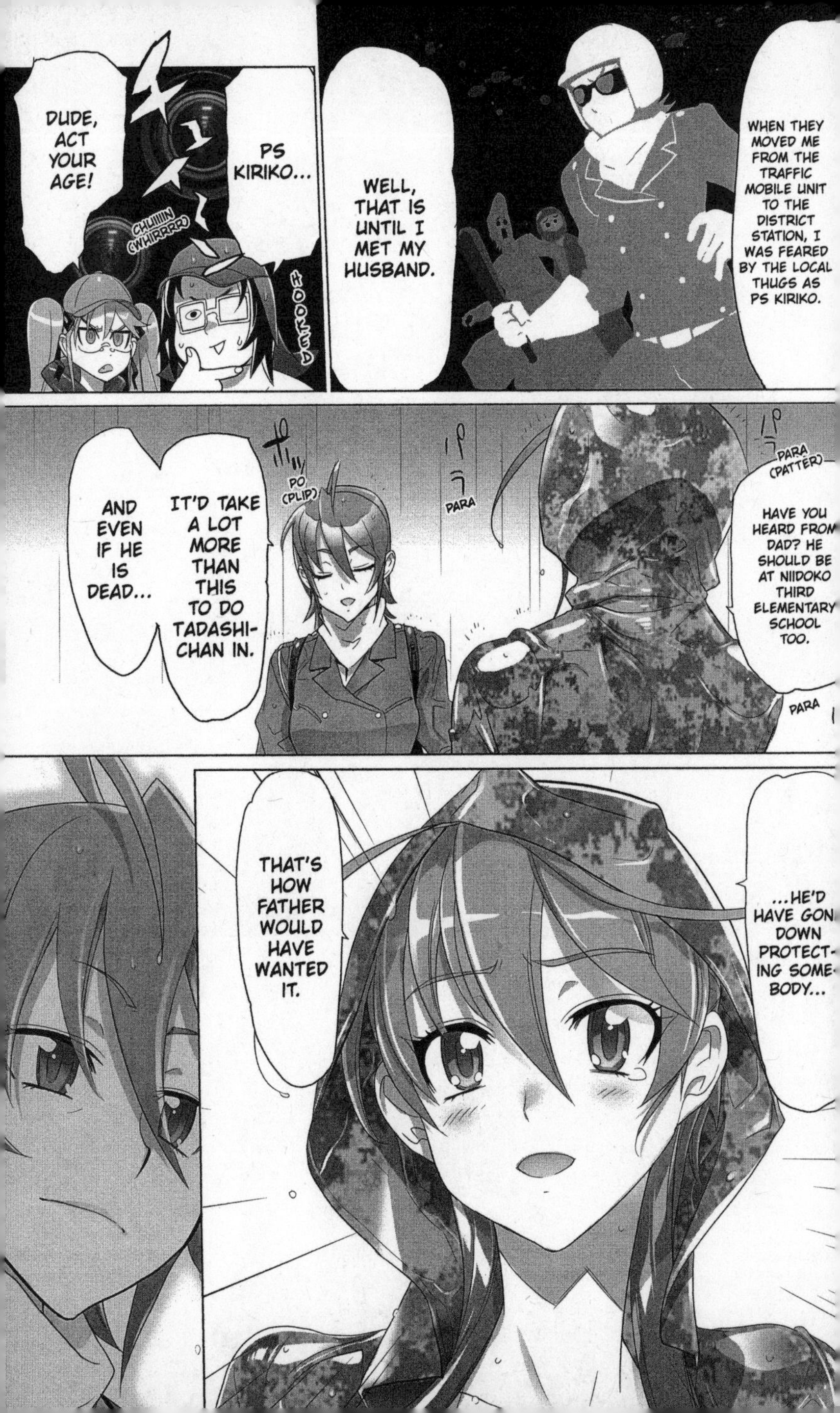
WHEN THEY MOVED ME FROM THE TRAFFIC MOBILE UNIT TO THE DISTRICT STATION, I WAS FEARED BY THE LOCAL THUGS AS PS KIRIKO.
WELL, THAT IS UNTIL I MET MY HUSBAND.
PS KIRIKO...
CHUIIIIN (WHIRRRR)
HOOKED
DUDE, ACT YOUR AGE!
PARA (PATTER)
HAVE YOU HEARD FROM DAD? HE SHOULD BE AT NIIDOKO THIRD ELEMENTARY SCHOOL TOO.
PARA
PARA
PO (PLIP)
IT'D TAKE A LOT MORE THAN THIS TO DO TADASHI-CHAN IN.
AND EVEN IF HE IS DEAD...
...HE'D HAVE GON DOWN PROTECTING SOMEBODY...
THAT'S HOW FATHER WOULD HAVE WANTED IT.

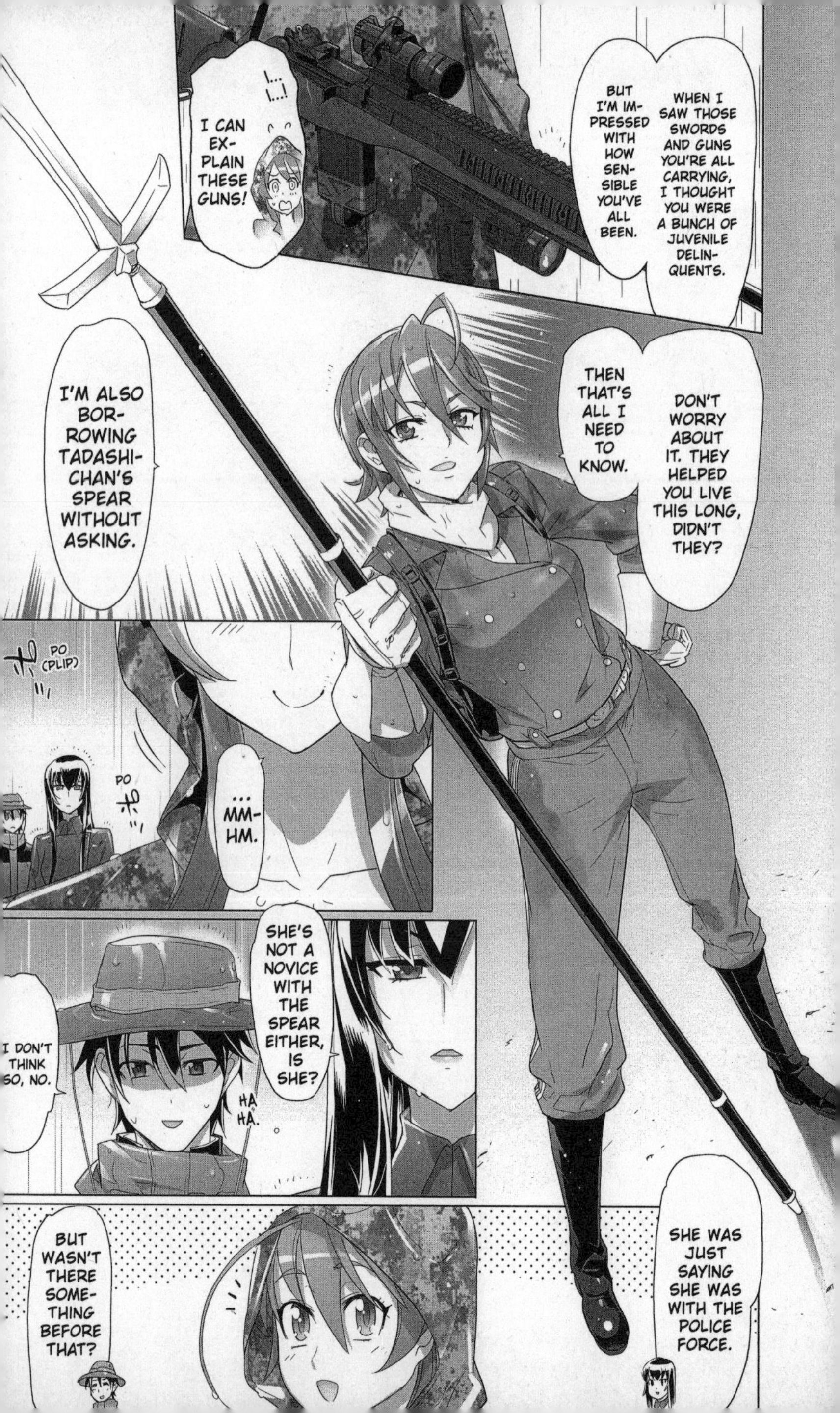

WHEN I SAW THOSE SWORDS AND GUNS YOU'RE ALL CARRYING, I THOUGHT YOU WERE A BUNCH OF JUVENILE DELIN-QUENTS.
BUT I'M IM-PRESSED WITH HOW SEN-SIBLE YOU'VE ALL BEEN.
I...I...!
I CAN EX-PLAIN THESE GUNS!
DON'T WORRY ABOUT IT. THEY HELPED YOU LIVE THIS LONG, DIDN'T THEY?
THEN THAT'S ALL I NEED TO KNOW.
I'M ALSO BOR-ROWING TADASHI-CHAN'S SPEAR WITHOUT ASKING.
PO (PLIP)
...MM-HM.
PO
SHE'S NOT A NOVICE WITH THE SPEAR EITHER, IS SHE?
I DON'T THINK SO, NO.
HA HA.
SHE WAS JUST SAYING SHE WAS WITH THE POLICE FORCE.
BUT WASN'T THERE SOME-THING BEFORE THAT?

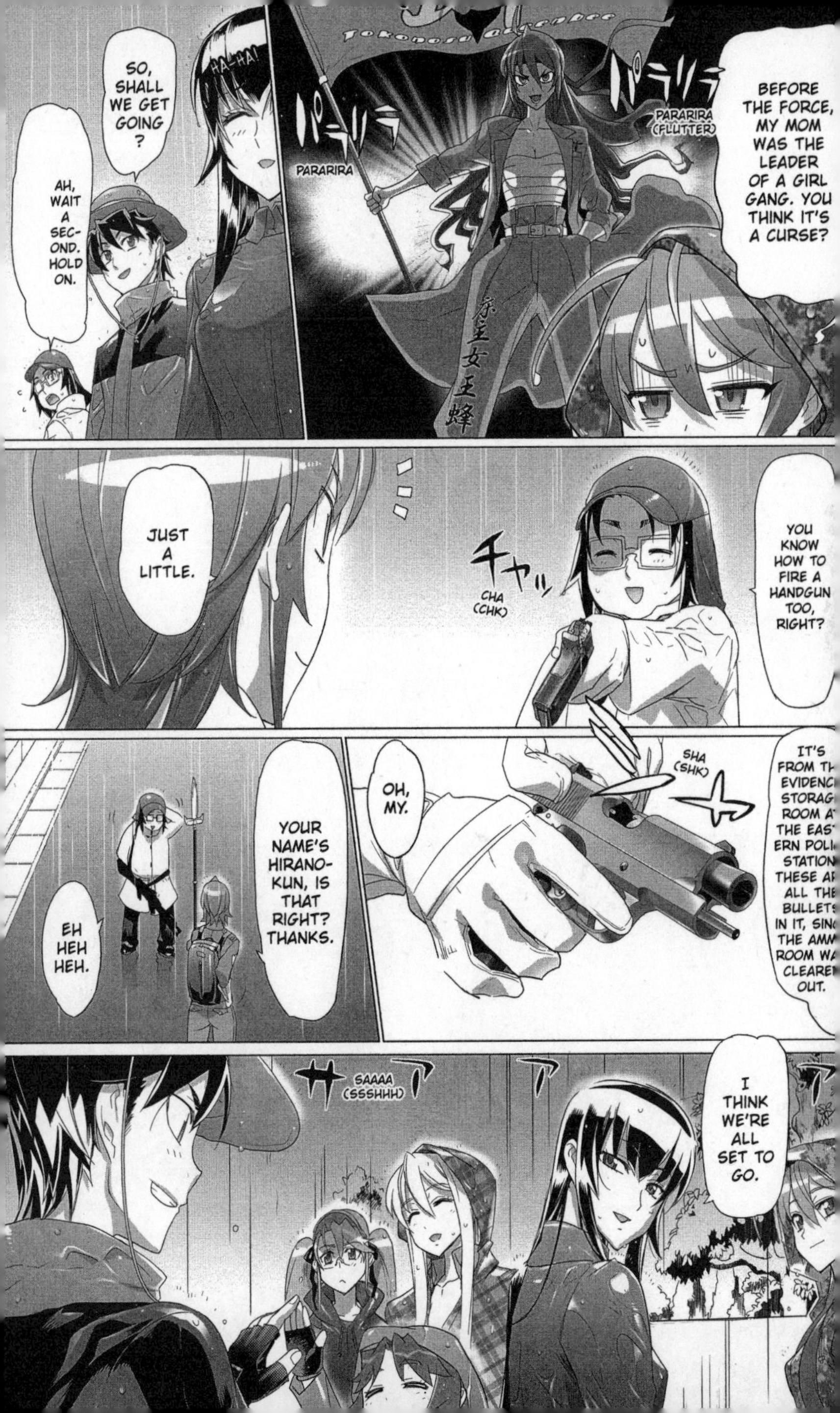
BEFORE THE FORCE, MY MOM WAS THE LEADER OF A GIRL GANG. YOU THINK IT'S A CURSE?
PARARIRA (FLUTTER)
PARARIRA
HA-HA!
SO, SHALL WE GET GOING?
AH, WAIT A SECOND. HOLD ON.
YOU KNOW HOW TO FIRE A HANDGUN TOO, RIGHT?
CHA (CHK)
JUST A LITTLE.
IT'S FROM TH EVIDENC STORAG ROOM AT THE EAST ERN POLI STATION THESE AR ALL THE BULLETS IN IT, SINC THE AMM ROOM WA CLEARE OUT.
SHA (SHK)
OH, MY.
YOUR NAME'S HIRANO-KUN, IS THAT RIGHT? THANKS.
EH HEH HEH.
I THINK WE'RE ALL SET TO GO.
SAAAA (SSSHHH)

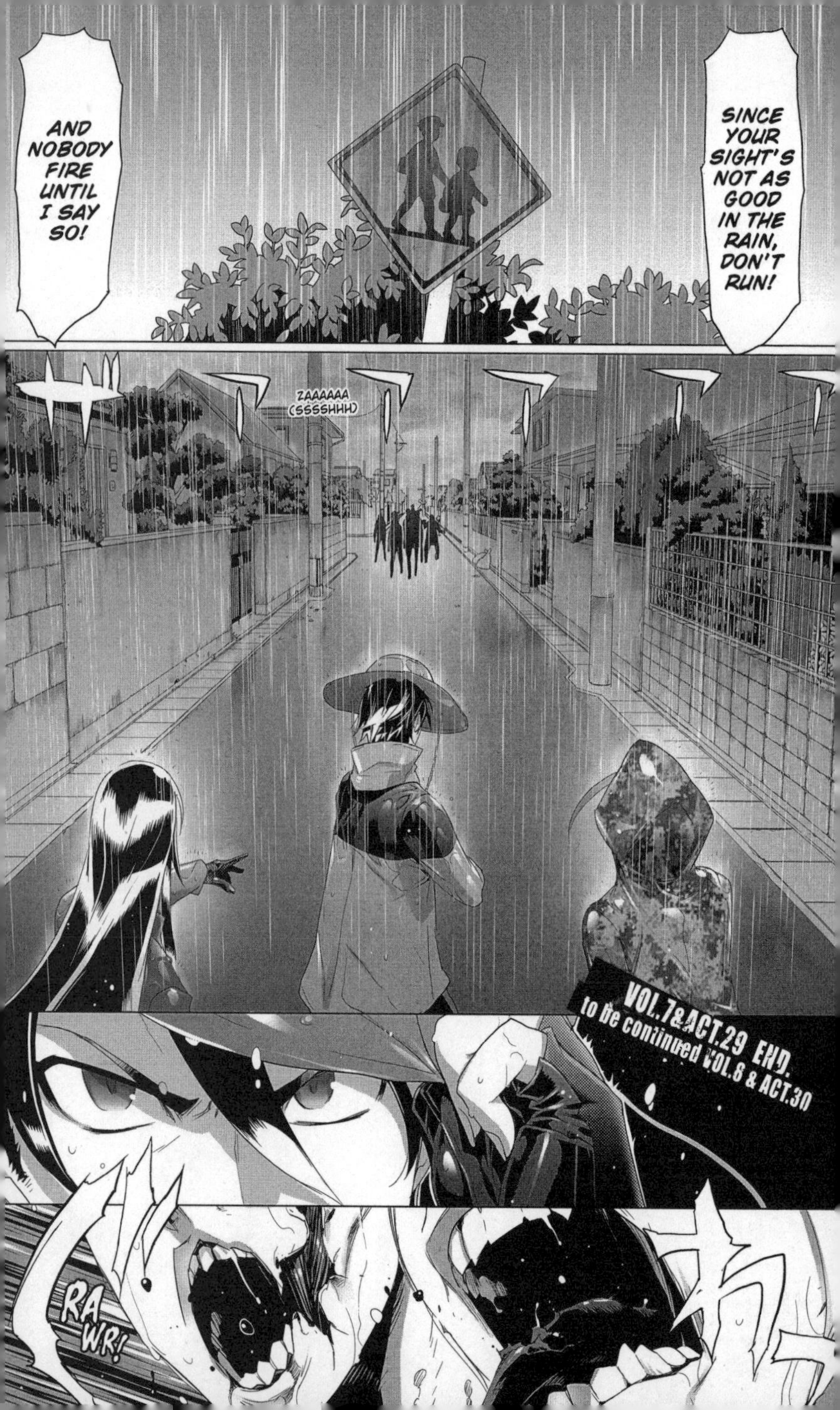
SINCE YOUR SIGHT'S NOT AS GOOD IN THE RAIN, DON'T RUN!
AND NOBODY FIRE UNTIL I SAY SO!
ZAAAAAA (SSSSHHH)
VOL.7&ACT.29 END.
to be continued VOL.8 & ACT.30
RAWR!

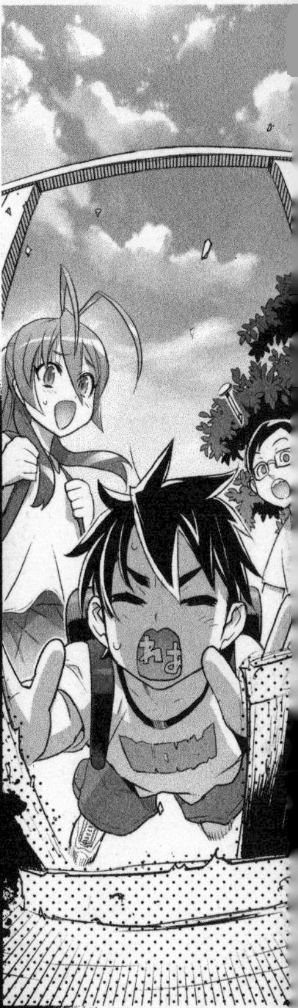

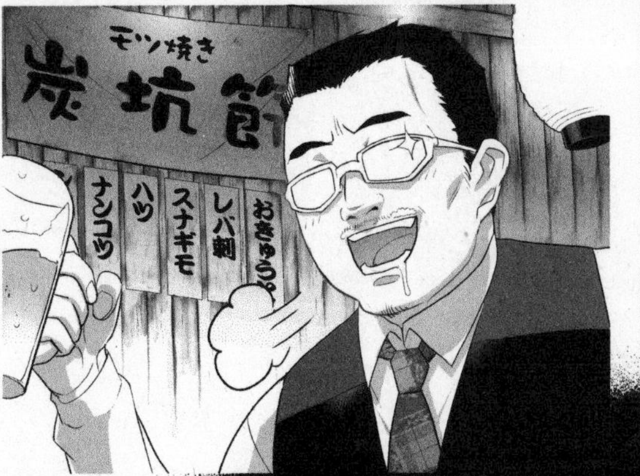
モツ焼き
炭坑館
レバ刺
スナギモ
ハツ
ナンコツ

H.O.T.D.

vol.7
STAFF

Original Story
Daisuke Sato

Illustrations
Shouji Sato
Hisayoshi Misasagi
Mirai Kobayashi
TEPPEI
OH-3

Special Thanks
Kouta Hirano
Inequality Ueki
Shouji Gato

Editor
Akira Kawashima
Takashi Harada
Masahiro Onai

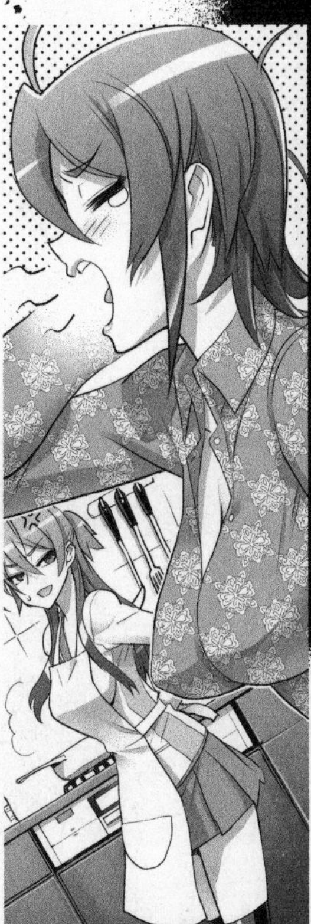

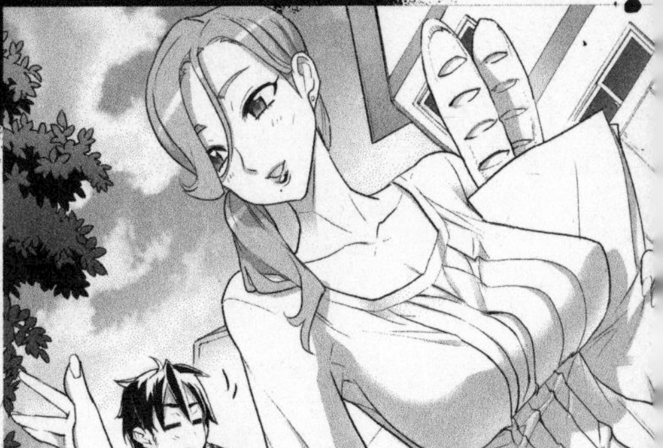

HIGHSCHOOL OF THE DEAD 7

DAISUKE SATO
SHOUJI SATO

Translation: Christine Dashiell

Lettering: Chris Counasse

GAKUENMOKUSHIROKU HIGHSCHOOL OF THE DEAD Volume 7 ©2011 DAISUKE SATO ©2011 SHOUJI SATO. Edited by FUJIMISHOBO. First published in Japan in 2011 by KADOKAWA CORPORATION, Tokyo. English translation rights arranged with KADOKAWA CORPORATION, Tokyo, through TUTTLE-MORI AGENCY, INC., Tokyo.

Translation © 2012 by Hachette Book Group, Inc.

Yen Press
Hachette Book Group
1290 Avenue of the Americas, New York, NY 10104

www.HachetteBookGroup.com
www.YenPress.com

Yen Press is an imprint of Hachette Book Group, Inc.
The Yen Press name and logo are trademarks of Hachette Book Group, Inc.

First Yen Press Edition: July 2012

ISBN: 978-0-316-20944-1

10 9 8 7 6

BVG

Printed in the United States of America